FABRICATING THE ANTIQUE

FABRICATING THE ANTIQUE

Neoclassicism in Britain, 1760–1800

VICCY COLTMAN

The University of Chicago Press : Chicago & London

VICCY COLTMAN is lecturer in the history of art at the University of Edinburgh.

The University of Chicago Press, Chicago 60637
The University of Chicago Press, Ltd., London

Printed in China
15 14 13 12 11 10 09 08 07 06 1 2 3 4 5

ISBN: 0-226-11396-5 (cloth)

Coltman, Viccy.
Fabricating the antique : neoclassicism in Britain, 1760–1800 / Viccy Coltman. — 1st ed.
p. cm.
Includes bibliographical references and index.
ISBN 0-226-11396-5 (cloth : alk. paper) 1. Neoclassicism (Art)—Great Britain. 2. Art, Britiash—18th century. I. Title.
N6766.5.N4C65 2006
709.41'09033—dc22

2005030541

This book is printed on acid-free paper.

CONTENTS

ILLUSTRATIONS

FIGURES

FOLLOWING PAGE 164

ACKNOWLEDGMENTS

In May 1786, Edward Gibbon wrote to his stepmother of his hopes for completing *The History of the Decline and Fall of the Roman Empire* later that year. He was overly optimistic: the sixth and final volume of his text would not be published until 1788. His letter contains the following authorial caution: "Let no man who builds a house or writes a book presume to say when he shall have finished. When he imagines that he is drawing near to his journey's end, Alps rise on Alps, and he continually finds something to add and something to correct." Having worked and reworked this manuscript, I can well understand Gibbon's Alps rising on Alps metaphor. In its earliest incarnation, this book was a Ph.D. thesis at the Courtauld Institute of Art, funded by the British Academy and supervised by the rigorous energy and devastating critical talents of Jaś Elsner. I am hugely indebted to Jaś for his continued guidance and support. The Henry Moore Foundation and the Paul Mellon Centre subsequently awarded me postdoctoral fellowships at the Courtauld. My gratitude to the trustees and the advisory council of both these institutions is considerable. As my host institution, the research fund of the Courtauld Institute offered some financial support, for which I am indebted to Robin Cormack and Rose Walker. Colleagues in History of Art Department at the University of Edinburgh, especially Tom Tolley and Richard Thomson, have offered advice in the latter stages, as have Malcolm Baker and Frank Salmon. Malcolm suggested the inclusion of material in chapter 5 and brought my attention to a number of relevant articles I had overlooked. I was extremely fortunate in having Christopher Johns as one of the readers of the manuscript for the University of Chicago Press. He offered a number of suggestions for revising the manuscript, which have improved the text considerably. Neither he, nor Malcolm, can be implicated into its shortcomings, however!

In addition, I would like to thank the staff at the many libraries, archives, and record offices that I have used. I acknowledge Sir R. M. Clerk Bt.; Lord Daventry; the Head of Leisure Services; Sheffield City Council; the Trustees of the British Museum; and the eighth Earl of Yarborough for permission to quote documents in their collections. The following individuals have offered invaluable assistance in one way or another: Keith Adam, Charles Avery, Lord Aylesford, Rosemary Baird, Jill Banks, Stephen Bann, Elizabeth Bartman, Keith Bennett, Melanie Blake, Stacy Boldrick, Susan Bourne, Lucilla Burn, Helen Burton, Edith Clay and the Clay family at Newtimber Place, Sir Robert Clerk, Helen Clifford, David Connell, Pandora Cook, Camilla Costello, Doris Dance, Christopher Date, Andrea Davies, Robert Eyre, Jane Fejfer, Kate Fielden, Geoffrey Fisher, Robert Fotheringham, Emma Gervasio, Georgina Jarvis, Ian Jenkins, Christopher Kelly, Alastair Laing, Valerie Lambirth, Emma Lauze, Arthur MacGregor, Andrea Martin, Michael Meredith, Lynne Miller, Susan Palmer, Martin Phillips, Mark Purcell, Lord St. Oswald, Maia Rigas, Lord Shelburne, Ruth Shrigley, Colin Shrimpton, Jacob Simon, Helen Smailes, Edmund Southworth, Elisabeth Stacey, Jane Stevenson, Nino Strachey, John Styles, Jeremy Tanner, Henry and Janet Tempest, Gary Thorn, Eleanor Tollfree, Sir Simon Towneley, Janet Wallace, Geoffrey Waywell, and John Yorke.

Earlier versions of chapters 1 and 3 were published as Viccy Coltman, "Classicism in the English Library: Reading Classical Culture in the Late Eighteenth and Early Nineteenth Century," *Journal of the History of Collections* 11 (1999): 35–50 and Viccy Coltman, "Sir William Hamilton's Vase Publications (1766–76): A Case Study in the Reproduction and Dissemination of Antiquity," *Journal of Design History* 14 (2001): 1–16. I am grateful to Oxford University Press for permission to reprint these articles.

It has been a privilege to publish this book with the University of Chicago Press. The professionalism of my editor and associate editor, Susan Bielstein and Anthony Burton, and their commitment to the book at every stage of the review and publication process have made them a pleasure to work with. The illustration costs were funded by a small project grant from the British Academy. The Carnegie Trust for the Universities of Scotland contributed toward the color plates, and the Moray fund provided a subsidy toward publication.

Finally, recognition must go to my family for their unwavering support and to Stuart.

INTRODUCTION

Getting into the Classical Mood

It was the Victorians who first coined the term "neoclassicism," applying it pejoratively and perfunctorily to what they perceived as the affectations of classical taste displayed by earlier generations.[1] In an article on Pompeii published in the *Quarterly Review* in April 1864, the British archaeologist A. H. Layard referred to instances of neoclassicism at the turn of the nineteenth century as a failed experiment. He maintained the reason for its failure was obvious:

> Too much was attempted. The true principles of application were misunderstood. The walls were overladen with colour and gilding, and comfort and utility were sacrificed to classic forms. Furniture, fire-irons, teapots, and the various objects of daily domestic use, made after the manner of the ancients, could scarcely be turned to their legitimate purpose, however well adapted they may have been to the sacrifices and ceremonies of a Greek or Roman temple. Chairs and sofas strictly made upon the model of the sella curulis, and the bronze bisellium, might have been comfortable in the forum, but were execrable in the drawing room. We were at last driven out of the classic mood.[2]

Layard's criticisms are levied at the imitation of ancient objects, specifically furniture, fire irons, and teapots and their installation into the domestic interior. In his opinion, the experiment failed by sacrificing the comforts of modernity in the too-rigorous pursuit of antique models, where ancient form failed to follow contemporary function. One of Layard's contemporaries was Adolf Michaelis, professor of archaeology at the University of Strasbourg and author of *Ancient Marbles in Great Britain* (Cambridge, 1882), a work devoted to ancient sculptures in private collections in Britain acquired between the seventeenth and nineteenth centuries. Like Layard on the furniture and furnishings of the neoclassical drawing room, Michaelis's archaeological agenda similarly misunderstood the principles behind the formation and arrangement of the neoclassical sculpture collection (fig 1). He famously wrote of Sir John Soane's early nineteenth-century house-museum at 13 Lincoln's Inn Fields in London:

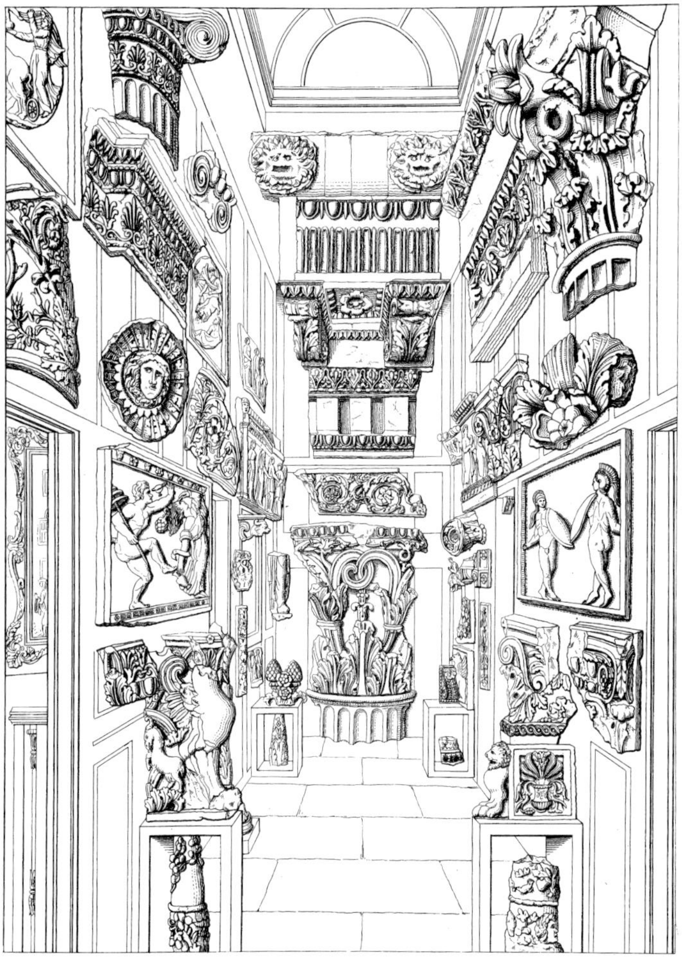

Figure 1 *(left)* "An immeasurable chaos of worthless fragments" (Michaelis): "View in the corridor (between the Corinthian Colonnade and Picture Room)," plate 9 of Soane's *Description of the House and Museum on the North Side of Lincoln's Inn Fields* (London, 1835). By courtesy of the Trustees of Sir John Soane's Museum.

Figure 2 *(right)* "View in the model room," plate 38 of Soane's *Description of the House and Museum on the North Side of Lincoln's Inn Fields* (London, 1835). By courtesy of the Trustees of Sir John Soane's Museum.

Non multum sed multa appears to have been his motto in collecting; for there is something of everything. Along with a few choice specimens of high value, or at least of considerable interest, there is an immeasurable chaos of worthless fragments, of all times, from all countries, of all kinds of art, originals and copies mixed together. All this is crammed into the narrow limits of a private house, and is arranged in so ingenious a manner that no corner, however dark, is left unoccupied. In this respect the architect has achieved marvels; nevertheless this labyrinth stuffed full of fragments is the most tasteless arrangement that can be seen; it has the same kind of perplexing and oppressive effect on the spectator as if the whole large stock of an old-clothes-dealer had been squeezed into a doll's house. For an appropriate situation has not been in all cases found for even the few good specimens. Two only are fairly well placed, the remarkable Egyptian sarcophagus discovered by Belzoni, and the Cawdor vase . . . in fact, many sculptures worthy of notice are rendered quite unavailable for enjoyment and study by their bad position. In such a shape has this cabinet of rarities, by the will of the collector, become the property of the State. It seems to find admirers: And certainly it enriches London by one curiosity the more.[3]

What to the late nineteenth-century German archaeologist seemed a most tasteless arrangement of worthless fragments was to its architect-collector Soane an architectural kaleidoscope. Soane's collection was not so much a doll's house as a model house, complete with a room devoted to architectural models (fig. 2), the chief of which in size (measuring about eight feet square) and interest, was a cork model of the entire site of Pompeii as excavated in 1820.[4]

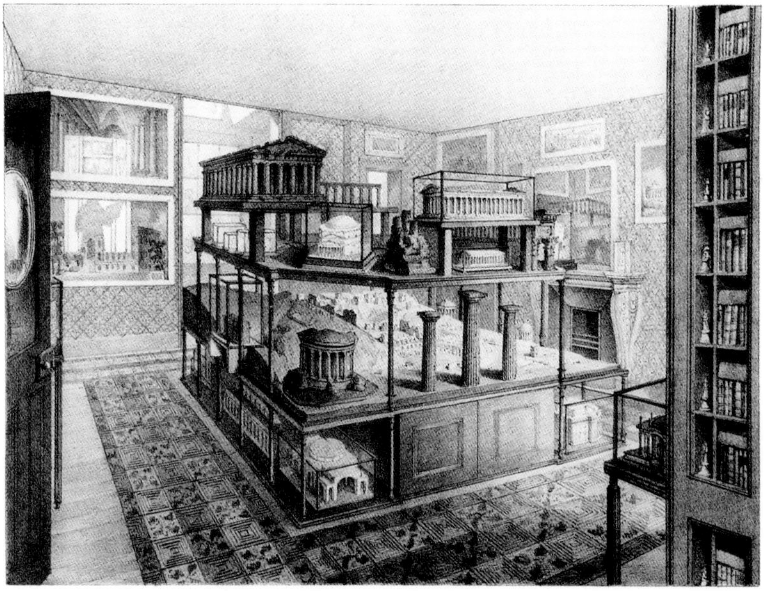

This book focuses on the material culture that Layard and Michaelis found problematic. The imitation antique objects and interiors of elite British drawing rooms and the ancient artifacts collected during the forty-year period from 1760 to 1800 (see fig. 3). In dealing with this material, it is not my intention to undermine the archaeological achievements of our two Victorian heavyweights. Rather,

I suggest that the material itself and the strategies of its display practiced by British collectors should be evaluated on their own, late eighteenth-century terms. Michaelis's bewildered critique of Sir John Soane's house-museum reveals more about his own professional and institutional baggage, as a university professor and an ancient Greco-Roman sculpture specialist, as it does about the kaleidoscopic Soanean collection. His isolation of individual ancient (master)pieces—the Egyptian sarcophagus and the Etruscan vase—indicates a nineteenth-century-object fetishization that misunderstands the heterogeneity of the neoclassical collection. The quotations from Layard and Michaelis summarily demonstrate how the specialized study of antiquity can subject works of art to a retrospective interrogation in which they are denied their own cultural codification.[5] They become unintelligible; their possessors, cast as incompetent; hence Michaelis's disbelief at Soane's collision of artifacts of disparate chronology, geography, and typology inside his London labyrinth.

Since the early period of penetrating archaeological investigation, specimens of neoclassical art of the later eighteenth century have provoked division, rather than dismay, within the academic community. A choice example is *Clytie* (fig. 4), a marble bust formerly in Charles Townley's London-based collection of ancient sculptures. She is known as Clytie after a nymph who fell in love with the sun god Helios and metamorphosed into a sunflower. In the bust, sunflower petals are enveloping her lower torso. One of Townley's Roman dealers, Thomas Jenkins, wrote to him after acquiring the marble in Naples in 1772 from the family of Principe Laurenzano of being "exceedingly glad the Lady increases in your Esteem. at the same time that it Proves her Excellence it's a Testimony of the warmth of your Passion."[6] In 1990, she was included with a number of ancient sculptures from Townley's collection in an exhibition at their permanent home, the British Museum, entitled *Fake? The Art of Deception.*[7] To designate *Clytie* a fake is, however, to impose a whole series of cultural and institutional biases that are governed by twentieth-century preoccupations. According to the text of the exhibition catalog, the bust is not an eighteenth-century fake but rather an ancient marble reworked to enhance her charms and to give her a new personality. Having been earmarked a fake for the purposes of the exhibition the accompanying catalog pronounces her to be in fact ancient but reworked. We might well ask *when* she was reworked: in antiquity or during the extensive postantique historical period? The issue of the identity of *Clytie* remains far from resolved and is divided into two opposing schools of thought. One school of thought as championed by former British Museum curator of Greek and Roman antiquities, Susan Walker, pronounces the bust to be ancient—a first-century A.D. Roman portrait of Antonia, the mother of the emperor Claudius.[8] The other camp, as represented in print by the postantique European sculpture specialist Nicholas Penny, claims her as a modern eighteenth-century creation by "a

Figure 3 Map showing the properties in Britain and Ireland discussed in the text.

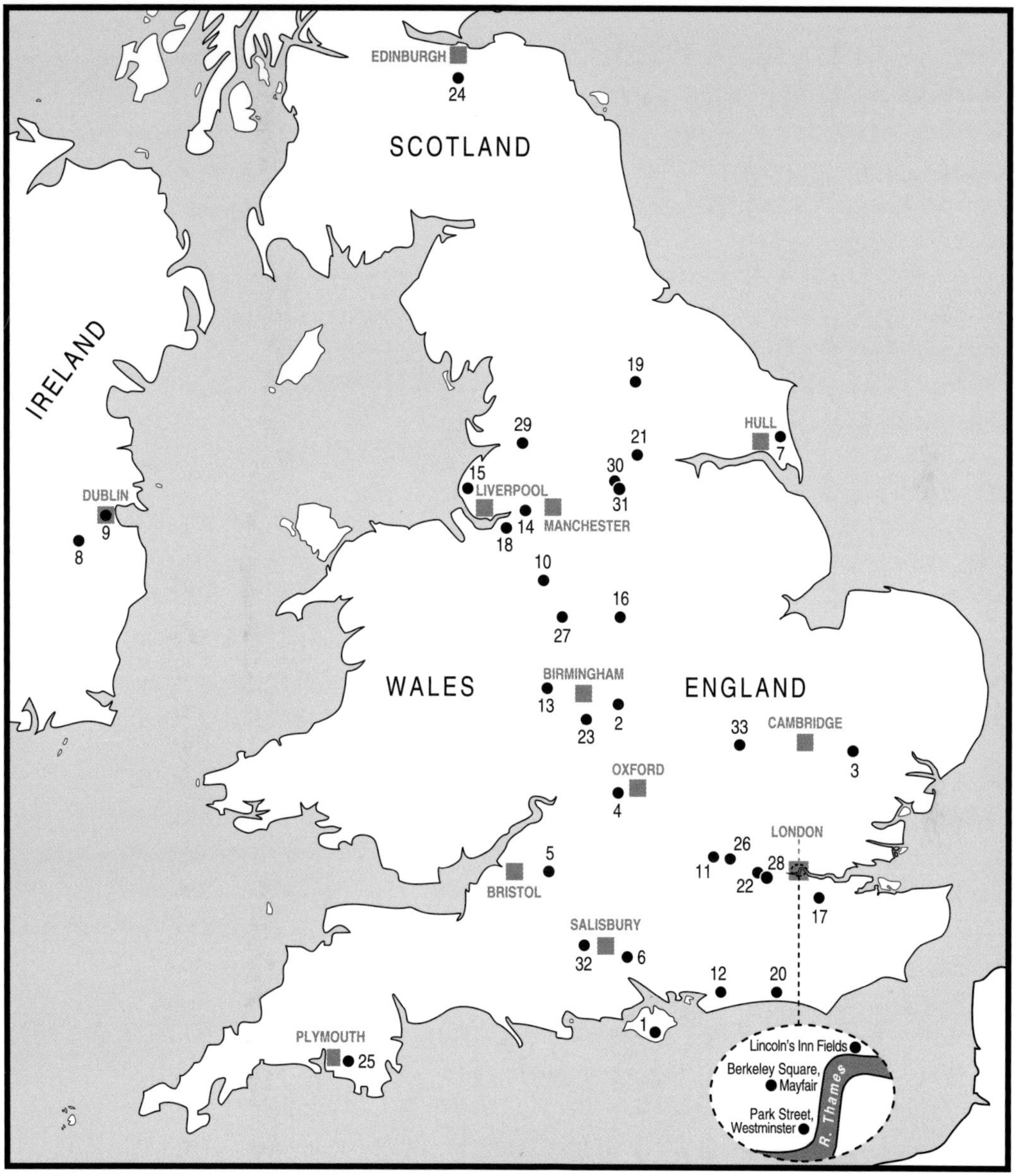

1 Appuldurcombe Park, Isle of Wight
2 Arbury Hall, Warwickshire
3 Audley End, Essex
4 Blenheim Palace, Oxfordshire
5 Bowood House, Wiltshire
6 Broadlands, Hampshire
7 Burton Constable, Yorkshire
8 Castletown House, Co. Kildare
9 Charlemont House, Dublin
10 Etruria, Staffordshire
11 Fawley Court, Henley-on-Thames
12 Goodwood House, Sussex
13 Hagley Hall, Worcestershire
14 Heaton Hall, Manchester
15 Ince Blundell Hall, Lancashire
16 Kedleston Hall, Derbyshire
17 Knole House, Kent
18 Mere Hall, Cheshire
19 Newby Hall, Yorkshire
20 Newtimber Place, Sussex
21 Nostell Priory, Yorkshire
22 Osterley Park House, Middlesex
23 Packington Hall, Warwickshire
24 Penicuik, Midlothian
25 Saltram House, Devon
26 Shirburn Castle, Oxfordshire
27 Shugborough, Staffordshire
28 Syon House, Middlesex
29 Towneley Hall, Burnley, Lancashire
30 Wentworth Castle, Yorkshire
31 Wentworth Woodhouse, Yorkshire
32 Wilton House, Wiltshire
33 Woburn Abbey, Bedfordshire

sculptor as thoroughly saturated in the antique as Bastianini was to be in the Quattrocento."[9] The end result is a kind of stalemate in which Clytie is variously cast in and cast out of the conflicting art historical traditions of antiquity and modernity, originality and fakery.

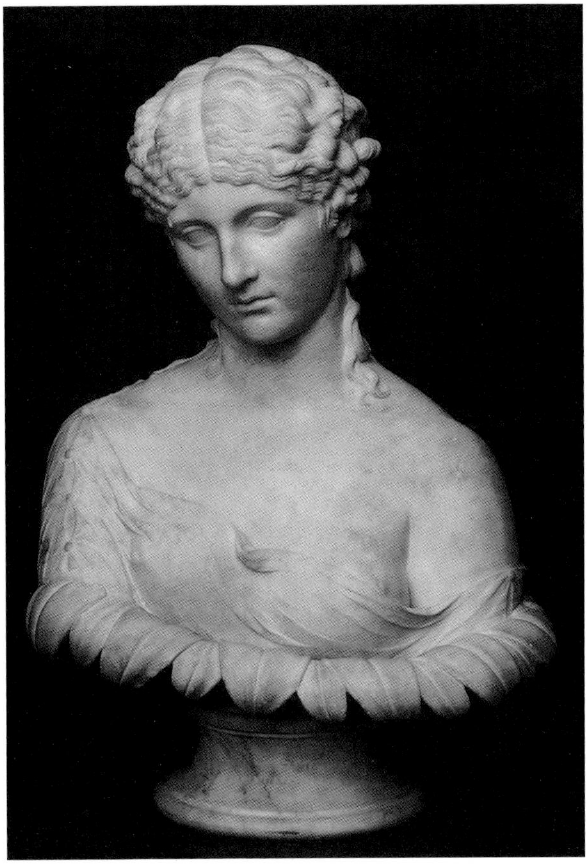

Figure 4 Charles Townley's bust *Clytie*. By courtesy of the Trustees of the British Museum.

This narrative rejects such partisan action and prefers to decipher objects according to the cultural codes of the later eighteenth century. Within the context of Townley's sculpture collection exhibited in his London house at 7 Park Street, Westminster, Clytie was no false female, but a thought to be ancient bust that Townley "used jocosely to call his wife."[10] In an undated letter to Clytie's "husband," the poet Samuel Rogers referred to "the pleasure [I had] to travel with you this morning thro' fairy-land, [when] I forgot to ask your permission to introduce some Lancashire friends to-morrow to a sight of *your august* family! a family not the less imposante for their vow of perpetual silence!"[11] "I hope all my acquaintance in your Museum with whom tho mute (& as Ovid says nec Vox nec Verba Sequuntur) I have so often conversed by the expression of their countenances are well—especially the Beautiful Clytie—I am happy in the thoughts of stealing a peep at them soon," wrote one William Sandys to Townley in 1780.[12] These quotations derive from letters preserved in Townley's extensive archive, which was purchased by the British Museum in 1992.[13] The evidence contained in the collector's notebooks and diaries, along with letters from his exhaustive number of correspondents sheds new light on Townley's august family during the collector's lifetime. This Who's Who of British neoclassicism is one of *many* unpublished archival sources that will be plundered, transcribed, and reproduced here in an attempt to contextualize and so better situate what Layard called the classic mood of late eighteenth-century Britain within its historical, cultural and intellectual context.

Existing studies that have informed my own have investigated instances of reference and reverence for different versions of the antique in the eighteenth century. Alex Potts's *Winckelmann and the Origins of Art History* (New Haven, 1994) is a tour de force of art historical erudition: Potts applied rigorous analysis and critical interpretation of the work of German-born, Rome-based scholar Johann Joachim Winckelmann on the ruins of the latter's pioneering system of classification for Greek and Roman art.[14] For Potts, Winckelmann's *Geschichte der Kunst des Alterthums* (Dresden, 1764) was at one level the bible of late eighteenth-century neoclassicism.[15] In chapter 6 I will feature Winckelmann's text in a discussion of the sculptures in Charles Townley's collection. Sam Smiles's *The Image of Antiquity: Ancient Britons and the Romantic Imagination* (New Haven, 1994) is a book about the pursuit and re-use of the past—published the same year as Potts's book on Winckelmann. In this study, Smiles explored how an archaic British past was collected, debated, and classified between 1750 and 1850 to produce *a version* of antiquity that was appropriate for what he describes as, the interests and needs of a *contemporary audience.* Though this may seem an obvious point to make–the refashioning of aspects of the past for the purposes of the present—it is always worth bearing in mind when studying aspects of the classical tradition. Where Smiles talks of the *image* of antiquity, he is acutely aware of how far this image was self-consciously constructed in a texture of verbal and visual language.[16] Philip Ayres's *Classical Culture and the Idea of Rome in Eighteenth-Century England* (Cambridge, 1997) takes the Glorious Revolution of 1688 as the starting point from which the ancient Roman ideals of liberty and civic virtue were appropriated by England's cultural and political elite. Ayres's book documents how aristocratic England referred to an *idealized* image of republican Rome; how they created their own "oligarchy of virtue" in a collaborative discourse of philosophy, aesthetics, archaeology, architecture, literature, and politics.[17] Like Ayres, my study is concerned with the educated elite of British society but in the more focused historical period of the later eighteenth century. It also hopes to penetrate and interrogate what he refers to as a classical frame of mind and, specifically, a Roman habit of mind. In a chapter entitled "The Illusion of Grandeur? Antiquity, Grand Tourism and the Country House" in her *The Georgian Country House: Architecture, Landscape and Society* (Sutton, 1998), Dana Arnold situates the productions of neoclassicism within a cultural and social history of the long eighteenth century. While Potts views Winckelmann in the context of the European Enlightenment, Arnold places souvenirs of the grand tour in the physical space of the English country house interior. She implicitly refutes the notion that neoclassicism represents a return to the preexisting historical models of Greek and Roman antiquity, offering instead "interpretations on the cultures which chose to cite" the antique.[18] The classical collections inspired by the grand tour, which are, she explains, too many and diverse for a complete discussion in her short chapter, represent a major component of this book.

Despite the methodological contributions of these four significant academic studies, the label "neoclassicism" continues to denote a predominantly *decorative* style; David Irwin writes that the architecture of Robert Adam and the pottery of Josiah Wedgwood are perhaps the best-known examples of English neoclassicism.[19] The problem of definition in some ways accounts for the identity crisis that surrounds the term. As Craske has recently pointed out, any use of the label is inevitably loaded with a multiplicity of modern meanings.[20] Modern scholarship has attempted to elicit further meanings by referring to instances of "high Neoclassicism," "orthodox neoclassicism," "uncompromisingly virilised neo-classicism," "a truly classical neo-classicism" and "the neo-classical band wagon," to cite only a few examples.[21] Such refinements seem to indicate a desire to recognize instances of neoclassicism more meaningfully and usefully than the label at present allows for. They also give weight to the suggestion that neoclassicism was not a monolithic enterprise but a pluralistic one.[22]

Certainly, there were national incarnations and variations.[23] In late eighteenth-century French visual culture, the classical aesthetic codified by Winckelmann in his writings on ancient art was politically nuanced by artists like David and Ingres in the service of the revolutionary cause. Winckelmann's construction of classical fifth-century B.C. Greece provided a model of utopian freedom and *desire,* a model in which, as Potts argues, neoclassical taste has as much to do with an erotic sensuality as with esoteric notions of noble simplicity.[24] The naked male body was dressed up with classical resonances of ideal beauty *and* politicized notions of a truly free subject. By the end of the eighteenth century, France's "political thought, her symbols and institutions were mainly Roman," proclaims Ridley.[25] Roman self-imaging has been seen as continuing to prevail under Napoleon—the modern Roman emperor cum living legend—if we swallow the hype of his own myth-making propaganda.[26] Christopher Johns's discussion of *Napoleon as Mars the Peacemaker* (1803–6; fig. 5) offers an insightful reading of the relationship between Napoleon and neoclassical culture as embodied in his colossal marble statue by Antonio Canova.[27] This martial image is exceptional in Napoleon's propagandistic art patronage as it is a classicizing monument to *himself* rather than part of the wider architectural and sculptural embellishments he initiated in the urban centers of Paris and Rome. Canova mixed the genre of portraiture with that of mythological sculpture in a bid to, as Johns reads it, camouflage the statue from potential political controversy. Its full-length nudity also offered an ideological smokescreen with ancient associations of physical perfection and aesthetic sublimity rather than contemporary political relevance. Nudity as visual shorthand for an ancient Greek mode of representation proliferated in images of Hellenistic rulers as an indication of heroic or semidivine status; in pose and conception Napoleon as Mars looks back to images of empire-building Alexander the Great. Whatever the sculptor's aims and innovations—and Johns is convinced that the subversion of Mars, the official god of war, to the antithetical role of peacemaker is Canova's own—the reception of the statue was the opposite of what Canova had envisaged: both controversial *and* political. Uncomfortable with his statue au naturel, Napoleon had it banished to the oblivion of a storage closet. When the British government purchased the work from Louis XVIII in 1816, they presented it to the victor of Waterloo, the Duke of Wellington. Napoleon as Mars still languishes trophylike in the stairwell at his enemy's former home, Apsley House, in London.

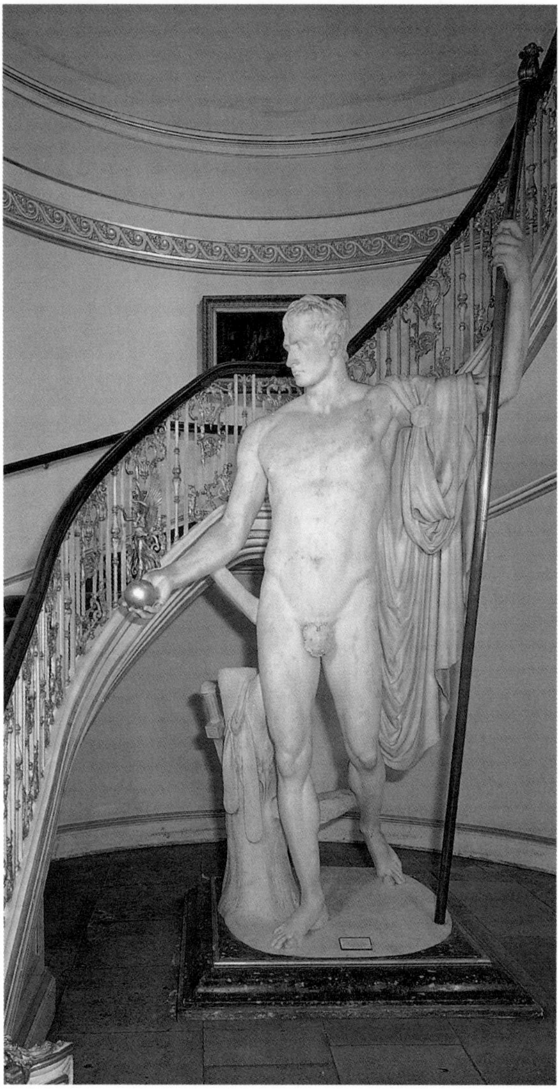

Figure 5 Antonio Canova, *Napoleon as Mars the Peacemaker*, 1803–6. V&A Picture Library.

In contrast with the French, whose conflated citations from ancient Greek, Hellenistic, and Roman antiquity into Napoleonic modernity were predominantly political, neoclassicism in late eighteenth-century Germany took the form of a cultural revolution by intellectuals. More often called "German philhellenism," the German brand of neoclassicism was essentially pedagogic.[28] Intellectuals looked to Winckelmann's literary construction of an ideal Greece rather than to ancient Rome, which had been conquered, both literally and ideologically, by invading French troops under Napoleon. Britain, meanwhile, remained what has been termed an ahistorical zone, in which Greco-Roman antiquity is said to have resisted historicization.[29] The antique was never called upon as a charged ideological force from which to mount a political or cultural project as it was in contemporary France and Germany.[30] Having never become a defining characteristic of the fabric of late eighteenth-century society, British fabrications of ancient Greece and Rome remain largely overlooked outside the specialist parameters of architectural history or the so-called decorative arts. Hence the architecture of Robert Adam and the pottery of Josiah Wedgwood *remain* its best-known manifestations.

This ahistorical position is not itself a precedent that we should apply to our study of the phenomenon. Nor should we be geographically unadventurous and retain a Eurocentric focus that compares and contrasts the culture of British neoclassicism with that of France or Germany. A more useful conceptual model derives from the other side of the expanding eighteenth-century world—the discourse of colonialism in which the material culture of the New World was historically refigured. In *Entangled Objects: Exchange, Material Culture and Colonialism in the Pacific* (Cambridge, Mass., 1991), Nicholas Thomas explains how indigenous artifacts became trophies reflecting the traveler's experience and mastery of a passage round the world in much the same way that the knowledge of Europe and of the sites of classical literature obtained during a grand tour was sometimes expressed in the acquisition and display of classical relics.[31] Benjamin West's portrait of Joseph Banks (c. 1771–73; fig. 6) represents the scientist accompanied and even enveloped by objects collected during his voyage to the South Seas. His cloak is a modified Polynesian bark cloth cape fringed with dog hair. On his left stands a Maori canoe paddle and a carved fighting staff decorated with feathers; below them is a basketry headdress as worn by Tahitian warriors. A comb and a Tahitian stone adze lie on the floor in the right foreground; behind them is an open folio of botanical drawings showing New Zealand flax and in so doing, signaling that the assembled artifacts are not merely ornamental but also collected for the purposes of scientific study. For Harriet Guest, West's portrait is a display of Banks's cosmopolitanism.[32] The indigenous artifacts, drawn from a dispersed variety of "exotic" cultures, are an indicator of authenticity, of the subject's firsthand and intimate experience of the material culture of the new worlds. The translation of knowledge into material artifacts is one aspect of colonialism—and of neoclassicism, as shall be elucidated in due course. Another is the dissemination of this translated knowledge into other forms of cultural expression. P. J. Marshall and Glyndwr Williams's *The Great Map of Mankind* (London, 1982) concludes with an overview of British perceptions of the world in the so-called age of enlightenment, as fashioned by travellers and explorers in their published letters and journals; by painters and illustrators of books who had represented it visually; by literary figures like playwrights, poets, or novelists; and by designers and craftsmen who had drawn upon it for new motifs.[33] Marshall and Williams focus attention on colonialist translation of exotic curiosities into a variety of texts, images, and artifacts. This process, in which modes associated with the exotic were assimilated and redeployed as models intelligible to a British audience, also characterizes late eighteenth-century

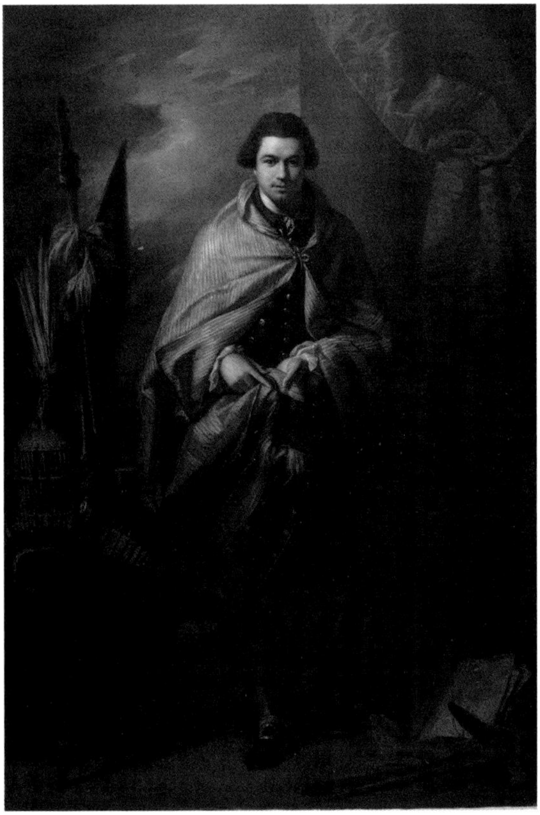

Figure 6 Benjamin West, *Joseph Banks*, c. 1771–73. Lincolnshire County Council—Usher Gallery, Lincoln.

neoclassicism. As will be demonstrated throughout this book, the material culture of the ancient Romans in Italy was similarly adopted and adapted, translated and transposed.

The analogy of neoclassicism and colonialism speaks to the mechanisms of translation, dissemination, and imitation that were applied to ancient artifacts and exotic curiosities. This does not adequately convey, however, the complicated ideological implications inherent in the British assimilation of ancient Roman artifacts from Italy. Early eighteenth-century Britain had already appropriated the ancients in the spheres of literature and architecture. Authors including Pope, Swift, Johnson, and Goldsmith wrote in what is conveniently called the "Augustan mode"—a label as loaded and as prone to misuse as "neoclassicism," with which it is often misguidedly lumped together.[34] The aristocratic architect Lord Burlington designed and constructed buildings in which ancient Roman architecture preserved in stone and on paper was reinterpreted through the sixteenth-century interpretations of the Italian architect Palladio.[35] From the early 1760s, however, Britain was no longer a peripheral European state paying lip service to ancient Rome via her literature and her architecture but instead an empire ready to take on the material legacy of that paradigm of empires. For its colonizers, the New World represented dispersed exotic cultures in geographically distant territory. This was far from the case for neoclassicism. As a result of their educational system, elite British men took on a distinctly "Roman" mind set. Their attitude to the spolia opima of their travels was proprietary rather than exploratory. They identified with the imperial Roman paradigm to such an extent that, rather than encountering the other, they seemed to be furnishing an indigenous tradition.

This account of fabricating the antique intends to rewrite neoclassicism in Britain, not as an ahistorical decorative style but as a style of thought. Our terminology comes from the German sociologist Karl Mannheim; our methodological framework, from the sociology of classical education.[36] The chapters that follow will investigate the proposition that "Classics formed part of the style of the English gentleman" by focusing on the culture of education, imitation, and competition through which the thought styles of a classical education were inculcated.[37] By situating classicism as a style of thought and neoclassicism as the material application of this process, this study will show how *together,* they shaped the lives of the peerage of eighteenth-century Britain both intellectually and physically—an idea posited but not developed by Cannon.[38]

Attention must focus on the intellectual makeup of members of the British aristocracy and gentry. In "Systems of Education and Systems of Thought," Pierre Bourdieu asserts that the patterns informing the thought of a particular period can be fully understood only by reference to the school system. It is this system, he argues, which establishes and develops, through practice, the habits of thought common to a whole generation.[39] The educational system that will be treated here is the English public school system, which included Eton, Westminster, and Winchester. Although there is no strict definition of what constitutes a public school, the term evolved in the eighteenth century when the leading old grammar schools sought to distinguish themselves from private schools.[40] These schools were public in the sense of not being privately owned, but they operated according to legal statutes drawn up by their founders. Boys paid fees and lived there as boarders.

As a form of what Bourdieu would call intellectual programming, the English public school system may be seen to represent a process of "Romanization." For eighteenth-century education at public school amounted to a prolonged and thorough exposure in, first, the languages of the ancient Romans and the ancient Greeks, and subsequently, to a selection of their literary works. It has been estimated that by the time a boy left Eton or Winchester, he would have read Virgil's *Aeneid* at least twice and all of Horace's poetry some two or three times, except the *Epodes,* some of which were too risqué for a schoolboy audience.[41] Using notes on the Eton curriculum made by the assistant master, Thomas James between 1766 and 1771, we can begin to understand how far a classical education patented the styles of thought for generations of British schoolboys. A rough timetable for an Eton student in the fourth form (fig. 7) shows how classics dominated the formal classroom teaching. Of the approximately twenty-seven hours of timetabled teaching, three were allocated to other subjects, which for a fourth former meant writing and arithmetic, with a further three allocated to church and prayers. This meant 88 percent of lesson time was allocated to the classics—twenty-one hours a week for an average of six years at public school between the ages of nine and fifteen. The classical content of the lessons was cumulative. Boys in the first year of the lower school were taught only Latin grammar. Having mastered Latin language and syntax early on, it then became the language of learning for ancient Greek.[42] By the fifth and sixth forms of the upper school, boys were construing, translating, and repeating passages from, among others, Homer, Lucian, Virgil, Horace, and the *Scriptores Romani* and the *Poetae Graeci*. In addition, these boys wrote verse compositions in ancient Greek and Latin, they staged classical plays, they spoke Latin during public debates and even—in the upper school at Westminster—in conversation.[43] It is no exaggeration to say that the minds of generations of educated schoolboys were quite literally steeped in the classics.[44]

What this book investigates is not so much the *content* of a classical education but rather the characteristics specific to what Bourdieu refers to as the intellectual universe of the English public school, the acquisition and framing of the styles of thought that were to map out itineraries for the many endeavors of the eighteenth

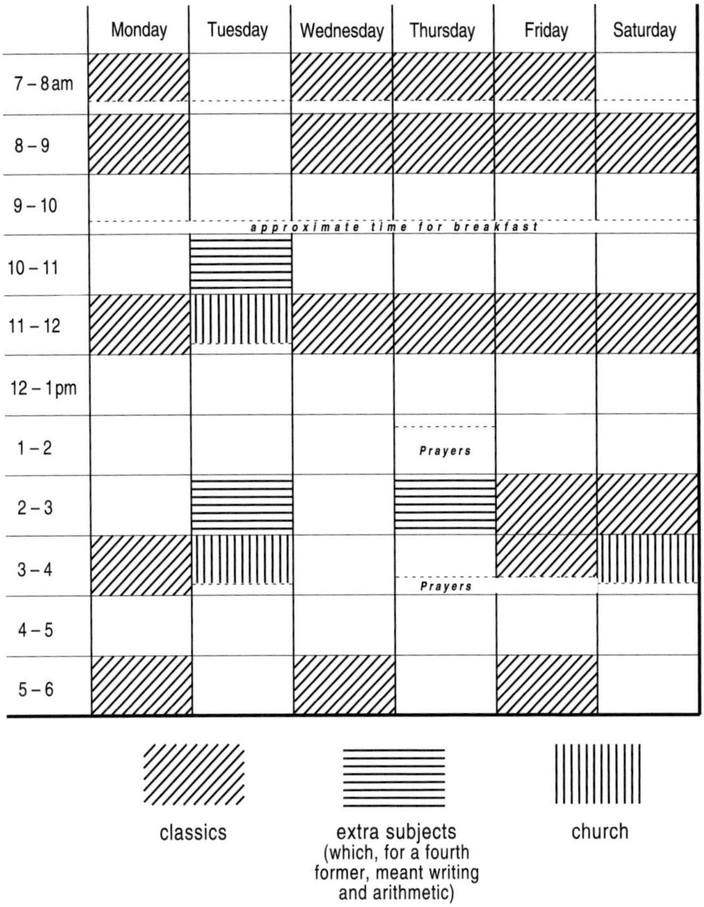

Figure 7 An estimated timetable for a fourth former at Eton based on notes taken by a master between 1766 and 1771. From M. V. Wallbank, "Eighteenth Century Public Schools and the Education of the Governing Elite," *History of Education* 8 (1979): 5.

century, including and especially for our purposes, neoclassicism.[45] A classical education imbued the practice of translation into its students: transposing words from one language into another and from one medium into another. In 1733, Lord Lincoln's tutor at Eton wrote to the boy's uncle, the Duke of Newcastle, that "[h]e has twice as much book and desire to play as ever he had in his life, and cant find a moments leisure: from construing and pearcing Greek he is gon to make verses, and from verses to prose, and from prose to Greek again."[46] The public school timetable incorporated different modes of translation on a daily and weekly basis. Thomas James describes lessons at Eton in which the sixth form construed passages in front of the fifth formers. The former turned Homer into Latin, while the latter parsed the words and quoted grammatical rules and parallel passages. The fifth form composed three original Latin exercises every week, as did the sixth, although their verses were longer and included Greek iambics.[47] For Bourdieu, school is a habit-forming force providing those who have been subjected to its influence with "that general disposition, generating patterns that can be applied in different areas of thought and action, which may be termed cultured *habitus*."[48] The schoolboy rituals of parsing, translating, and imitating the classical authors patented styles of thought among the British elite. It is these styles of thought inculcated by a classical education that I am calling classicism.

Having already surveyed the reverberations of antiquity in early modern Europe, the late eighteenth-century French context is once more relevant to our discussion of classical education. H. T. Parker's *The Cult of Antiquity and the French Revolutionaries* (Chicago, 1937) studies the development of the revolutionary spirit, devoting an entire chapter to the education of men of the revolutionary generation including Robespierre, Desmoulins, Danton, and Courtois in the quarter century from 1763 to 1788.[49] Questioning what these men thought of antiquity, from the high school to the guillotine, Parker investigates the classical curricula taught throughout the French system of *collèges*. Primary emphasis was placed on the works of Cicero, which were studied during a four-year period; after Cicero, prominence was given to Horace and Virgil, studied for three out of the six years of secondary education. According to our critical model, "school . . . maps out itineraries, that is to say methods (in the etymological sense) or programmes of thought."[50] Parker's chapter proceeds to look at instances of classical authors or modern authors like Montesquieu and Rousseau citing ancient history being referred to in the debates of the National Assembly, the Legislative Assembly, the National Convention, and in newspapers. As a group, participants in the Revolution cited in maturity particular classical works they had probably studied in their youth. These works were Roman, rather than Greek, classical texts and were composed within the time frame from 80 B.C. to A.D. 120, in which the present was unfavorably contrasted with the golden age of the republican past. The Roman republic's dual devotion to country and liberty spoke volumes to the French revolutionary generation.

Parker's discussion provides a coeval example of the educational context in revolutionary France that this book deals with for neoclassical Britain. Given that instances of neoclassicism are historically determined and nationally configured, so we should not be surprised by its different incarnations beyond the classrooms of France and Britain. When the British elite left public school with their minds steeped in the classics, it was customary for them to travel throughout Europe on the grand tour. While in Italy, they encountered a classical heritage with which they were already intimately connected: thanks to their educational programming, it was "their" cultured habitus. Much has been written on the grand tour in the period of its so-called golden age in the eighteenth century from a multiplicity of geographical perspectives, be it *The British Abroad* or *The Lure of Italy*.[51] Yet the specific relationship for British tourists between their classical education and the classic ground of Italy has been consistently underplayed. Following Bourdieu's work on the sociology of education, this book will argue that when classically educated British tourists encountered the antique firsthand in Italy, the thought styles that had become second nature through endless ritualized repetition at school were no longer latent but blatant. Their classical education was both fleshed out once on classic ground *and* imaginatively played out before their eyes.[52] We will encounter many instances of this in chapter 1. In a similarly novel approach to what constitutes neoclassicism, the attitude of British tourists toward the material culture of the ancients will be seen as an extension of the styles of thought inculcated at public school. Ancient artifacts like "Etruscan" vases (the focus of chapter 3), sculptural casts and copies (chapter 5), and restored ancient marbles (chapter 6), may be seen to represent the raw materials. We shall see how these raw materials were parsed, translated, and imitated by a nexus of dealers, artists, and manufacturers who received commissions from our classically educated British aristocrats and gentlemen. Through the networks of patronage and collecting, the ancient artifacts were transposed from one cultural context and, in many cases, medium and appropriated into another.

Fabricating the Antique deals then with the packaging and repackaging of the material culture of the ancients; how ancient culture came to be isolated and dislocated from its original contexts in Italy for the purposes of possession and exhibition by a British audience. With its focus on material culture, this book is intended to compliment existing studies within this expanding interdisciplinary field. The range of materials that constitute material culture in this study—paintings, sculptures, books, furniture, and furnishings—follow Prown's broad system of classification with its six sequential categories that range from the more decorative to the more utilitarian.[53] The theories and methodologies of design history are freely applied here to preindustrial, handmade objects traditionally the preserve of the fine arts, in addition to their more conventionalized application for the industrial productions of mass manufacture. In a recent review of the relationship between material culture and design history, Judy Attfield defines the former as a new kind of investigative approach that takes into account the new products, practices, and spaces of modernity.[54] Similarly for Vincentelli, design history is concerned with objects, technologies, and ideas.[55] Steven Shapin and Simon Schaffer's *Leviathan and the Air-Pump: Hobbes, Boyle and the Experimental Life* (Princeton, 1985) argues that three technologies were involved in the production and validation of matters of fact in the seventeenth century: material, literary, and social. The workings of each of these technologies depended on the other two. The laboratory, designated by Shapin and Schaffer a special space, was the domain in which experimental, discursive, and social practices were collectively controlled.[56] This study borrows two of Shapin and Shaffer's technologies—material and literary—to investigate how the late eighteenth century repackaged the material culture of the ancients as a series of *possessions* through the regimes of collecting and of representation. Both these regimes are understood as extensions of the intellectual itineraries or styles of thought inculcated by a classical education at English public school.

The regime of collecting is represented by an assortment of ancient artifacts belonging to a number of well-known collections, including Sir William Hamilton's "Etruscan" vases and Charles Townley's ancient marble sculptures. That of representation is concerned with two types of books: travel literature and antiquarian publications. An impressive number of recent studies have explored the popularity and significance of travel literature within the eighteenth century, many of them being as interested in the *representation* of travel as the act itself.[57] Travel literature devoted to Italy is conceptualized as a series of textual guidebooks, a literary counterpart to antiquarian publications like *Le Antichità di Ercolano esposte* and *Collection of Etruscan, Greek and Roman Antiquities,* whose engraved plates represent pictorial guidebooks to collections of ancient artifacts in Italy.

The relationship between the regimes of collecting and representation brings us back home to Britain following the grand tour in Italy and into the elite interior. Having been packaged in book form, the contents of published folios like *Collection of Etruscan, Greek and Roman Antiquities* were then repackaged when their accompanying plates were utilized as pattern books by architects, manufacturers, and craftsmen, including the ubiquitous Robert Adam and Josiah Wedgwood, in producing interior schemes and collectable artifacts. The special space that unites the two regimes of collecting and representation—and hence may be seen to embody the neoclassical enterprise—is the elite British library. The library is figured by authors and artists alike as the prime site or repository for the reception, preservation, and display of antiquity. According to the Shapin and Schaffer model, the library may be seen to encapsulate the neoclassical enterprise as the laboratory had for the experimental life a century before. So it is with a portrait, *Sir Rowland and Lady Winn in the Library at Nostell Priory* (plate 1), by the Irish artist Hugh Douglas Hamilton that we will begin our exploration of neoclassicism in Britain.

Certainly one of the greatest ornaments to a gentleman or to his family is a fine library.

Thomas Coke,
first Earl of Leicester, 1715[1]

1 (Neo)classicism in the British Library

Hugh Douglas Hamilton's painting *Sir Rowland and Lady Winn in the Library at Nostell Priory* (1767–68; plate 1) imag(in)es the British aristocrat and his wife on display in their recently refurbished library. Just as the wheat field in Gainsborough's *Mr. and Mrs. Andrews* (c. 1748–49) functioned seen as a backdrop for the landed classes, so the library here forms a backdrop for the aristocracy's intellectual property.[2] Its furniture signifies the elite privileges of learning and travel: consisting of a wall of bookshelves lined with books (which in this case create a literary landscape) and a globe displayed on the vast library desk. When we learn that this desk was supplied by the firm of Thomas Chippendale at a cost of seventy-two pounds, here is proof of Sir Rowland's patronage of the most fashionable—and costly—of contemporary furniture makers.[3] An architectural plan and other building tools deposited on the desk further denote the aristocratic couple as architectural patrons. But most strikingly, the painting is an evocative representation of aristocratic Britain's taste for the antique. The library bookcases, with their rectangular columns and pediments surmounted by busts of classical statuary, replicate the architectonic forms of ancient buildings. The busts surmounting the bookcases cannot be identified, although the one immediately behind Sir Rowland bears an uncanny resemblance to him. Another bust, at once identifiable as a copy of the "first lady" in the canon of ancient art, the *Medici Venus* (fig. 8), is installed in the far left of the painting, where she is displayed on a reproduction antique pedestal in wood with carved bull's heads and leafy garlands. To the right of the bust a framed chalk drawing, again of the head and neck of the *Medici Venus*, rests on a chair and is propped up by Sir Rowland.

Even with its vividly material depiction, Hamilton's painting is more than an inventory of imitation antique furnishings and furniture since the space and the contents of the library at Nostell Priory have been distorted.[4] Like the faux door composed of mimic volumes, which to all intents and purposes is another bookshelf, the painting is and is not what it seems. While it represents *an* image of the country house library at Nostell Priory as designed by the architect Robert Adam, its furnishings have been artfully adapted. The right hand wall of the actual library, for example, housed not two pedimented bookcases as shown in the painting, but one (on the right-hand side of fig. 9). In addition, the prominently placed bust of the *Medici Venus* appears to have been positioned with other plaster busts of famous antique statues like the *Apollo Belvedere*, the *Belvedere Antinous,* and a second bust of the *Medici Venus* along the cornice of the bookcases. Hamilton's surviving bill to Sir Rowland, dated 1767–69, explicitly refers to "a Bust of the Venus de Medicis & 2 packing Cases 1½ guineas."[5] From a memo dated 11 April 1773, it would also appear that the larger series of busts after the antique were not incorporated into the library scheme until some time after the painting was completed. Headed "To write to Mr Adam about under," the memo lists "Busts for Library" along with "the Rain coming into Sub Hall" and "Colouring of Saloon Seiling and sides."[6] Consequently, it must have been the artist who orchestrated the prominent installation of the bust of the *Medici Venus* into his double portrait of Sir Rowland and Lady Winn in their library.

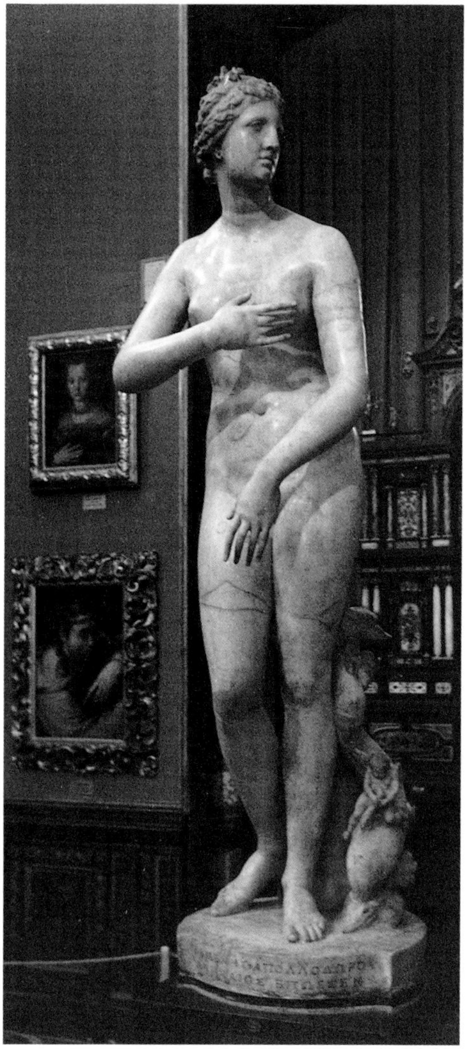

Figure 8 The *Medici Venus* "esteemed to surpass . . . any piece of sculpture throughout the whole world." The Conway Library, Courtauld Institute of Art. Photograph: Dr. Nicholas Penny.

By incorporating the plaster bust and the chalk drawing of the *Medici Venus*, Hamilton depicts not (only) the newly furnished country house library but Lady Winn as the aristocratic patron's greatest ornament. Sir Rowland's French-Swiss wife, Sabine Louise d'Hervart of Vevey, is imaged as the living, or in this case painted, incarnation of that "perfect model of female beauty," the *Medici Venus* (fig. 8 above), an ancient sculpture "esteemed to surpass not only all the statues in [the

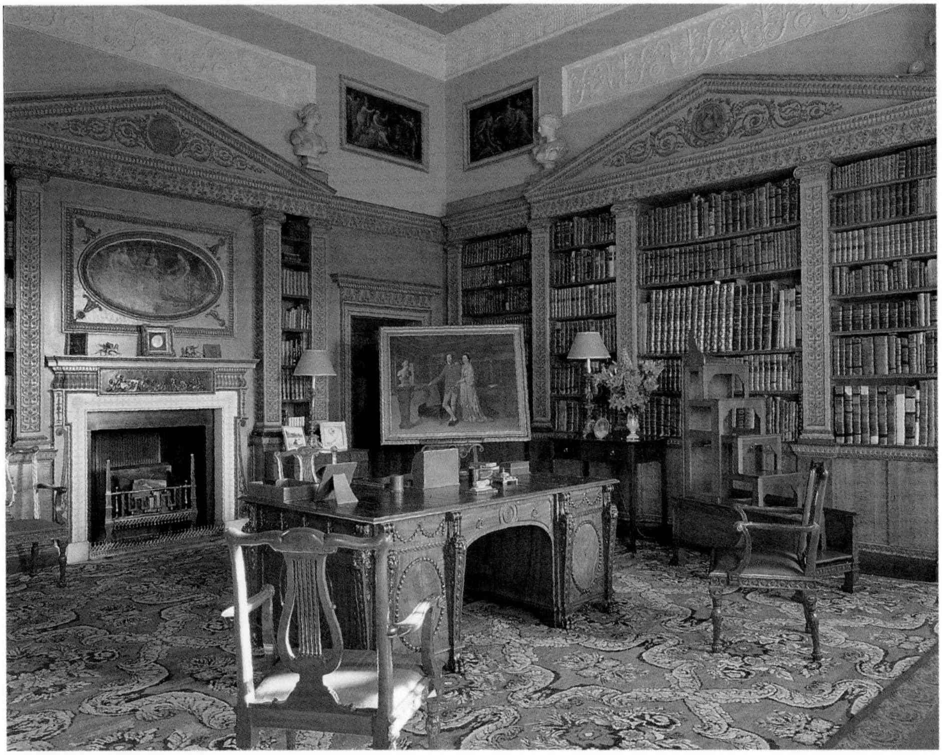

Figure 9 View of the library at Nostell Priory, designed by Robert Adam, 1766–76, with furniture by Thomas Chippendale and bookcases surmounted by plaster busts of classical sculptures. National Trust Photographic Library / Andreas von Einsiedel.

Tribuna in] Florence, but any piece of sculpture throughout the whole world."[7] As such, the Nostell Priory conversation piece is not an inventory and an unreliable one at that, but a fantasy: a fantasy located within a representation of a neoclassical library and played out by manipulating that library's imitation antique furniture.[8]

Until recently, this painting had no profile beyond the confines of its country house context. Then in 1997 it was launched from obscurity to celebrity when it was reproduced as the dust jacket for John Brewer's *The Pleasures of the Imagination: English Culture in the Eighteenth Century*. With its visual evocation of the library space, Hamilton's portrait of Sir Rowland and Lady Winn invites comparison with another, more famous, painted library: Johann Zoffany's *Charles Townley's Library at 7, Park Street, Westminster* (1781–83/98; plate 2).[9] When Zoffany painted this image, Townley's collection of ancient sculptures was one of the sights of late eighteenth-century London. Visiting the capital in 1786, Sophie von la Roche thought 7 Park Street "a fine house with some of the rarest and most costly ornamentations."[10] The fame of the collection extended to Townley himself, who was reportedly regarded by the public as a "Model of Taste."[11]

Zoffany's *Charles Townley's Library* has been described as perhaps the most evocative of all visual documents of the taste for the antique at the end of the eighteenth century.[12] Yet my goal in juxtaposing the Zoffany and Hamilton paintings is not to discuss their varying evocative qualities, but rather to assess them as two visual representations of the late eighteenth-century *library* as a repository for the antique. Both paintings offer us different versions of the library space and its classical contents. Zoffany's *Townley* is located in the library of the Roman Catholic gentleman's London townhouse. The antique is represented by his exhaustive collection of ancient marble sculptures, most of which were excavated, restored, and exported from Rome. In Hamilton's portrait of Sir Rowland and Lady Winn, the aristocratic library of the Winn's country house outside Leeds provides the backdrop for their painted portraits. Here too is another version of antiquity: not ancient artifacts transported from Italy, but rather antique architecture and sculpture imitated and translated into an interior scheme by the British architect Robert Adam.

As far back as the Renaissance curiosity cabinet, libraries and collections of works of art were understood as depositories of wisdom, whose aim was to encapsulate and perpetuate literary and material remains. John Britton describes Sir John Soane's collections at 13 Lincoln's Inn Fields, London, within this Renaissance paradigm in *The Union of Architecture, Sculpture and Painting* (London, 1827):

> To the Artist and to the Author, works of art and of literature are indispensible: they are necessary monitors, companions, friends. They are the depositories of wisdom; the legacies bequeathed by genius and talent to advance science and perpetuate information. By these we hold converse with Raffaelle, Michel Angelo, Vitruvius, Shakspeare. We consult with them for information: we associate with them for pleasure. In what they have said, we recognise the progress and effect of their studies: in what they have done, we behold evidences of their own experience engrafted on acquired knowledge. Hence libraries, and collections of works of art, are of inestimable value. They bring to "our own homes and bosoms" the learning, the talent, and the taste of distant nations and of distant ages.[13]

A late eighteenth-century ideology of the library space is articulated for us by the Reverend Alison in his *Essays on the Nature and Principles of Taste* (Edinburgh, 1790):

> The antiquarian, in his cabinet, surrounded by the relics of former ages, seems to himself to be removed to periods that are long since past, and indulges in the imagination of living in a world, which, by a very natural kind of prejudice, we are always willing to believe was both wiser and better than the present. All that is venerable or laudable in the history of these times present themselves to his memory.[14]

While relics from a miscellany of historical periods surrounded the Reverend Alison's antiquarian in his cabinet, Charles Townley and Sir Rowland Winn are imaged in their libraries surrounded with relics and imitation relics from the former ages of ancient Greece and Rome.[15] Like the antiquarian's cabinet, the library evokes an antique world that exists only in the imagination but is given tangible form in collections of works of art *and literature*.

Study of the impact of (what Britton calls) the learning, the talent, and the taste of Greek and Roman antiquity on the modernity of the late eighteenth century is, however, problematic, particularly in regard to works of literature. Experts on reading estimate that in the last two-thirds of the eighteenth century an unprecedented number of private libraries were established, but the majority of these collections are now wholly or partly dispersed.[16] The dispersal of the library is one chapter in the sorry story of the demise of the English country house, when owners struggling to retain their ancestral heritage began to sell off their collections. Once indispensable monitors, companions, and friends (to cite Britton again), books were all too dispensable and often the first to reach the salerooms.[17] The fate of the library collection formerly at Osterley Park House in Middlesex is one such case (fig. 10). This collection had a shelflife of well over a century, beginning in 1756, when Francis Child bought the entire library from the estate of Bryan Fairfax for two thousand pounds. Like Sir Rowland Winn's library at Nostell Priory, its equivalent at Osterley

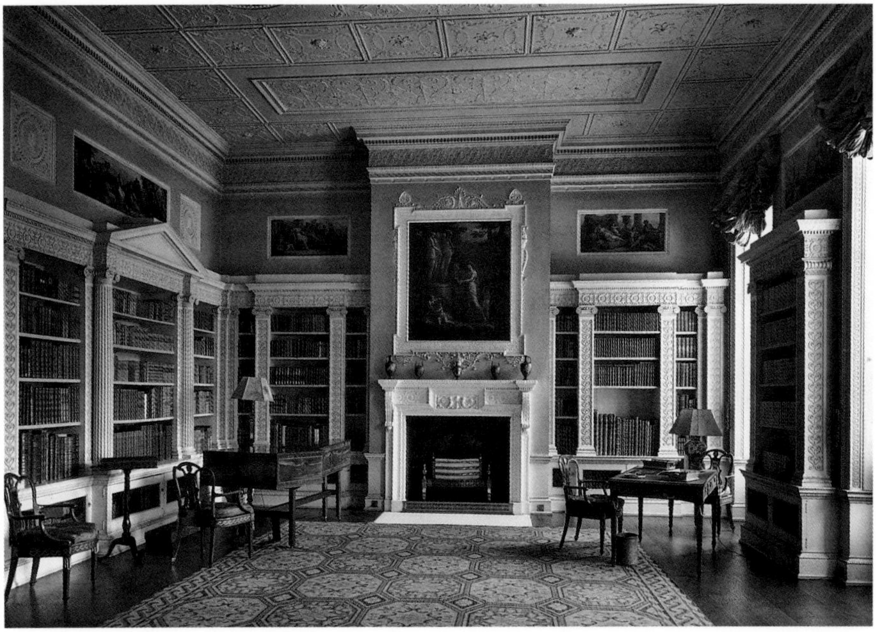

Figure 10 "Mr. [Robert] Adams has lavished all his taste in ornamenting every part": The library at Osterley Park House, Middlesex. The National Trust. Photograph: A. F. Kersting.

comprised a suite of rooms designed by the Adam. Visiting the property in 1772, Agneta Yorke thought the library "a charming room. It is filled with fine books, and Mr. Adams has lavished all his taste in ornamenting every part. It is plain white. The tables, desks and chairs are all of the fine inlaid work of different woods, and you cannot imagine how very elegant they are, and must have cost a great deal of money, but indeed one sees that no expence has been spared anywhere."[18] In May 1885, the fine books, by then the property of the Earl of Jersey, were sold at Sotheby's in an eight-day sale that raised over thirteen thousand pounds for urgent renovations to the property. Although printed catalogs of English private libraries pre-1800 are said to be few and far between, the library at Osterley Park House was cataloged and published in twenty-five copies by the Reverend Dr. Morell as *Catalogue Librorum in Bibliotheca Osterleiensi* (London? 1771).[19] All too often, the much later sales catalogs of auction houses are all we have to reconstruct the contents of eighteenth-century private libraries, and they make for difficult reading.

Excluding the books, the contents of the libraries of Sir Rowland Winn and Charles Townley have subsequently become the property of national institutions. In 1953, Nostell Priory was conveyed to the National Trust. The series of rooms designed by the architect, Robert Adam, are preserved, including the library, although its bookcases were grained circa 1826 to resemble painted wood. Hamilton's portrait of Sir Rowland and Lady Winn has become a prominent piece of furniture in the library it represents, being displayed on an easel behind the Chippendale desk (plate 1). Unusually, the books have not been dispersed but have been long neglected as literary wallpaper; as early as 1775, Edward Harwood wrote in *A View of the Various Editions of the Greek and Roman Classics* that "of late years books have been converted into a species of expensive furniture."[20] After Charles Townley's death in 1805, his collection of marble sculptures was purchased en bloc for the nation for twenty thousand pounds and deposited in the British Museum. With the opening of the Wolfson Galleries in 1984, Townley's sculptures have once again been displayed *as a collection* accompanied by a reproduction of Zoffany's painting of the collector's library. The original painting is the property of Towneley Hall art gallery and museum, formerly the Townley family's Lancashire home. The literary content of Townley's library, meanwhile, is long dispersed. It was inherited by his uncle, John Townley, himself a collector of rare and valuable books and was auctioned as the bibliotheca Townleiana in a number of sales held at the top and tail of the nineteenth century.[21] The Townleian collection of drawings, books, books of prints and British topography (some 1291 articles) was sold by a Mr. King in May 1816.[22] Two catalogs of Charles Townley's library, one from his house at Whitehall, dated 1771, the other from Westminster, undated and now in Chetham's Library at Manchester, make it possible for us to extrapolate the contents of his library from the sale catalogs of that of his uncle.[23] Only once this has been undertaken can we judge how far the folios, quartos, octavos, and duodecimos in Townley's book collection and his collection of ancient artifacts *operated together* in enabling their possessor to converse with what John Britton later called the learning, the talent, and the taste of ancient Greece and Rome.

Having identified possible leads in the specialist field of book history, let's continue our discussion of (neo)classicism by turning from contemporary paintings of the elite library to its books, by borrowing and reading a "classic" work of the late eighteenth-century by one of Sir Rowland Winn's and Charles Townley's contemporaries: Edward Gibbon's *The History of the Decline and Fall of the Roman Empire* (1776–88).

In the last section of chapter 6, in the final (sixth) volume of *The Decline and Fall*, Gibbon reviews the revival of classic literature in fifteenth-century Europe under the rubric the "Use and Abuse of Ancient Learning."[24] According to Gibbon's summary, the more perfect idioms of Greek and Roman texts enlightened the barbarians by introducing their previously vulgar manners to a "new world of light and science; to the society of the free and polished nations of antiquity." While this idealized polish rubbed off onto humanist scholars, Gibbon suggests that "from the first experiment, it might appear that the study of the ancients had given fetters, rather than wings to the human mind." By imitating the ancient models so faithfully, the moderns had cast themselves as slaves, fashioning their thoughts, speech, and beliefs on those of antiquity. While this period produced "a crowd of Latin imitators, who decently repose on our shelves," no work of invention or eloquence in the vernacular tradition was produced. Only once the soil of learning had been "deeply saturated with the celestial dew" could the classics of Athens and Rome inspire not only poetry and fiction but also "the light of speculative and experimental philosophy," first in Italy and later in France and England. The chapter ends with Gibbon's thoughts on education and imitation: "Genius may anticipate the season of maturity; but in the education of a people, as in that of an individual, memory must be exercised, before the powers of reason and fancy can be expanded; nor may the artist hope to equal or surpass, till he has learned to imitate, the works of his predecessors."[25]

This passage on the use and abuse of ancient learning, framed within the narrative of decline and fall, tells yet another story fundamental to Gibbon's methodology—that of classicism. Here, Gibbon emphasizes the *ideal* status of the antique, that culture of freedom and polish, canonized by the ideologically charged classicizing tradition. Also evident is the practice of intertextuality, which was central to works produced within this tradition in imitation and emulation of antique models—where writers of modern texts are readers of the texts of their predecessors.[26] In reminding his readers of the Latin imitators occupying their bookshelves, Gibbon locates this passage and, by implication, his *Decline and Fall*, within the intellectual and physical space of the *library*.

Purporting to review the place of classical learning within fifteenth-century Europe, the ironic and playful tone of this passage constructs the monument that is Gibbon's *Decline and Fall* both within and outside the traditional framework of humanist classicism. His reading of Renaissance humanist texts locates his work within a genealogical tradition starting with Petrarch and Boccaccio.[27] Yet in seeking a work of invention or eloquence in the popular language of the country, Gibbon implies that his readers need look no further than the text in front of them—Gibbon's own *Decline and Fall*! We should recall that the last two volumes in the series were written in "retirement" in Lausanne, when Gibbon's status as the historian of the Roman Empire was securely established.[28] Even the first volume, published in February 1776, sold a thousand copies by 26 March and was lauded by Horace Walpole in a letter to William Mason:

> Lo, there is just appeared a truly classic work: a history, not majestic like Livy, nor compressed like Tacitus; not stamped with character like Clarendon; perhaps not so deep as Robertson's *Scotland*, but a thousand degrees above his *Charles*; not pointed like Voltaire, but as accurate as he is inexact; modest as he is *tranchant* and sly as Montesquieu without being so *recherché*. The style is as smooth as a Flemish picture, and the muscles are concealed and only for natural uses, not exaggerated like Michael Angelo's to show the painter's skill in anatomy; nor composed of the limbs of clowns of different nations, like Dr. Johnson's heterogeneous monsters. This book is Mr Gibbon's History of the Decline and Fall of the Roman Empire.[29]

Gibbon's thoughts on genius and education may be read then as a playful and prophetic epitaph to his life's work. As Walpole's comment demonstrates, Gibbon's classic volumes came to represent a literary artifact of the elite culture of learning, both a product of the humanist classical tradition *and* an original text that formulated an ancient story for a modern British society. Indeed, Walpole confirms its classic status by reference to both literary and art historical comparanda. In any gentleman's library, like that of Horace Walpole, Gibbon's text would join those of immortal men on the bookshelves whose collected works represented an amalgamation of the elite culture of learning.

How then can we use Gibbon's *Decline and Fall* to formulate *our* understanding of eighteenth-century classicism? Surely Johann Joachim Winckelmann, hailed as the hero of the classical revival and whose name has become synonymous with the art historical movement known as neoclassicism, is a more obvious case study.[30]

Admittedly, the art historian reading Gibbon's text is rarely confronted with visual or archaeological finds—the arch of Constantine, "a melancholy proof of the *decline of the arts*," being the notable exception.[31] Yet Gibbon's epitaph at the close of chapter 66 represents a theoretical maxim applicable to both literary and material (neo)classicisms of late eighteenth-century Britain. Classicism is a learned process where "memory must be exercised, before the powers of reason and fancy can be expanded; nor may the artist hope to equal or surpass, till he has learned to imitate, the works of his predecessors."[32] And as a process it is "framed" in the library: (just) like the portraits of Sir Rowland and Lady Winn (plate 1) and Charles Townley (plate 2). While we know of Winckelmann's early career as a teacher and librarian, his work for Cardinal Albani in Rome, whose library was apparently entirely at his disposal, the books and bibliography that molded his encyclopedia of the art of antiquity have been largely overlooked by his commentators.[33] With Gibbon's classicism, by contrast, detailed footnotes accompany the text of the *Decline and Fall*, while his *Memoirs of My Life* in some seven revised versions are as much an autobiography as a comprehensive bibliography—the lifetime's reading of a critical historian, who saw it as his "right" and "duty" "to collect, to weigh, to select the opinions of his predecessors."[34] For Gibbon, this duty was realized by the contents of his library—some 6,000 volumes (in c. 1789) that he described as "the tools of my historical manufacture."[35] In a kind of literary premonition, in his early *Essai sur l'étude de la littérature* (1761), Gibbon described the scholar in his study surrounded by his own intellectual society—an image that he himself would later realize:

> Follow the man of letters into his study, you will see him surrounded by the literary productions of all ages; his library is stocked with them, and his mind informed without being overburdened by their perusal. He looks about him on all sides; nor is the author, whose writings may have the most distant relation to the subject of his thoughts, forgotten: he may happen to meet there with some accidental and striking passage, to confirm the discoveries of the critic, or stagger his hypotheses.[36]

From this we can construct an image of Gibbon as a literary archaeologist, exploring and excavating the stratified and, at times, previously fossilized layers of received classical learning. Take also a passage from the *Decline and Fall*—

> The confusion of the times, and the scarcity of authentic memorials, oppose equal difficulties to the historian, who attempts to preserve a clear and unbroken thread of narration. Surrounded with imperfect fragments, always concise, often obscure, and sometimes contradictory, he is reduced to collect, to compare, to conjecture: and though he ought never to place his conjectures in the rank of facts, yet the

> knowledge of human nature, and of the sure operation of its fierce and unrestrained passions, might, on some occasions, supply the want of historical materials.[37]

Gibbon's library was as much a monumental site to his erudite learning as his classic *Decline and Fall*. If Gibbon was a literary archaeologist, according to the passage quoted above, he was also a collector-connoisseur, "surrounded with imperfect fragments" or textual ruins. In response to Gibbon's characterization of the historian's methods, we can also begin to capture something of the *scientific* tone of eighteenth-century erudition. The library, in this account, becomes not merely a repository of ancient learning but also a site with clear contemporary resonances—where Gibbon's books are his tools and his library, the site of his experiments. Like any experiment, Gibbon's work and, particularly, his novel methodology were open to criticism. In response to the criticisms of Henry Davis concerning what he perceived as Gibbon's misrepresentation of the source material, it is as if Gibbon is inviting him, by invoking the textual furniture of his London library at 7 Bentinck Street, to come and see the test conditions under which his work was formulated:

> I cannot profess myself very desirous of Mr. Davis's acquaintance; but if he will take the trouble of calling at my house any afternoon when I am *not* at home, my servant shall shew him my library, which he will find tolerably furnished with the useful authors, ancient as well as modern, ecclesiastical as well as profane, who have *directly* supplied me with the materials of my History.[38]

Criticism of Gibbon's text did not necessarily apply to the contents of the library that formulated his *Decline and Fall*. On the flyleaf of his copy of volume 4, William Beckford inveighed against Gibbon's "almost ludicrous self-complacency . . . your affected moral purity peking up every now and then from the corrupt mass. . . your tumid diction, your monotonous jingle of periods."[39] Yet Beckford the bibliophile, in what has been described as his most flamboyant gesture as a book collector, purchased Gibbon's entire library for nine hundred and fifty pounds in the winter of 1796–97.[40] The library at Bentinck Street was not only tolerably furnished with books, since its interior was refurbished in the 1770s in the fashionable, so-called neoclassical style, as lavished (so Agneta Yorke described it) by Robert Adam on the libraries at Nostell Priory and Osterley Park House. In a letter of 1772, Gibbon describes the program of redecoration: "Ireland the Upholder visited it with me this morning, and to omitt other particulars talked of Bookcases, quite agrees in the proscription of Mahogany. The paper of the Room will be a fine shag flock paper, light blue with a gold border, the Bookcases painted white, ornamented with a light frize: neither Doric nor Dentulated . . . but Adamic."[41]

His work not yet complete, Gibbon's retirement to Lausanne in 1783 witnessed the removal en bloc of his indispensable books; without such tools at his side, he wrote that he would be deprived of good company and bibliography for the last volumes.[42] While he envisaged making use of "private and public libraries which will be freely opened for the use of a man of letters," Gibbon later boasted that his personal library was "superior to any in the Pays de Vaud, and more compleat and valuable than it formerly was in Bentinck street."[43] Via subscription and contact with London booksellers, Gibbon was constantly acquiring new books for his library. The librarian of the Duke of Hanover and travelling companion to the Prince, Ernst Langer, describes in the 1780s being granted unsupervised access to Gibbon's "treasury of learning" and its accompanying catalog. He noted Gibbon's "good fortune and his fine taste in every thing, the elegance of the bindings, the exteriors of his books, [which] bespoke their value, was to be expected."[44] Gibbon's display of knowledge was matched only by his display of books—books themselves becoming not only sources of evidence, but as material evidence of the historian's social and intellectual powers. Thus, Gibbon would be crowned by the tourist John Owen as "the *grand monarque* of literature at Lausanne": a bibliophile who, according to the Duchess of Devonshire, was consulted "as the best book in his Library."[45]

To read Gibbon's *Decline and Fall* is for the "patient reader" to confront a literary monument whose publication would ensure that the volumes of Gibbon's library would never be wholly dispersed.[46] Even the first volume in the series was received in 1776, as has already been noted, as a classic text. The range and depth of the *Decline and Fall* gives that reader privileged, albeit secondhand access to an ocean (to invoke the epigraph from Livy on the title page of vol. 1) of learning: the *Decline and Fall* as a miniature library constructed from the textual fragments that are represented by Gibbon's extensive collection of books. Indeed, this miniature library would itself become a collectable. In Gibbon's lifetime it was translated into French, Italian, and German.[47] Almost prophetically, Gibbon wondered in his *Memoirs* whether his text "may, perhaps, an hundred years hence, still continue to be abused."[48] How fitting then that at the end chapter 66 in volume 6 of the *Decline and Fall*, Gibbon actually characterized what we have called classicism as the use and abuse of ancient learning.

In our study of late eighteenth-century classicism, Gibbon's *Decline and Fall* provides us with a definition, a methodological framework based on education and, imitation, and a location: the library. The problem with Gibbon as a spokesman (so to speak) for eighteenth-century classicism is that as a package—the library, the books and bibliography, the *Decline and Fall*—it is too good to be true; too much to be typical. "Almost everybody that reads has purchased [the volumes of the *Decline and Fall*]," wrote Gibbon to his stepmother on 13 April 1781, "but few persons (comparatively) have read them; and I find that the greater number, satisfied that they have acquired a valuable fund of entertainment, differ the perusal to the summer, the country, and a more quiet period."[49] Gibbon's six-volume work was a valuable fund of entertainment, not a formulation of British classicism. "He has . . . give[n] interest and amusement to, a period of history, which, till he undertook it, lay buried under a heap of Gothic rubbish, which scarce any one was bold enough to touch, and which he, by touching, has changed to gold," claimed the *Pamphleteer* when recommending Gibbon's *Decline and Fall* for the formation of a select and small library.[50] Being concerned with Gibbon's attitude to antiquity rather than his historical feats of literary alchemy, we might turn again to his literary debut for clarification. In a passage in the *Essai sur l'étude de la littérature* (London, 1761), Gibbon writes explicitly and emphatically, "An acquaintance with antiquity is the only true comment on the writings of the ancients: but what is still more necessary, is a certain turn of mind, which is generally the result of it; a sentiment not only making things known, but familiarizing them to our ideas, and inducing us to regard them with the eyes of the ancients."[51] Again, Gibbon's "eyes of the ancients" mark him out from among his contemporaries as atypical. But he, like so many of them, *did* possess what is characterized in this passage as "a certain turn of mind" for Greek and Roman antiquity. And in order to understand where this derived from, we need to go back to school.

"Rome is the school for the whole world," wrote J. W. von Goethe, quoting Winckelmann's letter to Francke.[52] For the British traveller in the late eighteenth century, the experience of visiting Rome was more akin to that of attending a finishing school. A classical education at English public school or the privilege of a personal tutor at home represented the British schoolboy's earliest encounter with the ancients via the classical languages of Latin and Greek. According to one of the seven versions of Gibbon's *Memoirs*, "a finished scholar may emerge from the head of Westminster [Gibbon's alma mater] or Eaton in total ignorance of the business and conversation of English Gentlemen in the latter end of the eighteenth century. But these schools may assume the merit of teaching all that they pretend to teach, the Latin and Greek languages: they deposit in the hands of a disciple the keys of two valuable chests."[53] With these keys the schoolboy could unlock the classical library since, as Christopher Stray has recently pointed out, the classics were materially embodied in books—as a corpus of school knowledge, especially in textbooks.[54]

Classical textbooks in the archive at Eton College confirm the emphasis on Latin and Greek language, which together constituted the entire formal curriculum. With titles like Thomas Bowles's *A compendious and rational institution of the Latin tongue* (Oxford, 1740) and John Clarke's *An Introduction to the making of Latin* (14th ed., London, 1747) we are left in little doubt as to the content of the educational diet. James Greenwood's *The London Vocabulary, English and Latin* (18th ed., London, 1782) was published specifically for schoolboys "to acquaint the Learner with Things as well as pure Latin Words." The 1741 edition of *The Odes, Epodes and Carmen Seculare of Horace*, which juxtaposed the Latin text with an English translation, was similarly pitched at a schoolboy audience. According to the preface, "Of all the Gifts of the Muses *Horace's Poems* are the most useful, and he is the only Poet who can form the Gentleman." Yet his "so very excellent, and so very useful" poems, which are said to offer their reader "the Fruits of Wisdom curiously set off with the most charming Flowers of Parnassus," are necessarily edited for his impressionable audience. The preface explains how *"nothing [is] translated contrary to the Rules of Decency or good Manners, or that can offend the chastest Ear"*: thus the eighth and twelfth poems of the *Epodes* remain untranslated, while some other sentences are rather loosely translated. In a telling example of the proprietorial nonsense of the classical literary tradition, such censorial measures are apparently justified by the "excellent Rule" of Juvenal (*Satires,* XIV, 44–45), "Nil dictu foedum visuque haec limina tangat / Intra quae puer est (Suffer no Lewdness or indecent Speech / The Apartment of the tender Youth to reach.")

The vast bibliography of Roman history was similarly presented in accessible volumes, such as that in a *question and answer* format *extracted from Ancient authors, and the most celebrated among the modern* (London, 1749). Atlases of ancient geography aided the schoolboy in retracing the paths of literary journeys like that of Aeneas, the founder of Rome, in Virgil's *Aeneid*. According to the preface of the *Geographia Classica* (London, 1712), such mapping made reading the ancient authors less tedious and enabled the student "with reasonable Exactness [to] judge of the Actions described by them."[55] These volumes give us a clear indication of the extent to which the study of Greek and Roman antiquity in the eighteenth-century classroom was materially embodied in classical textbooks, including vocabularies, translations, grammars, and atlases.

This narrative is less concerned with the *content* of a classical education than with its *impact* on the material possessions collected and commissioned by classically educated Britons. Stray's proposition that "Classics formed part of the style of the English gentleman" may be refined into the position that eighteenth-century classicism was a style of thought inculcated by a classical education.[56] Bourdieu's work on the sociology of education provides us with a useful methodological framework in which the styles or programs of thought of any given period can be fully understood only by reference to the school system, which is alone capable of establishing them and developing them.[57] The classical curriculum of the English public school established and developed distinctive styles of thought through endless ritualized repetition. For approximately twenty-one hours a week during an average of six years at public school, boys parsed, translated, and imitated the classical authors. These exercises implicitly patented the styles of thought that I am calling classicism. As a form of intellectual programming, classicism provided a "cultured *habitus*" among members of the British elite.[58] So what we, following a passage in Gibbon's *Decline and Fall*, have called classicism—the use and abuse of ancient learning—was in fact a technology of public schooling; a style of thought instilled by the classical curriculum of an elite public school education and embodied in its textbooks.

According to Bourdieu, school maps out itineraries.[59] Having been patented by the educational patterns of the English public school system, classicism was transformed by the possibilities of foreign travel in Italy. Once on classic ground, the styles of thought that had been implicit and latent in the classroom became explicit and blatant.[60] In his *Letters from a young painter abroad to his friends* (London, 1750), for example, James Russel acknowledges how "the smack of poetry, which I contracted at Westminster, has contributed not a little to the pleasure, I have frequently enjoyed" in Italy.[61] A pleasure, as he notes in another letter, "not to be felt by any one confined within the walls of a study, or a chamber."[62] For the Earl of Mornington, were it not for recurrences to the "old ideas of Eton and Oxford," then "the journey through Italy would lose the greatest part of its amusement."[63] The grand tour in Italy transplanted the student onto actual classic ground that he had so often encountered in textbooks in the classroom. Lord North made this observation in a letter of 1–19 September 1753, to his tutor at Eton, Charles Dampier:

> You know, that ye road from Rome to Naples abounds with Classical amusement: I can assure you that ye road from Naples to Paestum is no less amusing in ye same way. There is scarce a town, a rivulet, a hill, or a valley, that is not mentioned & even distinctly pointed out in some of ye antient writers. Those travellers, who are well read in them, & who have already made ye same journey several times in their imaginations, are highly-pleased to find themselves in a well-known Country: Almost every spot they see, & every step they take, recalls or refreshes, confirms or clears up some old Idea.[64]

Edward Gibbon's grand tour represents this conflation of schoolboy text and enlightened travel; in his *Memoirs* he recalled his literary campaign (the library, his headquarters) for conquering Italy:

> My studies were chiefly preparations for my Classic tour—the Latin poets and historians, the science of Manuscripts, medals, and inscriptions, the rules of Architecture, the Topography and antiquities of Rome, the Geography of Italy, and the military

> roads which pervaded the Empire of the Caesars. Perhaps I might boast that few travellers more compleatly armed and instructed have ever followed the footsteps of Hannibal.[65]

Gibbon's *Decline and Fall* can be read as an imaginative grand tour, where chapters and volumes represent the course of a journey through centuries of Roman history: "In a composition of some days, in a perusal of some hours, six hundred years have rolled away, and the duration of a life or reign is contracted to a fleeting moment."[66] With Gibbon as *cicerone*, the historical pilgrimage ends, in keeping with the course of actual tours, in contemporary Rome. Yet in many ways, the actual paths of the grand tour in Italy may also be seen as a type of pilgrimage, where "a new race of pilgrims from the remote, and once savage, countries of the North," as Gibbon put it, followed in the footsteps of a cast of ancients immortalized in Roman literature.[67] Furthermore, the eighteenth-century pilgrim travelling to Rome necessarily followed in the footsteps of the medieval pilgrim. While the former's goal was not largely a Christian one, the notion of an archaeological pilgrimage integrates the historical fabric of Western society into the grand tour. The classic tourist's baggage consisted of the texts of ancient authors either carried to or obtained in Italy to act as his guides and guidebooks. We know that in Gibbon's library, for example, a mahogany box housed twenty-four volumes of the classical authors (fig. 11) published by J. Brindley.[68] This outlook was seconded by the Reverend Eustace in his *A Classical Tour through Italy* (London, 1813):

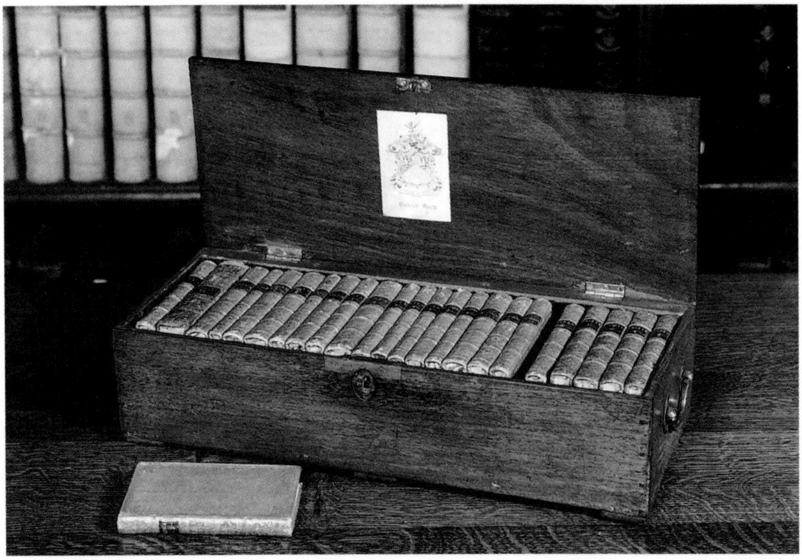

Figure 11 Edward Gibbon's travelling library. By courtesy of the Governing Body of Christ Church, Oxford.

> Virgil and Horace, Cicero and Livy, ought to be the inseparable companions of all travellers; they should occupy a corner in every carriage, and be called forth in every interval of leisure to relieve the fatigue and to heighten the pleasure of the journey. Familiar acquaintance or rather bosom intimacy is evidently the first and most essential accomplishment of a *classical* traveller.[69]

The portability of the travelling library undoubtedly affected the way such classics were read. In other words, while the texts referred to in the course of a journey were the same as in the classroom, not only the setting but also the reader would have been changed by the fact of travel, and this would have opened up a different range of possible responses. The physician Lucas Pepys, for instance, wrote from Rome that he had "read the six last books of Virgil lately and they appear to me in quite a new light as being on the spot, and having the Scene of Action before my eyes. For the future I shall not only understand better, but be more interested in reading the Latin Classics, so many places being mentioned in them with which I am now so well acquainted."[70]

Prior to embarking on their grand tours, our British pilgrims were already acquainted with the texts of ancient authors, as much for their lessons in polite behavior as for those of Roman history. Old Etonian William Pitt extolled this aspect of a classical education in a letter of 12 October 1751. Replying to his nephew's letter than was written in Latin, Pitt rejoiced to hear he had begun reading Homer's *Iliad* in Greek having made "so great a progress" in Latin with Virgil. The letter continues:

> I hope you will taste and love those authors [Homer and Virgil] particularly. You cannot read them too much: they are not only the two greatest poets, but they contain the finest lessons for your age to imbibe: lessons of honour, courage, disinterestedness, love of truth, command of temper, gentleness of behaviour, humanity, and in one word, virtue in its true signification. Go on, my dear nephew, and drink as deep as you can of these divine springs: the pleasure of the draught is equal at least to the prodigious advantages of it to the heart and morals. I hope you will drink them as somebody does in Virgil, of another sort of cup: "Ille impiger hausit spumantem pateram."[71]

As Samuel Sharp more concisely put it in his *Letters from Italy* (London, 1766): "*Rome* . . . which from our cradles, we have been taught to adore."[72] In many ways, the story of the grand tour is the story of how this adoration was both formative and transformed. In the same way the books of classical authors, having returned home after the tour, became the memento of the journey as well as its guidebook.

Edward Gibbon's first impressions of Rome—or rather, Gibbon's memories written in later life of his arrival in the eternal City—are well known:

> My temper is not very susceptible of enthusiasm, and the enthusiasm which I do not feel I have ever scorned to affect. But at the distance of twenty-five years I can neither forget nor express the strong emotions which agitated my mind as I first approached and entered the *eternal City*. After a sleepless night I trod with a lofty step the ruins of the Forum; each memorable step where Romulus *stood*, or Tully [Cicero] spoke, or Caesar fell was at once present to my eye; and several days of intoxication were lost or enjoyed before I could descend to a cool and minute investigation.[73]

Describing his experience as unforgettable but also somehow inexpressible, Gibbon actually articulates the memory of his arrival by imitating Ammianus Marcellinus's account of the imperial *adventus* of Constantius II. In the *Decline and Fall*, Gibbon described the fourth-century A.D. Roman historian as "an accurate and faithful guide, who has composed the history of his own times, without indulging the prejudices and passions, which usually affect the mind of a contemporary."[74] According to a passage in Ammianus's *Res Gestae* (16.10, 15), the emperor Constantius was overwhelmed at the sights of Rome, as Gibbon was fourteen centuries later. At the forum of Trajan "he stood fast in amazement, turning his attention to the gigantic complex about him, beggaring description and never again to be imitated by mortal men." By invoking Ammianus's description, Gibbon maps the memory of his own arrival in Rome onto that of Constantius. In doing this, he practices his maxim for the classicizing tradition in which the artist cannot hope to equal or surpass the works of his predecessors until he has learned to imitate them.[75] As Gibbon admits, in writing these memories of his memories of Rome, his powers of cool and minute reasoning were wholly supplanted by idealized fancy or, as he describes it, by enthusiasm.

Undeterred by the ruinous presence of antiquity in contemporary Rome, the classical pilgrim saw not the archaeological present, but visions of an ancient past imposed by his reading of classical literature. Take a passage on entering Rome from the Reverend Alison's *Essays on the Nature and Principles of Taste*, which aptly demonstrates how grand tourists not only travelled miles in the geographical sense over the Italian countryside but also seemed to travel back in time to ancient Italy:

> It is not the scene of destruction which is before him. It is not the Tyber diminished in his imagination to a paultry stream . . . It is not the triumph of superstition over the wreck of human greatness . . . It is the country of Caesar, and Cicero, and Virgil, which is before him. It is the mistress of the world which he sees . . . All that the

> labours of his youth, or the studies of his maturer age have acquired with regard to the history of this great people, open at once before his imagination, and present him with a field of high and solemn imagery which can never he exhausted.[76]

Outside the imperial capital, where "you may quote at least a hundred verses from different parts of Horace and Virgil," the topographical landscape of Naples still resounded with classical allusions.[77] James Boswell wrote to John Johnston on 19 March 1765 that

> Naples is indeed a delicious spot; *praeter omnes ridet*. I have been near three weeks here and have been constantly employed in seeing the classical places all around. Is it possible to conceive a richer scene than the finest bay diversified with islands and bordered by fields where Virgil's Muses charmed the creation, where the renowned of ancient Rome enjoyed the luxury of glorious retreat and the true flow of the soul which they valued as much as triumphs?[78]

Like Gibbon's account of his arrival in Rome, Boswell's letter quotes from the texts of the classical literary tradition. This includes not only the first-century B.C. poet Horace on Naples, which "smiles beyond all others" (*Odes* II. vi. 13–14), but also Alexander Pope's imitation, *The first satire of the second book of Horace* (first published in 1733): "The feast of reason and the flow of soul" (I. 128). These quotations represent an elite dialogue between the classical and classicizing authors, the educated tourist and his readers at home. The classical pilgrim (re)wrote Italy with the classical library as his bibliography, just as he viewed the archaeological sites with the classical texts as his guides.

> Our early studies, as Gibbon justly observes, allow us to sympathize in the feelings of a Roman; and one might almost say of every school boy not insensible to the sweets of his first studies, that he becomes in feeling and sentiments, perhaps even in language, a Roman. Is it not then wonderful, that when in a riper age he visits that country and beholds those very scenes which he has imagined to himself so long before, he should feel an uncommon glow of enthusiasm, and in the moment of enchantment, should add some imaginary to the many real charms. Besides, the scenery of Italy is truly classical, I mean, it is such as described by poets and historians.[79]

So wrote the Reverend Eustace in *A Classical tour through Italy* (3rd ed., London, 1815), a guidebook that drew attention to each and every ancient nuance. While Boswell advised his late eighteenth-century audience to "Read all Virgil and Horace in Italy," Eustace prepackaged the ancient authors in the early nineteenth century.[80] Had Gibbon by this time become the British classical pilgrim par excellence —as Goethe was for his German audience?[81] Writing to his mother from Rome on 3 November 1802, Thomas Robinson described his commitment to "improving my Talents & finishing my education. I have made considerable progress in Connoisseurship of Statues, Pictures & Gems. I have been zealously pursuing the study of drawing... I have taken some practical lessons by observations on architecture, & I have been perusing the Works of Gibbon. *Don't say I came to Rome for nothing.*"[82] In paraphrasing a footnote from the *Decline and Fall*, Gibbon's modern text is quoted by Eustace with the authority of its ancient counterparts.[83] On Eustace's account, a classical education in Britain amounted to a process of Romanization. Saturated with Roman literary culture in youth, the British pilgrim came to Rome after years of exposure to it with preconceived ideals. It is the paradox of an English public school education that its process of Romanization—"a set of the best *roman* virtues deeply engraven on your heart"—was understood to have taken place outside Rome.[84] Indeed, the firsthand experience of Rome often became the climax of a process where the classical traveller became Roman.[85] After visiting the house of Cicero, James Boswell describes being "seized with enthusiasm" and being resolved to speak in Latin: "harangu[ing] on Roman antiquities in the language of the Romans themselves."[86]

Such outpourings of classical enthusiasm are not idiosyncratic, insists Conyers Middleton in *A Letter from Rome* (London, 1741), "but common to all men of reading and education" in pursuit of "the pleasure of finding out and conversing with *those ancient Sages* and *Heroes*, whose characters they have most admired."[87] The classical traveller already intimate with the ancients experienced Italy at a distance: a distance created by education and expectation. The grand tour was a form of classical pilgrimage that traced the cult of ancient Italy, where every visual sight and archaeological site was used to refer to an ancient hero, event, or text. Ruins traditionally associated with ancient authors became their workplaces, homes, or even tombs according to the pervading influence of the classical tradition. Here is Eustace again, on the topographical landscape around Naples, which may,

> have never been... the theatre of heroic achievements, or the stage of grand and unusual incidents; but they have been the residence of the great and the wise; they have aided the meditations of the sage, and have awakened the raptures of the poet; and as long as the Latin muse continues to instruct mankind, so long will travellers visit with delight the academy of Cicero, the tomb of Vergil, and the birth-place of Tasso.[88]

However, the educated eighteenth-century culture that so delighted in revisiting the antique has been posthumously greeted with derision. According to Ludwig Curtius,

> For the cultured upper classes in the eighteenth century the classical era was no more than an object of study for antiquated pedantry or something of a random collector's piece, nothing more than a decorative background for operas, processions and garden parties. It could, of course, also serve to provide quotations or as material for didactic and moralising works for the edification of young gentlemen or to embellish political treatises.[89]

Paradoxically, Gibbon's *Decline and Fall* has retained its classic status. Indeed, in the preface of the most recent 1994 edition, it is promoted as "one of the greatest narratives in European literature."[90] Just as Gibbon's narrative is far removed from antiquated pedantry (although William Beckford might disagree), so this chapter has attempted to show how the classical tradition in the eighteenth century *was* an object of study, not for antiquated pedantry but for establishing and developing the thought styles of a classical education. The style of thought inculcated by the English public school system was classicism—the use and abuse of ancient learning. Neoclassicism, in turn, was not the random collector's piece or the decorative background that Curtius would have us believe it was. Rather, it was the application of this formative style of thought onto the material culture of the ancients.

In *Letters from a young painter abroad to his friends in England* (London, 1750) James Russel refers to the pleasure deriving from standing on classic ground in Italy:

> This pleasure I endeavour to repeat and increase at home, by calling to mind those many persons, so illustrious in arms or arts, of whose great actions, residence, or retirement these places had been the scenes. Here I give the reins to my imagination, and fancy to myself, how they fought, or spoke, or studied, or diverted themselves, in this or that particular spot. And to impress the remembrance both of the places and of the passages the deeper, I divert myself now and then in attempting a translation, or rather imitation, of the latter. The consequence of which is much the same with that, which always attends my copying some pieces of the most famous Painters, a greater admiration of the graces of the originals.[91]

Consciously attempting to impress the memories of his classical tour, Russel attempted a translation, or rather, imitation of the relevant passages from the ancient authors. In diverting himself in what was effectively a schoolboy ritual, he exercises the thought styles, which had been instilled by his classical education at Westminster school. In this letter, Russel explicitly aligns the educated act of translating or imitating a classical text with the aesthetic art of copying works by famous painters. In both cases, Russel's copy enhances "the graces" of the original. As we will see in the following chapters, in the acquisition of material artifacts like Etruscan vases, restored ancient sculptures and plaster casts, the classically educated British aristocrat or gentleman was able to, as Russel put it, "impress the remembrance both of the places and of the passages the deeper." In other words, he was able to translate and transpose his classical education and grand tour in Italy into material possessions. Here is the Reverend Alison again in his *Essays on the Nature and Principles of Taste* describing the reigning taste of the 1780s that we would call neoclassicism: "The taste which now reigns is that of the ANTIQUE. Every thing we now use, is made in imitation of those models which have been lately discovered in Italy; and they serve. . . to occupy our imagination, by leading to those recollections of Grecian or Roman Taste, which have so much the possession of our minds, from the studies and amusements of our youth."[92] To repeat a phrase already borrowed from Bourdieu, a classical education at English public school mapped out itineraries or programs of thought.[93] These itineraries were both literal *and* figurative, being later realized through firsthand encounters with the antique: on classic ground in Italy and then translated and transported back home to Britain. What the Reverend Alison refers to as "so much the possession of our minds," the formative thought style that was classicism, was transferred into material possessions: into neoclassicism.

Having already provided us with a definition of classicism as the use and abuse of ancient learning, a subsequent chapter in the final (sixth) book of Gibbon's *Decline and Fall* deals with the plunder of the "vast and various mine" that was ancient Rome under the rubric "The Use and Abuse of the Materials."[94] Gibbon traces the systematic destruction of the city and its ancient edifices by "foreign and domestic rapine," from the barbarian invaders, who "usurped in a moment the toil and treasure of successive ages" by the removal of precious materials like marble, to the later recycling of its structures by "every call of necessity or superstition" of indigenous Romans. Following Gibbon, our working definition of neoclassicism will be the use and abuse of the materials.

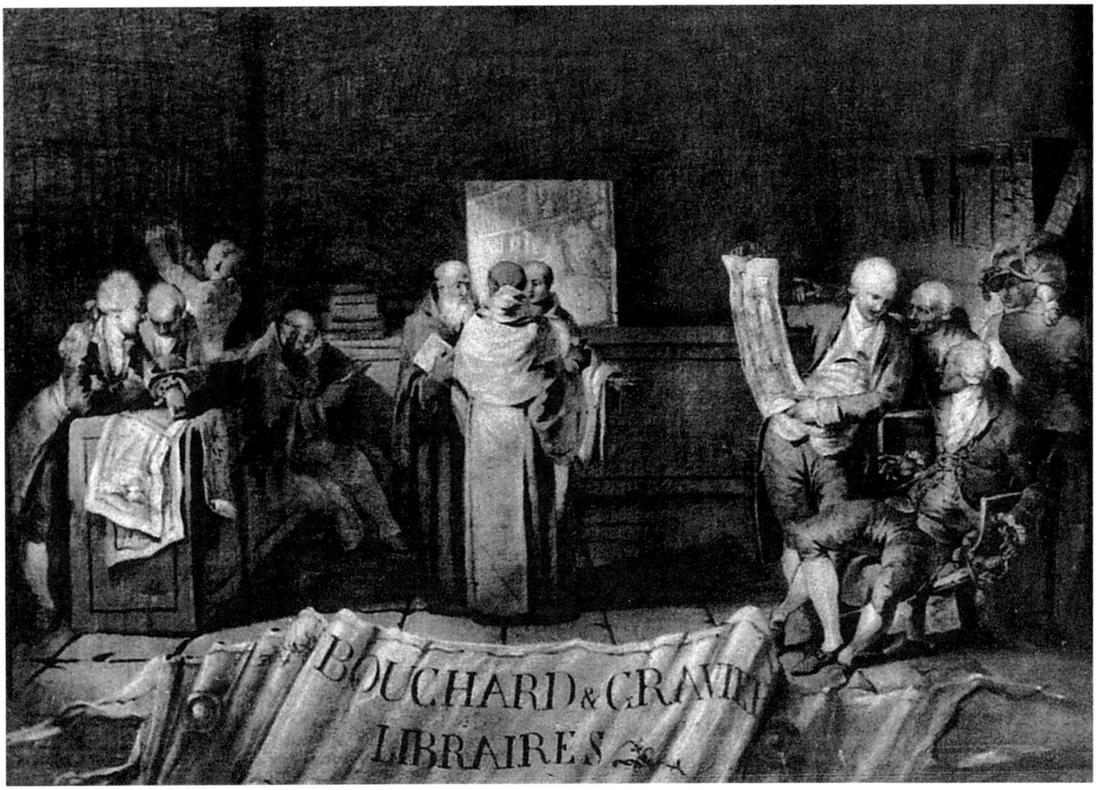
BOUCHARD & GRAVIER
LIBRAIRES

There is a kind of superiority which books give one better than horses.

Viscount Palmerston[1]

2

"Worth looking at with reflection"

Monuments as Texts and Texts as Monuments

A painting of the *Interior of the Bouchard and Gravier Bookshop in Rome* (c. 1774; fig. 12) reminds us that while on classic ground in Italy, the foreign traveller collected more than memories. Against the dimly lit bookshelves stacked with rows of folio volumes we see the bookshop's customers, consisting of a group of monks in the center and foreign tourists to either side. In the same way that the painting *An Antiquary's Shop in Naples* (1798) has become synonymous with the vogue for Etruscan vases in late eighteenth-century Naples, so the figuring of a shop selling books and prints—items worthy of perusal and conversation *in* the painting—signals the significance of such goods for the tourist in Rome.[2] The name of the bookshop situated in the Via del Corso is inscribed onto an unraveled scroll in the foreground of the image, the scroll being a literary format particularly associated with the ancients. The Tate Gallery's *Grand Tour* catalog notes that the shop is best known as the publisher of Giovanni Battista Piranesi's works from the *Carceri* (1745) to the *Antichità Romane* (1756). Certainly, the engravings overhanging the left-hand counter and that being displayed to the group of tourists assembled on the right depict examples of the ancient monuments in Rome engraved by Piranesi: the pyramid of Cestius and a triumphal column. As representative of *The Lure of Italy in the Eighteenth Century*, this anonymous painting causes us to consider to what extent the

Figure 12 Anonymous, *Interior of the Bouchard and Gravier Bookshop in Rome*, c. 1774. Private collection.

grand tour was an opportunity for collecting not only material artifacts but also for literary collectables.[3]

Archival evidence of the British tourist buying books during his travels in Italy is preserved in the grand tour accounts of Sir Roger Newdigate, which are located in the Warwickshire County Record Office. Newdigate, who was classically educated at Westminster school, made two tours of Italy: the first in 1739–40 at the age of (just) twenty, the second from 1774–75 when in his fifties. The accounts of this second tour show that Sir Roger's book buying totaled £407-more than what he spent on any other category of grand tour souvenir, including marbles, paintings, drawings, "Intaglias," and plaster casts.[4] An inventory headed "Books Marbles Medals Casts & c purchased from July 1774 to Jany 1776" (fig. 13a) is organized according

Figure 13a *(left)* List entitled "Books Marbles Medals Casts &c purchased by Sir Roger Newdigate from July 1774 to January 1776." Warwickshire County records office, CR136 / B 3014B.

Figure 13b *(right)* List, detail.

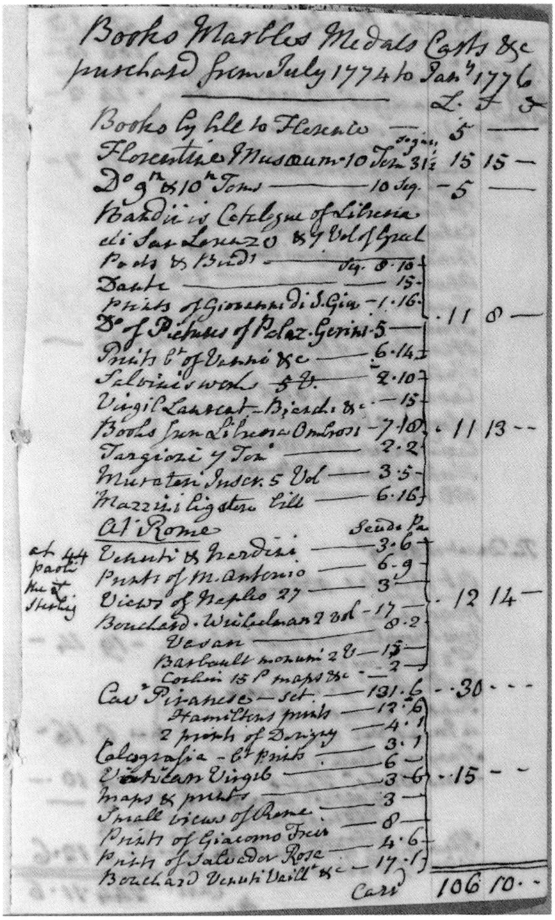
Books Marbles Medals Casts &c
purchased from July 1774 to Jany 1776
L. s. d.
Books by bill to Florence 5 —
Florentine Museum 10 Tom 31½ 15 15 —
At Rome
Cav^r Piranese — set 131.6
Carr^d 106 10 .

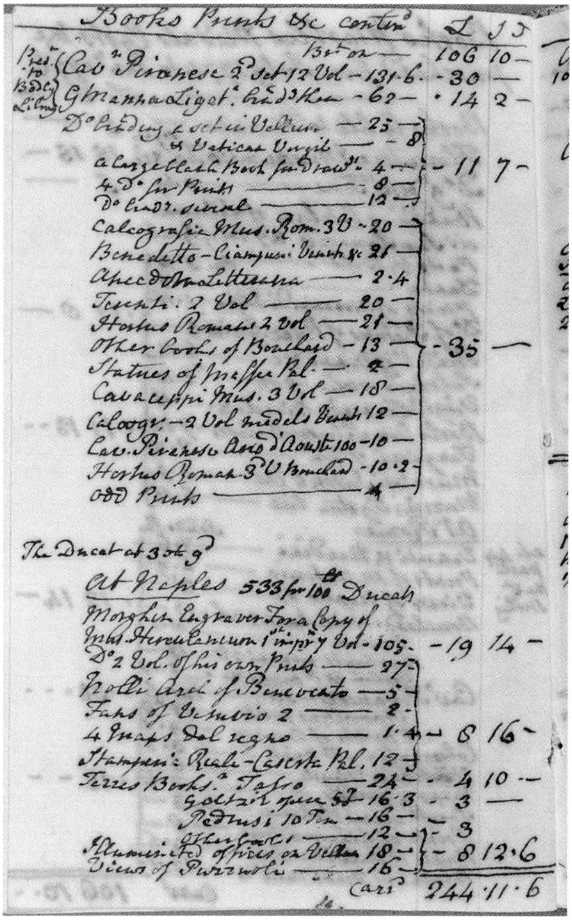
Books Prints &c contin^d L s
Cav^r Piranese 2^d set 12 Vol — 131.6 — 30 —
At Naples 533 for 100 Ducats
Carr^d 244 11 6

to the cities in Italy—Florence, Rome, and Naples—where Newdigate was buying books. For instance, books bought in Rome from the bookseller Bouchard included Winckelmann, Vasari, Barbault and Cochin, two sets of Piranesi's engravings, Hamilton's prints, Statues of the Maffei Palace, and Cavaceppi's museum.

After completing this second tour, Newdigate continued to obtain foreign publications through the agency of his cousin Charles Parker, who wrote in 1783 that "whenever I buy any Prints, Drawings, Pictures &c. it is with a view to your Library" at Arbury Hall in Warwickshire.[5] Later that year, on 22 November, Parker was

> willing to proceed cautiously, & not buy things, that you have already. I think it best to send you an Acc.[t] of what things are come out in Rome since -75- that you may judge what is worth your having & send me word in time to get them bound & ready before I leave Rome. Inclosed is a list of Piranesi's works, publish'd both by Father and Son since 75. The Son has published some things in the Stile of his Father that are well done, but of late he has alter'd his Stile & taken to engraving statues. The Father made another engraving of your Candelabro with the Cranes—in the Inscription he speaks handsomely of the Purchaser, but I want to add a few words more & say that it is placed in the Radcliffe Library at Oxford. I shall take for you a dozen copies of your Arch & a Dozen of the Candelabri. Send me also the Armament of the Backs of your Piranesi's that I might have these bound the same. The 4 antique Paintings you have are not done by Mirri, but by a Man whose name is Camillo Buti. The 4 first were engraved by Mengs, & are much better than the latter one's, but as you have begun, you must go on with the work. I cannot get them a jot cheaper than 5 sequins each . . . there will be 12 in all, but only 7 are published—I have never been able to see any of the Originals, they were cut out of the walls & sold—Mirri has left off the Painted Ceilings He has published a complete volume of all the Ceilings of Titus' Baths in Print, but as you have the best of them colour'd I suppose you would not chuse that. He has also publish'd a new Work, call'd Museum Clementinum—the first volume only come out, it is principally composed of the additions this Pope has made to the Vatican Museum which he has enrich'd very considerably, the Apollo & 9 Muses found at Tivoli are in it, the statues are well done, but the misfortune is its being a growing Work, so that you will have to send for the Volumes over as they come out. Volpato's Prints of Raphael's Pictures in the Vatican I have taken for you . . . send me word, what is the last volume of your Museum Capitolinum, that I may get you the Remainder, that Work was completed this year—Hortus Romanus—is already order'd . . .[6]

Another of Parker's letters demonstrates how contemporary publications of antiquity served a variety of functions: as grand tour guidebooks, souvenirs of a grand tour, and as editions of classical texts and collections of images.

> You ask me about Horace's Sabine villa, I believe the learned are agreed about the site of it, which is that which we saw—There is a very pretty Treatise coming out upon it—with Views taken of all the Places he mentions in that Country, which besides illustrating the Work, make a pleasant Collection of landscapes. It will be finish'd the end of this year, & I will venture to order a Copy for you.[7]

Any well-ordained eighteenth-century library, like that of Sir Roger Newdigate at Arbury Hall, had a section devoted to travel literature.[8] Parker informed his cousin in a letter of 30 January 1784, "I have also two folio volumes of Cluverius upon ancient Italy, which I shall send off when I leave Rome. His Germany I cannot get here, which completes the Work. But tis probable that I shall find it in Holland—He is the first writer for Classic Learning—& I find most of Mr Addison's Quotations upon Italy taken from him."[9]

James Byres's surviving correspondence with William Constable of Burton Constable in Yorkshire further demonstrates how the contact abroad—in Constable's case, his dealer in Rome—supplied the tourist who had completed the grand tour with an up-to-date bibliography of recent publications. Byres's letter of 11 June 1785 mentions a number of volumes, either published or in the course of publication; many of which Charles Parker drew to Newdigate's attention in his epistolary account. Here is Byres:

> You know that since you left Rome a great Museum of antient Monuments have been collected at the Vatican by the late and present Pope, a publication of which is going on, but I am affraid will not do justice to so noble a collection, being in the hands of a Sig.^{r} Mirri an illiterate man, who employes the cheapest artists he can find to execute this work. The same Mirri published some years ago the antient paintings of Titus's Baths in plain and colour'd prints which might have been a good and useful work, had it been well executed. Sig.^{r} Volpato is now finishing his excellent Engravings of Raphael's Room at the Vatican, which may be had either colour'd or plain. They are extremely well executed but the colourd ones come very high. I would rather recommend them plain. He has likewise published many Views of Rome and the neighbourhood which do best colour'd and are reasonable.—young Piranesi has published a plan of Hadrians Villa at Tivoli and is publishing a collection of forty of the best antient statues, they are well done.—

> Sig.[r] Camillo Buti is publishing colour'd prints of the decoration of an antient House found about eight years ago in the Villa Negroni, they are by far the best in that way I have seen . . .[10]

The contents of six cases shipped to Constable in Yorkshire are listed in an undated inventory compiled by Byres and include books—"Venuti's Roma Antique & moderns" in four volumes, two volumes of Terence, three volumes of Virgil, and Piranesi's works in seventeen volumes—among the scagliola statuettes and copies of paintings. These books exported from Italy formed part of a library collection at Burton Constable of around 9,600 books, although this figure is unreliable, being quoted in inventories of 1775 *and* sixteen years later in 1791.[11] As well as being a book collector in his own right, Constable inherited in 1747 his father's collection of books, manuscripts, and library bookcases.[12] However, as is the case with so many country house library collections, the books were dispersed at auction in the late nineteenth century.[13]

Unlike former English public schoolboy Newdigate, Constable was educated at a college on the continent. With Roman Catholic schools barred from England up to 1778, Constable and many of his Roman Catholic contemporaries attended the Catholic seminary and school of Douai in northern France.[14] Their humanities curriculum as preserved in the *Prefect of Studies* book for 1750–94 had much in common with the classical curriculum in English public schools, although the timetable incorporated Mass first thing in the morning with prayers and litanies later in the day.[15] At Douai, the School of Humanities was divided into five schools, from the lowest to the highest: rudiments, grammar, syntax, poetry, and rhetoric. Though the system of teaching was differently structured from that of English public schools, the content of the Douai curriculum, being predominantly classical, was markedly similar. Like the intellectual universe of the English public school, the style of thought inculcated by the educational patterns at Douai was classicism.

In the same way that classicism was embodied in classical textbooks, so the books collected during and after the grand tour of Italy functioned as an extension of the itineraries mapped out at public or Roman Catholic school. Volumes bought on classic ground in Rome included editions of works by ancient Roman authors like Horace and Virgil—works with which the classically educated traveller was already intimately acquainted. But in addition to the schoolboy texts of ancient authors, the bibliographical sources in the Newdigate and Constable papers are dominated by contemporary publications devoted to the *material culture* of the ancients: their architecture, sculpture, and painting.

As early as 1719, the French antiquarian Abbé Bernard de Montfaucon had established a philological approach to the remains of antiquity in his ten-volume *L'Antiquité expliquée et représentée en figures* (Paris, 1719–24). In the preface to volume 1, written in French and Latin, Montfaucon describes the division of ancient monuments into two classes: the first that of books; the second of statues, bas reliefs, inscriptions, and medals. For him, these two classes, the literary and the material, lend each other mutual assistance. Similarly, Count Caylus opens volume two of his six-volume *Recueil d'antiquités egyptiennes, etrusques, grecques et romaines* (Paris, 1752–67) with the claim that works in sculpture and painting tell us as much about the genius of a people, their morals and turn of mind, as their surviving books.

A classical education at a English public school or at the Roman Catholic school at Douai focused exclusively on one of Montfaucon's classes of ancient monument: the literary corpus, albeit a tailored and toned-down version. It was not until the mid- to late nineteenth century that ancient artifacts were incorporated into the curricula and collections of English public schools. In Cecil Torr's *Catalogue of the Classical Antiquities from the Collection of the Late Sir Gardner Wilkinson* (Harrow, 1887), for instance, the knowledge derived from books which "can be read when and where one pleases" is said to be enhanced "by having a few things constantly at hand."[16] The grand tour of Italy by educated Britons in the second half of the eighteenth century extended the classical curricula of their school days onto Montfaucon's second class of ancient monuments: the material culture of the ancients. While the classical literary tradition was canonical by this time, from "the chosen study of men of letters" to "the enforced study of youth," as Torr's *Catalogue* puts it, the material corpus of the ancients was still in the process of being excavated, classified, collected, and published.[17] As far as we can reconstruct them from the archival sources, the libraries of Newdigate and Constable contained a bibliography of grand tour volumes devoted to ancient architecture, sculpture, and painting. As a result of the styles of thought inculcated by their classical education, antiquity was already part of their intellectual makeup; what Bourdieu terms their cultured habitus.[18] Packaged in books collected in the libraries of their country houses, it became part of their own architectural and sculptural and, in Newdigate's case, painted habitus.[19]

By looking in more detail at a number of eighteenth-century grand tour folios, we can begin to understand how far the packaging of antiquity in collectable and consumable form—in books for the library—created an elite, cosmopolitan intellectual culture. The volumes under review here maintained the classically educated British collector's reference to and reverence for Greek and Roman antiquity as part of the fabric of the educated mind as well as the furniture of the well-ordained library. But for their authors, these folios often served a multiplicity of purposes.

The volumes lining the shelves of, say, Newdigate's or Constable's country house libraries were produced by authors of different nationalities and from different levels of the social hierarchy, including professional architects, learned antiquarians, and aristocratic collectors. The publications they produced enabled them to participate in what Robert Wood in his *Ruins of Balbec* (London, 1757) called "the Re-publick of Letters, which knows, or ought to know, neither distinction of country, nor separate interests."[20] Members of Wood's republic of letters followed the philological agendas of Montfaucon and Caylus by textualizing ancient monuments, transforming them from material objects into reading material and monumentalizing texts, in which the process of transformation was reversed.[21]

Montfaucon's *L'Antiquité expliquée et représentée en figures* (Paris, 1719) was a pioneering publication in which its author attempted to collect, classify, and condense the two classes of surviving ancient monuments: books and artifacts.[22] In the preface of volume 1, Montfaucon refers to the almost infinite number of published books on the subject, many of which were large and difficult to procure; even when obtained, they could barely be read during a man's life. Critical of those authors who delay publication to polish and retouch what they have collected, Montfaucon's ten-volume work represents a medium between these two extremes. On the one hand, it is an encyclopedic survey of ancient monuments—"I have reduced into one body all antiquity"—a work not to be read cursorily but over a couple of years.[23] On the other, he insists, his enterprise is not the product of an exhaustive search, given the vast number of ancient pieces and monuments as well as those concealed in cabinets or yet to be unearthed. In the preface of the *Supplement* (Paris, 1724), Montfaucon writes of the need for authors to be concise, to publish only what is curious and new and in doing so to avoid swelling or multiplying volumes with repetitions. He goes on to explain how multiple volumes represent a stumbling block for students in all kinds of disciplines, when it is the knowledge of antiquity that is the entrance into all the arts and all the sciences.

Specialist knowledge about the material culture of the ancients was distributed among a cast of professional artists, architects, engravers, and intellectuals for whom the packaging of antiquity in book form became their own entrance into the republic of letters. Take, for example, a volume devoted to an ancient imperial monument produced by the Scottish architect Robert Adam, the *Ruins of Dioclesian's Palace at Spalatro in Dalmatia* (1764). The promotional role of Adam's deluxe folio has been discussed many times, drawing extensively on the Adam brothers' surviving correspondence in the National Archives of Scotland in Edinburgh.[24] Well aware of the impact of publication as a means of self-promotion and "hop[ing] to make more of being here [in Rome] than any body would imagine," Adam considered a number of architectural projects before selecting a volume devoted to the palace of the third-century A.D. Roman emperor Diocletian.[25] Subjects considered and subsequently abandoned included a monograph on Hadrian's villa, a corrected edition of Palladio's drawings of the baths of Caracalla and Diocletian ("a magnificent work, though not a profitable one") and an English version of Desgodets's *Les Édifices antiques de Rome* ("a work of years").[26] With Spalatro, financial and esoteric concerns were interwoven. It was apparently the only unpublished site that Adam could afford to visit from Rome.[27] It was not only unpublished, but like two of his proposed projects, it was the site of an ancient imperial monument and a rare surviving example of the private architecture of the ancients. Hints of the former magnificence of such edifices were preserved in classical texts, "accidental allusions in the ancient poets [and] some occasional descriptions in their historians" as well as the "more accurate accounts" in Vitruvius and Pliny, as Adam notes in the preface of *Ruins*.[28] But having "never been observed with any accuracy or drawn with any taste," Diocletian's palace at Spalatro was considered by Adam to be "a most propper subject for gaining applause & character in England," a nation of classically educated aristocrats and gentlemen for whom antiquity was part of their shared cultured habitus.[29]

The book that Adam envisaged as "a great puff, conducive to raising all at once one's name & character," the result of a five-week detour to Spalatro in Dalmatia on Adam's grand tour, took some seven years to produce.[30] This drawn-out production process gave the Adam brothers the opportunity to fête those patrons whose association with such a work in the form of subscription or presentation copies would be mutually beneficial: it became their own entrance into an elite world. How this reciprocal relationship operated is articulated in a proposal to present a copy of the *Ruins* to Frederick the Great of Prussia: "I know [wrote Adam] he loves books of this here nature greatly, so that it will rather oblige him to give him an opportunity of showing his taste. The éclat of his name would sell 100 coppys in the City."[31] On 30 September 1760, James Adam wrote of the importance of a subscription list for the volume with "high sounding [names] & [which] will read well in England."[32] The titles of potential Venetian subscribers were to be left in Italian "as people are fond of things misterious." For an audience without funds to purchase the complete volume, James Adam suggested the sale of pairs or sets of views, "so adjusted as to addorn the side of a Dressing room extremely well."[33] The fragmentation of the volume into collectable prints would "be a real source of profit," explained James, and "wou'd at the same time extend our names as travellers to the uttermost ends of the earth." With "distant names engrav'd under them, [they] might induce the publick to prefer them to all other ornamental prints, strange [i.e., exotic] only excepted." Ever-anxious to puff the book, Robert Adam replaced the "too nationall" dedication to the Scottish family patron, the Duke of Argyll, with a "more showy" dedication to King George II.[34] When a rival volume devoted to the ancient architecture of Greece—Stuart and Revett's *Antiquities of Athens*—was published in 1762, Adam was forced to postpone publication of the *Ruins* for eighteen months.[35] In the preface of *Ruins* he writes of being far from comparing his own undertaking with that of Dawkins, Bouverie, and Wood, authors of *Ruins of Palmyra* (London, 1753) and *Ruins of Balbec* (London, 1757): "one of the most splendid and liberal that was ever attempted by private persons."[36] In this statement of false modesty, Adam deliberately contrives to remind his reader of the positive reception of similar publications, particularly the *Ruins of Palmyra* and the *Ruins of Balbec*. In private correspondence with his brother, however, Adam derided Wood's volumes for being "as hard as Iron; & as false as Hell."[37]

In a portrait of Robert Adam attributed to David Martin (fig. 14), the sitter rests in his lap what is thought to be a copy of his literary debut: the *Ruins of Dioclesian's Palace at Spalatro in Dalmatia*.[38] If indeed, the vast folio—"little better than more reputable cushions to promote our repose," as Edward Young characterized them—represents a painted copy of the *Ruins*, then the image realizes Adam's desire that the expense and effort expended on a publication of this kind would elevate "all at once one's name & character."[39] For Adam looks straight ahead at the viewers, inviting them to admire his authorial and gentlemanly repose.

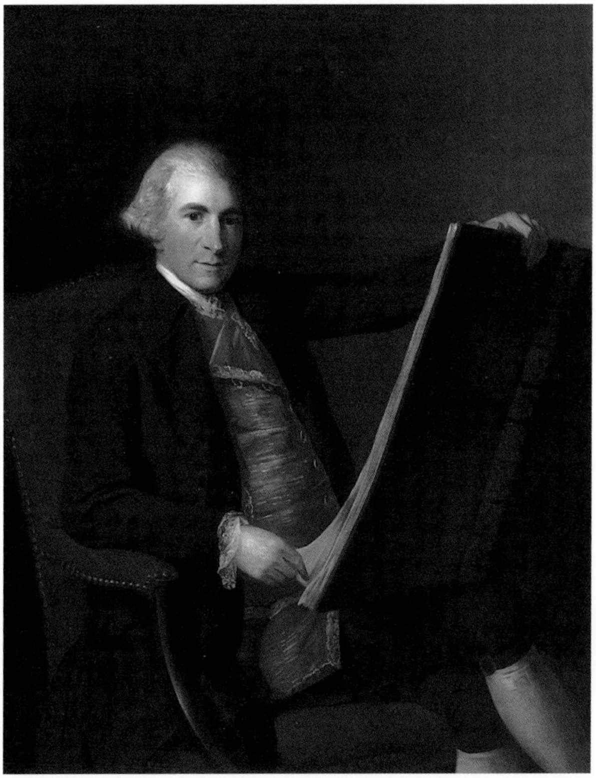

Figure 14 *Robert Adam*, attributed to David Martin. National Portrait Gallery, London.

The libraries of Newdigate at Arbury Hall and Constable at Burton Constable both contained the sets of volumes produced by an Italian contemporary of Robert Adam's who he once described as someone "who may be said, alone to breath the antient air."[40] In fact, Newdigate's grand tour account for books purchased at Rome between 1774 and 1776 (fig. 13 above) records that he bought a duplicate copy of "Piranese 2d set 12 Vol" and presented it to the Bodleian Library at Oxford. We have already seen, with reference to Adam's *Ruins of Dioclesian's Palace at Spalatro in Dalmatia*, how far the publication of an ancient monument was intended to puff one's professional status. Piranesi's *Antichità romane*, published in 1756 by the Bouchard & Gravier bookshop in Rome, is credited with having established his reputation in Europe as the leading protagonist of Roman archaeology.[41] Unlike Robert Adam, who spent just five weeks at the site of Spalatro, Piranesi's four-volume edition on the antiquities of Rome was the product of eight years of study.[42] Producing and distributing such a luxury publication entailed huge costs—the sale of Winckelmann's *Monumenti Antichi inediti* (Rome, 1767) had not produced sufficient income to make him financially independent.[43] The *Antichità romane* project was financed in its early stages by an Irish aristocrat then in Rome, James Caulfield, first Earl of Charlemont.

In recognition of Charlemont's patronage, the title page of volume 1 bears a dedication to him inscribed in Latin onto an engraving of an ancient relief (fig. 15). By chiseling the dedication "in stone," in the language of the ancient Romans, Piranesi transformed the title page of a book of monuments into a permanent monument to Charlemont, a monument erected and dedicated in the ancient Roman tradition. When Charlemont returned home to Ireland and failed to provide further financial support, Piranesi's revenge took a similarly ancient Roman form. In a pamphlet published in his defense, *Lettere di giustificazione scritti a Milord Charlemont* (Rome, 1757), Piranesi committed an act of *damnatio memoriae* by erasing Charlemont's name from the monuments he had previously erected in the pages of the *Antichità romane* in his honor.[44] As we see from plate 7 of the *Lettere* (fig. 16), the large relief from the frontispiece of volume 1 and the other monuments dedicated to Charlemont have had their inscriptions removed.[45] The deleted dedications preserve for posterity Charlemont's dishonor. In the following plate (fig. 17), three

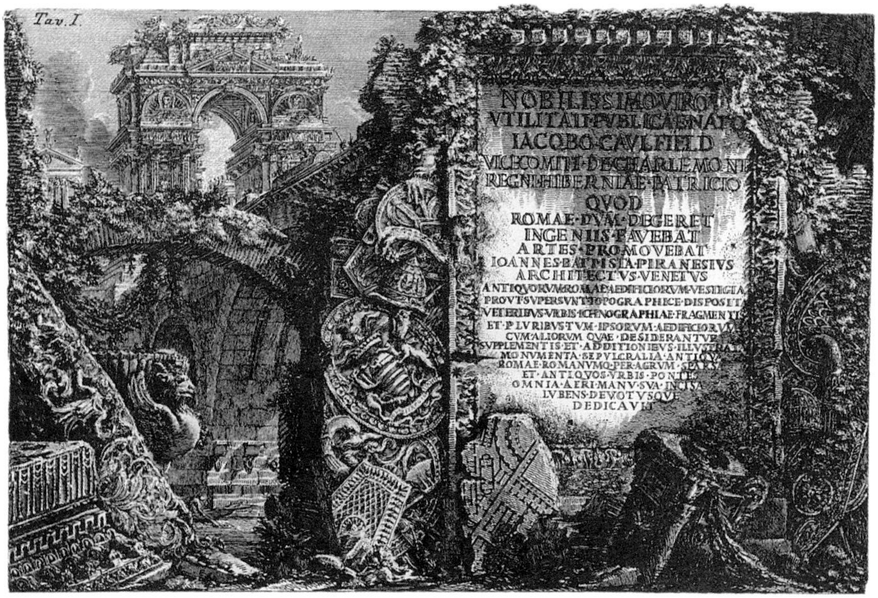

Figure 15 Giovanni Battista Piranesi, *Antichità romane* (Rome, 1756), vol. 1, title page, with an engraved relief monument dedicated to James Caulfield, Viscount Charlemont. The Warburg Institute.

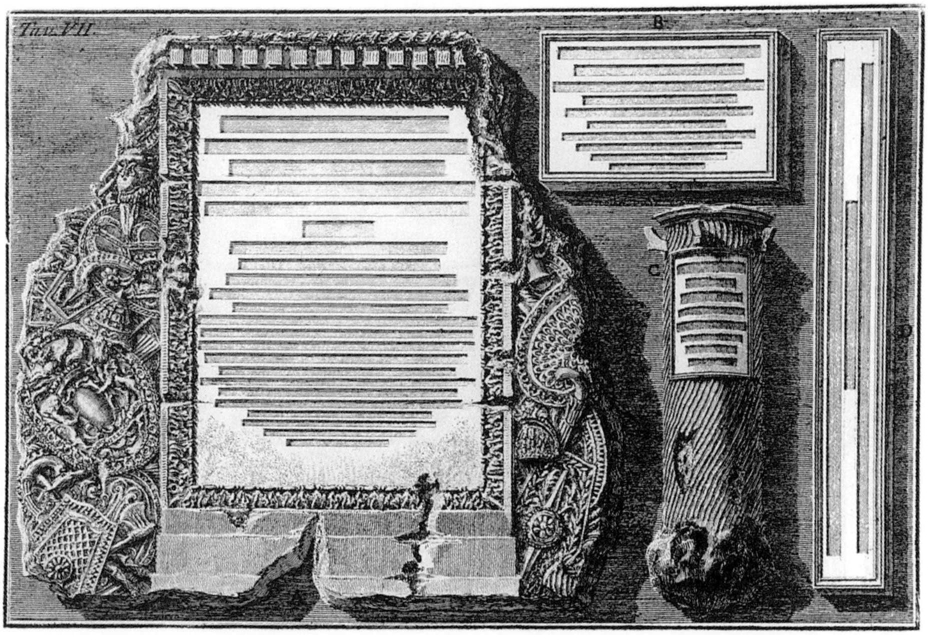

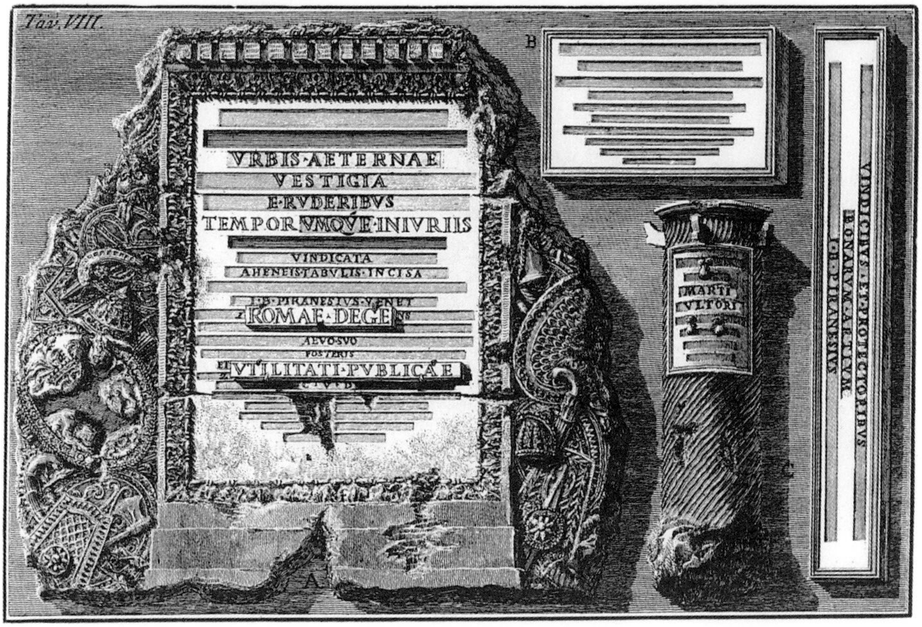

Figure 16 Giovanni Battista Piranesi, *Lettere di giustificazione scritti a Milord Charlemont* (Rome, 1757), plate 7, with inscriptions to Lord Charlemont deleted from the engraved monuments. The Warburg Institute.

Figure 17 Giovanni Battista Piranesi, *Lettere di giustificazione scritti a Milord Charlemont* (Rome, 1757), plate 8, with monuments rededicated to the public. The Warburg Institute.

of the monuments are rededicated to the public, reminding the classically educated audience of a quotation from Martial: "Pleasure that belonged to a master now belongs to the people" (*De Spectaculis* II.12). But the recutting of the relief and the blank spaces still visible is a telling reminder that the monument has suffered another form of ruin: the loss of reputation.[46]

In *Lettere di giustificazione* Piranesi writes of the *Antichità romane* as his literary monument; as a volume, which like the ancient Roman monuments it reproduced in engravings, would not remain buried but would enjoy longevity.

> I believe that I have completed a work which will pass on to posterity and which will endure so long as there are men curious to know the ruins which remain of the most famous city in the universe. . . This work is not of the kind which remains buried in the crowded shelves of libraries. Its four folio volumes comprise a new system of the monuments of ancient Rome. It will be deposited in many public libraries throughout Europe, and in particular in that of the Most Christian King. And there is reason to suppose that the name of its author will pass on to posterity together with his work.[47]

In this passage, Piranesi explicitly invokes the elite cosmopolitan library as the prime site for the reception of his *Antichità romane*. His volume represents a new system of one of the most revered institutions of the learned world—the monuments of ancient Rome. As such, being deposited in the library institutions of that learned world would ensure its longevity rather than its burial. Invoking the many public libraries throughout Europe including that of the "Most Christian King," Piranesi composed an ideal subscription list. One surviving copy of the *Lettere* actually preserves a register of names believed to be a kind of mailing list drawn up by Piranesi.[48] Intended readers included Sir William Hamilton, Sir Horace Mann, the Earl of Mansfield, Mengs, sculptors like Filippo della Valle, painters, architects, and members of the Roman aristocracy—in other words, not only Piranesi's artistic contemporaries in Rome but also the aristocracy and prominent foreign patrons.

Piranesi's four-volume *Antichità romane* became a kind of portable guidebook to the largest museum in the learned world, a museum that contained what Lady Miller describes as "whole labyrinths of curiosities. . . was I to mention them all I should send you folios instead of letters."[49] The British traveller Tobias Smollett, who "longed to view the remains of antiquity by which this metropolis is distinguished," recorded that "a hundred zequines will not purchase all the books and prints which have been published at Rome on these subjects. Of these the most celebrated are the prints of Piranesi, who is not only an ingenious architect and engraver, but also a learned antiquarian."[50] The widespread distribution of Piranesian prints meant that many travellers experienced Piranesi's Rome before ever setting foot on classic ground. This reproductive experience was indelibly colored by what Horace Walpole recognized as

> the sublime dreams of Piranesi, who seems to have conceived visions of Rome beyond what it boasted even in the meridian of its splendor. Savage as Salvator Rosa, fierce as Michael Angelo, and exuberant as Rubens, he has imagined scenes that would startle geometry, and exhaust the Indies to realize. He piles palaces on bridges, and temples on palaces, and scales Heaven with mountains of edifices.[51]

A "stranger, arriving here [Rome] with the expectations raised by those prints, will be infallibly disappointed," wrote Joseph Forsyth.[52] Joseph Farington records that Flaxman's first impression of Rome was one of disappointment because the ruins were "less striking than he had been accustomed to suppose them after having seen the prints of Piranesi."[53] For Goethe, on the other hand, the Cloaca Maxima was "even more colossal than Piranesi's designs had led me to expect."[54]

While Piranesi's engravings transmitted an image of Rome that Charles Brown described in the 1820s as "full of poetry and lies," the publication of ancient monuments beyond Rome was seen as a necessary means to ensure their future preservation.[55] In the proposal drawn up in Rome in 1748 for publishing *The Antiquities of Athens*, James Stuart writes of the multiple volumes devoted to Rome's structures and sculptures published by Desgodets, Palladio, Serlio, and Santo Bartoli. He goes on to explain how although the original monuments they reproduced had been since destroyed, these volumes ensured that their memory and the form would not perish: as a result of the industry of the artists, representations of the originals had been dispersed throughout all the polite nations of Europe. In contrast with those of Rome, however, the monuments of Athens had been largely neglected. Hence the pressing need for a volume devoted to them. As Stuart explains, "unless exact copies of them [monuments in Athens] be speedily made, all her beauteous Fabricks, her Temples, her Theatres, her Palaces, now in ruins, will drop into oblivion: and Posterity will have to reproach us, that we have not left them a tolerable Idea of what was so excellent, and so much deserved our attention; but that we have suffered the perfection of an Art to perish, when it was perhaps in our power to have retrieved it."[56] Fourteen years after the book proposal was composed and circulated, Stuart informed one of his British architectural patrons, Thomas Anson of Shugborough in Staffordshire, that

> Count Caylus in the 6th Volume of his Antiquities which as he informs the Reader closes & completes that Work, has made honorable mention of me, & of

> my Antiquities of Athens. . . I had set a person to translate my first Volume into French, but found him unequal to the Task, Lord Hardwicke has wrote to Sir Joseph Yorke on that subject. & is of opinion that amongst the writers of a litterary journal there, who give an account of Books published in England, & occasionally translate passages out of them some one may be found able & willing to give a good translation of my Book.[57]

Here we see the so-called republic of letters at work. The French antiquarian, Count Caylus, refers to Stuart's publication in volume 6 of his *Recueil d' Antiquités Egyptiennes, Etrusques, Grecques et Romaines*, while the author-architect is assisted in translating the work into French by one of his aristocratic British patrons, the Earl of Hardwicke.

Stuart is credited with having "introduced into Britain the knowledge of a style of art, which, though among the oldest in existence, was new to this country."[58] *The Antiquities of Athens* would preserve for posterity representations of the ruins that had survived since the fifth century B.C. But while the memory of ancient Athenian ruins were being prolonged by publication, the ancient Roman cities of Pompeii and Herculaneum in the Kingdom of Naples were being excavated and published for the first time since their burial in antiquity. "Tis certainly an advantage to the learned world, that this has been laid up so long," thought Horace Walpole.[59] It was as much of a *disadvantage* to the learned world that when the sites were excavated and the unearthed finds published, access was in both cases restricted. Guards prohibited visitors from making drawings or taking notes either at the sites or in the royal museum at Portici where the disinterred artifacts were displayed. James Russel described how those tourists admitted to see the paintings "are watched very narrowly, and are not permitted to make use of a pencil. All therefore that I could do, was to range them in my memory, as well as I could; and from thence to commit them to paper the same day. This I did twice."[60]

When the paintings were officially published as engravings in volume 1 of *Le Antichità di Ercolano esposte* (Naples, 1757), the accompanying text, written by persons described as being "long eminent in the republic of letters," hoped the appearance of this first volume would sufficiently meet the public's expectations.[61] Yet the public's expectations were to be prolonged even further, for the volumes that formed this museum without walls (fig. 18) were not for public sale—at least not initially.[62] The eight folios were what Charles Parker in his 1783 letter to Newdigate termed a "growing work," published between 1757 and 1792 and organized typologically. So volumes 1–4 were devoted to ancient paintings, volumes 5 (1767) and 6 (1771) to bronzes, volume 7 (1779) to additional paintings, and finally volume 8 (1792), to lamps and candelabra. At first, they were distributed as gifts of royal favor to princes, foreign universities, and travellers of distinction, at an enormous cost to King Charles III, of 12,000 ducats.[63] While Rome was the classroom for the masses, "the school for the whole world," wrote Goethe quoting Winckelmann, the publication of a collection ranked above all other ancient monuments functioned as a monument to its royal possessor.[64] A review in the *Gentleman's Magazine* for 1773 complained that "the engravings of most of those valuable remains of antiquity [are confined] to the libraries of those only to whom his Majesty has been pleased to present them."[65] However, after unsuccessful attempts to prohibit the publication of rival editions, the volumes were available for sale from the Royal Printing House. Newdigate's grand tour accounts (fig. 13 above) reveal that he purchased "a Copy of the Mus. Herculaneum 1st impr 7 Vol" in Naples in 1775 for 105 ducats.

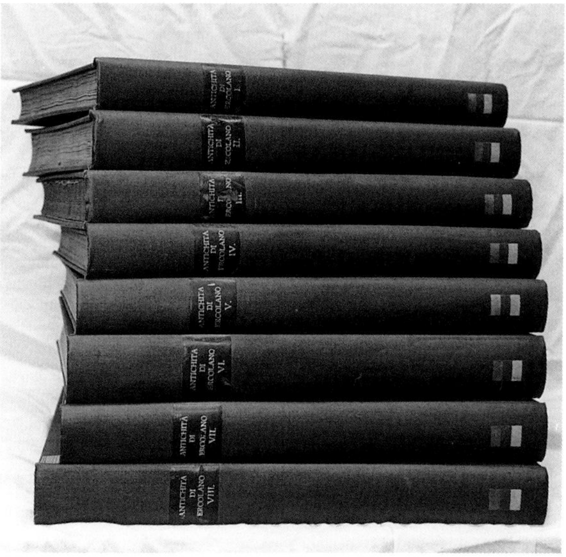

Figure 18 "A museum without walls": *Antichità di Ercolano esposte*, 8 vols. (Naples, 1757–92). The Warburg Institute.

In addition to being collected for the libraries of British grand tourists like that of Newdigate at Arbury Hall, one of the *Antichità di Ercolano* volumes figures in Angelica Kauffman's portrait of the gentleman John Byng (1764; fig. 19). Like many grand tour portraits, Kauffman's image locates the foreigner in Italy in a recognizable topographical landscape. In this case, Byng is standing in front of an open window with Naples harbor and Mount Vesuvius in the distance. He is represented turning the page of a painted copy of volume 2 (1760) of *Le Antichità di Ercolano esposte*, which lies open at plate 9, an engraving of an ancient painting of Urania, the muse of astronomy. The sentence at the top of the proceeding page reads "merita di essere guardata con riflessione" (worth looking at with reflection), an instruction that has been taken to refer simultaneously and wittily to the book, ancient art, the heavens, the city of Naples, *and* Kauffman's portrait of Byng. Certainly, the muse Urania may have had some special significance for Byng, who died in Bologna just months after his portrait was painted. Being accompanied by volume 2 of *Le Antichità* suggests much more than Byng's fashionable worldliness and his familiarity with the latest discoveries of antiquity, which is how the painting has been read.[66] Instead, it casts Byng as a recipient of volume 2—socially elevating him into the constellation of privileged royal favor. Two years after volume 2 was published, Sir Horace Mann wrote to Horace Walpole that he was still endeavoring to procure the new volume for Walpole's library at Strawberry Hill. "Much fewer copies were

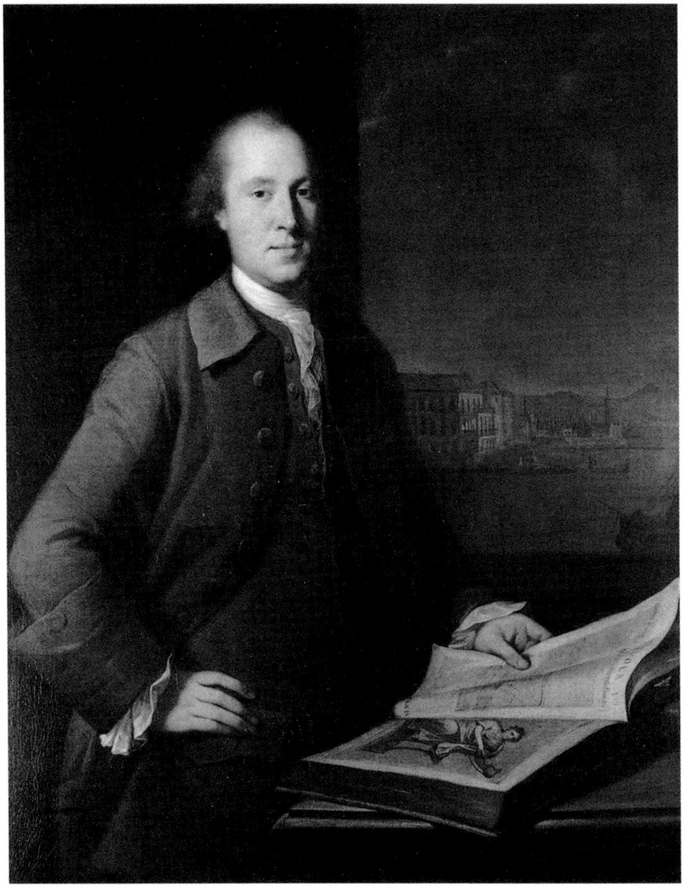

Figure 19 Angelica Kauffman, *John Byng*, 1764. Private collection. Photograph: The Paul Mellon Centre for Studies in British Art.

made of this than of the preceding volumes, the King of Spain having heard that many to whom they were given had sold them. This makes them very difficult to get," explained Mann.[67] No wonder then that Byng's portrait is worth looking at with reflection.

Equally worth looking at with reflection is a copy of volume 6 (1771) of *Le Antichità di Ercolano esposte* installed in Zoffany's famous painting *Charles Townley's Library at 7, Park Street, Westminster* (1781–83/98; plate 2). The volume rests on the plinth of an ancient marble sculpture of a drunken faun and is opened to plate 42, an engraving of a similar sculpture in bronze excavated from Herculaneum and displayed in the royal collection at Naples (fig. 20).[68] We know from his grand tour account for books that Townley, who like William Constable was educated at the Catholic school of Douai, subscribed to black market copies of the first six volumes of *Le Antichità* in Naples in March 1768 for the considerable sum of 240 ducats.[69] By

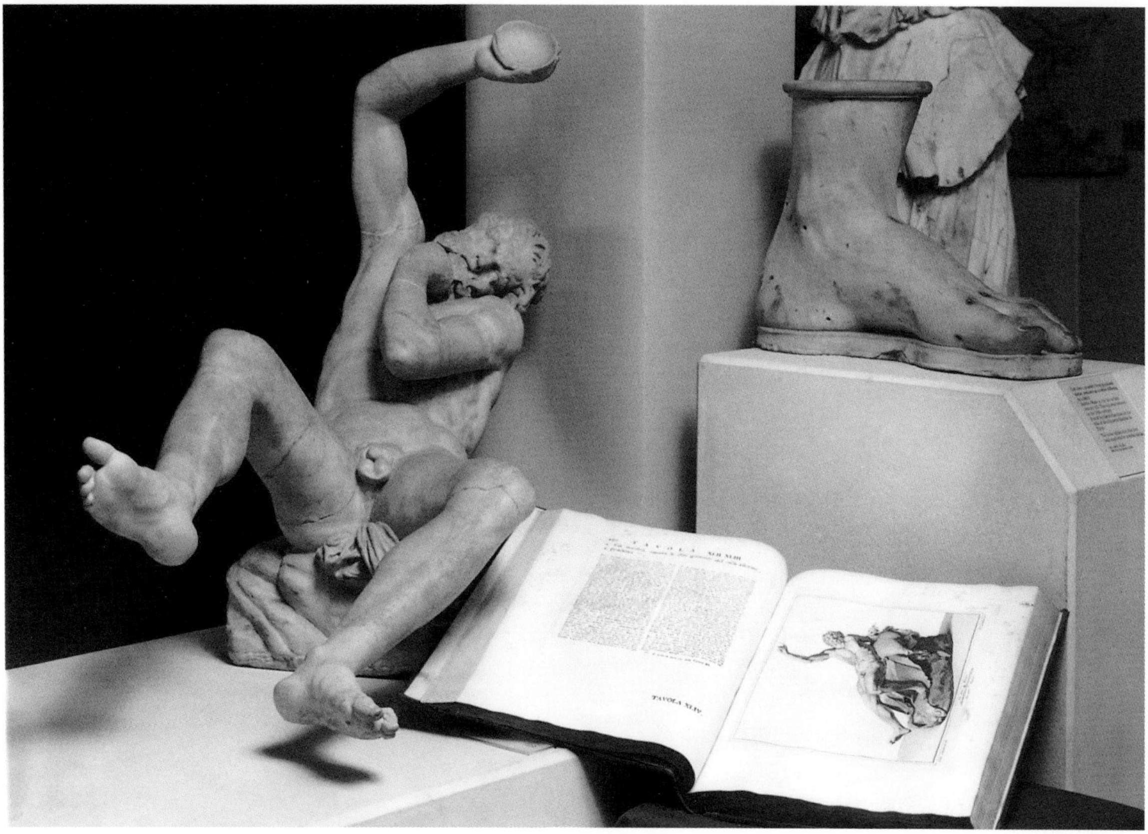

Figure 20 Townley's marble statue of a drunken faun with volume 6 open to plate 42 of *Antichità di Ercolano esposte* (Naples, 1771). By courtesy of the Trustees of the British Museum.

the beginning of 1770, Townley was informed by one of his dealers in Rome that the work was now available to the public at 12 ducats a volume with any outstanding volumes priced at 18 ducats.[70]

The juxtaposition of Kauffman's portrait of John Byng and Zoffany's painting of Charles Townley's library encapsulates the dissemination and display of the *Antichità* volumes: transported from Naples, the site of their production, to the library of the ancient sculpture collector in metropolitan London, the site of their consumption. In Zoffany's painting it is the library, out of all the exhibition rooms in Townley's house at 7 Park Street, that is represented as the prime site for the reception and preservation of antiquity in both its excavated and published forms, as material *and* textual artifacts.[71]

In Joshua Reynolds's portrait *Sir William Hamilton* (1777–82; fig. 21), the British envoy at Naples is painted for posterity *not* in his formal diplomatic role but as a possessor and publisher of a collection of ancient Etruscan vases.[72] The folio resting on

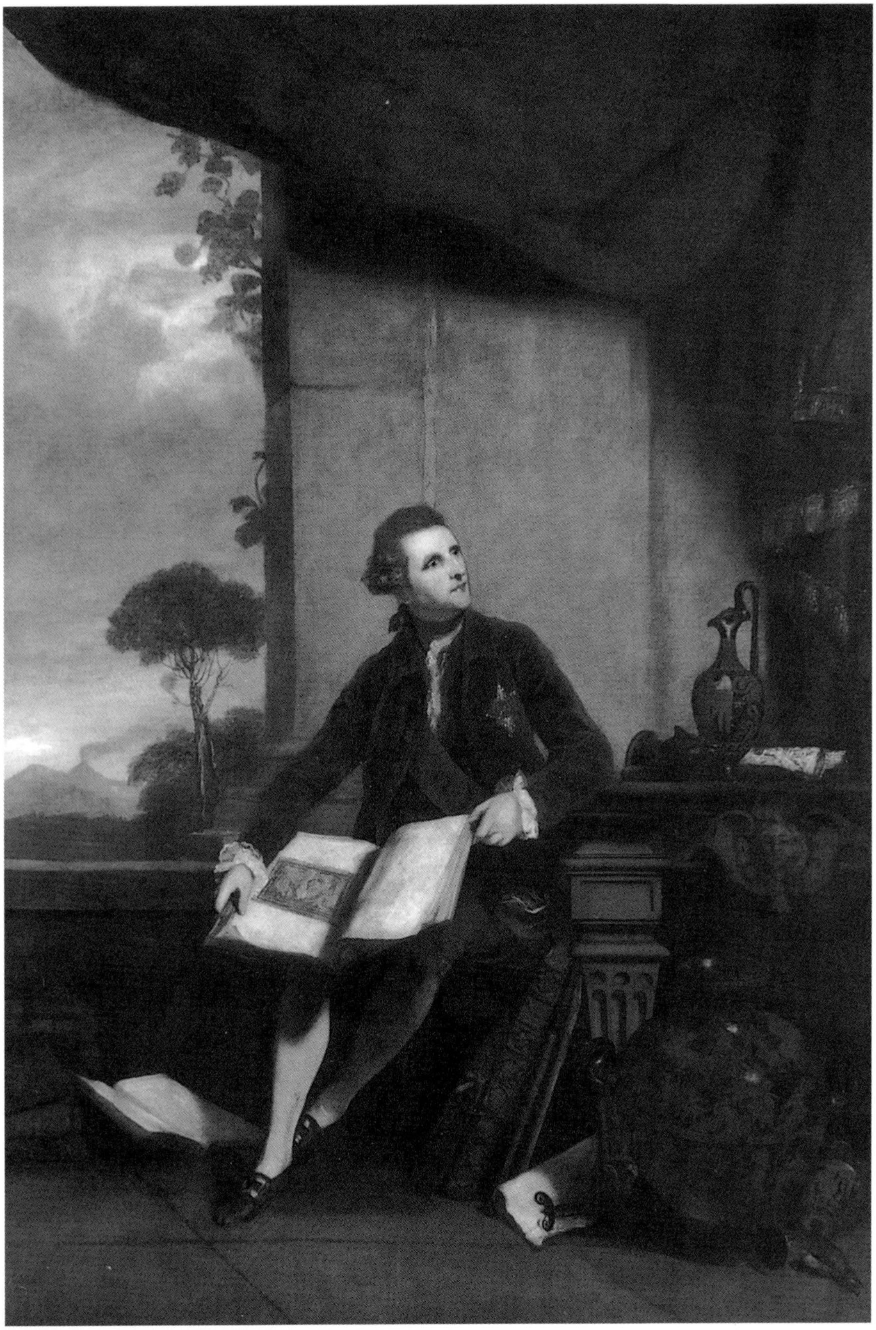

Figure 21 Joshua Reynolds, *Sir William Hamilton*, 1777–82. National Portrait Gallery, London.

Hamilton's knee is a painted copy of volume 1, open at plate 71, of the four-volume edition of Hamilton's *Collection of Etruscan, Greek and Roman Antiquities* (Naples, 1766–76). "Not having leisure himself, from the occupations of his employment," Hamilton recruited the self-styled Baron d'Hancarville to oversee the publication of his collection of ancient vases.[73] According to the preface in English and French of volume 1, Hamilton was said to be less flattered with the privilege of possessing such "precious Monuments of the Genius of the Ancients" than with "rendering them useful to Artists, to Men of Letters and by their means, to the World in general."[74] D'Hancarville explains:

> for whatever Father Montfaulcon may think, collections of this kind are very scarce even in Italy, and are hardly of any utility to the Artists, because those who possess them will not venture their vases into the hands of those, who from awkwardness or heedlessness, would not take as much care of them as their fragility requires, and it is natural for the possessor of a fine piece to apprehend the loss of it. Thus designers cannot have their just proportions, being scarcely allowed time sufficient to take a slight idea of their forms. As to the Paintings, they would require still more time to be seen and drawn with precision. In this manner these collections lose the greatest part of their merit, remaining (as one may say) buried in Cabinets and become rather Monuments to the luxury of the possessors, than of utility to the progress of the Arts.[75]

Having already encountered part of the proposal for Stuart and Revett's *Antiquities of Athens*, we know how far a publication of ancient monuments was seen as a means of enhancing their survival chances.[76] Hamilton himself wrote to the Earl of Hardwicke in October 1769 of wanting "to preserve at least the memory" of the drawings on his ancient vases, "their fragility endangering them to continual accidents."[77]

Collection of Etruscan, Greek and Roman Antiquities not only conserved the fabric of the ancient vases and preserved a memory of them in print but also simultaneously excavated rare examples from other private cabinets. In volume 2 the Hamiltonian collection is embellished with ancient vases from the private cabinets of the pope, the grand duke of Tuscany, the prince of Biscari, and the king of France. Thus, ancient vases from the royal and elite collections of Europe are united in an ideal cabinet or phantom collection of reproductions. The mass production of engravings said in the advertisement for the volumes to be "suitable to furnish an apartment, or to enrich a porfolio of engravings, or to take their place in a library," gave artists unrestricted access to the choice vase collections of Europe, replicating the experience of visiting and the luxury of possessing the vases through their engraved reproductions.[78] According to d'Hancarville, by the means of engraving, "the Artists of every country will have these fine forms under their eyes, almost as well as if they were in the very Cabinet which contains the originals, and had the liberty of disposing of them at pleasure."[79]

The Hamilton publications also claimed to provide a more authentic image of the ancient vases than that presented in the books of their learned predecessors (fig. 22):

> for we believe it will be readily acknowledged that it is not sufficient to have a general idea of the Vases of the Ancients, as they are given us in the Books of the Count de Caylus and Father de Montfaulcon: These works at the utmost only shew what members the Ancients employed in the composition of their Vases, but do not indicate their relative proportions, and one should succeed as ill in copying them after these vague notions, as one should do in attempting to imitate Greek architecture with success, without having first studied it's proportions.[80]

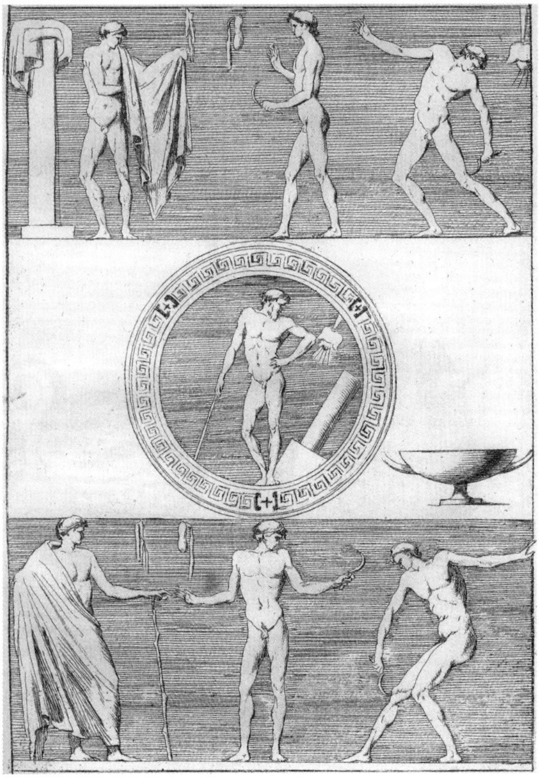

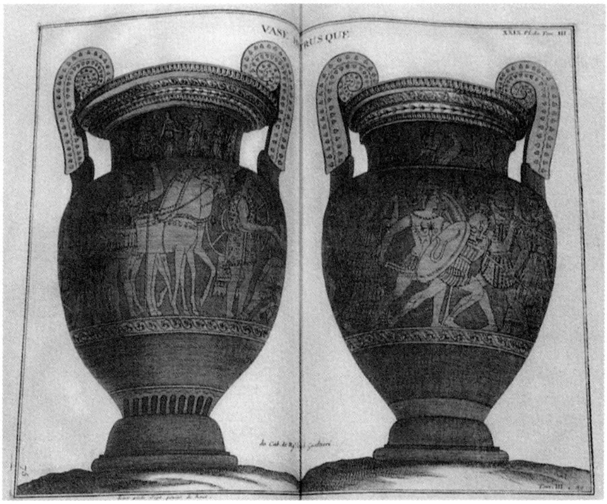

Figure 22a "A general idea of the Vases of the Ancients": Caylus, *Recueil d'Antiquités Égyptiennes, Étrusques, Grecques et Romaines,* vol. 2, plate 37.

Figure 22b Montfaucon, *Antiquité Expliquée,* supplement ,vol. 3, plate 29. The Warburg Institute.

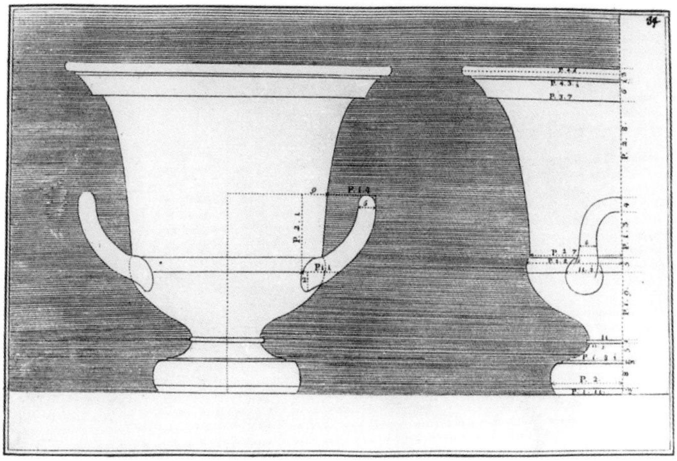

Figure 23 Engraving from *Collection of Etruscan, Greek and Roman Antiquities* showing the relative proportions of an ancient vase. Institute of Classical Studies Library.

The colored engravings of Hamilton's vases are accompanied by outline drawings recording the shapes and measurements of their architectural forms (fig. 23). Investing importance in the proportions of the vases, the Hamilton volumes place themselves in competition with the works of Caylus and Montfaucon and also borrow strategies for measuring and delineating ancient monuments from the plates of architectural volumes like Stuart and Revett's *Antiquities of Athens*. The reference to those successful imitations of Greek architecture alludes to this work of ancient architectural scholarship.[81]

The visual and textual strategies employed throughout the Hamilton volumes locate the work within a tradition of antiquarian and architectural scholarship that it emulates and attempts to surpass. While volume 1 is dedicated to the British king George III, d'Hancarville's text acknowledges the influence of its royal, Neapolitan counterpart, the *Antichità di Ercolano*:

> It is perhaps to this rich collection, to the ideas with which it has furnished us, to the comparisons which it has enabled us to make, that we owe the most valuable part of our work, and the place from whence we write is perhaps also, that of all Europe, the most proper to favour our intention of treating of these matters; for what place can be found where ideas are more continually produced, nourished and strengthened by the presence of the objects, and where is the collection comparable to that of the King of the Two Sicilies?[82]

As well as being a product of the intellectual community of late eighteenth-century Naples, *Collection of Etruscan, Greek and Roman Antiquities* has wider, more cosmopolitan, points of reference. As has been pointed out, its French title, *Antiquités etrusques, grecques et romaines* (deliberately?), echoes Count Caylus's *Recueil d' antiquités egyptiennes, etrusques, grecques et romaines* (Paris, 1752–67).[83] In the preface, "Lovers of the Art, Artists and men of Letters" are explicitly referred to the erudition and illustrative examples in Winckelmann's *Geschichte der Kunst des Alterthums* (Dresden, 1764) and his *Monumenti antichi inediti* (Rome, 1767).[84] These bibliographical cross-references are both textual *and* visual. Engravings of ancient artifacts published in the volumes of Montfaucon, Winckelmann, and the *Antichità di Ercolano esposte* are reproduced in the lengthy prefaces, with vignettes and initial letters borrowed and miniaturized from Piranesi and, on two occasions, from Robert Adam's *Ruins of Dioclesian's Palace at Spalatro*.[85]

In summary, *Collection of Etruscan, Greek and Roman Antiquities* preserved an ideal collection of ancient vases, the art of making which was said in its pages to be dependent upon architecture in "the proportions it employs, upon Sculpture by the outlines, & on Painting by the designs with which its productions are adorn'd."[86] By bibliographical reference and material quotation, the volumes also preserved fragments of the contemporary literary monuments devoted to the architecture, sculpture, and painting of the ancients. The survival chances of this collective monument were enhanced by being interred into libraries throughout Europe; libraries that Goethe, writing about Winckelmann's literary career, characterized as real treasure-houses.[87] The contents of these treasure-houses would determine the preservation of ancient monuments collected and published in eighteenth-century texts in the same way that ancient library collections had predetermined the survival of the classical literary tradition. In *The History of the Decline and Fall of the Roman Empire* Gibbon writes of the fate of libraries in antiquity:

> I sincerely regret the more valuable libraries which have been involved in the ruin of the Roman empire; but when I seriously compute the lapse of ages, the waste of ignorance, and the calamities of war, our treasures, rather than our losses, are the object of my surprise. Many curious and interesting facts are buried in oblivion; the three great historians of Rome have been transmitted to our hands in a mutilated state, and we are deprived of many pleasing compositions of the lyric, iambic and dramatic poetry of the Greeks. Yet we should gratefully remember, that the mischances of time and accident have spared the classic works to which the suffrage of antiquity[88] had adjudged the first place of genius and glory: the teachers of ancient knowledge, who are still extant, had perused and compared the writings of their predecessors; nor can it fairly be presumed that any important truth, and useful discovery in art or nature, has been snatched away from the curiosity of modern ages.[89]

While perusing and comparing the works of his predecessors, d'Hancarville orchestrates his own apotheosis into the constellation of celebrated antiquaries.[90] In the frontispieces of volumes 2 and 3 of *Collection of Etruscan, Greek and Roman Antiquities*, ancient monuments are erected and dedicated with Latin inscriptions as memorials to Winckelmann and Caylus.[91] For the former, a top-lit, pantheonlike tomb, lined with columbaria, contains a gigantic sarcophagus raised on huge stone blocks. The valedictory inscription records d'Hancarville's grief at Winckelmann's murder in 1768, a loss visually reiterated in the tiny mourning figure in the right foreground. Count Caylus is similarly remembered by d'Hancarville with an inscription on what looks like a broken lid of a square sarcophagus. In the background, Caylus's head appears in gemlike profile on a brick pyramid. Later in volume 3, d'Hancarville inscribes, in lettering that is less chiseled and more graffiti, his *own* epitaph onto an engraving of a modest, freestanding funerary altar (fig. 24): he inters himself into his own text as if it were his *Res Gestae*. Explaining, "The Publick does not forget, that a right has been given me, to look upon myself as an author that does not exist for some years past; not being at a loss, if needs must, to name the places where I have been burry'd, and the People who have instigated my burryal, I think my self impowered to hold my former opinions, to be them of a man dead this long time."[92]

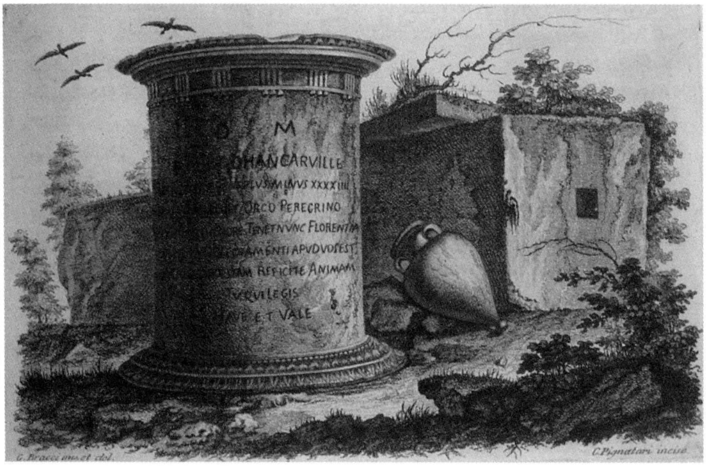

Figure 24 Engraving of d'Hancarville's "tomb" from volume 3 of *Collection of Etruscan, Greek and Roman Antiquities*. Photograph: The British Museum.

As both text and monument, *Collection of Etruscan, Greek and Roman Antiquities* was Janus-like. While looking backwards into the ancient past from the late eighteenth-century present, it also looked *forward* into the future when it would be emulated by later collectors of rare monuments. The preface makes this latter point explicitly: "If it should not serve as a model to those which may hereafter be printed, we flatter ourselves it may serve as an example, and if the example should be found good, one step will have been made towards perfection. We think well enough of Mankind to believe that those who possess rare Monuments of this nature will be desirous of communicating them."[93] Sir Richard Worsley's two-volume *Museum Worsleyanum* (London, 1796–1804), is a collection of antique basso relievos, bustos, statues, and gems, with views of places in the Levant taken on the spot in the years 1785–87, collected, and published in the Hamiltonian tradition. Though Worsley would write to Hamilton that he thought his own publication "the finest printed Book I have yet seen," in 1791 he purchased "most of the finest Gems" that Hamilton had collected.[94] Worsley spent a prolonged period of two years travelling from Rome to Greece and Egypt through the Near East and onto Russia accompanied by an English artist, William Reveley, "to make drawings of Architecture & of the most interesting Ruins," as Worsley's surviving travel journal informs us.[95]

During his extensive and extended travels abroad, Worsley became "so great a dabbler in Virtù" as his "Brother Virtuoso," Sir William Hamilton.[96] Like Hamilton,

Worsley published his collection, the text in English and Italian, with the assistance of Ennio Quirino Visconti, the keeper of the Capitoline museum in Rome. "It will consist principally of things relative to the arts of Design," Worsley explained in a letter to Sir Joseph Banks, "I had the good fortune while at Athens, Paros, Egypt & Constantinople to find & purchase some very fine things in that way."[97] The views of places in the Levant published in the *Museum Worsleyanum* "make a kind of Itinerary of my Travels, of about 18,000 miles," so Worsley informed fellow sculpture collector Townley.[98] They were accompanied by engravings of the antique basso relievos, bustos, statues, and gems, making a kind of itinerary to Worsley's collection of ancient artifacts housed at the family seat of Appuldurcombe Park on the Isle of Wight.

When the Earl of Yarborough, who inherited the collection by marriage, published a new edition of the *Museum Worsleyanum* in 1824, the original folio was described as "not published but printed by Sir Richard for his friends." Yarborough's edition was intended "to spread the fame, & keep up the character of the original, which will thus be always the object of curiosity and value."[99] Like the early volumes of the *Antichità di Ercolano*, the one hundred fifty copies of the first edition of the *Museum Worsleyanum* were not for public sale but were distributed by their collector-publisher. With its limited print run and restricted distribution, Worsley ensured that his collection in its published form would be a rare literary collectable and would be preserved in the libraries of select institutions and elite individuals. Letters acknowledging the receipt of volumes 1 and 2, dated 1798 and 1804, respectively, are bound in a volume preserved with the Worsley papers in the Lincoln Record Office.[100] Of the one hundred fifty copies printed, volumes were presented to the libraries of the following institutions: the British Museum, the Bodleian Library, Oxford, the Royal Academy, the Society of Antiquaries, and the Royal Society. Brother virtuosi on Worsley's mailing list included Hamilton ("disappointed in not finding any of my Gems engraved yet"), Townley, and Richard Payne Knight. In addition, Prime Minister William Pitt at Downing Street, his political adversary C. J. Fox, Lord Nelson, King George III, the Prince of Wales, and the Duke of York all received copies. As well as revealing the roll call of some fifty-nine names on Worsley's exclusive mailing list, the letters of acknowledgement give us an indication of how the work itself was received. Worsley's alma mater, Winchester, considered volume 1 "not only as a Proof of the elegant and Scientific Taste of the author, but also as of his attachment and polite attention to the Wiccamical Body, which has the Honour of ranking him amongst the Number of it's Members." Eton College thanked Sir Richard for "so costly so rare & so Classical a Present." A "richer [present] does not, in my [Symmons] judgment, grace the shelves of any Library in Europe." The vice chancellor of All Souls College, Oxford, had "already deposited it in the Bodleian Library, where it will remain a Monument of the Taste of its accomplished Donor." The Earl of Bute wrote that he would "always value it as one of the principal ornaments of my library at Luton Park."

The two volumes of the *Museum Worsleyanum* were variously and effusively described in the letters of acknowledgement as a work which "will do honour for this Age & Nation": as one of the "Classics of this Country." "The exquisite beauty of the Engravings, together with the very splendid manner in which Antiques are so long concealed, or only imperfectly known, are now exhibited, reflect *Lustre* on *Him*." One Dr. Moseley did "solemnly think the *Museum Worsleyanum* the perfection of human taste, and industry; and will immortalize its Author. It illustrates, and also perpetuates, parts of ancient history, and events, which otherwise would remain in obscurity, and be lost." Richard Bull wrote to Worsley that his daughter studied the volumes that "give the world proper ideas of your invaluable collections . . . [and] is become quite knowing in the history of Greece and Rome." That these letters have been preserved with Worsley's papers and bound into a single volume, demonstrates the extent to which the *Museum Worsleyanum* was conceived and received as an "object of curiosity and value."[101] In other words, it stood as a textualized version of ancient material monuments—"a Gem in itself"—and a monument to Worsley's "Elegant Taste and extensive research": "a Specimen of English Spirit matured and perfected by observation of the most majestic works of Classic Antiquity."

Chapter 1 established the library as the heart of the (neo)classical enterprise; a classical education was understood as being materially embodied in books, especially in school textbooks. Chapter 2 has argued that the grand tour in Italy was embodied in books for the library—in deluxe folios in which the material culture of the ancients was packaged in collectable and consumable form. By looking at a number of volumes devoted to ancient architecture, sculpture, and painting, dating from Montfaucon's *Antiquité Expliquée* (1719–24) to the contents of the *Museum Worsleyanum* (1796–1804), this chapter has explained how, through the mechanics of publication, ancient monuments were "textualized" by being reworked as engraved plates in collectable folios. These textualized monuments were themselves implicated into a process of "monumentalization," not only for the ancient artifacts they preserved through engraved reproductions, but also for the creation and affirmation of reputations for authors like Robert Adam and their aristocratic collector-patrons like Sir William Hamilton. The packaging of antiquity in book form created an elite, cosmopolitan, intellectual culture, a republic of letters that disseminated, or—in the case of the selectively distributed *Antichità di Ercolano*—restricted the privileges of learning and collecting. As the repository for the antique, the elite library is cited by authors and artists alike, including Piranesi and Zoffany, as the prime site for the reception, preservation, and display of these textualized monuments and monumentalized texts. In chapter 3, we will proceed to investigate how these folios were repackaged when their plates were imitated by British architects and craftsmen as pattern books for the interior and its contents, especially in the library.

In every Art, good models give birth to ideas, by exciting the imagination, theory furnishes the means of expressing those ideas, practice puts these means in execution and this last part, which is always the most common is also the easiest.

D'Hancarville, *Collection of Etruscan, Greek and Roman Antiquities*[1]

3

"Fitt to furnish 2 or more rooms"

The Influence of Sir William Hamilton's Vase Publications on English Country House Furnishings

"To sit for one's picture," wrote Jonathan Richardson, "is to have an abstract of one's life written, and published."[2] In her *Memoirs,* the artist Elisabeth Vigée-Lebrun characterized the life of one of her sitters as a genre of popular literature: "The life of Lady Hamilton reads like a romantic fiction."[3] "Mrs. Hart was born and lived in the lowest situation till the age of 19, and since that in no higher one than the mistress of Sir W. Hamilton," wrote Lady Elizabeth Foster in 1791, précising the romantic novel that was at that moment the rags-to-riches story of Emma Hamilton (née Hart).[4] Life and art were inextricably combined in Sir William Hamilton's relationship with Emma. Given that "every man . . . wishes to purchase, what is good, let it be in marble, painting, a horse or a dog," so "picture-mad" Hamilton commissioned paintings of Emma from the artists Joshua Reynolds and George Romney while she was the property of his nephew, Charles Greville.[5] Having commissioned her painted representations, Hamilton was later offered the portrait subject; the exhibit that had inspired the painted imitations was to be loaned on a more permanent basis.[6] Greville wrote to Hamilton that this latest acquisition would complement the latter's collection of classical artifacts, being "a Modern, who will not render your criticism of the Antique less pure."[7]

When performing her famous attitudes, Emma was a living incarnation of her collector-husband's affair with antiquity. Through a rapid succession of staged poses she inverted the Pygmalion myth by metamorphosizing into a series of sculpted and painted artifacts as well as examples of historical, mythological, and literary heroines. Visiting Sir William's secret treasure vault in 1787, Goethe described how he was greatly intrigued by a chest large enough to hold a standing figure, whose front had been removed, the insides painted black, and the whole set in a gilt frame. Apparently, "not content with seeing his image of beauty [Emma] as a moving statue, this friend of art and girlhood [Hamilton] wished also to enjoy her as an inimitable painting, and so, standing against this black background in dresses of various colors, she had sometimes imitated the antique paintings of Pompeii, or even more recent masterpieces."[8] The similitude of performance transformed the living Emma into a sculpture or painting, and it also transformed her socially. Though said to be "coarse and ungraceful in common life," as a performing artifact she was "highly graceful, and even beautiful": a kind of guided tour to an ideal collection.[9] As Goethe wryly observed,

> The old knight idolises her and is enthusiastic about everything she does. In her, he has found all the antiquities, all the profiles of Sicilian coins, even the Apollo Belvedere. This much is certain: as a performance it's like nothing you ever saw before in your life. We have already enjoyed it on two evenings. This morning Tischbein is painting her portrait.[10]

"Sir William perfectly idolises her and I do not wonder he is proud of so magnificent a marble, belonging so entirely to himself," remarked Lady Palmerston.[11] As Hamilton's exclusive possession, he exercised the proprietorial privilege of the collector by inviting prestigious foreign guests to view his prize artifact on display. As a result, Emma's attitudes became one of the unmissable sights on the grand tour of Naples and are preserved for us in the accounts and letters of contemporary tourists. These include Goethe, who witnessed her performances on three recorded occasions, and the British sculpture collector, Henry Blundell, who never enjoyed the privilege himself but whose written itinerary of Naples still included a description of them. In a letter to Charles Townley, Blundell listed Pompeii, Portici, the coast of Baia and Capodimonte as places he had visited near Naples

> with great pleasure and lament nothing, but not having seen ye celebrated Mrs. Hart in her attitudes, singing &c; all ye Eng.^{h} who saw her were in raptures at her performances; some Ladies visited her, others too squeamish: It made a kind of party affair Sr Wm Hamilton often entertains his company with her performances, which

> they say are inimitable. It consists in taking off attitudes of antique statues, characters &c. She has dresses for purpose, one a chemise, light & plaeted here & there, so as to shew limbs; her person very fine and a most expressive countenance.[12]

This textual platform preserved and transmitted Emma's attitudinal celebrity beyond the confines of Hamilton's invited company of "Ambassadors, Nuncios, Monsignoris, Envoys, Residents, and the first quality of *Naples.*"[13]

At the same time as he was entertaining his company with his wife's performances, Hamilton was also orchestrating the reproduction of his ideal collectable. In 1787, Emma wrote to Greville that she was being copied by artists and craftsmen into a variety of collectable artifacts like paintings, gems, and clay and wax sculptures:

> Sir William is very fond of me, and very kind to me. The house [Palazzo Sessa] is ful of painters painting me. He as now got nine pictures of me, and 2 a painting. Marchant is cuting my head in stone, that is in cameo for a ring. There is another man modeling me in wax, and another in clay. All the artists is come from Rome to study from me, that Sir William as fitted up a room that is calld the painting-room.[14]

For the cosmopolitan artistic community based in Rome, Emma's attitudes were not a touristic sight, as they would have been for Blundell (had he seen them), but an academy of imitative models. Vigée-Lebrun wrote in her *Memoirs* that she could have copied Emma's different poses and expressions and filled a gallery with paintings.[15] The German artist Friedrich Rehberg preempted Vigée-Lebrun by producing a portable gallery of engravings of Emma's attitudes—a series of twelve outline drawings entitled *Drawings faithfully copied from Nature at Naples,* published in 1794 with a dedication to Hamilton (fig. 25a). The artist and dealer James Irvine wrote of having "heard much" of Emma's talents, especially from Irish sculptor then in Rome Christopher Hewetson, "who is all raptures when she is the theme. He says he is to attempt something from her."[16] These enraptured artists would not all have been employed by Hamilton; some worked without commission while others came to Naples at the request of foreign patrons.[17] Emma was reported by Goethe to be "regarded as the proper model for all heroines and demi-goddesses," so her reproduction was part of an artist's training as well as his or her economic livelihood.[18] The painter Alexander Day, for example, thanked Sir William Hamilton

> for the favor which you did me in leaving Lady Hamiltons portrait with me. I have had the inexpressible pleasure of copying it in a variety of ways. I have made one Copy in Oil the size of the Original. I have also made several Copys in miniature

> with variations &c one of which I have taken the liberty to send for your approbation. Lord Cole has done me the favor to take the charge of it. It has given great satisfaction to every one here [Rome] that has seen it.[19]

If we subscribe to Richardson's claim that to sit for one's picture is to have an abstract of one's life written and published, then based on this brief survey, Emma Hamilton's biographers would include the following painters: Elisabeth Vigée-Lebrun, Alexander Day, Friedrich Rehberg (fig. 25a), Joshua Reynolds, George Romney, and J. H. W. Tischbein (fig. 25b), the sculptor Christopher Hewetson, and the gem engraver, Nathaniel Marchant (fig. 25c).[20] These artists condensed Emma's life into a whole range of aesthetic media: stone, wax, clay, and paint; they communicated it in various sizes—Day's letter refers to miniature copies (as in fig. 25d)—and in different series: from individual commissions by Hamilton to Rehberg's mass-produced engravings. In fact, Emma's rags-to-riches and back-to-rags story (she died a penniless alcoholic) has been told and retold in pictures and in print by countless biographers.[21]

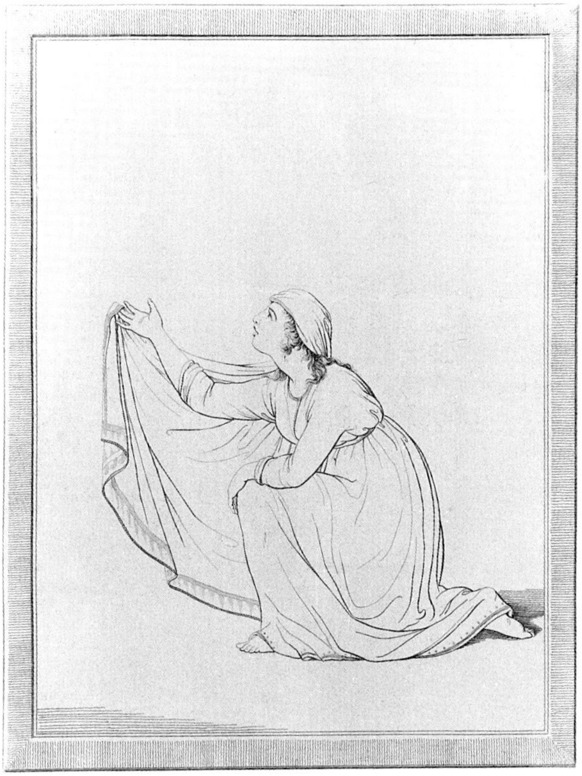

Figure 25a *(left)* Friedrich Rehberg, *Emma as Cleopatra. Drawings faithfully copied from Nature at Naples and with permission dedicated to the Right Honourable William Hamilton* (London, 1794). The Warburg Institute.

Figure 25b *(right top)* Wilhelm Tischbein, *Emma as a Sibyl*, c. 1788. Weimar, Stiftung Weimarer Klassik und Kunstsammlungen Museen.

Figure 25c *(far right top)* Nathaniel Marchant, head of Emma Hamilton, carved chaldecony. Metropolitan Museum of Art, New York.

Figure 25d *(right bottom)* Enamel miniature by Henry Bone dated 1803 after Elisabeth Vigée-le Brun's 1790 oil painting *Emma as a Bacchante*. Wallace Collection.

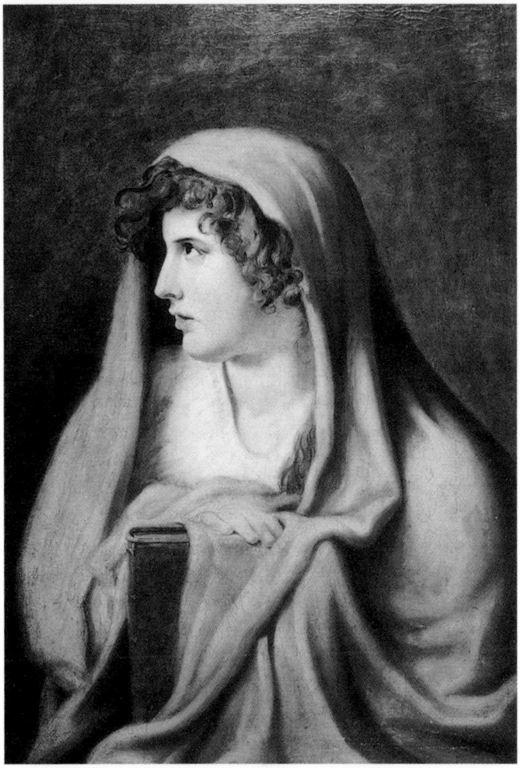

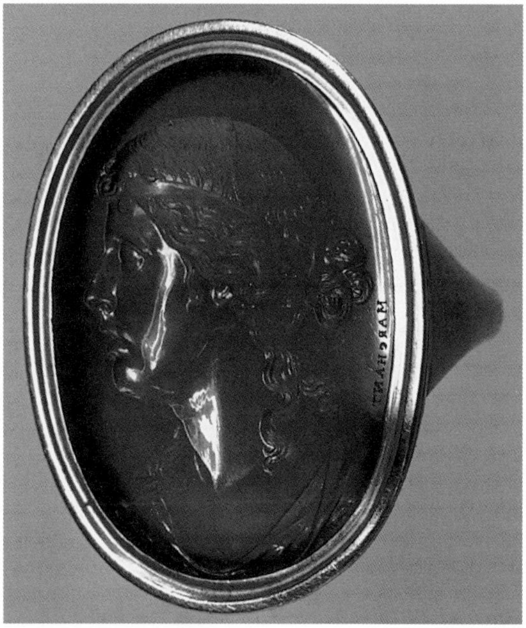

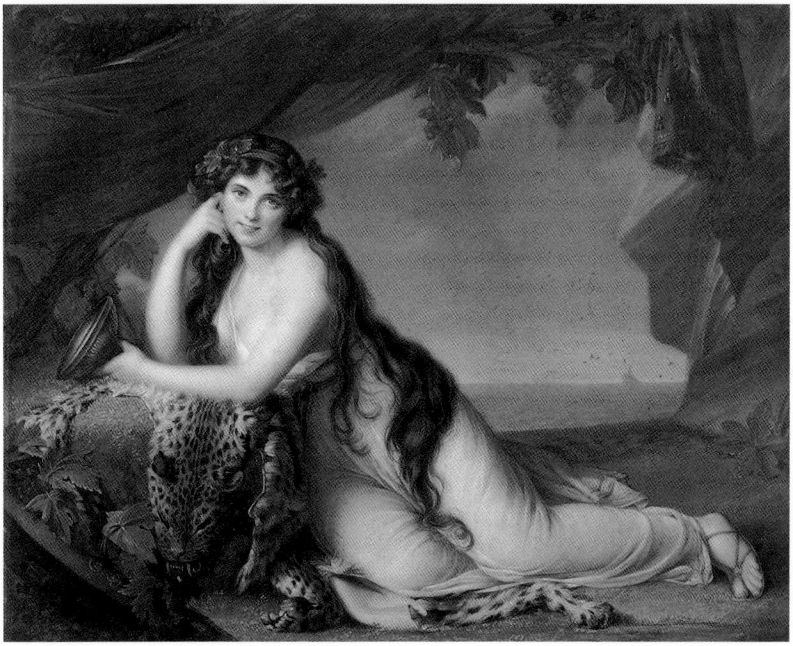

As opposed to the artistic or literary biographer, the art historian understands the transformation of Emma, from ideal collectable into a series of reproductive collectables, as a repetition of another type of aristocratic performance: the publication of Hamilton's collection of ancient vases and its influence as pattern books on British artists and craftsmen. In the same way that Charles Greville was reported by the Comtesse de Boigne to have found no difficulty in bringing the young Emma upstairs from the kitchen and installing her in his drawing room, so it has been said that Emma's attitudes brought antiquity into the drawing room.[22] In this chapter we will see how Hamilton's vase publications, *Collection of Etruscan, Greek and Roman Antiquities* (Naples, 1766–76) brought antiquity in the form of painted wall schemes, furniture, and collectables into the drawing rooms, halls, and especially the libraries of English country houses.[23]

Sir Joshua Reynolds's sixth discourse provides a theoretical insight into the artistic practice of imitating antiquity. In this sixth of his fifteen lectures delivered at the Royal Academy between 1769 and 1790, he describes the works of the ancients as a "magazine," a storehouse of "common property, always open to the public, whence every man has the right to take what he pleases."[24] In reality, however, the antique past was not always so accessible to its eighteenth-century public. In the preface written in English and French on facing pages of volume 1 of *Collection of Etruscan, Greek and Roman Antiquities,* Hamilton's editor, d'Hancarville, refers to the nonvisibility of antiquities: excavated pots in private collections, for example, were perceived as "remaining (as one may say) buried in cabinets," in which case they were of as little utility to artists as when buried in tombs.[25] Hamilton's vase publications set out to exhume the pots from collectors' cabinets and make them visible to the artist "as if he had the original in his possession."[26] The text continues,

> We think also, that we make an agreeable present to our manufacturers of earthenware and china, and to those who make vases in silver, copper, glass, marble etc. Having employed much more time in working than in reflexion, and besides being in great want of models, they will be very glad to find here more than two hundred forms, the greatest part of which are absolutely new to them; then, as in a plentiful stream, they may draw ideas which their ability and taste will know how to improve to their advantage, and to that of the public.[27]

The contents of the Hamilton volumes are presented as much-needed models to contemporary manufacturers. They are not only models in the sense of providing over two hundred new patterns, but serve as paradigms furnishing craftsmen with, as the preface puts it, a "plentiful stream" of ideas: ideas that their ability and taste will improve to their personal and public advantage. In this passage, we encounter two different ways of imitating antiquity, "working," or faithful quotation, and reflection, imaginative interpretation and the improvement of the original. Reynolds's sixth discourse expands on this idea of different ways of imitating the antique:

> He who borrows an idea from an antient. . . and so accommodates it to his own work, that it makes a part of, with no seam or joining appearing, can hardly be charged with plagiarism . . . But an artist should not be contented with this only; he should enter into a competition with his original, and endeavour to improve what he is appropriating to his own work. Such imitation is so far from having any thing in it of the servility of plagiarism, that it is a perpetual exercise of the mind, a continual invention.[28]

Reynolds's program of improving rather than slavishly imitating the model itself emulates theories of imitation from the classical and classicizing traditions. From the first-century A.D. Roman orator Quintilian (*Institutio Oratoria,* IV.X ii, 6–7, 10), to Vasari fifteen centuries later in *Life of Mino da Fiesole* and following Reynolds's discourse in Gibbon's *History of the Decline and Fall of the Roman Empire* (6: 1788):[29] "Genius may anticipate the season of maturity; but in the education of a people, as in that of an individual, memory must be exercised, before the powers of reason and fancy can be expanded; nor may the artist hope to equal or surpass, till he has learned to imitate, the works of his predecessors."[30] When dealing with the subject of imitation in his monumental history Gibbon evoked the practice of the *artist*; similarly Horace Walpole defended Reynolds against charges of plagiarism by citing the practice of the *author*:

> Sir J. Reynolds has been accused of plagiarism for having borrowed attitudes from ancient masters. Not only candour but criticism must deny the *force* of the charge. When a single posture is imitated from an historical picture and applied to a portrait in a different dress and with new attributes, this is not plagiarism, but quotation: and a quotation from a great author, with a novel application of the sense, has always been allowed to be an instance of parts and taste; and may have more merit than the original.[31]

This tension between working and reflection, sanctioned by ancient texts but with a clear contemporary relevance, is central to understanding the transference of the Hamiltonian vases: from ancient pots to engraved and mass-produced prints.[32] The accompanying text purported to provide imitative models that were not only excellent but that were as exact as possible to their original models.[33] In order

> that the Artists who would invent in the same stile, or only copy the Monuments which appeared to him worthy of being copied, may do so with as much truth and precision, as if he had the Originals themselves in his possession. It is by this means, that the present work may contribute to the advancement of the Arts, and make the masterpieces that are worthy of imitation understood as they deserve to be.[34]

By keeping their copies as close as possible to the originals, the Hamilton publications claimed to provide a more authentic image of the past than a general idea of the vases as presented in the volumes of Caylus and Montfaucon (figs. 22a and 22b above) and by which antiquarians and artists have, it is claimed, been cruelly misled.[35]

However, far from being faithful to their ruined or fragmentary condition in Hamilton's collection, the ancient vases are reconstructed and improved in their published form. Take an engraving from volume 1, plate 117 (fig. 26) of a vase (fig. 27), which depicts a female figure throwing a ball. In the transference from ancient

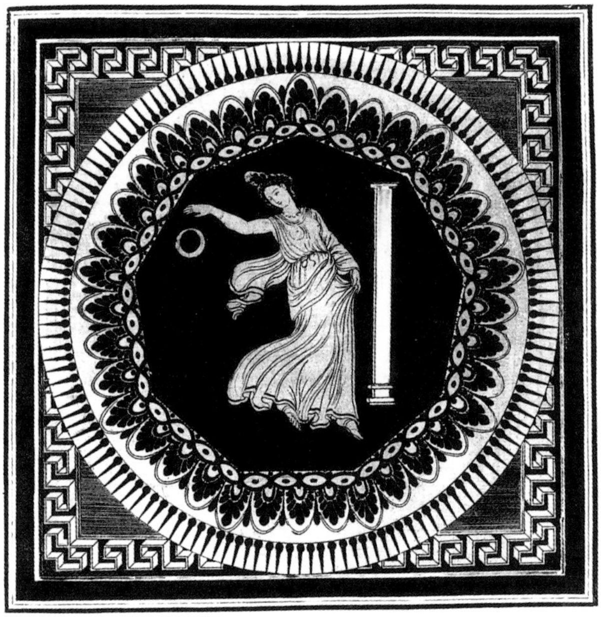

Figure 26 Engraving of Apulian lekane. D'Hancarville, *Collection of Etruscan, Greek and Roman Antiquities*, vol. 1, plate 117. Institute of Classical Studies Library.

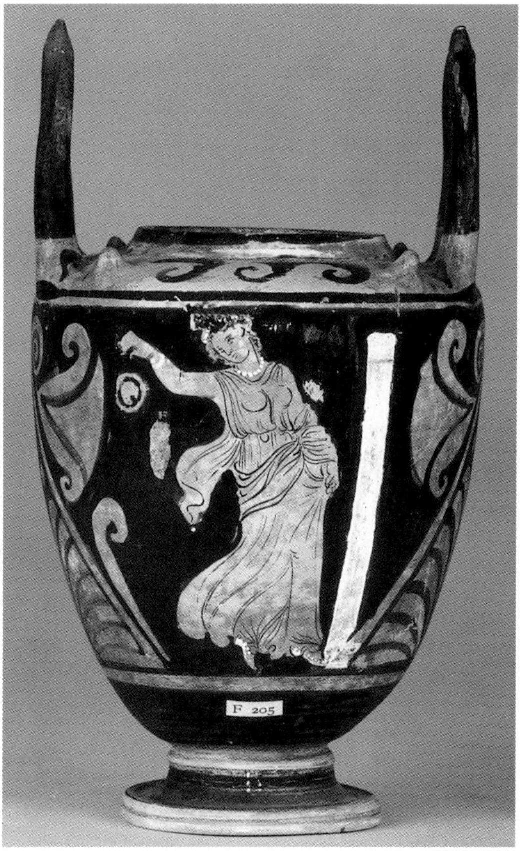

Figure 27 Apulian lekane (BM F205). © Copyright The Trustees of the British Museum.

pot to late eighteenth-century print, the painted figure has been isolated from its clay surface, surrounded by an elaborate circular and square frame and flattened onto the page.[36] The ancient painting has been improved: look at the details of the figure's facial features and her clothes, the now-slender column on her right. There is no indication of where the handles once joined the pot or even intercepted the decoration. Therefore the accompanying text, which claimed to have exercised such unprecedented fidelity in the engraved copies, is exposed as a fallacy. The vases are purportedly published as exquisite models for artists to improve to their advantage, yet it is the original vases that have been significantly improved by the engravers.[37] The idealizing engravings have transformed the ancient vase paintings into two-dimensional canvas paintings: just as Emma was transformed in her portable chest from moving statue into inimitable painting. The claims by the text to the fidelity of the copies are more rhetorical than realistic; the engravers have practiced the very notions of competition and improvement that Quintilian, Vasari, and Reynolds extolled.[38]

According to the accompanying text of *Collection of Engravings from Ancient Vases,* devoted to Hamilton's second vase collection, the ancient vase paintings were not only aesthetic masterpieces and, as such, worthy of imitation, but were themselves creative imitations of ancient wall paintings. "I am convinced [writes Hamilton] that the study of them wou'd be of more use to Artists, than they are at present aware of, for it is highly probable . . . that the drawings on many of these [vases] were originally taken from paintings of the very first Master's in Greece."[39] Such rhetoric justifies the study of the vase paintings by situating the ancient pot painter and his modern imitator in a genealogical tradition of copying: an aesthetic exercise that forever attempts to recoup the masterpieces of antiquity. But while this rhetorical strategy served to situate the ancient and modern artist in a venerable tradition, it was a tradition that was wholly fabricated. It created an ideal classical exemplum, which enhanced the ancient pot painter and his artistic creations by comparison with ancient Greek wall paintings that had not survived.[40]

Undeterred by the lack of archaeological evidence, d'Hancarville's text unearthed a more accessible but no less ideal comparison: the masters of the Italian Renaissance, in particular Raphael: "An examination of the Pictures of Raphael must be of infinite service to the study of the Antique, as this . . . teaches us to be more sensibly touch'd with the beauties of Raphael, whom we dare to insert amongst the number of the Ancients, of whom he has been the great admirer, and faithful Disciple."[41] Drawing the reader's attention to the last plate of volume I (fig. 28), an engraving of the upper scene of the Meidias hydria,[42] d'Hancarville challenged his readers, "I ask those who have well examined this little piece, if it is possible to execute it better, or if one could have expected more of Raphael himself, supposing one had given him two figures [Atalante and Hippomene] to compose and execute, with all the difficulties . . . which our Artist must necessarily have overcome."[43] Reading ancient vase paintings with Renaissance-tinted spectacles was a strategy d'Hancarville borrowed from Winckelmann. In his *Geschichte der Kunst des Alterthums* (Dresden, 1764), Winckelmann had written that given the quality of the figures on ancient vases, they "might deservedly have a place in a drawing by Raphael."[44] To demonstrate this observation visually, plate 22 of volume 2 of *Collection of Etruscan, Greek and Roman Antiquities* reproduced a reworking of the final plate in volume 1 as if it had been executed by Raphael (fig. 29).[45] The artist, M. Pecheux, transformed the engraving, instructed and restrained in his adaptation by d'Hancarville. D'Hancarville advises the viewer to compare the prints of the original vase and the reworking. He points out that Pecheux has engraved the figures with more detail and has rearranged their positions, in order that a clever man can see the profits of improving antiquity—a noble simplicity of which the greatest modern painters have been imitators.[46] Thus, Pecheux's reworking represents an example to artists of how to adapt the ancient vase paintings in the manner of Raphael, himself a great admirer and faithful disciple of the ancients. But as we have already seen, with reference to the Apulian lekane, the published engravings of the vases were themselves *improvements* of the ancient artifacts.

Figure 28 Engraving of the upper scene of the Meidias hydria. D'Hancarville, *Collection of Etruscan, Greek and Roman Antiquities*, vol. 1, plate 130. Institute of Classical Studies Library.

Figure 29 M. Pecheux's improved version of the upper scene of the Meidias hydria. D'Hancarville, *Collection of Etruscan, Greek and Roman Antiquities* vol. 2, plate 22. Institute of Classical Studies Library.

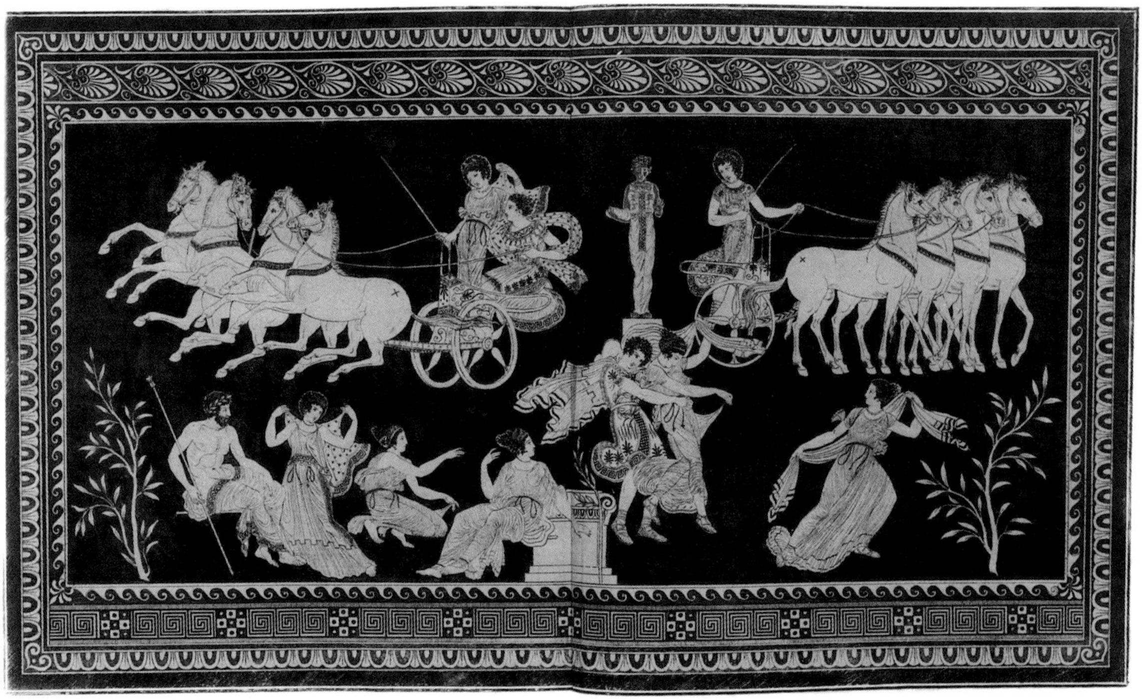

In the preface to *Collection of Engravings from Ancient Vases,* Hamilton wrote, "It is well known that Antiquarians have been often misled by drawings from Statues, Basrilievos, and Vases that have been modernly repaired, and their Dissertations have turned entirely upon certain attributes and Additions that did not exist in the Originals."[47] The engraved vases published by d'Hancarville do appear as if modernly repaired: the ancient past improved and intact. As a result of such creative restorations, d'Hancarville's text situates ancient vase paintings in an ideal tradition of ideal works of arts, a tradition fabricated and disseminated by the vase publications.

The deluxe engravings were explicitly targeted in the preface to *Collection of Etruscan, Greek and Roman Antiquities* as prints and drawings copied from the most ancient designs extant.[48] According to d'Hancarville,

> as in a gallery of Pictures, one endeavours to unite those of the Masters from Cimabue, Andrea Tassi, Gaddo Gaddi, Margariton, and Giotto down to our time, so in this collection one may see the stiles of different periods in the Art of the Ancients; consequently it is not without reason that we have said, that this Collection is equally proper for the compleating of well understood Collections of Prints and

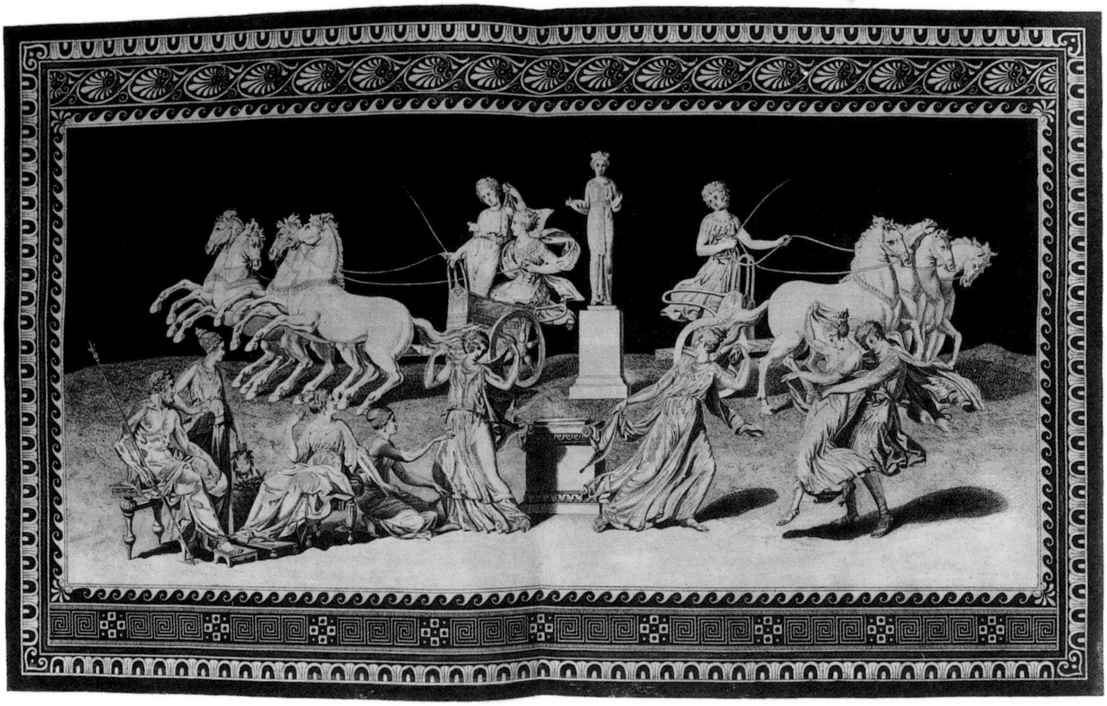

> Designs, or to furnish in a manner not only agreeable, but usefull and instructive, the Cabinet of a Man of Taste and Letters: since by its assistance, he may see as in a kind of Geographical chart, the whole progress, and count as it were every step of human industry, in the most agreable art of its invention.[49]

As part of the transformative strategy of the publications, the varying styles of the vase paintings represented were equivalent to the exhibition of pictures in a gallery. The Hamilton volumes were marketed not only as prestigious pattern books for artists but also as a gallery without walls, luxury collectibles fit to furnish the cabinets of men of "Taste and Letters." For Winckelmann, who classified ancient art into its distinctive periods, a collection of ancient vases was a real treasure of drawings.[50] The Hamilton volumes literally transformed and disseminated the original vases as a storehouse of collectable drawings.

As a summary of an aristocratic collection of ancient vases, the collectable prints were bound in lavish volumes and acquired as collectables for the elite, cosmopolitan library. Writing to his mother from Naples on 24 February 1767, Lord Kildare actually described *Collection of Etruscan, Greek and Roman Antiquities* as a very good ornament to the library:

> I mentioned in a former letter a book of Etruscan vases printed here by subscription, under the direction of Mr Hamilton. I have not yet subscribed, as I waited for an answer. But as the time of my departure draws near, I hope the Duke will not disapprove of my subscribing. It is about ten guineas, and it will be a very good ornament to the library, and a pleasant book to dip in, as there is very pretty figures, and vases to draw from. It'll also oblige Mr Hamilton, who has been very civil to me. Will you be so good as to mention it to Lady Louisa, as I am sure it is a sort of thing she would like, as she is fond of pretty ornaments, etc.[51]

In a later letter from Turin, Kildare thought it "amazing how one picks up our old Eton acquaintances abroad. I have dare say I have met above forty since I have been in Italy."[52] One of Kildare's fellow old Etonians he encountered in Italy who also subscribed to the Hamilton volumes was Lord Fitzwilliam. Like Kildare, Fitzwilliam (begrudgingly) subscribed as a token of esteem to Hamilton:

> one of the truest Dilettantis of every sort of virtù that we know: there is now publishing under his protection an account of the forms & ornaments of the antient Etruscan vases: the work is a very pretty one, & perfectly well executed, but excessively dear, as must be expected, when a gentleman Dilettanti is engaged in it: for in that care the work is prosecuted as far as the Gentleman's passion carries him; and

> every thing that pleases him, he looks upon as useful to the publick: this seems to me to be the present case: Artists will find many elegant ornaments in it, and things to be follow'd; but the price far exceeds the utility that can be deriv'd from the work however one must subscribe to it, to please Mr Hamilton, because he deserves to be pleas'd; but I own the subscription sticks in my stomach, for I could lay out the money much more to my own satisfaction.[53]

Other subscribers recognized the commercial possibilities of the volumes, not as ornaments for the aristocratic library but as pattern books for craftsmen mass producing a whole range of luxury collectables for an elite British market. One such subscriber was P. J. Wendler, who wrote to his employer, Matthew Boulton, the Birmingham-based manufacturer of decorative metalwork, of having

> been in Naples and subscribed in your Name & for yr acc.^{t}, for ab^{t} 456 prints in folio divided in 4 volumes; the first will appear in ab^{t} 2 or 3 weeks, & th' other successively in about a years time with an english & Italian explication of the ancient Etrurian Vases, fitt to furnish 2 or more rooms & to chuse from the said Prints handsome Designs & patterns for the Birmingham Manufactorys. It is reckoned a fine piece of work as being printed with colours imitating the said vases. Mr. Hamilton the English minister residing in Naples bought the Cabinet of the said vases & dedicats the Prints to His Brittish Majesty. Knowing you a Lover of such kind of Curiositys I thought I cou nt do wrong to subscribe for the same, as they only cost 16 oncies neapolitan money, which makes ab.^{t} £9. 10. I am certain, that Mr. Taylor & all our chief manufacturers & likewise Mr Baskevile would be very glad to have those Prints, for they may be very usefull for Birmingham.[54]

Wendler saw the utility of the Hamiltonian prints as providing designs and patterns for the Birmingham manufactories. As well as containing a vast repertoire (456) of color prints with the cachet of foreign antiquities, the volumes possessed a prestigious British stamp, given that Hamilton was the British envoy in Naples and the prints were dedicated to the king. The acknowledged aim of the Hamilton volumes was to serve "as an example, and if the example should be found good, one step will have been made towards perfection."[55] Yet the volumes acquired by British manufacturers like Matthew Boulton and Josiah Wedgwood, as we shall see presently, were utilized first and foremost as an ideal standard rather than as a possible example. The inventive fabrications of the volumes were stamped with the prestige of the collector and his collection of ancient artifacts: a prestige that the craftsmen literally subscribed to in their reproductive craft. For example, in 1772, Matthew Boulton wrote to Mrs. Montagu of his attitude to the process of reproduction: "Ye present age distinguishes it self by adopting the most Elegant ornaments of the most refined Grecian artists, I am satisfy'd in conforming thereto, & humbly copying their style, & makeing new combinations of old ornaments without presuming to invent new ones."[56] Boulton had no need to presume to invent anew. That process had already begun in the Hamilton volumes, the source of shapes for some of Boulton's silver wares and the source of his reverence for the "most Elegant ornaments of the most refined Grecian artists."[57]

As well as furnishing artists and craftsmen with a "magazine," to use Reynolds's phrase again, of idealized engravings that the accompanying text situated in an ideal tradition of ideal works of art, the Hamilton volumes also provided a framework for transforming these designs into a novel range of imitation antique furniture. In other words, the volumes covered all possible angles—the models, the theory, and the suggested practice. Wilhelm Tischbein, the editor of *Collection of Engravings from Ancient Vases,* demonstrated in material form d'Hancarville's conjecture that the collected prints of the volumes were equivalent to a picture gallery. In Naples in the early 1790s he decorated a cabinet, described in a letter of 18 December 1792, to Duchess Amalia. "Arranged according to the narrations so that one can have an instant overview," the framed prints could be purchased individually or in sets according to the tastes and space of a cosmopolitan audience:

> I had a similar cabinet constructed for the Imperial Ambassador, Esterhazy, which makes a pleasant impression, and a number of foreigners have ordered some. To go to England, Russia, Portugal and Vienna. I am pleased that these items are becoming more generally known and I hope this will make a great contribution to the return of good taste. I have arranged it that all the pictures are of a uniform size, with ornamentation and frame, so that they are easy to dispatch and each costs one ounce of Neapolitan gold. Each person can then, according to his liking, choose as much as he wants to decorate a room. The whole collection consists of a hundred items.[58]

As late as 1829, Peter Langford-Brooke purchased one such set on his grand tour of Naples. His account book for 10 March, "For Paintings of vases at Studio," records payment of 60 ducats for ten large (102.8 x 77.5 cm) prints and 16 ducats for twenty small (31.8 x 43.8) prints.[59] These

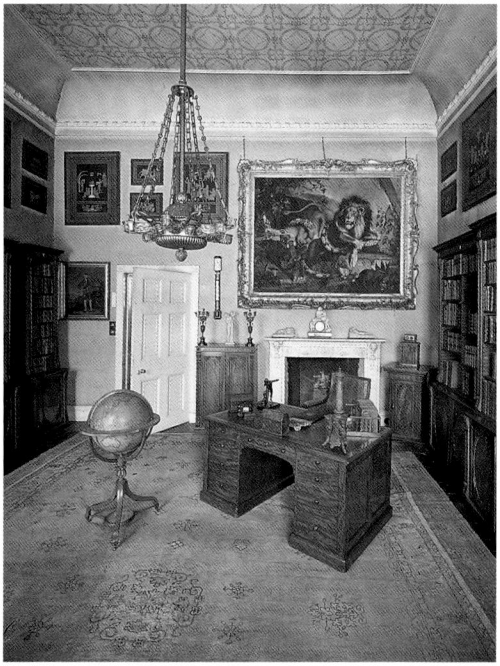

Figure 30 The library at Mere Hall, Cheshire, decorated with deluxe prints from *Collection of Etruscan, Greek and Roman Antiquities*. Christie's Images Ltd.

deluxe versions with their elaborate frames were then hung above bookcases in Langford-Brooke's library at Mere Hall in Cheshire (fig. 30).[60] On 4 April 1796, Charles Heathcote Tatham wrote to his employer, the architect Henry Holland, about Tischbein's cabinet.

> Referring again to internal Decorations, I had almost forgot a modern invention set on foot by a Man at Naples of the name of Tischbein, who has published certain prints, bordures, hangings & such like, in the etruscan style, precisely copied from Sir Will.[m] Hamilton's Vases & adapted to small Rooms and Cabinets, he has himself fitted up a room as a specimen with which I was so much pleased, that I procured specimens of the ornaments with their prices, you can scarce imagine how successful and new such ornaments appear—they are used in the way of our modern paper hangings, & are suited as well to the walls of a room as to the whole furniture throughout—figures, ornaments, symbols of every kind are copied from the real vases, representing them in their exact colours—the bordures are for panelling etc, (as I have sent you a scrap) and the figures are destined for the centre of pannells in a wide open field of dark colour—I will write you more details of this new & tasty method of fitting up rooms hereafter.[61]

It is one of the paradoxes of the spirit of continual invention that something ancient could appear new. Indeed, Tischbein's model room, decorated with an ensemble of Hamiltonian prints transferred from pattern book to showroom, is echoed in the furnishings of the outer hall at Newtimber Place in Sussex. Little is known about the history of the property purchased by one Nathaniel Newnham in 1741, even less about how the painted murals dated circa 1796 came to be there. Given their estimated date and the geographical location of Newtimber Place, Biagio Rebecca and John Francis Rigaud are possible contenders, based on the familiarity of Rebecca's work to the Sussex gentry and Rigaud's predilection for archaeological themes.[62] Enlarged reproductions of two plates, the nuptials of Paris and Helen (2: plate 32) and Pecheux's interpretation of the upper scene from the Meidias hydria (2: plate 22) dominate the west (fig. 31) and north walls. In panels distributed around the room, we witness the transference of the Hamiltonian designs from pot to print to picture gallery. Here the influence of the Hamilton volumes is unmediated; the prints are lifted as seen from the page and painted on the walls in the manner of a picture gallery or print room. For other panels, particularly those of the doors, single or pairs of figures have been isolated from their plates: "destined for the panells in a wide open field of dark colour," as Tatham observed of Tischbein's model. As in Tischbein's showroom, the Hamilton plates in the outer hall at Newtimber are applied to both walls and furniture. The engraved patterns have been reworked as

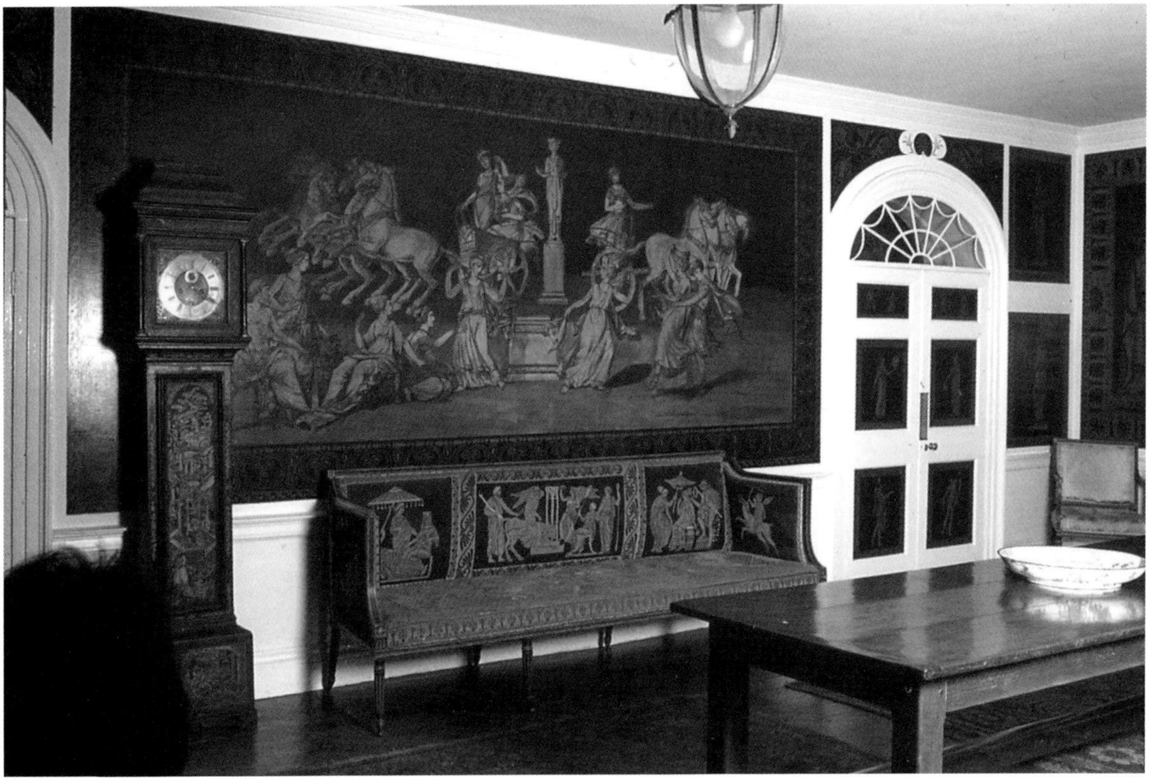

Figure 31 "From pot to print to picture gallery": the west wall of the outer hall at Newtimber Place, Sussex, decorated c. 1796, with an enlarged reproduction of *Collection of Etruscan, Greek and Roman Antiquities*, 2, plate 22. Photograph: The British Museum. By courtesy of Mr. Andrew Clay.

embroidered tapestries for the chairs, a settee, and a stool. Quotations range from faithful reproductions of the figural plates to free improvisation for the decorative frames.

In the outer hall at Newtimber Place, the totality of the furnishings and furniture is "Hamiltonian": engravings from *Collection of Etruscan, Greek and Roman Antiquities* are reproduced in painted *and* embroidered versions in an assortment of shapes and sizes. Regarding size, the *scale* of the influence of the Hamilton plates can be seen in their polarized uses in the outer hall at Newtimber Place and the Cupola Room at Heaton Hall near Manchester, home of the first Earl of Wilton. In the narrow vertical panels of the Cupola Room designed by James Wyatt and painted by Biagio Rebecca around 1772–84 are miniature painted versions of the Hamilton plates (fig. 32), drastically reduced in size from the two largest murals at Newtimber Place. Therefore the reproduction of the Hamilton prints, from gigantic to miniature, could be writ both large and small. At Heaton Hall their scale is miniaturized and incorporated into a broader decorative scheme that represents the influence

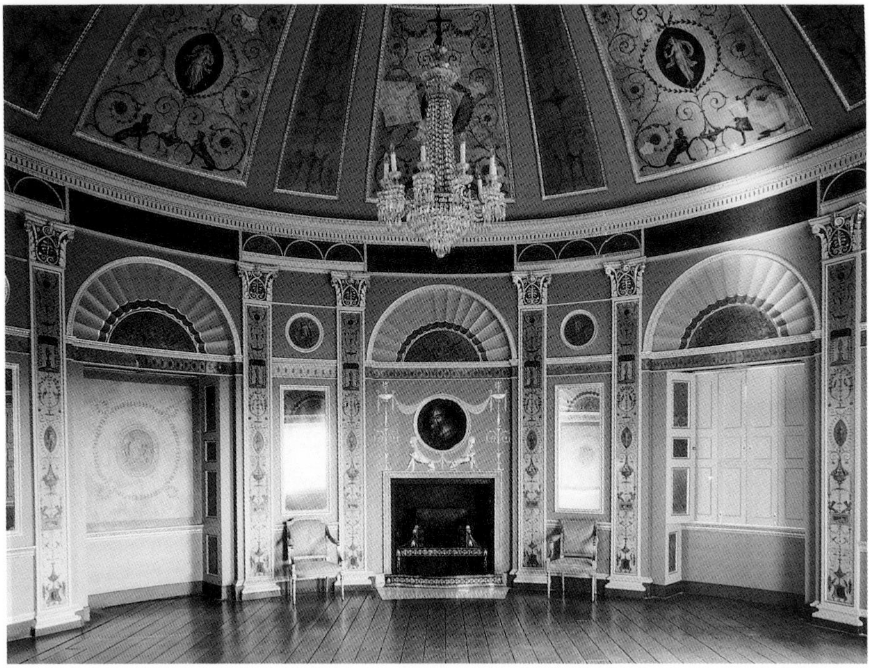

Figure 32 View into the Cupola Room at Heaton Hall, Manchester, designed by James Wyatt and painted by Biagio Rebecca, c. 1772–84. Manchester City Art Galleries.

of not (just) one prestigious pattern book but a choice bibliography. Plates copied from the Hamilton volumes are integrated into a painted composition with reproductions of plates from the *Loggie di Rafaele nel Vaticano* (Rome, 1776), engraved by D. Savorelli and P. Camporesi, and *Le Antichità di Ercolano esposte* (8 vols.; Naples, 1757–92).[63]

Writing to his patron Lord Arundel on 27 August 1774, Father Thorpe described the influence of the engravings of Raphael's loggia (fig. 33), which were incorporated into the scheme at Heaton. The plates had already been circulated to craftsmen in Rome prior to publication.

> Since the Vatican Pilasters have been printed & coloured, their ornaments are now put upon every thing. Coaches, Picture Frames, & all kinds of furniture are dressed up with them: I have seen Priests Vestments & the Antependiums of Altars composed entirely of them. These Ornaments & others in the Etruscan stile engross all the taste of the Gentry in this country; many of the little orders for Chimney Pieces intended for England are to be executed after the Etruscan manner in coloured Scagliuola, a platform for a grand Desart is just finished in the same material and manner.[64]

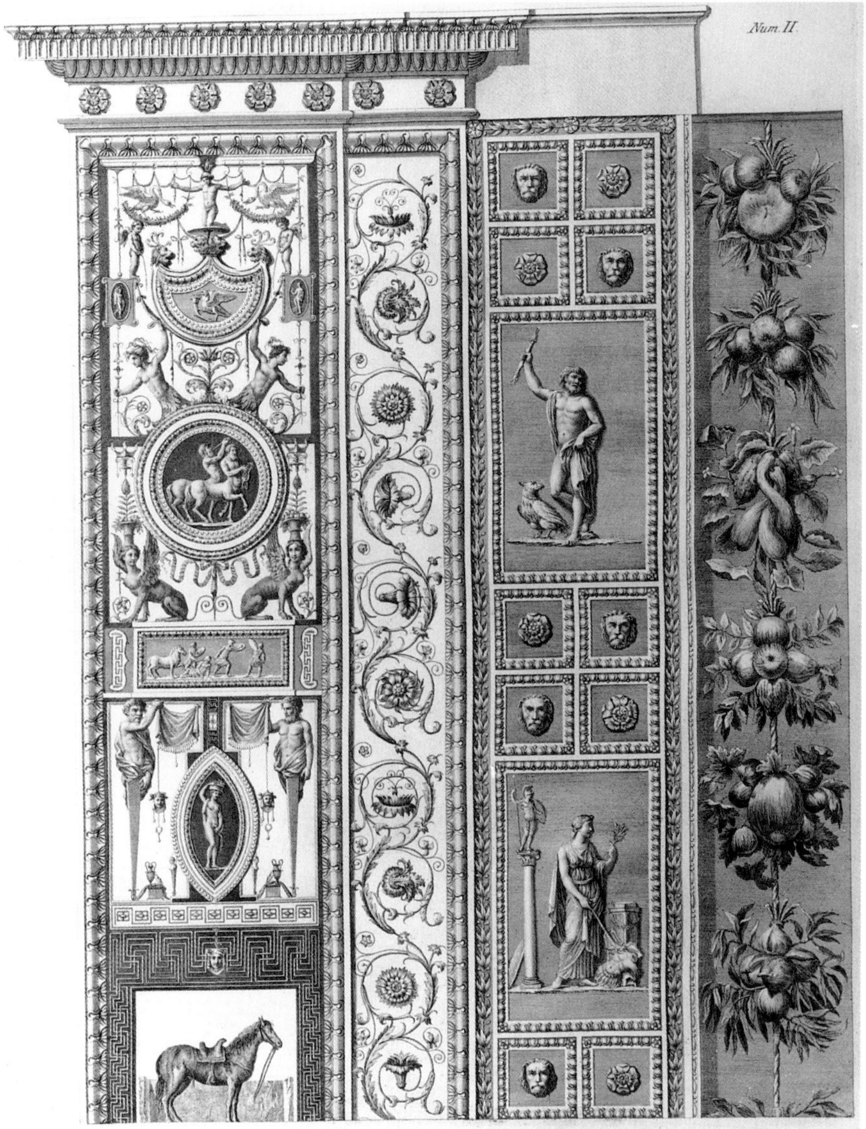

Figure 33 Plate from *Loggie di Rafaele nel Vaticano* (1776), engraved by D. Savorelli and P. Camporesi. By courtesy of the Trustees of Sir John Soane's Museum.

Thorpe's letter recounts that Roman craftsmen were busy transferring the engravings of the Vatican pilasters onto an exhaustive series of luxury objects, both domestic *and* religious, for consumption in Italy and export abroad. The eighteenth-century classification of styles under blanket labels like "Etruscan," to which Thorpe refers, will be addressed in the next chapter in relation to ancient paintings excavated from Pompeii and Rome. In the same way that the Vatican engravings were being utilized as patterns by contemporary artists, so the decorative scheme of Raphael's loggia was influenced by ancient grotesque paintings discovered by accident in the late fifteenth century in Rome.[65] Viewing the paintings in the subterranean rooms on the Esquiline Hill, Charlotte Eaton described them as the source from which Raphael had taken the idea of the ornaments to adorn the Vatican loggia. "To Raphael [she writes] these exquisite figures were a school of art. He transfused much of their soul and spirit into his own compositions, but made no slavish copy of them."[66]

The reproduction of Raphael's painted interior scheme in engravings and their dissemination throughout cosmopolitan Europe meant that the style said by Father Thorpe to "engross all the taste of the Gentry" in Italy was exported and replicated by foreign craftsmen. For instance, in 1767, the abbé Ferdinando Galiani wrote to the Neapolitan minister of internal affairs in an attempt to persuade him to reprint copies of the *Antichità di Ercolano esposte,* not for "rich antique dealers or literati" but for French

> goldsmiths, costume-jewellery makers, painters of carriages and ornamental panels [who] need this book. Did Your Excellency know that everything these days is made à la greque, which is the same as saying à Erculanum? . . . All the bronzes, engravings and paintings are copied from *Ercolano.* I have seen that painting of a woman selling cherubs as chickens at least ten times. So Your Excellency can see the importance of a reprint of *Ercolano* as, without the whole book, the poor artists have to cope with just bits and pieces.[67]

According to Galiani's letter, Parisian craftsmen were like their Roman counterparts, imitating the engraved plates of another grand tour folio to manufacture all manner of luxury goods "à la greque" or "à Erculanum." For the Cupola Room at Heaton Hall, James Wyatt transferred bits and pieces from his pattern books and united them in a composition that transformed the room into an evocative recreation of Italy, a kind of pictorial guidebook to the painted highlights of the grand tour. Moreover, by amalgamating copies of ancient vase paintings with copies of ancient wall paintings from Herculaneum and Pompeii with Renaissance frescoes by the master Raphael, the decoration of the Cupola Room visually demonstrates d'Hancarville's contention that ancient vase paintings are the product of a genealogical tradition of copying painted masterpieces.

The preface to *Collection of Etruscan, Greek and Roman Antiquities* already noted that the volumes were explicitly offered as a present to manufacturers of earthenware and china and to vase makers proficient in different media. A unique commission for a set of silver "Hamiltonian" vases was orchestrated by the classically educated aristocratic patron, Nathaniel Curzon, first Baron Scarsdale. Scarsdale, who owned copies of the first two Hamilton volumes, commissioned the London silversmiths Louisa Courtauld and George Cowles in 1771 to produce a set of three silver condiment vases (fig. 34) for his dining room at Kedleston Hall in Derbyshire, designed by Robert Adam.[68] Figures from the celebrated Meidias hydria were selected from their published engravings (*Collection,* 1: plates 127–30) and transferred onto this set of silver vases. In the spirit of continual invention advocated by d'Hancarville and demonstrated by Pecheux, key protagonists were isolated from their plates and their positions were rearranged so as to form novel compositions. According to d'Hancarville's accompanying disquisition, which draws on a library of classical literary sources including Diodorus Siculus and Ovid, Heracles received the golden apples from the Hesperides in Africa: hence the innovative suggestion on the vases of a tropical landscape with palm trees and the distinctive facial features of some of the figures. In addition, it has been suggested that the shape and decoration of the Kedleston vases may have been influenced by Josiah Wedgwood's First Day Vases produced in June 1769 to celebrate the revival of the arts in Etruria

Figure 34 Set of three silver condiment vases by Louisa Courtauld and George Cowles, 1771. Courtesy, Museum of Fine Arts, Boston. Reproduced with permission. © 2004 Museum of Fine Arts, Boston.

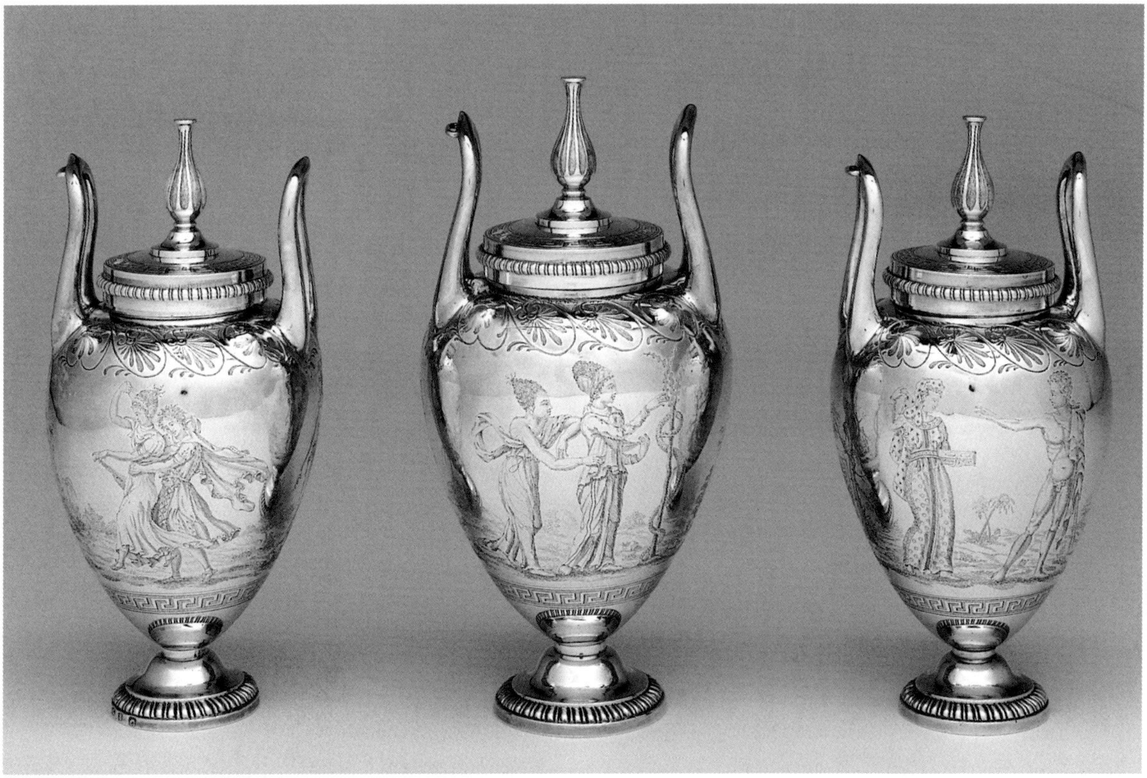

("Artes Etruriae revascuntur," which is how they were inscribed) in industrial, eighteenth-century Britain.[69]

It is well documented that Josiah Wedgwood, the Staffordshire potter and entrepreneur, employed the Hamilton volumes as a prestigious pattern book for his reproduction Etruscan wares.[70] Also well known is the fact that Wedgwood first acquired proof sheets from Hamilton's brother-in-law, Lord Cathcart, while another of his aristocratic patrons, Sir William Watkins Wynne, gave him a copy of volume 1. Wedgwood seems to have met Hamilton in the early 1770s, and they corresponded over a period of twenty years until Wedgwood died in 1795.[71] This contact between the aristocratic collector in Italy and the Midlands manufacturer gave Hamilton the opportunity of "superintending the Arts in England," a superintendence that also gave Wedgwood's reproduction Hamilton vases their original collector's stamp of approval.[72] While Hamilton had "flattered the old Pott painters very much," wrote Wedgwood, he, in turn, flattered and courted the patronage of members of the aristocratic English establishment, like Sir William Hamilton.[73] Thanks in part to his network of aristocratic contacts, Wedgwood was provided with the tools to manufacture both material objects *and* social opportunities.[74]

In *A Vindication of some passages in . . . the History of the Decline and Fall of the Roman Empire* (London, 1779), Edward Gibbon cites the manufacturer as a metaphor for himself, the historian, requesting that "if my readers are satisfied with the form, the colours, the new arrangement which I have given to the labours of my predecessors, they may perhaps consider me not as a contemptible Thief, but as an honest and industrious Manufacturer, who has fairly procured the raw materials, and worked them up with a laudable degree of skill and success."[75] Later in the *Vindication,* Gibbon insists "it is the right, it is the duty of a critical historian to collect, to weigh, to select the opinions of his predecessors."[76] As we saw in chapter 1, for Gibbon, this right and duty was realized by the contents of his library, a space he characterized as "my peculiar domain."[77] Gibbon's library contained the books that he considered to be "the tools of my historical manufacture," "the foundation of my works, and the best comfort of my life both at home and abroad."[78] So too, for the manufacturer Wedgwood, books like Hamilton's *Collection of Etruscan, Greek and Roman Antiquities* formed part of the firm's library collection and were utilized as tools in their material manufacture and mass production of the antique.

In a letter of 6 August 1770, Wedgwood wrote to his partner, Thomas Bentley, asking him to draw up a catalog of the books belonging to the firm.[79] This request arose as a result of a visit to the manufactory at Etruria by a Mr. Wilbraham of Nantwich in Cheshire. Wilbraham, whose forthcoming publication devoted to the mausolea and caves in Italy the firm had already subscribed to, asked Wedgwood whether they had copies of the *Antichità di Ercolano esposte* and other volumes, "all which I [Wedgwood] told him we had, at which he seem'd both pleas'd & rather surpris'd, but as I am often ask'd these questions & do not know the titles of all our books I sho.^{d} be glad to have a Catalogue when you have so much leisure." The catalog Bentley compiled, dated August 10, 1770, now forms part of the Wedgwood archive deposited at Keele University library (fig. 35).[80] This bibliography of thirty-one items, including prices for the majority of the books, reveals the number of folios devoted to ancient architecture, sculpture, and painting that were acquired as pattern books by the Wedgwood firm. Folios in their library included "L'Antiquité Expliquée par Montfaucon 15 Vol^{s} 1722," "Hambleton's [Hamilton's] Etruscan Antiquities 2 Vol^{s}," "Hambleton's Etruscan Antiquities 1 Vol S^{r} W[illiam]W[atkins]W[ynne]," "Gemma Antiquae Museum Florentinum 1st Vol," "Antiquities of Herculaneum. 6 Vol^{s} (Sheets)," "Caylus's Antiquities 7 Vol^{s}," "Stewarts Athens," and "British and Irish Peerage 3 Vol^{s}" (the latter "to find out *lines channels & connections*").[81] We see from this list that the library of the Wedgwood firm possessed as pattern books copies of the volumes acquired as ornaments for the country house libraries of Wedgwood's classically educated aristocratic patrons. In the *Monthly Review* for June 1770, Bentley described the Hamilton volumes and the works of Gorius, Montfaucon, Caylus, and Winckelmann as mines in which artists "must search for hidden treasure" and "expect to find just and beautiful ideas."[82]

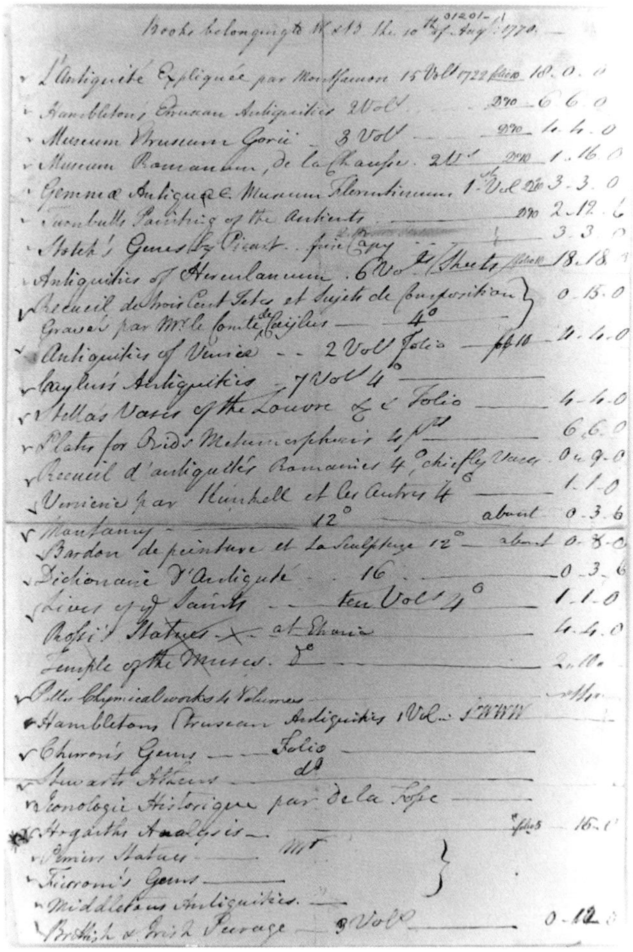

Figure 35 List entitled "Books belonging to Wedgwood Bentley, 10 August 1770." Keele, E1/31201. By courtesy of the Wedgwood Museum Trust, Barlaston, Staffordshire, (England).

The correspondence between the Wedgwood firm and two of their aristocratic customers sheds light on the creative use of the pattern book, in this case "Hambleton's Etruscan Antiquities," and the nature of an early nineteenth-century aristocratic commission. Having relied so far on the evidence afforded by the different *material* reproductions of the Hamilton plates at Newtimber Place, Heaton Hall, and in the condiment vases formerly at Kedleston Hall, these letters actually articulate the process by which the manufacturer mined the treasures from the Hamilton volumes and transferred them into and onto ornaments for the elite library. The third Marquis of Lansdowne ordered his Wedgwood vases in 1813 for his library at Bowood House in Wiltshire, designed by Robert Adam, with later additions by C. R. Cockerell (fig. 36).[83] The intended location of the vases is made explicit in Lansdowne's first letter to Josiah Wedgwood II, dated 14 May 1813:

> They are to be placed upon book cases at a considerable height near the ceiling which inclines me to prefer the taller ones. Perhaps however if you have enough, 16 to 22 inches will be sufficient—those (two of them) that are to stand at the corners I

Figure 36 The library at Bowood House, Wiltshire, designed by Robert Adam, with alterations by C. R. Cockerell. Country Life Picture Library.

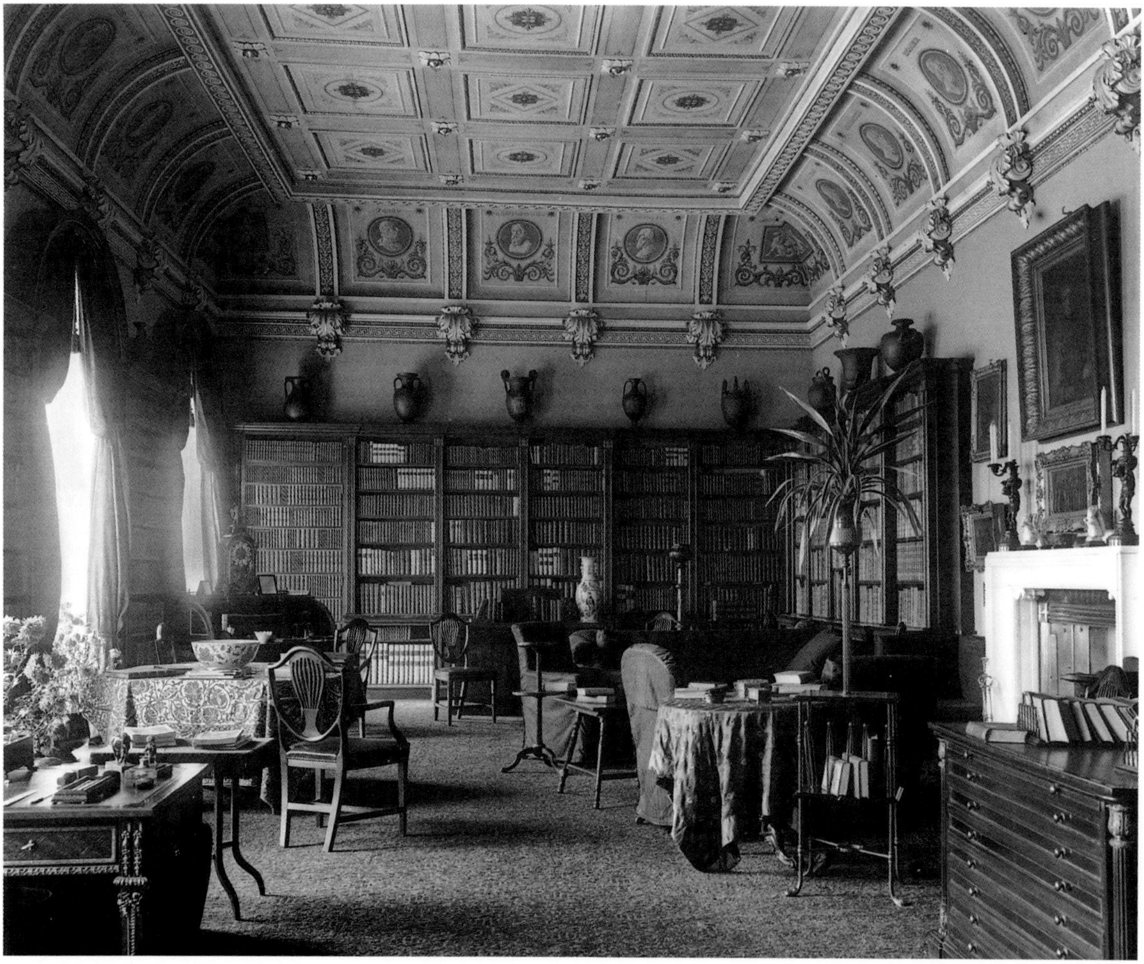

should wish to be rather broader than the rest . . . I should be glad to have as great a variety of shape as possible within the above limits.[84]

Here we see how the reproduction antique vases are to be tailor-made to the patron's requirements. Despite the inclusion of measured outline drawings in the Hamilton volumes (fig. 23 above), a feature said to make the work "absolutely new," the marquis prefers taller and broader examples.[85] The practicality of Lansdowne's specifications is significant: the reproduction ancient vases are required to fit into the existing scheme of his library. Three months later, in August 1813, the marquis replied to the firm from "a remote part" of his estate in Ireland, regarding the decoration of the vases:

> I think it will be sufficient to paint the vases on one side with figures, as they will stand upon bookcases, where only one side will be completely seen.
>
> With reference to the selection, I can give no opinion at present as I have no means of referring to Sir W. Hamilton's designs; but I should be sorry to have the execution delayed on that account, & shall have no hesitation in leaving it to your discretion, as I am confident you will make the best choice for me, & you are aware of the situation for which they are intended.[86]

Despite their three dimensionality, they are still effectively flattened ("paint the vases on one side with figures") into the library scheme of which they are a part. In leaving the selection of the Hamilton designs to Wedgwood II, Lansdowne relies on the discretion of the manufacturer. "Confident that you will make the best choice for me," Wedgwood II becomes, in aesthetic matters, the equal of his aristocratic patrons.

This practice of the patron selecting his own patterns from the Hamilton volumes is expanded in the correspondence between Wedgwood II and Lord Dartmouth, dated 1820. In this instance, the Hamilton volumes function as a catalog.

> [Dartmouth requests] to be supplied with forty five vases, from one foot to two feet in height, copied from the most approved Etruscan patterns,—to ornament the tops of book-cases. . . If Mr. Wedgwood can send any sketches or printed patterns of forms of vases to Lord Bagot's [at Blithfield in Staffordshire], L[ord] D[artmouth] will select those which he likes the best.[87]

Having made his selection, Dartmouth wrote to Wedgwood II on 31 January, that he had returned by coach

> your copy of S^{r} W Hamiltons work and I inclose here in a memorandum of the numbers of those vases represented in the plates,[88] the former of which I would wish to have imitated. Pray let me have one of each of these in the first instance—there is in the royal museum at Naples a very large collection of Etruscan, Greek and Roman vases, no two of which are exactly the same form, but I do not recollect to have seen any Drawings or engravings from them. It is to be hoped that some such representations of them may be sent to this Country.[89]

Hamilton had voiced the same concern in the preface to *Collection of Engravings from Ancient Vases:*

> I likewise flatter myself, that the Example of this Publication may promote others of the same Nature in this City [Naples] and that by Such means the Public may hereafter be in possession of a great number of Drawings after the most curious Vases in the Royal Collection at Naples, and in a rich private collection at Nola.[90]

By April 1820, Wedgwood II writes to Dartmouth that he has "prepared several pairs of Vases & am obliged to trouble your Lordship for some information before I proceed with them."

> The original order was for 45 vases from one foot to two feet in height . . . I should wish to know whether I should understand the dimensions given to refer to the vessel, or to the handles & tops . . .
>
> I must also inquire whether your Lordship would have each Vase painted like the original or whether I may select groups of figures & borders for them. Your Lordship will allow me to mention that probably the expense will be considerably diminished by painting them with no more figures than will be visible in the situation in which each will be placed, as was done with a number of large Vases I made for the Marquis of Lansdownes library—It is obvious that the painting on not more than half of each Vase can be seen when placed on the tops of the Bookcases.
>
> I have further to ask whether your Lordship would have twenty two pairs, each pair different from all the others, and one Single Vase, or sets of Vases, or of five vases, consisting of one, or two pairs, and a centre vase or what other arrangement.[91]

Here, Wedgwood II refers to the process of reproduction as practiced by the Wedgwood firm. His agenda echoes that outlined in the Hamilton volumes: faithful quotation ("painted like the original") or imaginative interpretation ("I may select . . ."). That this was the aesthetic policy of the Wedgwood firm, a policy endorsed by Sir

William Hamilton himself, is stated in a letter of July 1789 from Wedgwood I to Erasmus Darwin.

> And first I only pretend to have attempted to copy the fine antique forms, but not with absolute servility. I have endeavoured to preserve the stile and spirit or if you please the elegant simplicity of the antique forms, and in doing so introduce all the variety I was able, and this Sir W. Hamilton assures me I may venture to do, and that it is the true way of copying the antique.[92]

The manufacturer's language reveals his absorption of the rhetorical strategies of the Hamilton volumes, which as we have seen created and diffused the "stile and spirit," "the elegant simplicity" of the vase paintings. In the same way that the Hamilton volumes transformed the ancient vase paintings into two-dimensional canvas paintings, so when Wedgwood transferred the engravings back onto reproduction pots, they were decorated on one side only: a modification based not on authenticity but on economics. Significantly, Wedgwood II explained this modification to Lord Dartmouth, not in terms of imitation and/or improving the antique but by reference to a similar aristocratic commission executed for one of Dartmouth's peers, Lord Lansdowne. Dartmouth replied to Wedgwood II's letter as follows:

> I have to remark that the dimensions which I formerly gave for the vases related to the *vesals only,* and that I have no objection to the handles and tops of covers of *some* of them considerably exceeding the height of 18 inches.
>
> I do not wish to have each vase painted like the originals, but request that you will select groups of figures and borders for them, and I would have them painted on one side only. I do not wish to have them in regular sets or even in pairs, as I have observed that in large collections of antique vases of this description, it rarely happens that any two are exactly alike.[93]

Here again we see the deferral of antiquarianism to aestheticization, where antiquity can be cropped, shaped, and made to fit according to the specifications of the patron and the practices of the manufacturer. Dartmouth's letter also elucidates the tension between the ancient original and the neoclassical copy. He strays from the original in his choice of decoration ("I do not wish to have each vase painted like the originals") and in the painting of one side only. Yet in resisting sets or pairs for his reproduction vases, Dartmouth seeks to imitate contemporary collections of ancient vases in which "it rarely if ever happens that any two are exactly alike." This tension encapsulates the true way of copying the antique as defined by Wedgwood, with Hamilton's approval: preserving "the stile and spirit . . . of the antique forms" while introducing "all the variety I was able."

In the Marquis of Lansdowne's library at Bowood House (fig. 36 above), we witness the tripartite role of the Hamilton volumes, a role that encapsulates circularity. Here, they represent source, pattern book, and catalog. The decoration of the Wedgwood vases is taken from engravings published in volumes 1 and 2 of *Collection of Etruscan, Greek and Roman Antiquities,* copies of which Lansdowne owned. Therefore in the context of his library, described by the Reverend Warner as "the receptacle of duplicates," the volumes represent a form of guidebook to the collection, encapsulating the original engravings on which the decoration of the Wedgwood copies is based.[94] Despite the considerable height of the sixteen vases on top of the library bookcases, they are produced in eight pairs of matching shapes and decorated with corresponding designs. We can use the decoration of these vases to follow the process of transference from published engraving to tailor-made pot and also to

Figures 37a, 37b A pair of Wedgwood pelikai (1813) from Bowood House, with figures selected and copied from *Collection of Etruscan, Greek and Roman Antiquities,* vol. 1, plate 130 (fig. 26 above). Photographs: Derek Parker. By courtesy of the Trustees of the Bowood Collection.

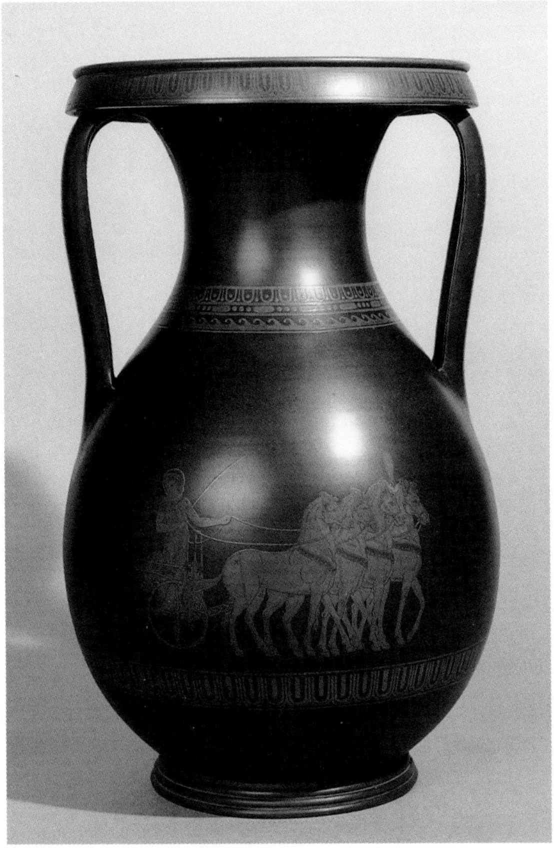

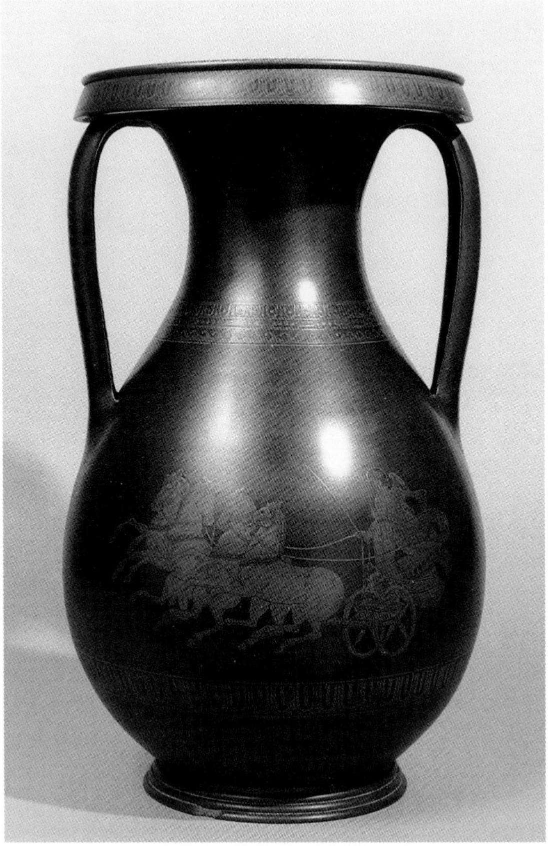

understand what Wedgwood I meant when he wrote of the "true way of copying the antique." For example, to decorate a pair of pelikai (figs. 37a, 37b), Wedgwood II selected the two chariot groups from the upper register of the Meidias hydria. By isolating these images (fig. 28 above) from their published source (vol. 1, plate 130), he plays with their authenticity just as the earlier transference from original pot to published plate had done. Surmounting bookcases in the library at Bowood, the vases provide an architectural function. Significance is derived from their place in the overall effect of the library. Just as each vase is a conflation of quotations from a pattern book, so the collection is itself a fragment of the aesthetic whole.

Horace Walpole's often-quoted letter of 1778 says much about the dissemination of Etruscan taste by contemporary manufacturers like the Wedgwood firm. He refers to the Etruscan room at Osterley Park House in Middlesex, designed by Robert Adam (fig. 38):

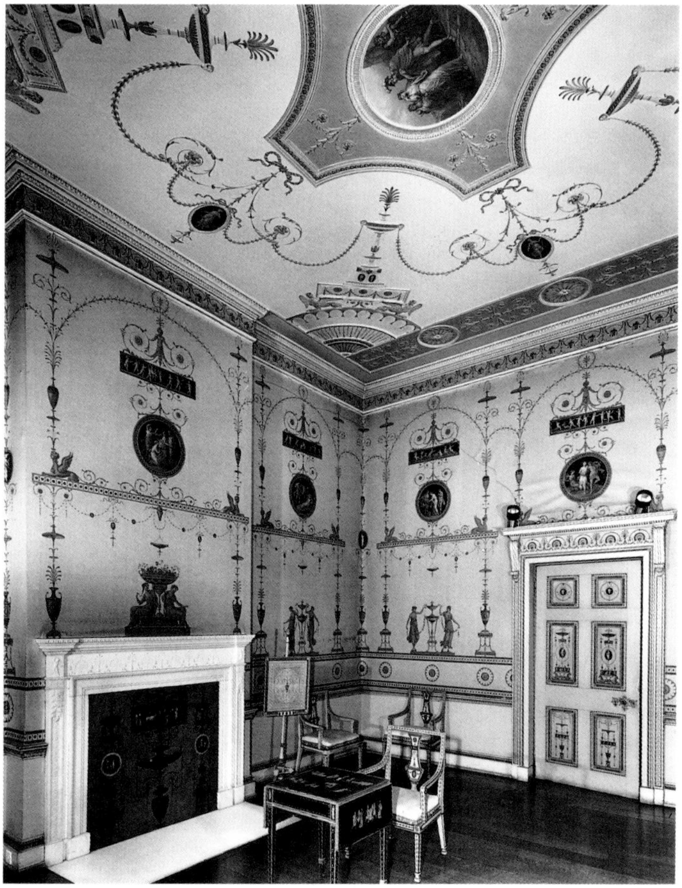

Figure 38 *(left)* Etruscan room at Osterley Park House, Middlesex, designed by Robert Adam, c. 1775–76. The National Trust. Photograph: A. F. Kersting

Figure 39 *(right)* "Ornamented in a very expensive manner": James Wyatt's "Wedgwoodian" temple interior at Fawley Court, 1771. Reproduced with the kind permission of Henley Royal Regatta Ltd.

> The last chamber . . . chills you; it is called the Etruscan, and is painted all over like Wedgwood's ware, with black and yellow small grotesques. Even the chairs are of painted wood. It would be a pretty waiting room in a garden. I never saw such a profound tumble into the Bathos. It is going out of a palace into a potter's field. Tapestry, carpets, glass, velvet, satin, are all attributes of winter. There could be no excuse for such a cold termination, but its containing a cold bath next to the bed-chamber:—and it is called taste to join these incongruities.[95]

In the text of their promotional *Works in Architecture of Robert and James Adam* (London, 1779), the brothers claim to have originated this type of decorative scheme "imitated from the vases and urns of the Etruscans."[96] However, the painted interior of an island temple on the Thames (fig. 39) exposes their boasts of innovation as invented fabrications. Executed by James Wyatt in 1771 for Sambrooke Freeman of Fawley Court, this is the earliest-known example of an Etruscan room and provides a precedent for the "waiting room in a garden" that Walpole imagines as more fitting for this type of "Wedgwoodian" scheme.[97] Listing the various improvements implemented at Fawley, Mrs. Lybbe Powys mentioned that "Mr. Freeman has erected an elegant building in his island, planned and executed by Wyatt, and the room is ornamented in a very expensive manner."[98] This "very expensive manner" of decoration involved the transference of the subject matter and coloring of the Hamilton plates, but in a mode popularized by Wedgwood's mass-produced range of Etruscan ware. The Wedgwood catalog of 1773 described their Etruscan ornaments as fit either for inlaying, as medallions in the panels of rooms, as tablets for chimney pieces, as ornaments in libraries, or as pictures for dressing rooms.[99] Wyatt adopted and adapted the Wedgwoodian

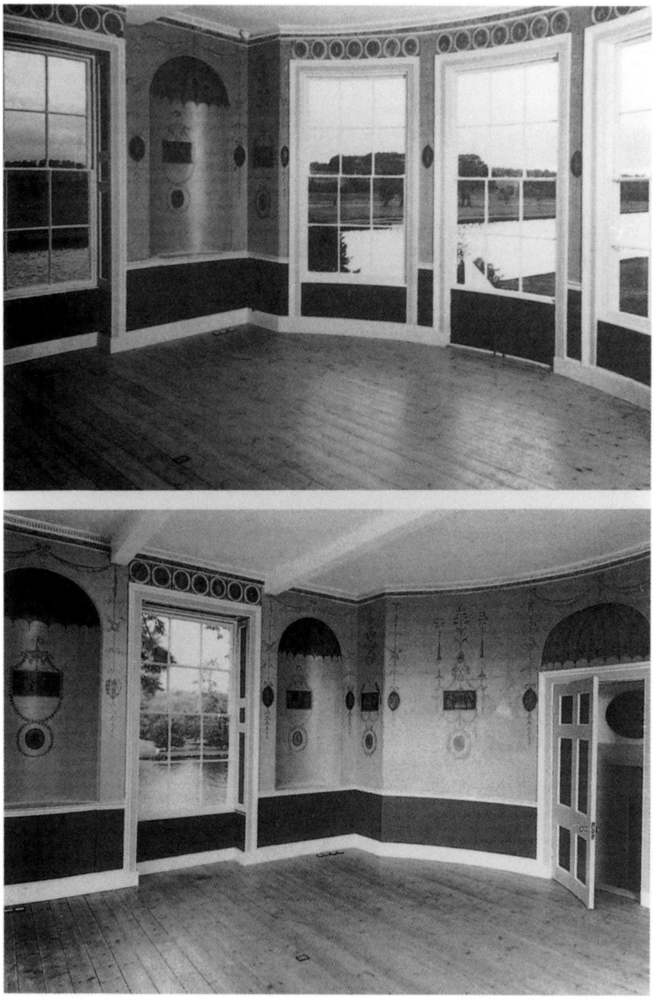

model by painting the Hamiltonian panels and their pendant medallions onto the pea green walls of the temple interior.

One item of furniture in the Etruscan room at Osterley Park House overlooked by Horace Walpole's list but recorded in the house inventory for 1782 is "A Pembroke table richly japanned by Clay" (fig. 40).[100] We learn from an account of a foreign visitor to Henry Clay's factory in King Street, Covent Garden, in 1775, that "they make their coffee-trays of paper and all kinds of other vessels, black with orange figures in the style of Etruscan vases, which are indescribably handsome."[101] The La Rochefoucauld brothers visited the Birmingham base of Clay's manufactory during their tour of England a decade later. There they met the proprietor and observed the manufacture and mass production of "every kind of thing that could possibly be made of paper-board," including buttons, trays, tea caddies, ladies' work-boxes, coffers, snuff boxes, breadbaskets and paintings: "all executed with the most exquisite taste."[102] Matthew Boulton's agent in Italy in 1767 had rightly predicted that the Hamilton prints would be very useful for all manner of Birmingham-based industry. The main panel of the Pembroke table at Osterley is decorated with figures after the engraving of the upper register of the Meidias hydria (fig. 28 above). Here there is no hint of competing with the

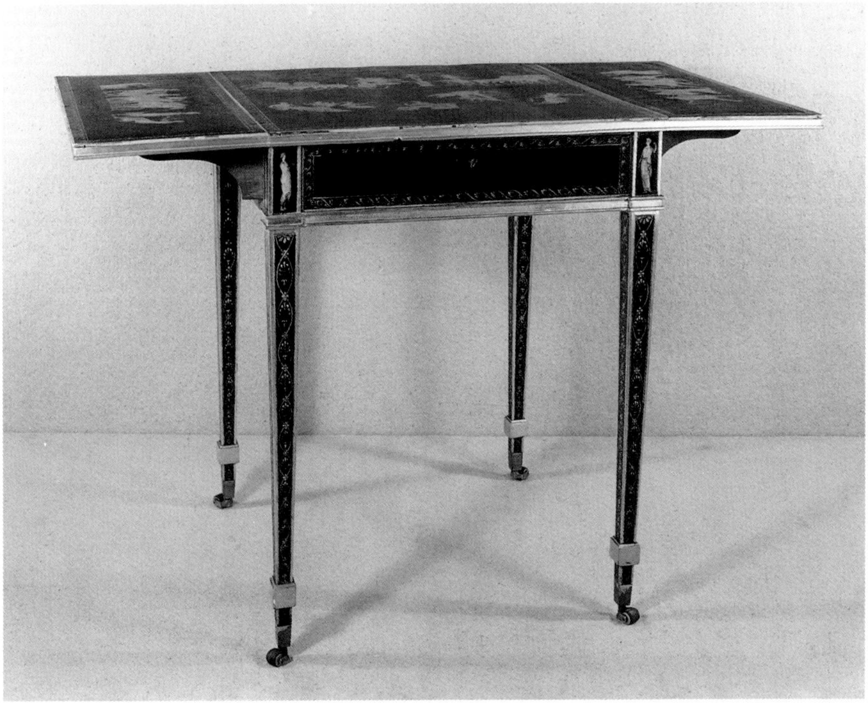

Figure 40 Etruscan Pembroke table by Henry Clay. V&A Picture Library.

source; unlike Pecheux as instructed by d'Hancarville or Louisa Courtauld and George Cowles in their silver condiment vases for Scarsdale, Clay has not embellished the scene. The two wings reproduce scenes engraved in volume 2, plates 106 and 129. However, the process of transference, from engraved print to paperboard table, is complex when the pattern book source is itself based on an earlier engraving of the ancient vase. The scenes reproduced by Clay for the table wings are taken from the obverse and reverse of a vase then in the Vatican collection. In this instance, Hamilton's engravers used not the vase itself as their source but the reworked engravings as previously published in Thomas Dempster's *De Etruria Regali* (Florence, 1723–26).[103] Predictably, Clay subscribed to the ideal standards of the Hamilton publications, writing, in a letter of 1 August 1775, to Hamilton that

> I must confess that I think myself, Messrs Wedgwood and Bentley and every Englishman (but particularly us) under still greater obligations to you for the usefull patterns which we have so abundantly in your Etruscan Publication, to which alone we are indebted for the gradual progress we have made in this kind of painting, so well and so deservedly received by the Publick. I am waiting very anxiously for the publication of the third and fourth volumes. I am much obliged to Your Excellency for the hint of snuff boxes of this taste: I have now put some in hand which will be exceedingly elegant and if it will not be obtruding too much I will beg the favour of you to point out to me a good shop in Naples where they will be well received.[104]

From this letter, we learn that suggestions from Hamilton influenced Clay's repertoire, a repertoire of imitation Etruscan objects mass produced in Britain and exported for sale in Naples. Similarly, when the British architect Thomas Hardwick dined with Hamilton in Naples in 1778, his journal records that he was shown "a little design for a snuff Box,—the Top and bottom stories copied from antique Painting and round it a frieze of figures copied from an Antique Hetruscan Vase, these were neatly drawn in Indian Ink, on Parchment."[105] These design initiatives represent Hamilton's ongoing desire of contributing to the improvement of the arts in his native country of Britain.

D'Hancarville draws our conclusion in his preface: "The Artist who would **invent** in the same stile, or only **copy** the Monuments which appeared to him worthy of being copied, may do so with as much truth and precision as if he had the Originals themselves in his possession."[106] Through the mechanics of publication, the Hamilton volumes disseminated idealized copies of an aristocratic collection of ancient vases. These volumes were acquired as collectables for the libraries of the classically educated elite and as pattern books for British architects, manufacturers, and craftsmen inventing and copying a whole range of Etruscan collectables for consumption at home and, in some cases, export abroad. The engraved plates were transferred into a variety of media like painted murals, tapestries, paperboard, pottery, and silver vases—some mass-produced, others specially commissioned as unique sets and schemes. In their various reproductions, the artists and craftsmen faithfully subscribe to the visual and textual strategies of the Hamilton volumes. Like Emma's attitudes then, the Hamilton volumes became a kind of elite performance in which truth and precision lay not in the relationship between the original and the copy but in the conviction of the performance and the skill of the operation.[107] In other words, truth and precision could be the truth and precision of invention as well as imitation. Both could share the status of the original and sustain the fabricated truth of the performance through its multiple reproductions.

At the beginning of the present century, any body would have imagined that the busts, statues, and pictures of Herculaneum had not a much better chance, than the persons they represent, of appearing again, within a few years, upon the surface of this globe.

John Moore, *A View of Society and Manners in Italy*[1]

4

"Under the sun there is nothing new"

(Re)constructing Pompeii and Herculaneum

During the course of the eighteenth century, excavations at the buried cities of Herculaneum and Pompeii unearthed a distinctly novel image of antiquity. By contrast with Rome, where according to one guidebook, you see the Romans only in public life and in public works, the ancient Romans at Pompeii and Herculaneum were literally entombed in their homes with their furniture and families.[2] The catastrophe of A.D. 79 had seemingly preserved the quotidian aspects of ancient life in their original locations and undisturbed by postclassical history. "There is nothing of the kind known in the world; I mean a Roman city entire of that age, and that has not been corrupted with modern repairs," enthused Horace Walpole of Herculaneum, which he visited in 1740.[3] The tantalizing possibilities of experiencing the ancient world untouched by time and barbarian invaders led to the saying "Roma non è che un vasto museo—Pompeii è un' antichità vivente" (Rome is but a vast museum—Pompeii is a living antiquity).[4] Lewis Engelbach articulates the idea of Pompeii as a site par excellence, one that surpassed the learned institutions, which were then the core of education and taste: "[Pompeii is] the gold mine of antiquity, the greatest classic jewel on earth. All the Museums in Europe, all the ponderous folios of a Montfaucon, a Lipsius, and the host of antiquarian authors, dwindle into insignificance when compared with the sight of an elegant Graeco-Roman town resuscitated from an oblivion."[5] Paradoxically, the gold mine of antiquity, which for Engelbach surpassed museums and learned folios alike, once resuscitated from oblivion, had its raw materials mined and refined for posterity.

The idea of the resuscitated sites as a living antiquity relied heavily on the excavation, restoration, exhibition, and publication of their material contents. The Bourbon monarchs controlled each aspect of this program, which the first half of this chapter will survey. The initial progress of the sites' excavations was determined to a large extent by the different types of volcanic matter that had buried them in antiquity. Herculaneum was entirely overwhelmed by solid layers of fused lava, which the workmen had to dig through to a depth of up to fifty feet. Access was easier at Pompeii, where the city was engulfed by a shower of ashes and pumice stone. On one level an act of restoration, the practice of excavation represented a process of decontextualization and fragmentation. Pompeii as a living antiquity became an artificially constructed model, with an emphasis not on the totality of the excavated material artifacts but rather on artistic masterpieces. Single wall schemes in the interiors of the exhumed houses were sawn apart to produce multiple paintings on plaster, while inferior examples were discarded and duplicates, destroyed.[6] The (to us) brutal act of sawing out the paintings was legitimized as being an ancient precedent: "This method was no modern invention; for, strange to tell, among the excavated remains of Stabiae, the workmen discovered an apartment with some paintings which had been separated, by the ancients themselves, from some wall (in Greece perhaps) with the obvious intention of being inserted in another place."[7] Once removed from their architectural and domestic contexts by being sawn out of the walls, the pictures were secured using mortar or cement into wooden frames, which were backed with slate and glazed.[8] The act of framing further presented the paintings, not as *part* of an interior scheme, but as individual masterpieces; examples from unrelated areas of the sites were paired or matched on purely aesthetic grounds.[9] Even attempts to conserve the pictures met with further damage, as Lady Miller explains:

> The glow of the colouring, which had been preserved for more than 1600 years, suffered much upon being exposed to the air, and a kind of whitish powder formed itself upon them: as a remedy for this accident, a Sicilian, named Moriconi, undertook to varnish them; this succeeded in some respects, but a new misfortune followed; for the varnish fretting the colours, which had been laid on with some kind of gum, great pieces shell'd off, so that many of the pictures have been much damaged, others quite spoiled.[10]

Damaged, yet protected, by burial for more than sixteen hundred years, on their recovery a more destructive process was unintentionally set in motion.

The burial of the sites in antiquity was, in many ways, mirrored in the eighteenth century by the royal agenda of censorship. To ensure that the artifacts excavated from Pompeii and Herculaneum would be the envy of cosmopolitan Europe, the king of the Two Sicilies, Charles III, strictly supervised access to them. When Lady Miller visited the site of Pompeii, the officers, soldiers, and spies whose job it was to watch visitors made it impossible for her to take a sketch of a house: "It is their business to see that no observations they can prevent should be made. They followed us closely, so that we could rarely evade their vigilance and impertinent curiosity," she recorded in her *Letters from Italy* (London, 1776).[11] In the museum of the royal palace at Portici, where according to one visitor in 1756, everything valuable was immediately sent, the contents of the cabinets were similarly patented and policed.[12] "Not a pencil must appear, so memory alone is all one has to trust to and each fine thing defaces the other in these transient views," remembered Charles Burney.[13] Having been recovered from oblivion by excavation, the artifacts were then (partly) reinterred in the royal museum. Lady Miller explained that the reason for the patent was on account of "a work published by order of government, which is already increased to seven or eight large folio volumes, embellished with engravings representing the various articles in this collection; but it is not yet near completed, on which account no person who visits this cabinet is permitted to take any sketch, note, or memorandum upon the spot."[14] The work Lady Miller refers to is the *Antichità di Ercolano esposte* (fig. 18 above). As we saw in chapter 2, these luxury folios were not initially for public sale but were instead selectively distributed by the Neapolitan monarch.[15] However, after unsuccessful attempts to prohibit the publication of rival volumes and translations, the work became more widely available by 1773.[16]

One such rival volume that defied the royal patent, was that published by the French engraver Charles-Nicolas Cochin and architect Jérôme-Charles Bellicard, *Observations upon the Antiquities of the town of Herculaneum* (London, 1753). In this work, they unofficially published examples of wall paintings from Herculaneum, explaining that although the plates

> are engraved after designs made from the memory, they pretty exactly represent the composition of the subject, and even the principal defects for which the originals are blamed . . . I am persuaded, that notwithstanding the defects in point of exactness, they will engage the imagination much more strongly than could possibly be done by simple description.[17]

Their plate 6 (fig. 41), an engraving of a large so-called historical painting of Theseus and the minotaur may well engage the viewer's imagination, but it does not escape the criticism of the authors.[18] They describe the composition as "very cold"; its principal figures, particularly Theseus, "seem to be copied from statues . . . the manner in these pictures is generally grand and the pencil easy. Otherwise this performance is unfinished, and cannot be considered in any other light than that of a forward sketch."[19] Elsewhere in their *Observations* they reiterate this idea of the paintings from Herculaneum as preliminary drawings, finding "almost all the pieces are unfinished, and painted pretty much like our decorations of the

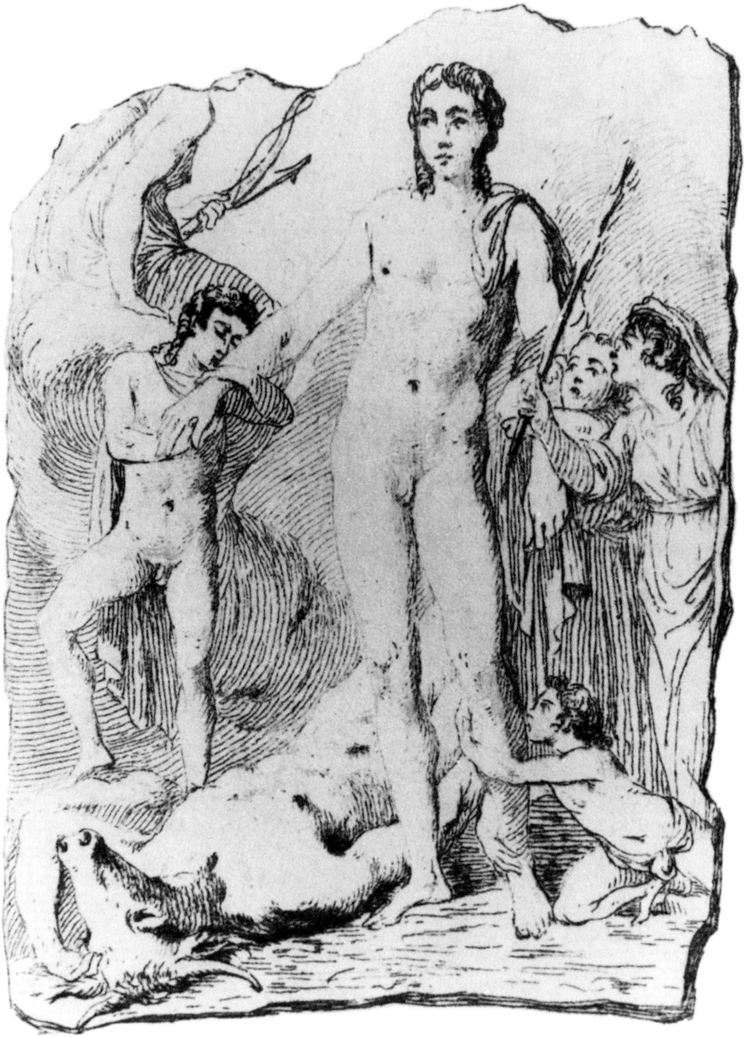

Figure 41 *(left)* C. N. Cochin and J. C. Bellicard, *Observations upon the Town of Herculaneum* (London, 1753), plate 6. Institute of Classical Studies Library.

Figure 42 *(right)* *Antichità di Ercolano esposte* (Naples, 1757), vol. 1, plate 5. Institute of Classical Studies Library.

theatre."[20] The miniature size of Cochin and Bellicard's plates, which one of their readers describes as that of a duodecimo, seems to confirm the lowly status of the paintings.[21] Compare, however, Cochin and Bellicard's sketchy and small-scale plate drawn from memory with the whole plate folio engraving published as plate 5 of volume 1 of the *Antichità di Ercolano esposte* (fig. 42). By juxtaposing the two engravings, we soon discover the similarity of Cochin and Bellicard's plate to the explanations of their text: the pencil is easy, the composition appears unfinished and like a forward sketch. In other words, their criticism is of themselves.

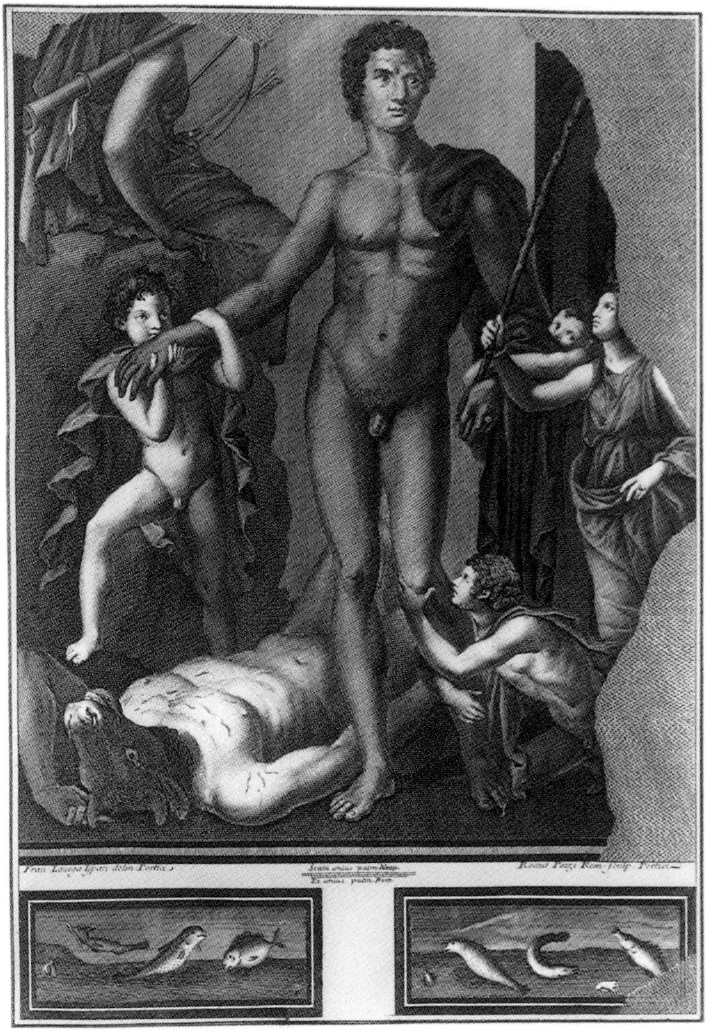

While Cochin and Bellicard's engraved plates are faithful to the underworked ancient paintings as they drew them from memory, those of the *Antichità* appear to have been overworked by the engravers. In these plates the antique is living in the sense that it is reconstructed and engraved as if in pristine condition. Repeatedly in travellers' accounts of Pompeii and Herculaneum, we encounter a rhetorical trope where the ancient paintings are described as being as fresh as when they were first painted, their colors as vibrant as if they were modern. However, the all-too-visible freshness of the paintings engraved in the *Antichità di Ercolano esposte* caused a Mr. Freeman at Naples to write to Lady Mary Capel as early as 1750:

> The king is now employing a person to take drawings of all the statues, and principal paintings, with an intent to publish them . . . The statues cannot be made to appear more beautiful than they really are: but the writer imagines the world will be vastly deceived with regard to the paintings. For the man is a very nice drawer; and has also managed the colouring to advantage, so that he has made exceedingly pretty things, from originals, which are miserable daubings. The company having seen the drawings first, were extremely disappointed, when they afterwards came to view the originals.[22]

In keeping with the idea that the collection enhances the collector, the ancient "miserable daubings" were engraved as "exceedingly pretty things." This policy of improving and idealizing the ancient artifacts was not only visual but also rhetorical. Camillo Paderni, curator of the royal collection of antiquities at Portici, explicitly compared the painting of Theseus and the minotaur with highlights from the art historical canon in a letter to Allan Ramsay of 20 February 1740. Paderni's letter was later read at the Royal Society and published in its *Philosophical Transactions*:

> Particularly one Piece, Eight Palms broad by Nine high, the Figures as big as Life, representing *Theseus* after having killed the *Minotaur*, which is wonderfully fine. You see the Figure of *Theseus* naked and standing, which, in my opinion cannot be more properly resembled to any other thing, than the *Antinous* of the *Belvidera*, both to the Attitude and Air of the Head. It is drawn and coloured with prodigious Elegance. The *Greek* Boys, who are represented as returning him Thanks for their Deliverance, seem, for their noble simplicity, the Work of Dominichino; and the Composition of the whole is worthy of *Raphael*.[23]

Paderni's hyperbole could not however be sustained against a more critical canon. The act of framing the wall schemes as individual pictures slotted them into contemporary critical debate, whereby the painted works of ancient Roman masters were comparable to those of the Renaissance. If it was an aim of Renaissance artists to equal, if not surpass, the ancients, to many eighteenth-century viewers it must have seemed as though they had succeeded. In a letter written on 18 April 1751, later read at the Royal Society, our Mr. Freeman takes a hostile view:

> Much the greatest part of them are but a very few degrees better than what you will see upon an ale-house-wall. They are all painted on plaister; which has been very carefully separated from the wall, in as large pieces as might be done. These pieces are now framed and there are above 1500 of them, but not above 20 that are tolerable. The best of them are 3 large pieces; one of which is a sort of history-piece, containing 4 figures, that have some expression in their faces; but even these best if they were modern performances, would hardly be thought worthy of a place in a garret . . . The designs of the greatest part of these paintings are so strange and uncouth, that it is difficult, and almost impossible, to guess what was aimed at. A vast deal of it looks like such Chinese borders and ornaments, as we see painted upon skreens . . . All the paintings are either upon black or red grounds: and such, that the writer cannot help suspecting that it is their antiquity alone, that has recommended them to their admirers, and atoned, in their eyes, for all their blemishes and defects; and possesses great amazement at the accounts, which have been sent to England concerning them.[24]

The sheer number of the ancient paintings and the diversity of the representations, on the one hand, sealed their fate: they could not all be ancient masterpieces when judged according to a modern critique. Although not all comparable with the works of Renaissance masters like Raphael, eighteenth-century viewers contrived to situate the paintings within an art historical framework more applicable to the study of Renaissance paintings. By these means, they attempted to understand the mass of previously unknown ancient paintings in terms of the existing canon.[25] This art historical model is based on the practice of artistic education, with "painters learn[ing] the elements of the art in a good school, and under masters who worked with ease."[26] It expounds a theory of provincial art in which the ordinary Pompeian painters are copying celebrated masterpieces.[27] The notion of Renaissance masters as an aesthetic tool for viewing ancient paintings may be said to be ultimately subversive. By idealizing images both unseen and seen, the unthinkable was realized whereby the Renaissance model proved, in many eyes, to be superior to its antique source. According to Cochin and Bellicard, for instance, "the antique paintings give room to doubt, whether the ancients were equal to several Italian,

Flemish and French masters, in the fire of genius, and force of imagination, either in composition, or the effect of light."[28] Ironically, viewers were forced into placing the paintings into a Vasarian notion of progress.

Paderni's advantageous comparison of the attitude and air of the painted Theseus with that of Antinous in the Belvedere Courtyard of the Vatican museum also situates ancient sculptural masterpieces in the conflicting critiques over the finds. The British traveller Charles Burney spoke for many of his contemporaries when he dubbed the busts and statues in bronze and marble uncovered at Pompeii and Herculaneum as "equally perfect with any of the finest statues in the world, such as those at Florence and the Belvedere."[29] But the sculptural excellence of works like the seated Mercury—"nothing just out of the mold could be more beautiful or perfect"—only served to heighten the deficiency of their painted counterparts.[30] As Mr. Freeman observed, unlike the paintings, the statues could not be perfected by publication. Travellers familiar from the classical literary tradition with the masterpieces of ancient Greek sculptors like Phidias and Praxiteles looked in vain at Portici for evidence of the handiwork of first-class painters like Apelles or Zeuxis. The excavated finds seemed to suggest an estrangement between the sister arts of painting and sculpture. Unable to contemplate that ancient authors would have bestowed equal praise on these art forms had one been inferior to the other, Henry Swinburne adopted the very argument that the entombed sites had apparently (not) refuted, namely, that the "capital productions of the ancient painters, being of more perishable materials than busts and statues, have been destroyed in the fatal disasters that have so often afflicted both Greece and Italy."[31]

A Renaissance art historical model dealing with masters and masterpieces in the sister arts of painting and sculpture was not always applicable to the exhaustive collection of ancient paintings, in particular the images classified as paintings of architecture. When describing this body of works, viewers resort not to comparison with the ideal productions of art history but with the aesthetic excesses of the foreign cultures of India, Arabia, and in particular, China. These stereotypically exotic, Eastern arts were more often defined by European tastes *in opposition* to the ideal classical canon.[32] Here, they became the substandard standard by which the ancient architectural paintings from Herculaneum and Pompeii were judged. Horace Walpole, for instance, recalled "a light and fantastic architecture, of a very Indian air, [which] made a common decoration of private apartments" at Herculaneum.[33] Lady Miller in turn observed that

> a strange mixture of the Gothic and Chinese taste [in the architectural paintings]; and some views in particular of country-houses or villas, situated on the margins

> of the sea (probably at Baja) where there appears Chinese ornaments, such as pales, bridges, temples &c. represented as belonging to gardens. That these people should have any knowledge of the Chinese and their gardens, ornaments, &c. is surprising. I observed one representation of a Chinese temple built on piles over a piece of water, and open on all sides.[34]

In his *Designs of Chinese Buildings* (London, 1757), a volume based on firsthand experience of Canton, the architect William Chambers observed a "remarkable affinity" between the architecture of the Chinese and the ancients; an affinity he describes as all "the more surprising as there is not the least probability that the one was borrowed from the other."[35] Chambers identified similarities in their architectural repertoires, including the use of pyramidal figures and the employment of columns for support and decorative fretwork. His attitude to the Chinese compositions is similarly frivolous: "I look upon them as toys in architecture: and as toys are sometimes, on account of their oddity, prettyness, or neatness of workmanship, admitted into the cabinets of the curious, so may Chinese buildings be sometimes allowed a place upon compositions of a nobler kind."[36] Chambers's placement of Chinese buildings within the gardens at Kew (1763) amounts to an attempt to realise the fantastic possibilities of the two-dimensional representations at Pompeii.[37] They are spectacular toys for the eighteenth-century aristocracy.

The text of the *Antichità di Ercolano esposte* accompanying plate 39 in volume 1 (fig. 43) outlines the official view of ancient architectural paintings:

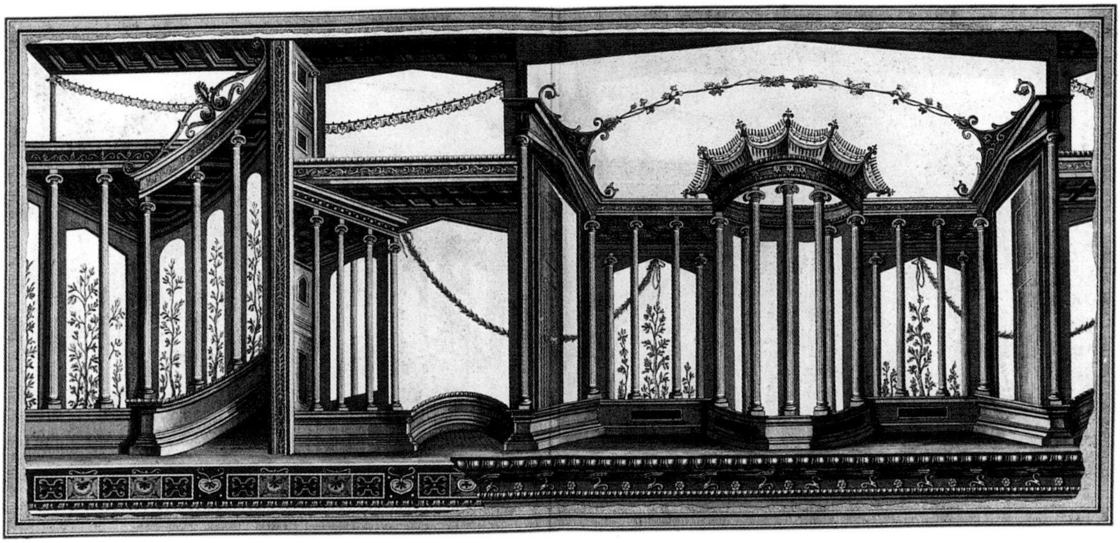

Figure 43 *Antichità di Ercolano esposte* (Naples, 1757), vol. 1, plate 39. The Warburg Institute.

It does not, however, follow, that because they are whimsical and irregular, they are therefore of no value . . . [The picture is] beautifully put together, by the hand of a painter indeed rather than of an architect. The festoons, which, with a variety of fancy, set off and unite the parts of this imaginary building, are elegant. The order bears a resemblance to the Ionic; but the errors and defects in the architecture disfigure it very much. This very deformity, however, adds a value to the piece, by giving us a view of that manner of painting which was the fashion in the time of *Vitruvius*, and against which he so much inveighs.[38]

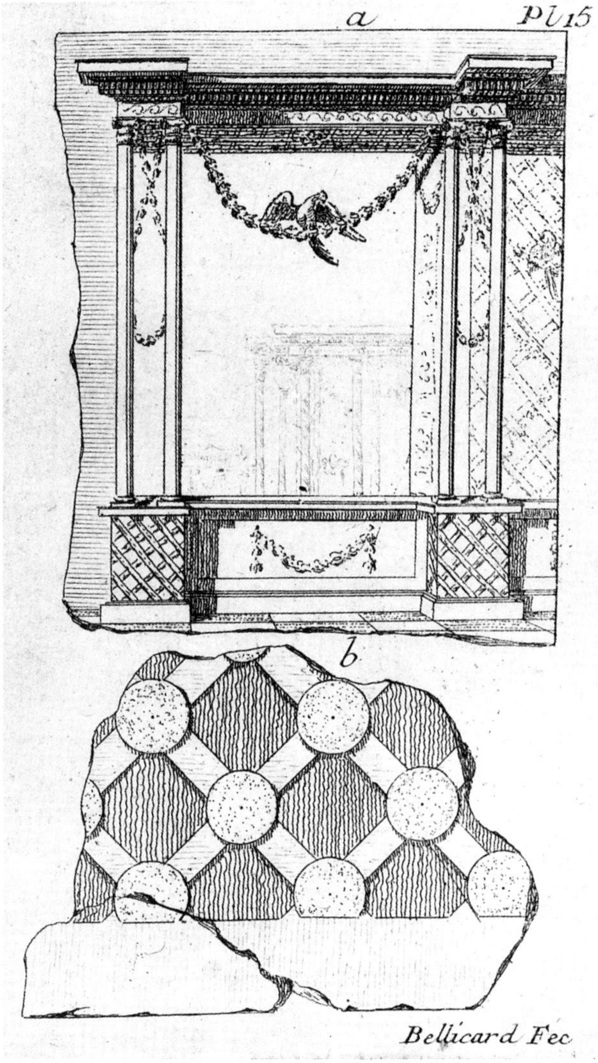

Figure 44 *(left)* C. N. Cochin and J. C. Bellicard, *Observations upon the Town of Herculaneum* (London, 1753), plate 15. Institute of Classical Studies Library.

Figure 45 *(right)* *Antichità di Ercolano esposte* (Naples, 1771), vol. 6, plate 96. The Warburg Institute.

The plates of *Antichità* not only restored the paintings to their former (or should that be contemporary?) glory, but the rhetoric of the text served simultaneously to fabricate their ideal reputation as representations of ideals. Cochin and Bellicard's *Observations upon the Antiquities of the town of Herculaneum* offers a far more critical view, where the architectural paintings are "altogether out of the proportion of the Grecian architecture. Generally speaking, the pillars are double or triple the length of the natural dimensions: the profil of the mouldings of the cornishes, chapiters and bases, is of a wretched Gothic taste; and most of the Arabic mixture in the architecture is as ridiculous as any Chinese design."[39] While Bellicard and Cochin cite the absence of Grecian architecture with its ideal proportions, the *Antichità* text observes a resemblance in plate 39 (fig. 43) to the Ionic order. To the former, the compositions are out of proportion, while the latter finds the picture "beautifully put together." The garlanded intercolumniations of Bellicard's plate 15 (fig. 44) are part of the Arabic composition, yet similar festoons are described as elegant in the *Antichità* text.[40] Perhaps most significantly, in criticizing this type of decoration, Cochin and Bellicard reiterate the opinion of the Roman architect Vitruvius in book 7, chapter 5 of his ten-volume work *De Architectura*. But even this ultimate damnation is no obstacle to the editors of the *Antichità* text. Rather, they use the authority of Vitruvius's text to add value to the very deformity of the excavated material evidence.

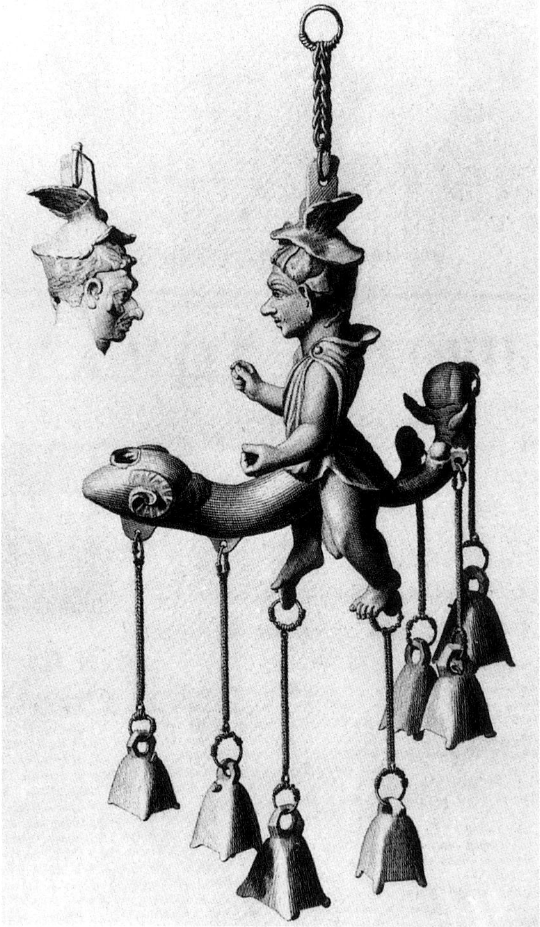

References to the exotic arts of China, India, and Arabia enabled European visitors to accommodate the ancient architectural paintings from Herculaneum and Pompeii within an aesthetic that was familiar to them but that at the same time was stereotypically foreign. Less easy to reconcile with enlightened, Christian notions of delicacy and propriety were some of the newly excavated erotic artifacts. The ithyphallic bronzes engraved in the final ten plates of volume 6 (1771) of the *Antichità di Ercolano esposte* (including fig. 45), for example, were described in the *Monthly Review* in 1775 as

> abominably indecent, the descriptions, with the *learned* and *copious* notes which accompany and

> explain them, cannot but astonish a Reader unaccustomed to the study of *such* antiquities. He may figure to himself a group of Herculanean Academicians composed chiefly of priests and lawyers; and, with an indignant smile, fancy he sees those gentlemen, so respectable for their profound erudition! laying their solemn heads together, poring over this obscene trash, citing Greek and Latin without mercy, calling ancient philosophers, poets, and historians, and what is stranger, saints and venerable fathers of the church, to their assistance, and puzzling through many a page for an illustration of what would be better consigned to oblivion, or left to such dilettanti, virtuosi, students and professors, as pursue their studies in the purlieus of Covent Garden.[41]

What this reviewer objected to so vehemently was the prostitution of the texts of the ancient and early Christian authors in the cataloging of risqué ancient artifacts: artifacts more suited to the "purlieus of Covent Garden" than to the territory of the republic of letters.[42] Rather than compromising the idealized literary canon—for the Reverend Eustace reader of works from the classical tradition conversed with "a species of gods and demi-gods"—travellers to Pompeii looked to the exotic and erotic other for a frame of reference: "The proofs are of the most extraordinary kind, and quite on a level with those which Captain Cook found in some of the South Sea Islands."[43] In his *Excursions in Italy* (London, 1838), James Fenimore Cooper aligns the mores of the ancient Pompeians with those of Cook's South Sea islanders. In this, the excavation of ancient Pompeii is mapped onto the recent discovery of foreign and distant lands.[44]

Closer to home, the most famous human casualty of the Vesuvian eruptions was the author of the *Naturalis Historiae*, Pliny the Elder. His nephew, Pliny the Younger, gave an account of his death in A.D. 79 in his letters to Tacitus (IV. 16, 20). Despite saying nothing about the site itself being overwhelmed, Pliny's letters were often quoted and, in some cases, reproduced, in eighteenth-century travel literature. James Russel reckoned they prepared the traveller for the most advantageous view of the ruins.[45] Long before the rediscovery of Pompeii and Herculaneum the works of the two Plinys were firmly ensconced in the classical literary canon; parts of Pliny the Elder's text will be treated in chapters 5 and 6. But with the unearthing of a library in a villa at Herculaneum, it seemed as though ancient texts previously lost to posterity or surviving only in fragments in later works had literally been resuscitated from oblivion. At first, the excavators discarded the carbonized scrolls as volcanic debris. Once they had been properly identified, the Neapolitan court faced the impossible task of unrolling their extremely fragile leaves and reading their contents. One Father Antonio Piaggio devised an ingenious but laborious machine for this purpose in 1756. The first scroll to be unrolled was found to be a tract in Greek on Epicurean philosophy, a bronze bust of the philosopher Epicurus having also been discovered in the library.[46] "Every lover of learning laments the slow way in which they proceed in opening these volumes," lamented Charles Burney.[47] Every lover of learning was to be further disappointed on discovering that the volumes were not the lost works of the classical literary tradition after all but were already known.

Although the particular appeal of Herculaneum and Pompeii was that they were untouched by time, as soon as the sites were rediscovered attempts were made to reappropriate and integrate them into contemporary Neapolitan history. The Bourbon monarch's manipulative control of these local collections would imply a genealogy of the Crown of Naples with an ancient heritage on the very site. It was vital therefore that all finds should be securely kept within the kingdom of Naples, since as Henry Matthews aptly remarked, "Travellers are the greatest thieves in the world."[48] The collection, classification, reproduction, and publication of ancient finds to authenticate the power structure had been long practiced by the papacy in Rome, but during the second half of the eighteenth century popes were fighting to control the foreign plunder of antiquities.[49] Partly to compensate for the total ban on the export of artifacts from Pompeii and Herculaneum, faux excavations were staged for the benefit of visiting dignitaries; a practice described by William Gell:

> It has been the custom to honour the arrival of illustrious personages by excavating in their presence some small portion of Pompeii: an enviable method of showing respect exclusively possessed by the court of Naples. For these occasions, an order is given that the earth should be left undisturbed to the depth of a foot or more, in several of the rooms of a newly-discovered house, and, on the day, appointed, these are cleared out for the amusements of the guests. It is seldom a fruitless search, as the overseers are previously aware that some curiosities exist, though they know not precisely what they may be.[50]

While distinguished foreign visitors could not take a souvenir from Pompeii back home, they were party to the resurrection of prepared areas of the site. Like travellers out of time, they were admitted into the homes vacated by those they characterized as the Pompeian elite.

The manner in which eighteenth-century travellers reconstruct the ancient sites inevitably tells us more about them than about the ancients. Indeed, a majority of visitors recreate Pompeian life according to a model of their own privileged social classes.[51] In a letter read at the Society of Antiquaries of London in 1771, Richard Fellowes describes the unearthed houses with their "mosaick Pavements and paintings in Fresco on the Walls" as "the residence of People of Fashion &

fortune": more eighteenth-century urban London than ancient Pompeii.[52] For Thomas Watkins, the scrolls excavated from Herculaneum must be the lost books of the Roman historian Livy, since "what private library in Britain is without the best histories of England?"[53] The recovery of an exhaustive inventory of ancient artifacts, in addition to the mosaics, paintings, scrolls, and sculptures also provided the focus for a series of debates. For Peter Beckford, the domestic paraphernalia from ancient dressing tables and kitchens was proof not only of the luxury of the ancients, but also their modernity; for him, the site gave the sense that there was nothing new under the sun: "Ladies will see mirrors of polished metal, combs, rouge and pins; earrings, necklaces, rings and bracelets: in short, every requisite to adorn their persons:—and a French cook might dress an excellent dinner with the very utensils he will find at Portici."[54] This sentiment was likewise expressed by Kenelm Digby:

> In the Museum of Portici (a City unknowingly erected on that of Herculaneum) and which certainly ought not to be entrusted with such curious & valuable relicks are besides statues & paintings, the minutest culinary utensils, with bread, eggs, fruit & grains existing in the same state not far short of two thousand years, when it appears the same vices, the same frauds were practiced as in these more social days, notwithstanding the eternal declamation we hear against the corruption of present times.[55]

Pompeii was characterized by its eighteenth-century visitors as "a town in miniature" whose main street was "so accurately preserved, that it resembles more a model of what *may have been*, than a monument of what really existed."[56] For Goethe, it was a model whose surviving structures "look[ed] more like architectural models or dolls' houses than real buildings."[57]

This survey of the reception of the sites and their excavated contents reminds us that Pompeii and Herculaneum were as much ancient monuments untouched by time as models (re)constructed by the eighteenth-century imagination. They were in fact part of a modern fiction long before Edward Bulwer-Lytton published his famous novel *The Last Days of Pompeii* (London, 1834), in which he described the town as

> the miniature civilization of that age. Within the narrow compass of its walls was contained, as it were, a specimen of every gift which luxury offered to power. In its minute but glittering shops, its tiny palaces, its baths, its forum, its theatre, its circus—in the energy yet corruption—in the refinement yet the vice—of its people, you beheld a model of the whole empire. It was a toy, a plaything, a showbox, in

> which the Gods seemed pleased to keep the representation of the Great Monarchy of Earth, and which they afterwards hid from Time, to give to the wonder of Posterity;—the moral of the maxim, that under the sun there is nothing new.[58]

Lytton's "account of its 'Last Days' has cast over it a more familiar garb, and peopled its desert streets with associations that greatly add to their interest," thought Mary Wollstonecraft Shelley, who visited Pompeii in June 1843.[59] To George Sala in 1869, "Bulwer has made Pompeii his own. The *Last Days* are the best possible guidebook to the disinterred city."[60]

In *A View of society and manners in Italy* (London, 1790), John Moore advocates a novel proposal for reconstruction in which one of the houses at Pompeii be re-roofed and its disinterred furniture, ornaments and utensils, re-installed in their original locations.[61] This "object of universal curiosity" would, he suggests, counteract for the dual exposure of the domestic residences of the ancients—to the negligence of the Neapolitan court and the injuries of the weather. In particular, it would, he insists, act as a means of protecting the "precious walls" of the ancient houses "which, were it possible to transport them to the various countries of the world, would be bought with avidity, and placed in the gardens of Princes!" With the royal embargo so rigorously enforced, transportation of the painted walls outside the kingdom of Naples was never an option, unlike the material reproduction of the wall schemes, which translated and transported an idea of Pompeii into the domestic interiors of late eighteenth-century British aristocrats. The gallery at

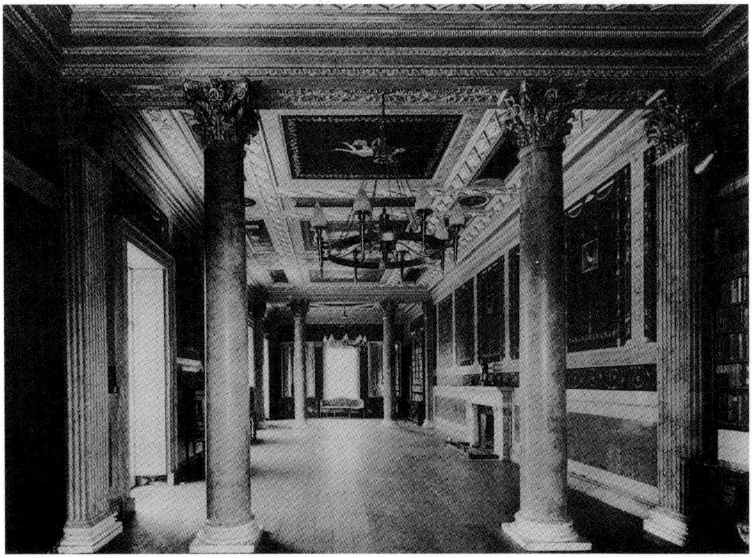

Figure 46 View of the "Pompeian" room at Packington Hall, Warwickshire, 1785–88. Reproduced by permission of English Heritage. NMR.

Packington Hall in Warwickshire (fig. 46) is said to be the earliest "Pompeian" room in Europe. It was designed in the late 1780s by its owner, the Earl of Aylesford and his architectural tutor, Joseph Bonomi.[62] The space of the gallery occupies the full length of the south wing of the house and is divided into three areas with screens of Corinthian columns at either end. Its painted decoration was executed by a team of artists including John Francis Rigaud, whose memoirs, written by his son, Stephen Rigaud, records the figural scheme for the ceiling:

> This is painted on the spot, in water and size colours, and in the style of Titus' baths, upon a black ground. They are flying figures, alluding to the Mysteries of Bacchus; according to the Mythology explained by D'Ankerville. At the two ends are figures flying on horseback. In the centre two figures, a man and woman holding a dish, and the mysterious veil; the other two are single flying females; one with a leopard skin and a crown of ivy, the other with a wreath of flowers.[63]

Stephen identified the ceiling decoration (fig. 47) as a representation of the mysteries of Bacchus according to the mythological thesis expounded by Baron

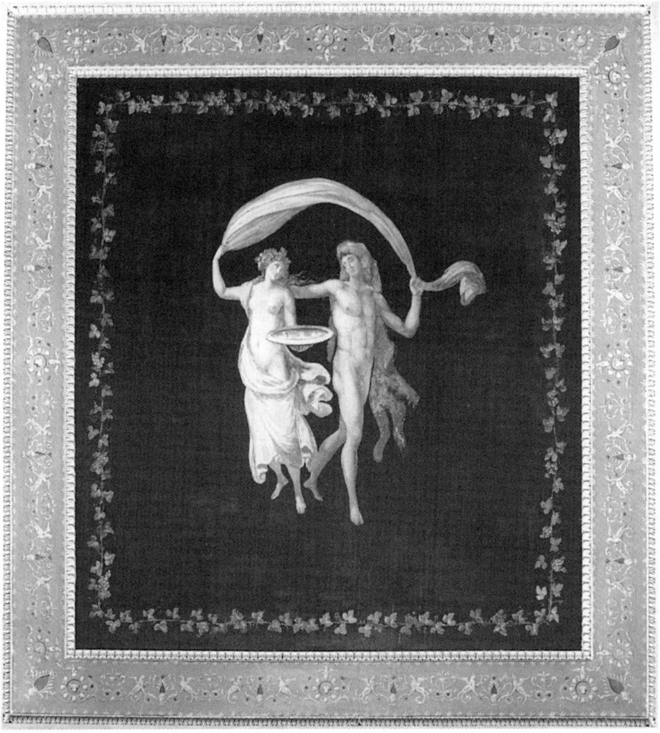

Figure 47 Center ceiling panel at Packington Hall. The Conway Library, Courtauld Institute of Art.

d'Hancarville in his *Recherches sur l'origine, l'esprit et les progrès des arts* (3 vols.; London, 1785–86).[64] One of d'Hancarville's readers, Richard Payne Knight, thought the volume "a very rich mine of learning and ingenuity, but I fear that prolixity & want of method will prevent it being so popular as he expects."[65] To Payne Knight, d'Hancarville's "wont of knowledge in the Greek language ... is so obvious that any Boy who has gone half way through Eton School must discover it."[66] While the theoretical basis for the gallery ceiling at Packington Hall derived from one library volume, the actual source of reference for the painted decoration derived from another deluxe folio: Nicolas Ponce's *Description des Bains de Titus; ou, Collection des Peintres trouvées dans les Ruins des Thermes de cet Empereur* (Paris, 1786).[67] The ruins of the Baths of Titus on the Esquiline Hill in Rome were misidentified in the eighteenth century, as they were in fact part of another imperial complex, Nero's Golden House. In a letter dated 25 April 1775, the Jesuit priest Father Thorpe described their ongoing excavation and organized illumination,

> The present opening of the ancient Baths of the Emp.r Titus, & the great discoveries already made in them, & more daily expected to be made, will both enrich & enliven ornamental painting. Accurate drawings are made of every part as soon as it is cleared from the earth & rubbish about it. These drawings are to be engraved, & then coloured from the Original paintings . . . four of the subterraneous Vaults were illuminated, & opened to all the Nobility, Gentry & Artists of the town. It was an entertaining sight to see Princesses & Ladies of quality squeezing their dresses through broken holes in walls deep under ground to admire these dirty remains of antiquity.[68]

Thorpe's account of this exclusive soirée at the excavated baths corresponds with the frontispiece of Ponce's *Description* (fig. 48), in which male and female tourists from the polite classes make their way towards one of the entrances to the baths. In the center of the doorway they are heading towards stands their guide with a lighted torch, flanked on either side by guards, including one on horseback. In the foreground, a group of four gentlemen, one with a magnifying glass, scrutinize a colossal fragment of painted plaster in much the same way that the reader is invited to do via the engraved plates that follow the frontispiece. The engraving also shows how the earth immediately surrounding the exterior of the baths had been removed to enable access, while the architectural ruins had been left overgrown with trees and foliage. The painted schemes of the baths that Thorpe anticipated would enrich and enlighten the repertoire of ornamental painting were described in Ponce's preface as being far superior to those at Herculaneum. Ponce's text is also keen to point out the cachet of these ancient paintings to the Renaissance master

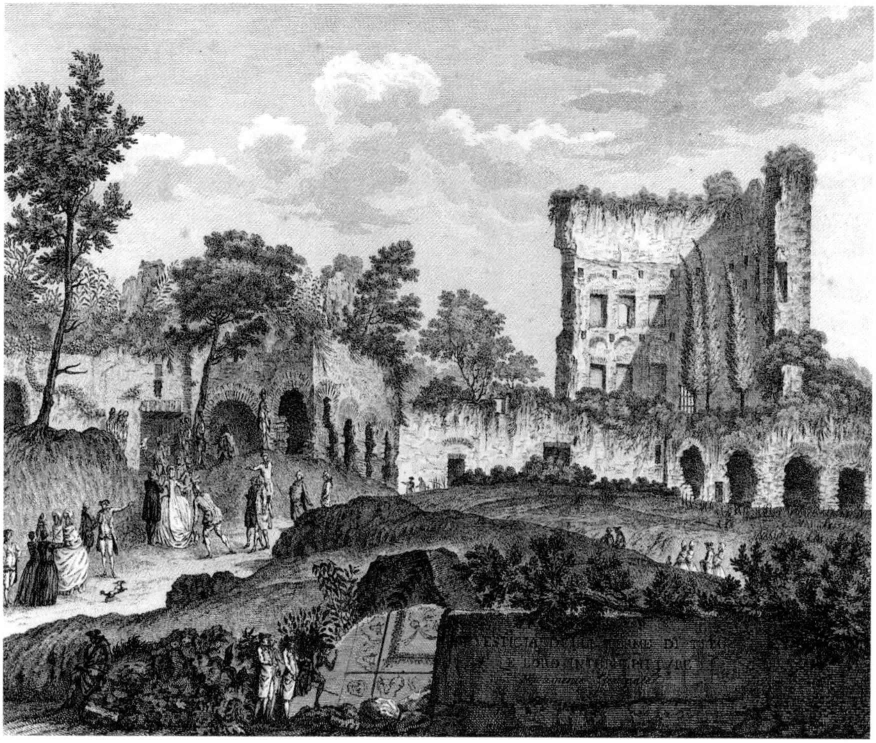

Figure 48 "Vue d'une des Exerdres des Thermes des Titus": Nicolas Ponce, *Description des Bains de Titus; ou, Collection des peintres trouvées dans les Ruins des Thermes de cet Empereur* (Paris, 1786), frontispiece. By permission of the British Library.

Raphael, who had incorporated them into his painted repertoire for the decoration of the arabesques of the Vatican loggia.

The Earl of Aylesford's gallery at Packington reproduced as paintings four of the sixty engravings published by Ponce: plate 1 was repeated for the wall scheme; plates 26 and 45, each depicting a naked youth on horseback, were painted in reverse for the two end panels of the ceiling; and his plate 51 (fig. 49), again in reverse, was used for the center ceiling panel (fig. 47 above). The two additional ceiling figures, which Stephen Rigaud described as single flying females, one with a leopard skin and a crown of ivy, the other with a wreath of flowers, do not appear to derive from Ponce's book; they may be invented or imitated from another unidentified source. The central panel reproduces Ponce's engraving of Ariadne and Bacchus (fig. 49), representing the apotheosis of Ariadne and thus the culmination of the Bacchic mysteries in the ceiling at Packington Hall. Published by Ponce as an example of an ancient painting from a Roman imperial monument in a lavishly decorated square frame with two borders, its transference from engraved print to painted ceiling is notably faithful.

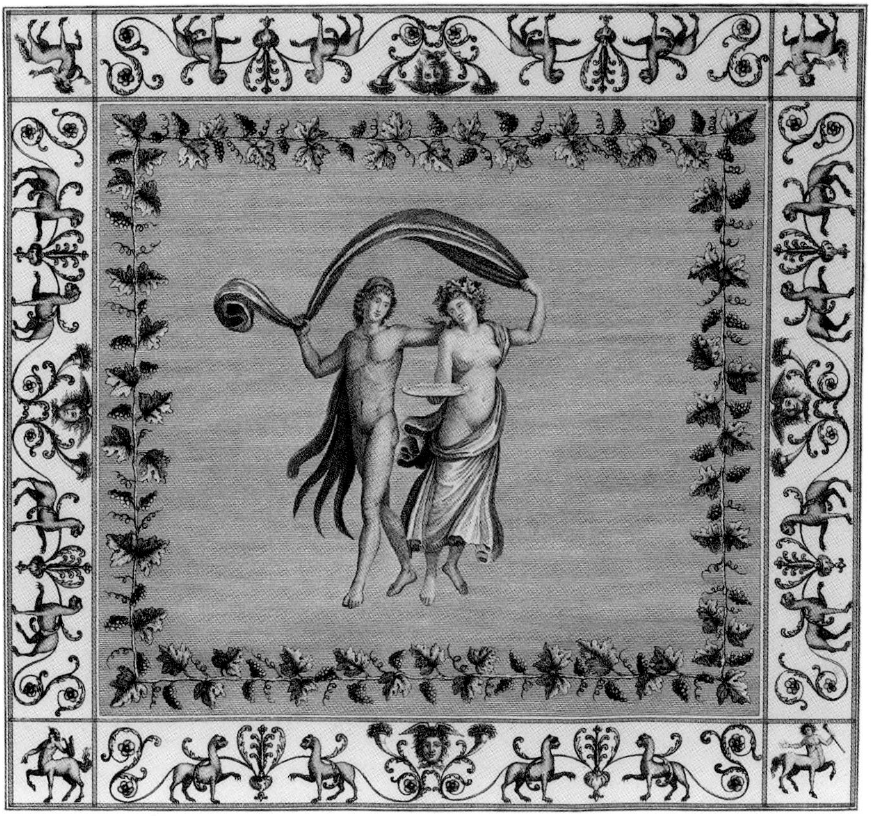

Figure 49 Nicolas Ponce, *Description des Bains de Titus; ou, Collection des peintres trouvées dans les Ruins des Thermes de cet Empereur* (Paris, 1786), plate 51. By courtesy of the Trustees of Sir John Soane's Museum.

But while this central ceiling panel may be seen to be faithful to Ponce's published engraving, how far the engravings themselves are faithful to their antique source depends largely on a neoclassical agenda of imitation and reproduction. We have already seen how far the plates of the *Antichità di Ercolano esposte* reproduced the unearthed paintings as if in pristine condition. The retrospective reception of the gallery at Packington as "Pompeian" is similarly problematic, since the published plates originate from the Baths of Titus—*in Rome*. Likewise the furniture, originally consisting of a set of seven or eight chairs, derives from the ancient *Greek klismos* type. What is striking about the decoration of the gallery at Packington is the dominance of two stereotypically "pompeian" colors: red and black. According to an account of Herculaneum published in the *Philosophical Transactions of the Royal Society* (1751–52), "All the paintings are either upon black or red grounds," with red "the brightest and best" of the ancient palette of colors.[69] In summary, the execution of the gallery scheme at Packington Hall represents a translation and transfusion of the *idea* of ancient paintings. The scheme and its furniture may, or indeed may not, be faithful to a specific ancient prototype. What is more striking is how far it is a contemporary reinterpretation of the antique that is conveyed by Lord Aylesford's interior: a little corner of Pompeii that is forever England.

Among news worth mentioning to his patron, William Constable in September 1777, the dealer James Byres describes the discovery on the Viminial Hill in Rome of an ancient house: "The plan, a number of small rooms round a square court about twenty feet below the surface in the middle of which appears to have been a fountain. the rooms are ornamented with Grotesque paintings. in a word the plan and decoration are exactly the same as those you saw at Pompeio."[70] The Welsh artist Thomas Jones visited the site earlier in the year, finding "the painted Ornaments much in the Chinese taste" and recording the progress of the excavations in a painting of 1779.[71] A permanent record of the ancient paintings, including plate 3, that were uncovered on the Negroni property was undertaken by Camillo Buti under the direction of Anton Raphael Mengs.[72] Buti's *Manifesto* outlines the motivation behind the copying of the antique frescoes:

> The idea which can be had of the ornaments of the ancients is so rare, or at least ornaments in this style, while the works so far published are either copied from detached pieces, and therefore do not give an idea of the whole, or are restored, and the additions confused with the true antique, or are copied with such thoughtlessness that they are not delicate enough: Wherefore our rooms are drawn (before being removed from the walls) with the most scrupulous exactness and with the same colours, in order that it can be seen what was the effect that the parts made with the whole, and finally so that one can form an idea of the taste of the ancients in this type of mixed ornamental and figural painting.[73]

According to Buti, the chief merit of his plates relied on their archaeological authenticity: being drawn while the original paintings were still in situ and being copied with scrupulous exactness. His emphasis on the totality of the scheme above fragmented images and their professed fidelity to the antique contrasts significantly with the improved reality of the paintings in the *Antichità di Ercolano esposte* volumes. However, the Negroni wall paintings were later fragmented and dispersed, so we are unable to compare the rhetorical niceties of Buti's text with the reality of his supposedly "delicate" engravings. Thomas Jenkins acquired the paintings—"Rome not abounding in Monuments of that kind, the stile . . . much like those in Hercolano"—from two of the four rooms.[74] Explaining in a letter to Charles Townley,

> a young man an architect who lives in the Villa has undertaken to publish them, but I fancy you will like to have the original colourd drawings, which shall be kept

> at your disposal. I have not yet, for want of Anders been able to get those paintings cleaned. would you wish to have the whole Room or is it a single picture only you desire. the idea of the Room and some ornaments by way of cornish and base, one of the Rooms having a much better piece of perspective than has hitherto appeard in antiquity. I have preserved one half of the end of the Room intire, which is in my opinion an interesting object.[75]

By 13 February 1783, Charles Parker wrote to his cousin, Sir Roger Newdigate, of his disappointment in finding the original paintings no longer *in situ* or intact:

> . . . the Pictures from which those 4 Beautifull Drawings you have were taken in the Villa Negroni—are carried off & dispersed over the World so there is no judging whether they are faithfully copied. There are 3 more come out which were engraved by Mengs—not equal to the first which were engraved—but fine things nevertheless. He asks me for 5 sequins each. but I hope to get them for 4.[76]

While the relationship between the ancient paintings and their engraved reproductions concerned Charles Parker in Rome, in the decoration of the English country house interior we see the paradox of the labeling of decorative schemes almost irrespective of their antique source. As we saw at Packington, the Roman becomes "Pompeian." The attribution of styles relied not only on contemporary taste but also upon the extent of contemporary knowledge and fashion. We can trace the beginning of this process at least as far back as Robert Adam, whose so-called Etruscan rooms proliferated in the homes of the English aristocracy in the latter part of the eighteenth century. Often the decorative scheme is the only constant, while the "style" is always changing: it seems that whatever was fashionable in the public eye could have a share in the naming. Visiting the Etruscan room at Osterley Park House, Middlesex (fig. 38 above) in 1786, Sophie von la Roche called it "the Etrurian cabinet, since its wall paintings are copied from one similar found in Pompeii; the chairs and tables are of Etrurian form, likewise the porcelain."[77] Two years later, Caroline Lybbe Powys reattributed the decorative scheme: "All the designs were taken from Herculaneum."[78] Sometimes the diversity of eighteenth-century labels is added to by modern research. Engravings published in Piranesi's *Diverse maniere d'adornare i cammini* (Rome, 1769), are seen as informing the scheme of Robert Adam's Etruscan room at Osterley.[79] According to a letter of Father Thorpe, Piranesi's published engravings furnished the artists of all countries with a plentiful library.[80]

One aristocratic English country house library whose imitation antique paintings were misidentified in the early nineteenth century is that at Goodwood House in Sussex. In *A Visit to Goodwood near Chichester, the seat of his Grace the Duke of*

Richmond (London, 1822), the librarian D. Jacques described the bases or closets of the bookcases in the grand library (fig. 50), with its 9,000 volumes, as painted in chiaroscuro from the drawings of Sir William Hamilton's Greek, Etruscan, and Roman vases found in the ruins of Herculaneum.[81] The ceiling decoration was

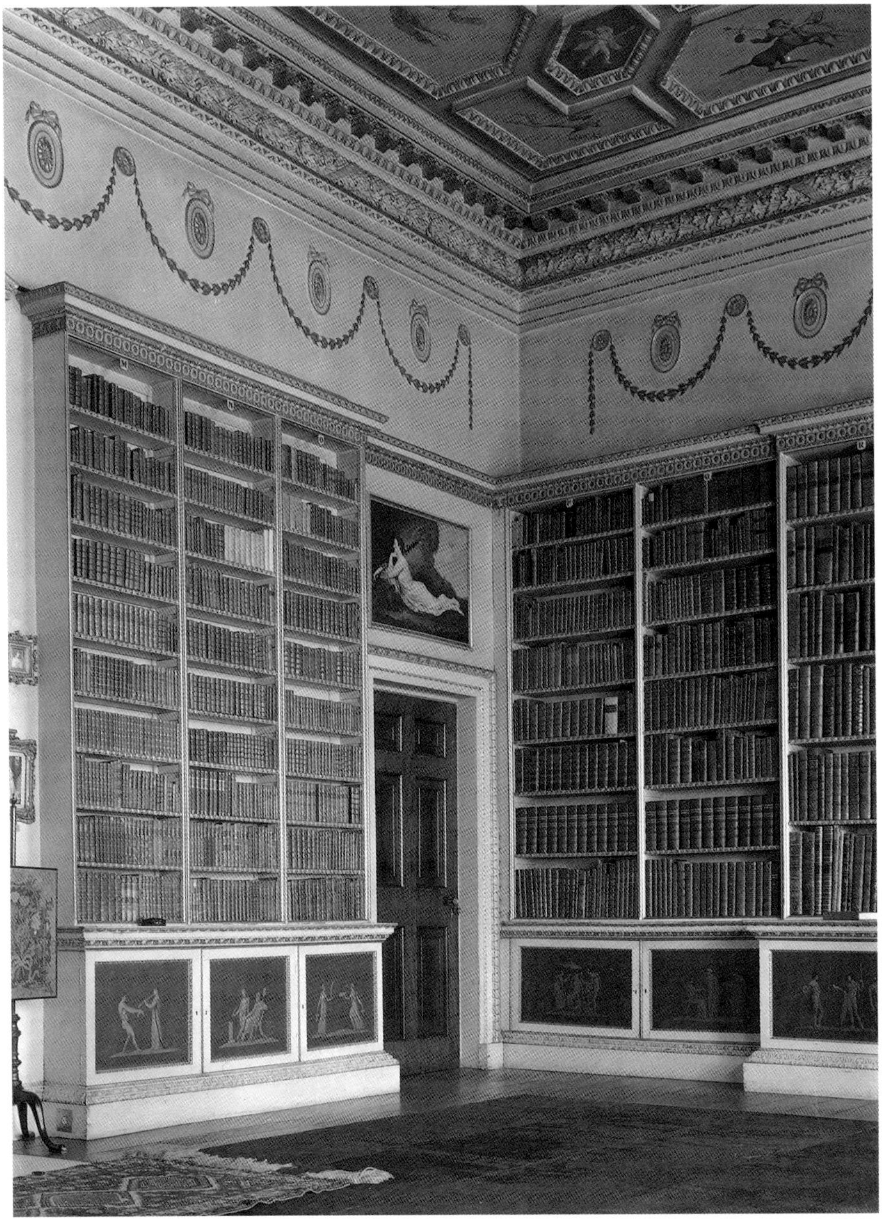

Figure 50 "One of the prettiest rooms I ever saw"—view of the grand library at Goodwood House in Sussex. Ceiling and library closets painted by Charles Reuben Riley in the early 1770s. Country Life Picture Library.

described as being executed by Charles Reuben Riley from paintings discovered in the baths of Titus at Rome. Sir William Hamilton's Etruscan vases were *not* found in the ruins of Herculaneum, and the ceiling paintings said by Jacques to derive from the baths of Titus at Rome are copied from engravings published in the *Antichità di Ercolano esposte*. Early in 1773, one of the Duke of Richmond's sisters, Lady Louisa Conolly, wrote to one of their other sisters, the Duchess of Leinster, that the library at Goodwood was "doing, and to my taste is one of the prettiest rooms I ever saw; if Mr. Conolly approves, I shall wish mightily to finish our gallery in the same manner."[82] After waiting impatiently for Riley to complete his work at Goodwood, by June 1775 she had him painting the Conollys' first-floor gallery at Castletown House, County Kildare in Ireland "in a most beautiful way."[83] In what was a creative collaboration, Lady Louisa was responsible for selecting the ornaments; her sister, Lady Sarah Bunbury, for uniting them within a composition; and Riley for painting them.

Like the painted scheme of the gallery at Packington Hall, that of its equivalent at Castletown House (plate 4) has been mislabeled as "Pompeian." In fact, the painted scheme of the Castletown gallery, the space described by Lady Caroline Dawson in 1778 as "150 feet long, furnished in the most delightful manner," derives from a library of eighteenth-century grand tour publications, including Montfaucon's *L'Antiquité expliquée*, the *Loggie di Rafaele nel Vaticano*, Sir William Hamilton's *Collection of Etruscan, Greek and Roman Antiquities,* and the *Antichità di Ercolano esposte*.[84] The largest single feature of the painted decoration is a lunette above the doors of the south wall after Guido Reni's *Aurora* (1614).[85] The pope's nephew, Cardinal Scipione Borghese, commissioned this early seventeenth-century painting showing the passage of the sun god's chariot for the ceiling of a summer house in the garden of his Palazzo Montecavallo (now Palazzo Rospigliosi) on the Quirinial Hill in Rome. For the eighteenth-century British tourist John Owen, the palazzo's reputation relied on Reni's Aurora; an image "so often engraved, that a transcript of its beauties—so far as frescoes can be copied into miniatures—is in the collection of every one who is at all an amateur of the fine arts."[86] Tobias Smollett reckoned the print by the Swiss engraver Jakob Johann Frey, which appeared as plate 5 in his *Icones Variae* (1721–27), "conveys but an imperfect idea of the beauty of the original."[87] The transcript of Reni's fresco in the long gallery at Castletown House was less ubiquitous and more exact, being executed on a large-scale canvas and in color. In fact, the Conolly gallery represents a union of the art of ancient painting and its postantique revival by Reni with the art of sculpture. On gilded wall-brackets distributed throughout the gallery are eight marble portrait busts, including the Greek poets and philosophers, Hesiod, Homer, Sappho, and Plato and the renowned Romans Cicero, Lucius Verus, and Caesar. A life-size marble statue of Diana the huntress is installed in a niche between the doors of the south wall and below the Aurora lunette. The significance of these types of material artifacts, especially to the neoclassical library, will be addressed in chapters 5 and 6.

One of the sources for the painted decoration of the Castletown gallery was the *Antichità di Ercolano esposte*, which was published in eight volumes over a period of thirty-five years beginning in 1757. This staggering of the publication replicated the act of excavation, since, as Russel tells us in his *Letters*, more and more painted, sculpted, and other rare artifacts were daily discovered at Herculaneum, creating "an immense treasure, continually receiving augmentation from an inexhaustible mine."[88] Though contemporary visitors to Osterley Park House erroneously identified the paintings in the Etruscan room by Robert Adam as taken from Herculaneum, Adam did make use of engravings in the *Antichità* volumes. For the ceiling of the Red Drawing Room at Syon House in Middlesex (fig. 51), home of Lord Northumberland, Adam created a visual précis of the *Antichità* by distributing its engraved contents into a mosaic of octagons and squares, executed on painted canvas and completed by Cipriani in 1764.[89] Adam's architectural rival, Sir William Chambers, inveighed against such fashionable ceilings which "excite no other idea, than that of a desert: upon the plates of which are dished out, bad copies of indifferent antiques."[90] Adam dished out a less explicitly Pompeian interior in the little drawing room at Audley End in Essex (c. 1770; plate 5), home of Sir John Griffin Griffin. Here, Adam reduced the mine of antiquity to key images (*Antichità*, 1: plate 24 and 3: plate 31 [fig. 52]). In these two surviving commissions by Robert Adam, we see the diversity of painted reproductions of Pompeii: from ceiling panoply to wall vignettes—a diversity that also characterizes the many (re)constructions of Pompeii in contemporary travel literature.

Writing to his father from Naples, William Blackett described the rooms in the houses at Pompeii as having "very small walls" and "painted in the manner of the Adams' from where they have taken many of their designs, the colours as fresh as if done only yesterday."[91] Using letters from travellers like William Blackett and published guidebooks of a tour in Italy, this chapter has documented the reception of the ancient sites of Pompeii and Herculaneum in the eighteenth century. Here was a *mass* of raw materials buried in antiquity and rediscovered sixteen hundred years later in situ and intact. Precisely because the sites and their contents had not been re-worked by postclassical traditions, their excavation, exhibition, publication, and reproduction may be seen as a model for the neoclassical enterprise. Although their appeal was that they had *not* been acted upon by later history, once they were exposed, repeated attempts were made to appropriate and integrate them into existing cultural, art historical, and intellectual traditions. We have seen how the Neapolitan monarchs attempted to make the finds their exclusive patrimony; how the debates

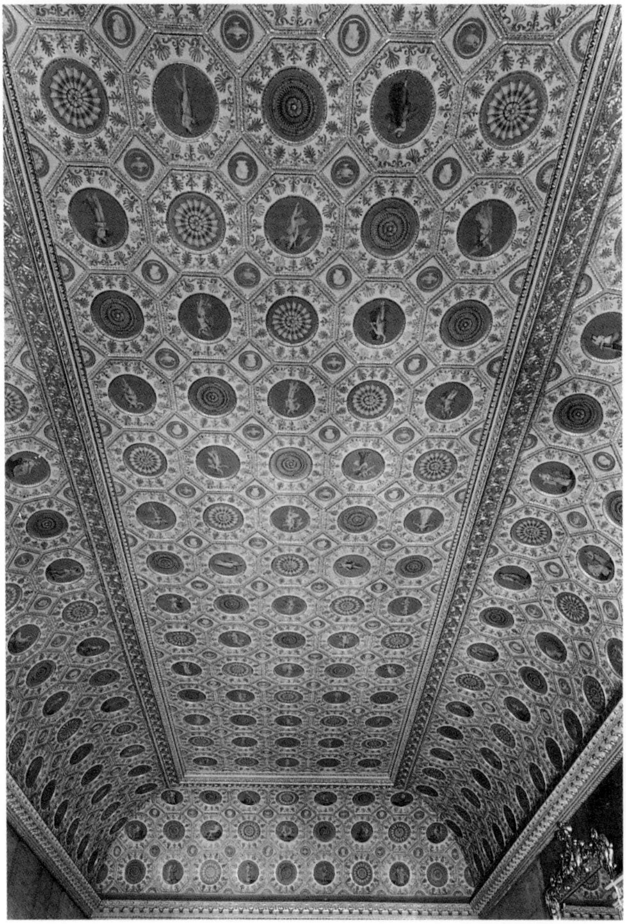

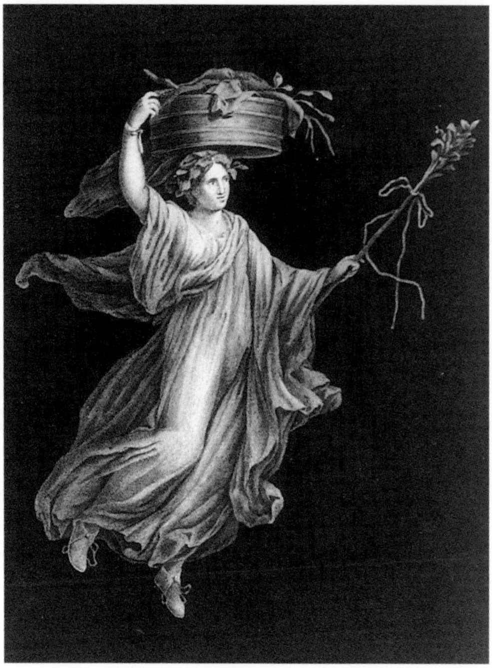

Figure 51 "A visual précis of the *Antichità di Ercolano* volumes"—view of the ceiling of the Red Drawing Room at Syon House, Middlesex, 1764–65: Photograph: A. F. Kersting.

Figure 52 *Antichità di Ercolano esposte*, vol. 3, plate 31. Institute of Classical Studies Library.

over the artifacts, especially the ancient paintings, conflicted and contradicted each other; and the extent to which the lives of the ancients were imaginatively reconstructed with a distinctly contemporary veneer. Blackett's description of the houses at Pompeii is an apt concluding statement for it draws attention to the final stage in the process of reception. For Pompeii to be a living antiquity, in diametric opposition to the vast museum that was Rome, required the reproduction of its ancient paintings in British interiors. Their colors as fresh as if they were modern.

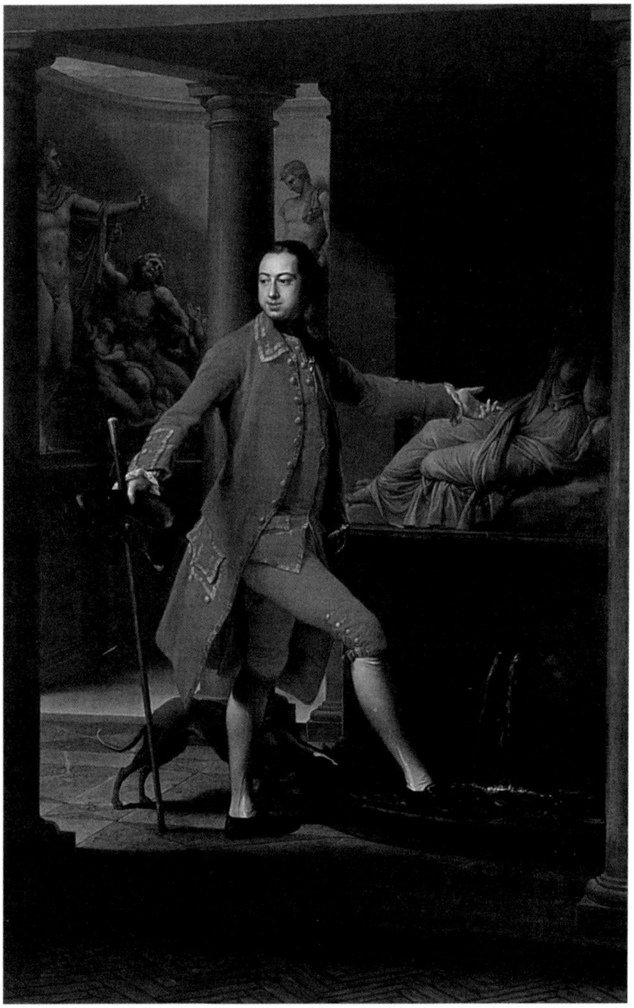

In the Palace [Villa Ludovisi] I must never forget that famous statue of the [Dying] Gladiator, spoken of by Pliny, and so much followed by all the rare Artists, as the many Copies and statues testifie, now almost dispers'd through all Europ, both in stone and metall.

John Evelyn, *Diary*, entry for 10 November 1644[1]

5

"Familiar objects in an unfamiliar world"

The Cachet of the Copy

Pompeo Batoni's portrait of Thomas Dundas (1764; fig. 53) represents the young British gentleman in Rome, a city hailed by a chorus of his contemporaries as the "most glorious place in the Universal World."[2] Dundas is accompanied in his grand tour portrait by four of the most celebrated antique sculptures in the city—the *Apollo Belvedere*, the *Laocoön*, the *Belvedere Antinous,* and *Cleopatra*. Following in the tradition of hyperbole established by Michelangelo, Thomas Martyn described the *Apollo* as "the finest single figure" and the *Laocoön* as "the noblest group in the world."[3] In Batoni's painting three of these four ancient sculptural masterpieces, the *Apollo*, *Laocoön,* and *Antinous*, are copied onto canvas from originals then in the Belvedere Courtyard of the Vatican museum: "a treasure beyond all price," so Thomas Broderick dubbed its classical contents.[4] Indeed, the architectural setting of the painting suggests an open courtyard beyond the painted pillars. Edward Wright, who travelled in Italy in the early eighteenth century, commented that the attitudes of the statues in the Belvedere Courtyard were "so well known, not only by the Prints, but Casts from them, or Models after them, which are in *England*, that I need only name them."[5] The reproduction of the ancient masterpieces and their repetition in prints, casts, and models disseminated the unique originals beyond the priceless treasure that was the Belvedere Courtyard in Rome. According to Wright,

Figure 53 Pompeo Batoni, *Thomas Dundas*, 1764. Private collection. Photograph: Photographic Survey, Courtauld Institute of Art.

these two- and three-dimensional copies were so well known at home in England that they were a stereotype of the originals. Such models, at hand or in mind, mediated between Wright's unique experience of viewing the originals in situ in Rome and the reader's secondhand encounter with them as textual figures in his published travel narrative.

In his *Travels through France and Italy* (1766), Tobias Smollett presumes his readers' familiarity with the original *Laocoön* in the Belvedere Courtyard through a series of innumerable reproductions in art *and* texts (as in fig. 54): "The work which we now see does honour to antiquity. As you have seen innumerable copies and casts of it, in marble, plaister, copper, lead, drawings, and prints, and read the description of it in Keyslar, and twenty other books of travels, I shall say nothing more on the subject; but that neither they nor I, nor any other person, could say too much in its praise."[6] Smollett refers here to a whole range of aesthetic casts and copies of the *Laocoön* executed in a variety of different media. As well as aesthetic reproductions, textual descriptions of the *Laocoön* proliferated in popular guidebooks, which were themselves reprinted and translated. One of the many travel accounts describing the *Laocoön* that Smollett explicitly mentions is Johann Georg Keysler's *Travels through Germany, Bohemia, Hungary, Switzerland, Italy and Lorrain* (London, 1760):

Figure 54 Engraving of *Laocoön*. Francesco Piranesi, *Choix des meilleures statues antiques* (Rome, 1792), foldout. By permisison of the British Library.

> Whether this piece consists of two or more blocks put together, according to the opinion of Michael Angelo when it was first found, is a question: and hence a doubt arises, whether it may be that mentioned by Pliny, who describes the groupe of Laocoön, &c. as made out of one single block. Fulvius Ursinus, also speaks of two pieces of serpents dug up in the same place, which may with greater probability be supposed to be part of Pliny's Laocoön. Be that as it will, the Laocoön of the Vatican is really admirable, whether considered as an original or as an antique copy; it being unreasonable to suppose that the first was not the only one those artists made.[7]

For Keysler, the Vatican *Laocoön* is really admirable whether it is the original Laocoön preserved and disseminated in the text of Pliny the Elder, or an antique copy produced by the same artists, Agesander, Polydore, and Athenodorus.[8] In making his aesthetic judgment, Keysler does not differentiate between the status of the original and the antique copy. For him, the canonical status of the literary and aesthetic traditions of antiquity is sufficient proof of their originality. Smollett, whose detailed account reproduces many of the points raised by Keysler, also describes the *Laocoön* as a work "which does honour to antiquity . . . neither . . . I, nor any other person, could say too much in its praise."

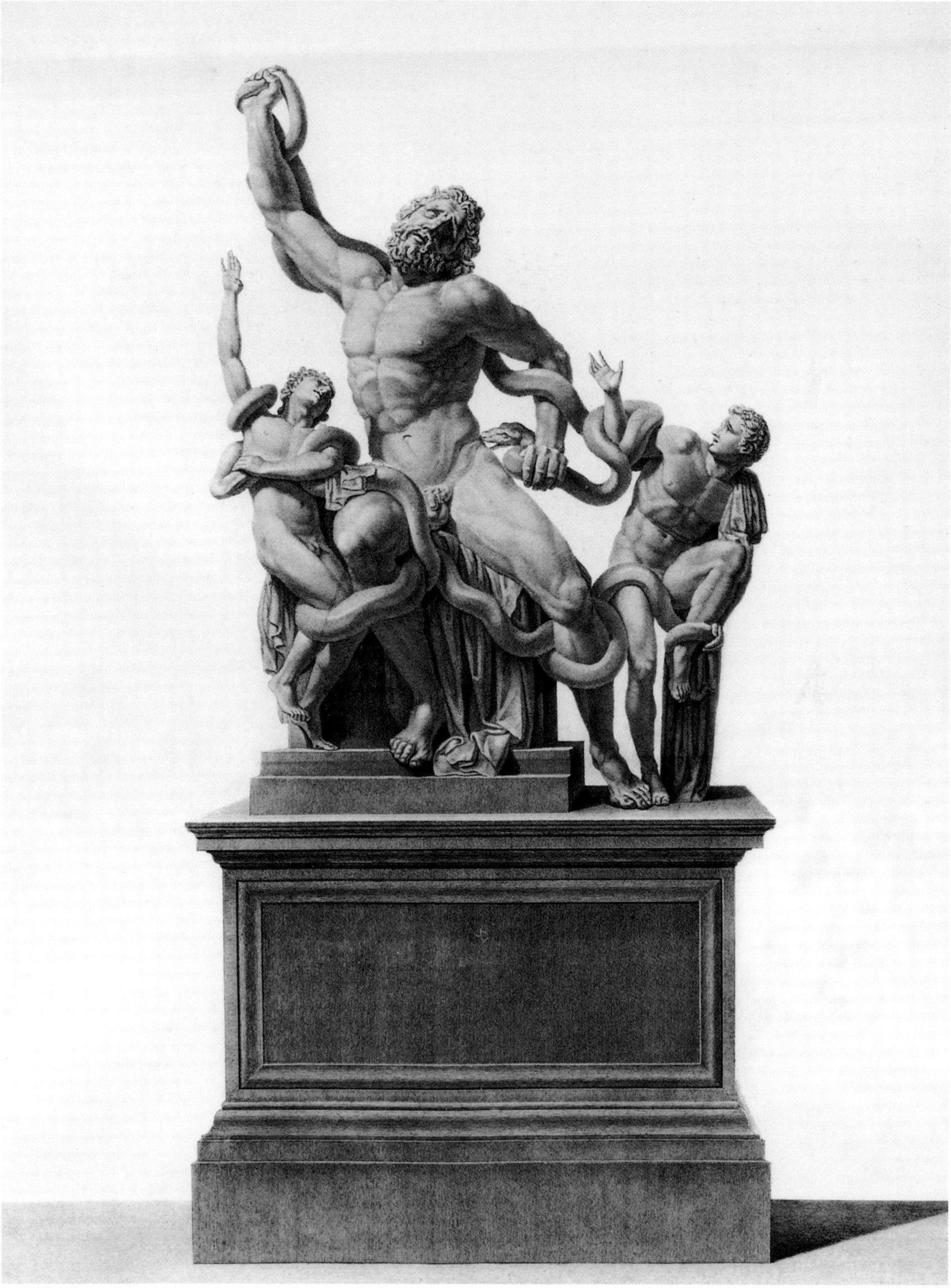

By their very nature, modern copies went some way to replicating a second-hand experience of antiquity outside the classic ground of Italy. Goethe, who visited in 1786 at the age of thirty-seven, described how his boyhood encounter with a replicated Rome at home affected his later vision of the original city:

> All the dreams of my youth have come to life; the first engravings I remember—my father hung views of Rome in the hall—I now see in reality, and everything I have known for so long through paintings, drawings, etchings, woodcuts, plaster casts and cork models is now assembled before me. Wherever I walk, I come upon familiar objects in an unfamiliar world; everything is just as I imagined it, yet everything is new.[9]

For Goethe, a city famous for its art objects was constructed and mediated through a multiplicity of copies of those art objects.[10] For Arthur Young, the sight of the *Medici Venus* in Florence (fig. 8 above) was anticipated by earlier encounters with her reproduction: "After all I had read and heard of the Venus of Medicis, and the numberless casts I had seen of it, which have made me often wonder at descriptions of the original, I was eager to hurry to the *tribuna* for a view of the dangerous goddess."[11] Yet when travellers came face-to-face with the ancient sculptures in Italian collections, the nature of the copies as substitutes for the originals often became controversial. John Boyle, for example, viewing the *Medici Venus*, explained in a letter, "Her head, as you may remember by the copies, turns a little towards the left shoulder."[12] Although the copy is a useful visual aid for the reader, Boyle proclaimed that no copy could ever reach the beauties of the original marble.[13] J. B. S. Morritt, writing home to his mother about the ancient marbles in the Farnese gallery at Naples, wondered how *best* to reproduce them: "A description of them is too like a catalogue, however, and will give you little or no idea of their beauties unless I can get drawings or casts of them, as perhaps I can of some."[14] Unable to translate their beauties into a written description, Morritt looked instead to obtaining drawings and casts. In this, he sets up a hierarchy of reproductive copies, where the aesthetic copy supersedes the textual translation. But the aesthetic copy was itself immediately superseded on coming face-to-face with the original model. Joseph Forsyth compared the ancient masterpieces in the Vatican Museum with sets of portable, engraved copies:

> Engravers have published the chief objects, rather as ornaments for a cabinet or a port-folio, than as documents for study. Piranesi's fine prints give the statues entire, and, when compared here before them, they even fail in resemblance. . . the details

> of a single statue would require fifty, and perhaps the sublime of the original would escape them all.[15]

The engravers to whom Forsyth refers had not produced an exhaustive catalog of the Vatican sculptures. Even Piranesi's engravings in which the statues are shown in single plate views are said to fail in their resemblance for neglecting multiple details. For Forsyth, the transference from three-dimensional plastic originals to two-dimensional paper copies, or from antique to tableau, would require fifty engraved prints, and even then, the sublime of the original might not be reproducible on paper.[16] Forsyth further differentiates between engravings for aesthetic use—as ornaments in a cabinet or portfolio—and as documents, which are more often textual than visual, for study. In this, he articulates an ambivalence about the *function* of the engraved copy as a reproductive tool.

Attitudes towards the reproductive process were equally controversial when the ancient sculptures were replicated as three-dimensional casts and copies. Edward Wright's narrative, which as we have seen invoked prints, casts, and models when describing the statues in the Belvedere Courtyard, continues:

> The Beauty of the Marble, and the Airs of the Figures in most of these are what no Copy can thoroughly represent; and indeed they are exquisite—For even in Casts, which must be esteem'd the most exact Copies of any, as these are taken off in several Pieces, when the Pieces come to be put together, it is great odds but that some little wrong turn at the setting on of the Head, or of an Arm or a Leg, may make the Statue not exactly suit with the Air of the Original.[17]

In Wright's reproductive hierarchy, casts are deemed as close to the original as any category of copy could be. Yet due to the techniques of their manufacture, which involved a process of breaking and remaking the copy, casts could transmute and even damage the originals. Viewing the "most amazingly fine" ancient sculpture of a fighting gladiatior in the Villa Borghese (fig. 55), Charles Burney explained how, "It has been formerly hurt and discoloured by the casts that have been made of it, and now, 'tis too late, crowned heads are refused the privilege of having it cast, the Empress of Russia among the rest."[18] In his grand tour journal, the British tourist James Martin described the casting process at work:

> saw there [at Jenkins'] the manner of making jesses by pouring liquid Plaister of Paris into a Mould in which it becomes dry in a very short time the jess of a Statue of natural size is formed in four moulds one of the Head & neck: the 2nd the Breast,

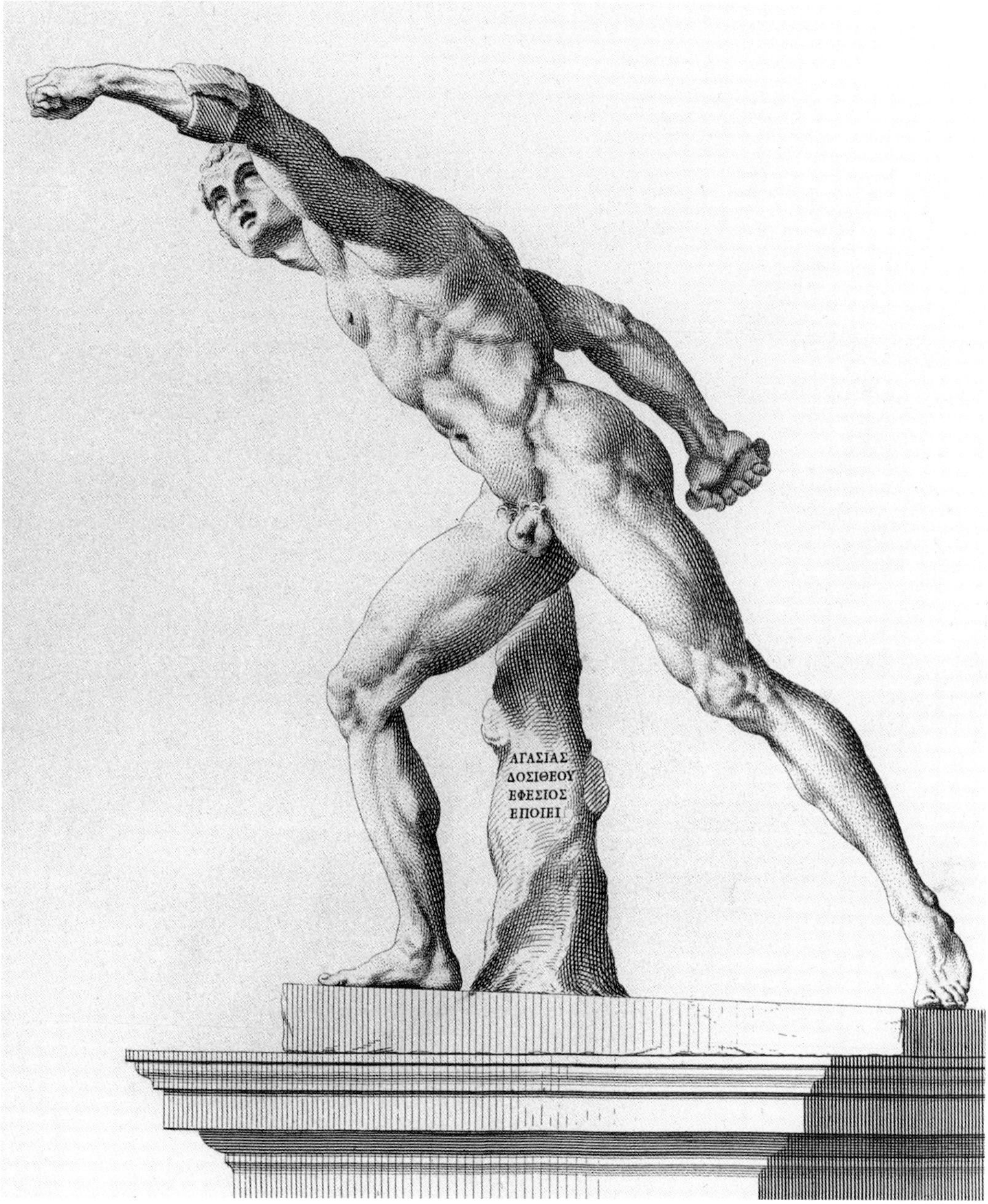

Figure 55 Engraving of the *Borghese Gladiator*. Domenico de Rossi, *Raccolta di statue di Roma* (Rome, 1704), plate 75. The Warburg Institute.

> Shoulders & Arms; the 3.d the lower Part of the Body with about Half the thighs; & the 4th the lower half of the thighs with the legs & feet. When these are finished there remains only to join them together which from the softness of the Matter is easily done without the joints being afterwards seen.[19]

The molds, which reproduced the original model, became the frame for a potentially infinite series of casts. Nevertheless, such casts were not necessarily identical with the original model or even with other casts in the series. To make a cast of a life-size statue, the statue was divided horizontally into four layers with a hollow mold for each portion being filled with plaster of paris. Once the plaster had dried, the four sections were released from their molds and reunited. But, as Wright pointed out, the act of piecing the fragments back together as a whole might make the cast "not exactly suit with the Air of the Original." In other words, the copy was never identical in every way with the original statue. The art of reproduction inevitably meant the displacement of the original. Indeed, in the act of casting, the cast was twice removed from its original, since it was produced from the molds.

In this hierarchy of modern reproductive copies, no imitation could ever reproduce in perfect form the reality of the original masterpieces.[20] Never mind: it might be argued that British collectors who acquired casts were not interested in questions of originality and authenticity when it was cheaper and easier for them to settle for modern copies.[21] Given this premise, let's look again at Batoni's portrait of Thomas Dundas (fig. 53 above). In *A View of Society and Manners in Italy* (London, 1790), John Moore describes Batoni as the best Italian painter then at Rome. Employed by young English and other foreigners, Batoni was "seduced from the free walks of genius, and chained by interest, to the servile drudgery of copying faces. Beauty is worthy of the most delicate pencil; but gracious heaven! why should every periwig-pated fellow, without countenance or character, insist on seeing his chubby cheeks on canvas?"[22] A Batoni portrait commissioned in Rome was certainly cheaper than a portrait by Sir Joshua Reynolds in London; in the 1750s and 1760s a half-length portrait by Batoni was about three-fifths of the price of a Reynolds.[23] In the 1780s, Batoni charged £50 for a full-length portrait; while Reynolds, £200. Although Dundas was (just) one of a generation of "periwig-pated" fellows to be reproduced on a full-length (298 x 196.8 cm) canvas, the fact that he was shown accompanied by a group of chef d'oeuvres of ancient sculptures in the Vatican museum, makes this portrait—if not entirely unique in Batoni's repertoire—then an original composition that was itself later imitated by its painter in another full-length (298 x 196 cm) portrait of the Russian tourist Count Razumovsky.[24] In 1766, Batoni painted Razumovsky in the company of the *Apollo Belvedere*, the *Laocoön*, the *Belvedere Antinous*, and *Cleopatra*: the very masterpieces that had been reproduced in Dundas's earlier portrait. While the *Apollo, Laocoön,* and *Antinous* are once again installed in an aedicula in an arrangement that reproduces almost exactly that in Dundas's portrait, *Cleopatra,* has been removed from her watery pedestal and turned right around. This arrangement and rearrangement makes Batoni's portrait of Razumovsky both an original invention and a copy of his Dundas.

The infrequent appearance of ancient marbles in Batoni's portraits has been described as surprising.[25] To paraphrase Goethe, we might say that they are familiar objects reproduced in an unfamiliar context and medium. Paradoxically, the painted copies are as we imagined or remembered them, but they are also *new*. The canonical masterpieces of antiquity have been reproduced and framed in a new context that manipulates their original material and size along with their later arrangement in the Vatican museum.[26] We have already seen that no copy, be it in paint, drawing, or cast, could reproduce in perfect form the reality of the original masterpieces. Rather, the copy reproduced however faithfully or unfaithfully the canonical original while simultaneously producing a variety of new associations.[27] Batoni's portrait of Thomas Dundas denotes the British tourist in "the most glorious place in the Universal World" that was Rome and at the same time connotes the travelling gentleman as a model of taste. Accounts of eighteenth-century visitors to museums in Italy frequently compared and contrasted the ancient statues before them; for Thomas Broderick, for instance, the *Belvedere Antinous* is a "statue which disputes among People of the first Taste, the prize with the Apollo [Belvedere]. The means of the comparison are open: both the statues stand in the same square, and they are equally perfect: both are of male figures, and both of the same age: the stature is much the same, and both seem to have been intended as models of perfection in the human frame."[28] Viewed in these terms, Batoni's portrait of Thomas Dundas is both a visual guidebook to refined taste in Rome and a souvenir to take home of its chef d'oeuvres—that include Dundas. In the definitive catalog of Batoni paintings, the seriousness of the antique theme is described as being belied by the light-hearted gaiety of Dundas's pose.[29] Admittedly, his pose seems artificial, but rather than contrasting Dundas with the sculptures, surely we as viewers are invited to compare the perfection of these painted copies of ancient sculptural masterpieces with the pretension of this British gentleman in his statuesque portrait.[30]

The kind of image that Batoni represented on canvas, itself a summary of highlights of the Vatican collection, was recreated throughout the eighteenth century in British country house interiors using casts and copies of ancient sculptures acquired in Italy. While on the one hand, plaster casts were recognized as being no substitute for their marble originals, on the other, as Goethe explains, "In Rome, when one is surrounded by such statues day after day, one becomes covetous and wishes to make them part of one's permanent surroundings, and the best way to do this is to acquire good plaster casts."[31] The published accounts and surviving correspondence are testimony to the paradoxical status of the copy; not as second-rate castoffs by sculptors reduced to the servile drudgery of copying statues but as acquisitions prized for their canonical *and* novel associations: what we might call the cachet of the copy.

Among the *Observations made in travelling through France, Italy &c. in the years 1720, 1721, and 1722* (London, 1730), Edward Wright, the tutor of George Parker, the second Earl of Macclesfield, describes a commission for bronze casts:

> When my Lord *Parker* was at *Florence*, and greatly delighted with these Statues, Signor *Pietro Cipriani*, an excellent Artist, and formerly a Scholar of *Soldani*, and his Assistant in casting those Statues for the Duke of *Marlborough*, undertook to make for him Copies in Copper of the [Medici] *Venus* and [Dancing] *Faunus*; which he engaged should at least equal *Soldani's*, and be the most exact that were ever made. He had the moulds of the several parts of them, and only desired that Leave might be obtained from the *Great Duke* for him to have Recourse to the Originals, for the more exact putting the Parts together (for want of which, Casts, often differ more from the Originals, than one would easily imagine; as has happen'd particularly in most of the Casts of this *Venus*.)[32]

Parker's grand tour provided an opportunity to purchase works of art for a gallery under construction at his home, Shirburn Castle in Oxfordshire. Thus, it is not surprising to find the would-be collector in the Tribuna of the Uffizi in Florence, "the greatest repository of curiosities in the world," according to Thomas Broderick.[33] What *is* striking about Parker's commission is how far it not only emulates highlights from the grand duke's collection of ancient marble sculptures but that it also replicates an earlier commission for casts executed by Massimiliano Soldani in 1710–11 for the British general John Churchill, first Duke of Marlborough of Blenheim (also) in Oxfordshire.[34] Here the cachet of the cast is related to the social prestige of its owners, where Parker is figured in an elite British tradition of collecting casts after the antique. In John Boyle's published account of the ancient masterpieces in the Tribuna, a note explicitly refers to these commissions for casts from the English aristocracy (figs. 56a–56c):

> The *Wrestlers*, the *Faun*, the *Slave*, and the *Venus de Medicis* were extremely well cast in copper by Signor *Soldani* for the great duke of *Marlborough* and are now at *Blenheim*. Copies of them by the same artist had been previously ordered by queen *Anne*, as a present to his grace, but a change in the ministry intervening, they were

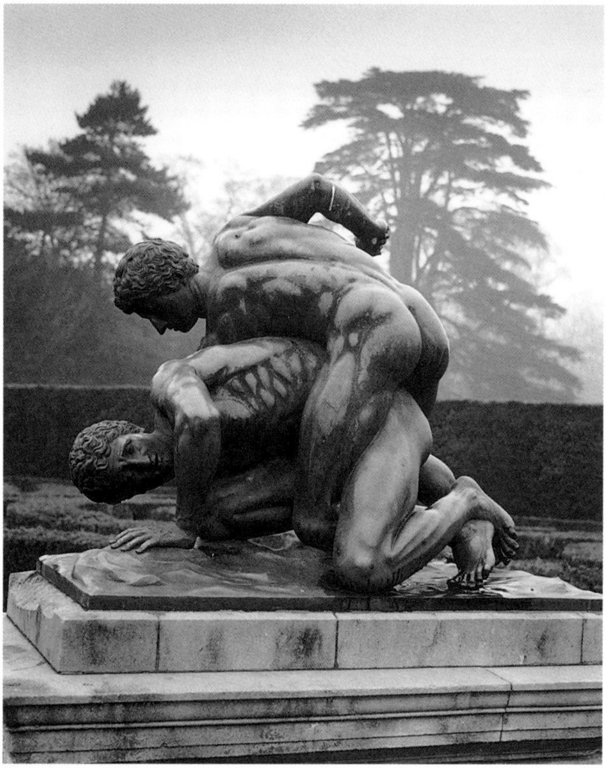

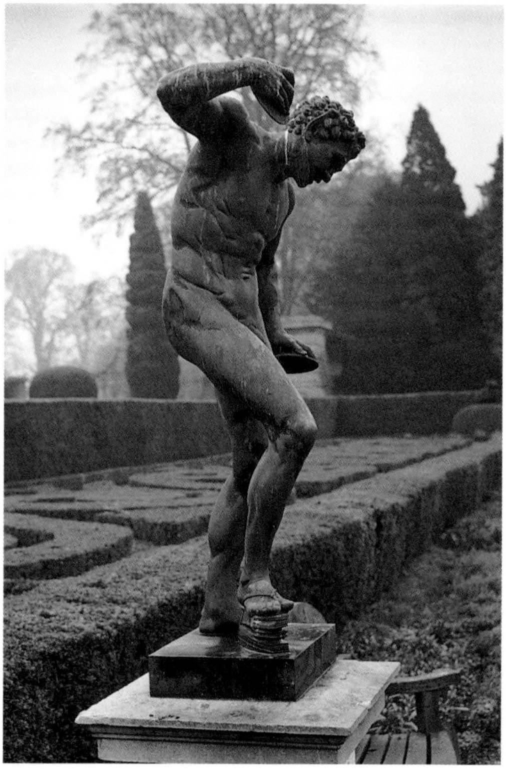

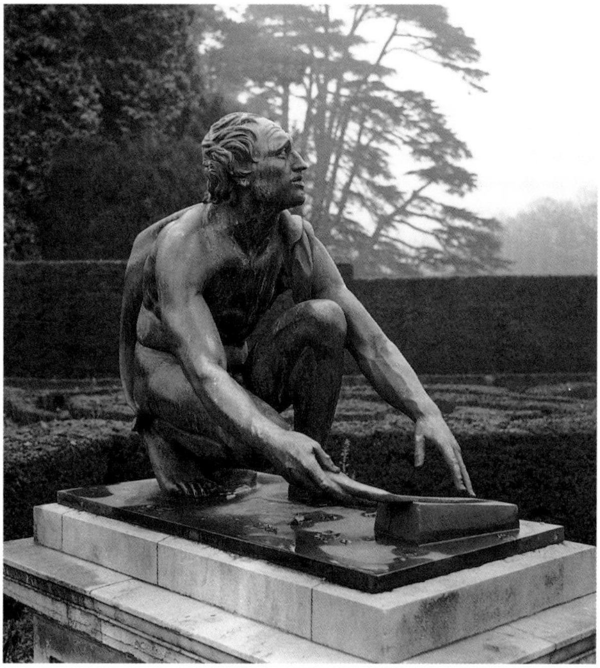

Figure 56a–56c Bronzes of the *Wrestlers (top left),* the *Faun (top right),* and the *Slave (bottom)* cast by Massimiliano Soldani, 1710–11, for the Duke of Marlborough at Blenheim. The Conway Library, Courtauld Institute of Art.

> countermanded, and still remain at *Florence*. The earl of *Macclesfield* also, at *Sherborn* castle, has admirable copies of the *Venus* and *Faun*, cast for the late earl by Signor *Pietro Cipriani*.[35]

While Marlborough's commission followed that earlier commission instigated as a gift of his royal favor by Queen Anne, Parker's commission replicates that of the Duke of Marlborough in the repetition of the subject matter of two of the statues, the *Medici Venus* and *Dancing Faun* and their material: bronze. That Cipriani was Soldani's assistant for the Blenheim commission is also significant; the curriculum vitae of the copier undoubtedly influenced the patron's choice of sculptor. For the Marlborough commission, Sodani had reused molds first made for copies for the Elector Palatine, but Cipriani, wanting his copies to "at least equal Soldani's, and be the most exact that were ever made," so Edward Wright tells us, made up new molds from the originals.[36] The process of bronze casting is described by James Martin:

> The moulds are made by making first the Figures in Wax which are then covered with a sort of Clay excepting that one Part is left open. They then make a sufficient Fire under it to melt the Wax which consequently runs out & leaves vacant Spaces, which being filled with melted bronze give the Representation according to the design of the Artist.[37]

In order that Parker's copies should be represented according to the design of the original marbles rather than that of the artist, Cipriani acquired the grand duke's permission to study the ancient sculptures firsthand so as to make his copies as close as possible to them. To further ensure fidelity in the copies, they were not executed in marble, the material of the original sculptures, but bronze. In a letter of 1695, Soldani wrote to one of his patrons that "to copy these statues in marble is not a good idea, because one can never in that way manage to copy them with that softness and grace of contours which are to be found in the originals, and, besides, marble copies are difficult to transport without breaking."[38] The medium of bronze satisfied both aesthetic and practical concerns. Ironically, in order for the copies to be as exact as possible to the familiar grand duke's originals, they were necessarily reproduced in an unfamiliar medium.

Along with copies of the *Medici Venus* and *Dancing Faun*, Parker also acquired tailor-made bronze casts of the busts *Plautilla* and *Geta*, wife and brother of the early third-century A.D. Roman emperor, Caracalla. Apparently the grand duke patented serial reproductions by insisting that the new mold for the Plautilla bust "should not be left at *Florence*, for the Cast to become common there, but should either be broken to pieces, or carried away by my Lord" back to England.[39] The cachet of the copy was determined as much by the social prestige of its owners as by the rarity of the molds. The proliferation of readymade casts of *Plautilla* in England would be sufficiently far away not to threaten the status of the original bust in Florence. Paradoxically, serial reproductions, which had initiated the very aura of the original, were the means by which that aura would potentially be threatened.[40]

Our next example concerns a commission for marble copies of the antique from later into the eighteenth century; but here the motivation behind the commission was not emulation, as it was with Parker's casts, but aristocratic competition. Writing in 1749 to his nineteen-year-old son Lord Malton in Rome, Lord Rockingham allocated him £400 to £500 to purchase marble tables and statues. This allowance for luxuries was accompanied by instructions relating to the requirements of the interior of their Yorkshire property, Wentworth Woodhouse: "there are eight niches in the Hall, the statues should be about six foot high."[41] By specifying the quantity and size of the statues he required instead of above considerations like subject matter or material, Rockingham conceived of them as articles of furniture, ordered to fit into the existing architectural scheme of his hall. In a letter of 19 August, Lord Malton related the progress of his sculptural shopping spree:

> As I hear it will be impossible to have antique statues, and as the Models made from them in plaister of paris are so easily broke and at best but have a mean look, and will never be proper for so fine a room as the Great Hall, I intend trying to get Copies done in Marble of the best antique statues. My Lord Strafford had 4 which cost him £500. But as those Your Lordship wants are a great deal less tho pure in proportion will be much smaller, when I am fully informed about the matter I shall let your Lordship know.[42]

Unable to obtain eight ancient statues, at the required height of six feet, Malton rejected plaster casts on the grounds that they were difficult to transport and that they were aesthetically inappropriate for their intended location. Opting instead for marble copies of the best antique statues and reminding his father that the latter's political opponent and aristocratic rival, Lord Strafford of nearby Wentworth Castle, had commissioned four marble copies at a cost of £500.[43] There were further developments from Florence on 1 September: "on seeing again the Gesses of the Statues, I [Malton] have resolved to send your Lord the Gesse ones—For copies in Marble at the cheapest would have been £100 a piece, I shall take home the copies of the Venus, Faun, Mercury and Idol. At Rome I shall take four more of the Copies of the finest Statues there."[44] When cost was the deciding factor, the cheaper, readymade, plaster cast overruled the handmade, marble copy.

That Rockingham immediately revised his son's allowance is proof of how far reproductions of famous antique statues figured in the competition between the Whig Rockingham and the Tory and Jacobite sympathizer, Strafford, to outcopy each other. Rockingham's reply explicitly compares Strafford's copies at Wentworth Castle with those he required for Wentworth Woodhouse:

> Eight Statues for the great Hall six foot High, those of Ld Strafforde's are larger but being of very course & spotted marble as they stand open so as you see every part make but an indifferent show. As yours will stand in Niches so that the backs will be in a manner out of sight, I would therefore wish you to have them frontward of the 1st Rate Statuary Marble, tho you may allow some specks in the Back parts. I am ready to pay the money for all these things.[45]

The demonstration of political rivalry between Rockingham and Strafford in monuments situated in the landscapes of their neighboring country houses has been well documented.[46] Here we see how in addition to being given physical form in a program of building, their rivalry was also given material form in the interiors of their country houses with a program of collecting copies modeled on the antique.

Malton's aim of obtaining copies of the finest statues in the urban centers of Rome and Florence was both realized and surpassed in the decoration of the Great Hall at Wentworth Woodhouse (fig. 57). In a bid to rival Lord Strafford's collection at nearby Wentworth Castle, the marble copies in the Great Hall emulated and, in some ways, exceeded the royal and elite sculpture collections of cosmopolitan Europe that possessed the ancient sculptural masterpieces. Executed by British and foreign sculptors in Rome, Rockingham's collection of marble copies included the *Callipygean Venus* (from the Farnese collection at Naples), the *Capitoline Flora* and *Capitoline Antinous* (Rome), the *Medici Venus*, *Dancing Faun,* and *Apollino* (Florence), *Germanicus* (Versailles), and *Faun with Kid* (San Ildefonso, Madrid).[47] This ideal collection brought copies of ancient statues dispersed in Italy and beyond and set them side-by-side in the English country house. Visiting a caster's workshop in Rome, Goethe wrote of the joy of watching "the exquisite limbs of the statues coming out of the molds one after the other. It gives one a completely fresh view of the figures. All the statues which are scattered over Rome can here be seen set side by side. This is invaluable for purposes of comparison."[48] In J. A. Galiffe's *Italy and its Inhabitants* (London, 1820), he recommended "bring[ing] to the Museum of the Vatican the finest of the statues kept in the Capitoline Museum, such as the real *Antinoüs*, the *Dying Gladiator*, the *Faun*, and the beautiful *Venus*; all which, with the statues of the Belvedere, would furnish out the most glorious, collection in the world."[49]

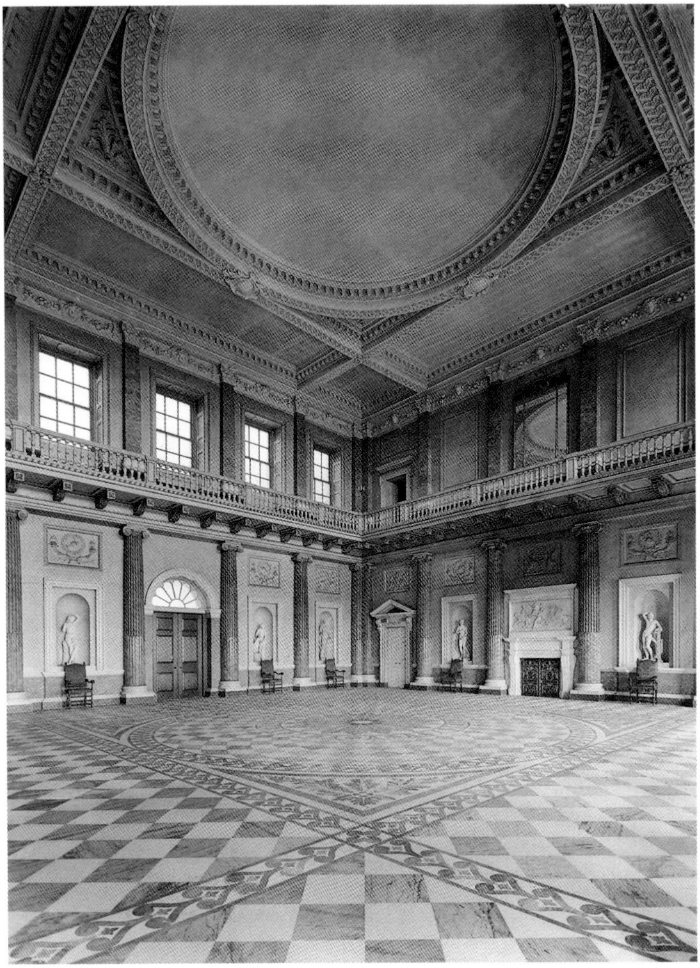

Figure 57 View of the Great Hall at Wentworth Woodhouse, furnished with "a most glorious collection" of marble copies. Country Life Picture Library.

The marble copies in the Great Hall at Wentworth Woodhouse represented a most glorious collection of reproductions. They not only physically united in one room marble reproductions whose originals were dispersed around Europe but were also uniformly united by being tailor-made (enlarged) to about six feet high. In the lower or pillared hall, Rockingham displayed the readymade collection of plaster casts that Malton had acquired in Florence; namely, the *Medici Venus*, *Dancing Faun*, *Mercury*, and *Idol*. For the marble copies of originals not housed in Rome, the copyists would have used plaster casts like these as their three-dimensional pattern books.[50] So more than half of Rockingham's marble copies were themselves copied and enlarged from existing plaster casts. The *Medici Venus* and *Dancing Faun* were represented in the collection at Wentworth Woodhouse as both readymade plaster casts *and* enlarged marble copies, tailor-made by Joseph Wilton and Simon Vierpyl from plaster casts.

The copies discussed so far for Parker and the Duke of Marlborough have had significant social cachet. Further north in Yorkshire, Rockingham's political rivalry with Strafford took material form in enlarged marble copies after the antique. While in Florence in 1749, Lord Malton also commissioned a marble sculpture whose prototype was not a masterpiece of Greco-Roman antiquity but instead of the Italian Renaissance and whose subject matter was not mythological as in the *Medici Venus* and *Apollino* but biblical. The work in question, Vincenzo Foggini's *Samson and the Philistines* (fig. 58), may be seen as a conflation of two earlier sculptural groups: *Samson and a Philistine,* executed by Giambologna in the late 1560s (fig. 59), and a projected composition of the same subject prior to Giambologna by Michelangelo.[51] Originally commissioned by the Medici in Florence, Giambologna's full-sized marble was passed from one European courtly circle to another. Presented to the king of Spain's chief minister by the Medici, the group was gifted in 1632 by Philip IV of Spain to Charles I, the Prince of Wales. The prince then presented the sculpture to his favorite, the Duke of Buckingham, where Samson stood "knocking his [the Philistine's] Brains out with the Jawbone of an Ass" in the garden of his property of York House in London and from 1714 to 1762, in the hall at Buckingham House.[52] Foggini's 1749 group for Wentworth Woodhouse evokes Giambologna's *Samson and a Philistine,* with its century-old aristocratic English provenance, while at the same time invoking the sculptural pedigree of Michelangelo. Michelangelo's *Samson and the Philistines* (as it is conveniently called) was never finished, but the composition is known to us, as it would have been to Giambologna and Foggini, in the form of bronze copies and drawings.[53] For Nicholas Penny, Foggini's group was the most important of the sculptures Malton acquired on the grand tour, with its genuflections to Giambologna, to Michelangelo, and back to an ancient sculptural tradition—where the figure of Samson is indebted to the *Laocoön* discovered in 1506 (fig. 54 above), the crouching Philistine, and the *Wrestlers* in the Medici collection in the Uffizi.[54] Bronze casts of the *Wrestlers* were part of Soldani's commission for the Duke of Marlborough (fig. 56a above); there were "so many copies of the Wrestlers in England [claimed Broderick in his *Travels,* published in 1754], that 'tis hardly necessary for me to say any thing about them."[55] Foggini's group, formerly at Wentworth Woodhouse, is however as much part of an assimilated and reworked Florentine sculptural tradition that harks back to antiquity as it is part of an elite tradition of *collecting*; of commissioning sculptures in Italy, as the Medici did from Giambologna, and displaying them in British properties, such as those of the Duke of Buckingham. This conceptual framework of collecting reworkings of renowned sculptures enables us to relate Foggini's *Samson and the Philistines* to the

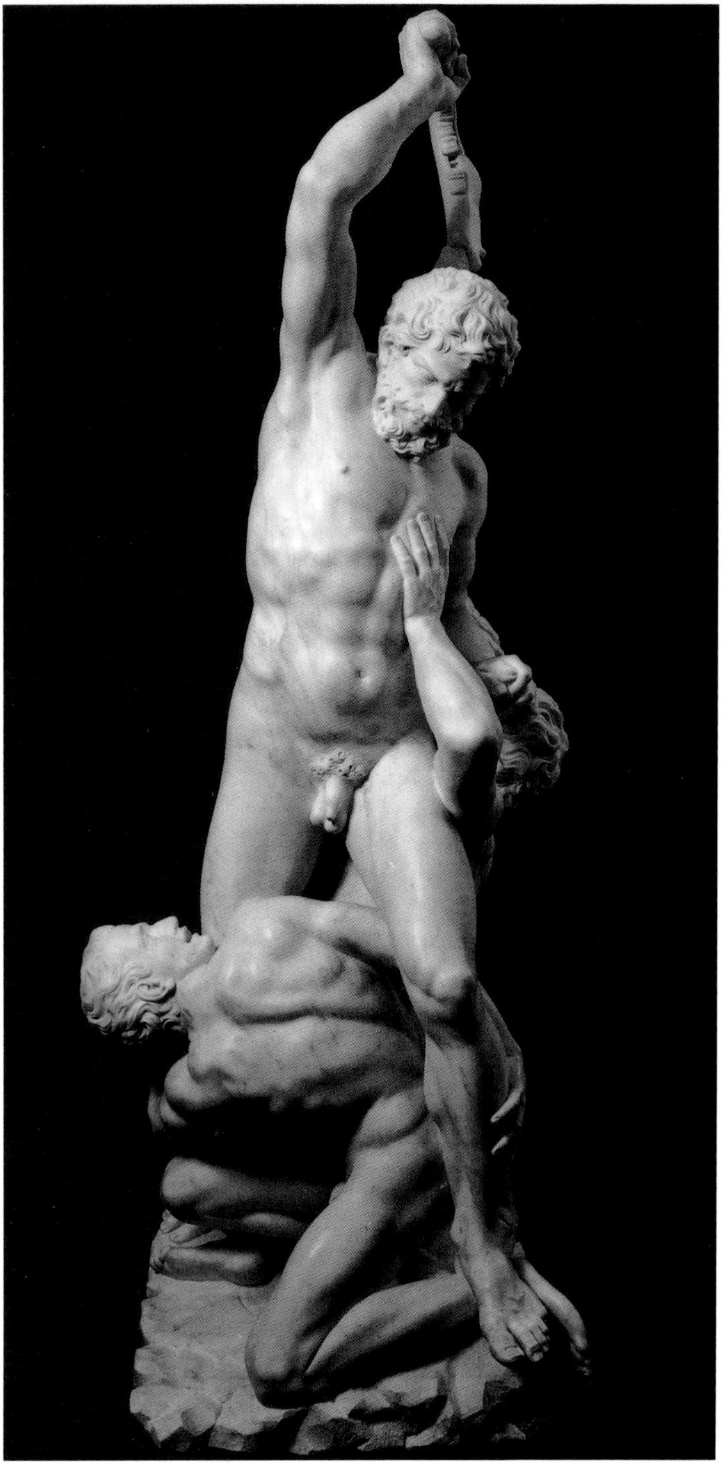

Figure 58 Vincenzo Foggini, *Samson and the Philistines*, 1749. V&A Picture Library.

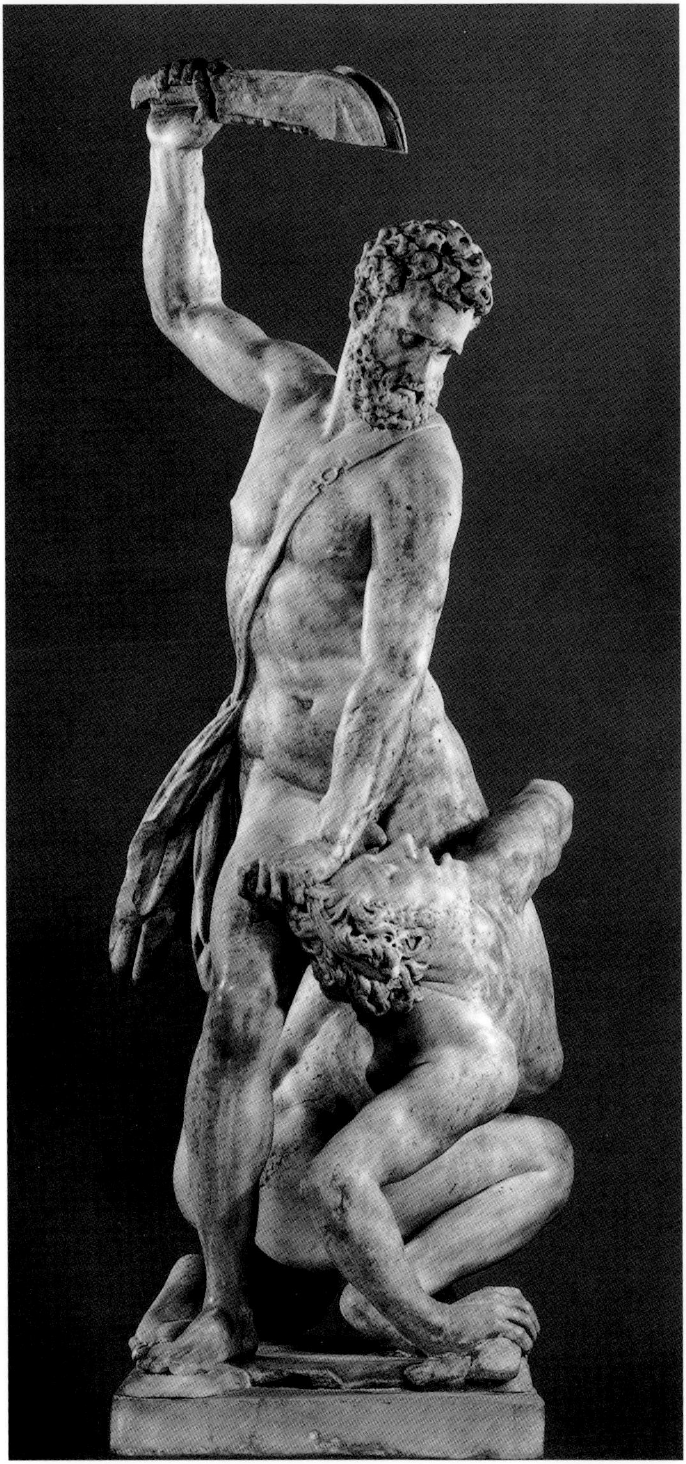

Figure 59 Giambologna, *Samson and a Philistine*, late 1560s. V&A Picture Library.

enlarged marble copies of ancient sculptural masterpieces that Malton commissioned in Italy at the same time.

From a letter of Horace Mann to Horace Walpole, we learn that the readymade collection of Medici antique casts that Lord Malton acquired for Wentworth Woodhouse in 1749 continued to be reproduced in Florence as part of a larger series that by 1756 included *Leda and the Swan*, *Venus Pulling the Thorn out of Her Foot,* and Sansovino's *Bacchus*—the last a Renaissance work esteemed in the eighteenth century as equal to classical statues.[56] On 18 March, Walpole wrote to Mann, the British Minister in Florence, with a commission for plaster casts from "no less a minister" than then-chancellor of the Exchequer, Sir George Lyttleton. Walpole named, with one exception, the repertoire of casts that Lyttleton wanted for his hall at Hagley Hall in Worcestershire: "the Venus, the dancing faun, the Apollo Medicis, (I think there is a cast of it) the Mercury, and some other female statue at your choice."[57] Mann was unable to realize the commission exactly, as he explained in a letter of 16 April:

> There is no gesso of the Apollo Medici, nor any female statue to accompany the Venus. The only female figure besides, are the Leda and the Swan, which is much less, and I think a disagreeable as well as a foolish idea, and the Venus pulling the thorn out of her foot, which is not only less too, but is a sitting figure, so that neither would serve as a companion for the Venus. There are, I think, but five figures in gesso of about the same size which are the Venus, the Faun, the Mercury, [Sansovino's] Bacchus, and the Idol, so that there is no choice if the hall requires five upright figures.[58]

The acquisition of readymade plaster casts depended on which statues in the Medici collection were already cast up from existing molds. But the repertoire of Lyttleton's casts was also restricted by their intended location in niches in the public space of the hall (fig. 60) which meant only standing figures and which ruled out conceptually inappropriate subjects like the rape of Leda by Zeus in the form of a swan. Lyttleton subsequently acquired four, rather than the full quota of five, casts: Sansovino's *Bacchus*, the *Dancing Faun,* and in the absence of a cast of the *Medici Apollo* or another female statue, the *Medici Venus* was accompanied by the *Mercury*.

Even though the mass-produced series, out of which Lyttleton acquired four types, was a stereotype of the unique model, nevertheless, plaster casts of ancient sculptures which proliferated in Italy were still rare outside Italy. Even the series was not as stereotypical as we might at first think. For example, in a letter of 26 July 1765, the sculptor Joseph Nollekens offered his patron Thomas Anson of Shugborough in Staffordshire first-time plaster copies of the *Furetti Centaurs*:

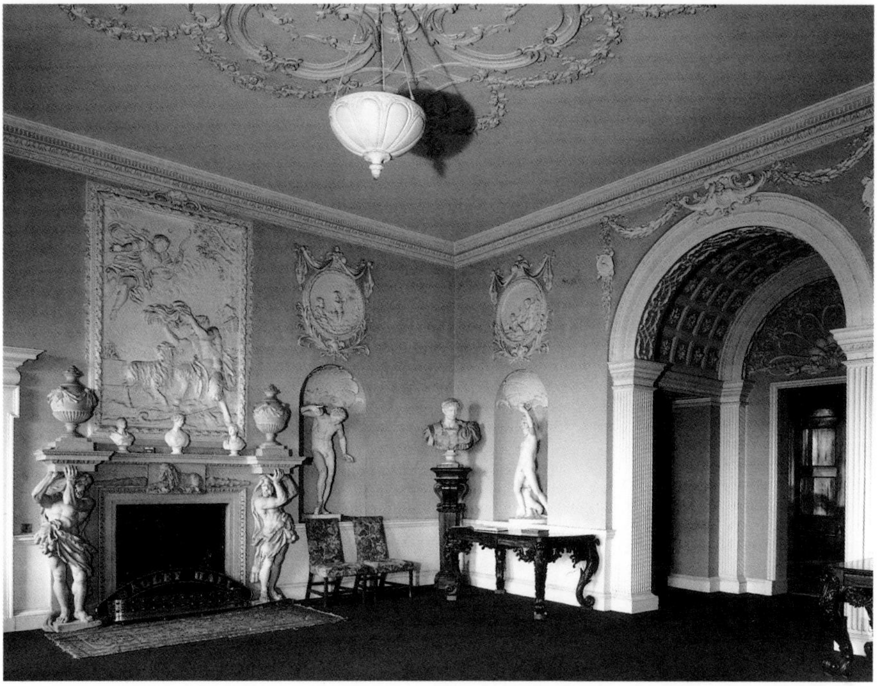

Figure 60 View of the hall at Hagley Hall in Worcestershire. Reproduced by kind permission of the Viscount Cobham. Photograph: Photographic survey, Courtauld Institute of Art.

> Casts of the two famous Centaurs of the late Cardinal Furiety which as bin Cast for the first time, for which they would not Sell Casts of them under the price of one hundred Crowns the pare which is very dear according to the Vallue of Plasters in Rome, but as I saw that there was others who agred to go to the same price & Casts that never was seen in England for both the raryty and fineness I thought you would not be against it. the origenals which are in Black Marble and of most Exquisite workmanship as with in this two month bin Sould to the Pope for the price of thirteen thousand Crowns the Pope as made them as a present to the Gallery in the Campidoglio. the Flavity Family as bin offered 20000 Crowns by som English I beleve it was commision for the king but they could not git licence to take them out of Rome.[59]

What an acquisition for the British gentleman-collector: to possess new plaster casts of a pair of ancient sculptures in Italy, where the rarity and fineness of the first-time copy is matched by the social cachet of the would-be *royal* possessor of the original.

The reproductions of ancient sculptures at Syon House in Middlesex are further testimony to the esteem of the copy as a means for the British aristocrat, in this case, Lord Northumberland, to rival—through reproductions—the royal and elite sculpture collections of cosmopolitan Europe. This ideal collection of copies contained in the entrance hall included a plaster cast of the *Apollo Belvedere* and a bronze cast by Valadier of the marble *Dying Gladiator.* This arrangement united the Gladiator, "one of the finest [sculptures] in all Italy" from the Capitoline museum with the Vatican Apollo, reportedly "the finest single figure."[60] In the adjacent anteroom (fig. 61), twelve verde antico columns are surmounted by gilt casts of antique statues, including the *Mercury*, the *Dancing Faun*, *Idolino*, *Medici Venus*, *Callipygean Venus*, *Celestial Venus*, *Belvedere Antinous*—and a cast of Canova's *Hebe* (a later replacement). In niches on the ground level the marble *Belvedere Antinous* is replicated in bronze, with another bronze cast of the *Borghese Silenus with the Infant*

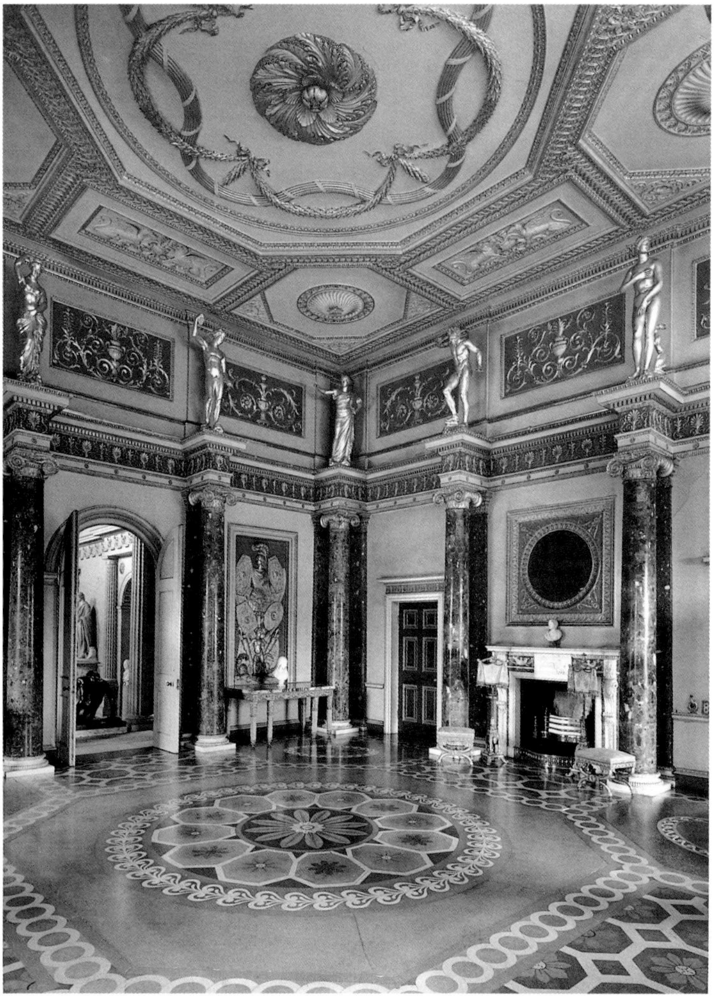

Figure 61 View of gilt casts in the anteroom at Syon House, Middlesex. Photo: A. F. Kersting.

Bacchus—the original of which is also in marble. The architect James Adam, who was overseeing Northumberland's commission from Italy while his brother Robert refurbished Syon House, wrote of the cost of commissioning a set of new molds for an original cast of the *Antinous*:

> Tell Bob [Robert] that I have prevented the Founder [Valadier] to cast the little Antinous in Bronze but cannot get him to agree for less for his Modell & Form or Mould than 280 C.[ns] which is near half of the entire price agreed for so that realy I shou'd think my L.[d] N.[d] wou'd yet do better to let him finish this in Bronze as tis a pity not to compleat a statue that will cost him so small an Additional sum. If my L.[d] shou'd not choose this, I suppose he will at least incline to have a plaister cast or two, taken from the mould, which will be a very trifling expence.[61]

Adam's letter articulates a tension between the handmade and the readymade copy. The mold for Northumberland's bronze cast of the *Belvedere Antinous* was handmade by Valadier at a considerable price—almost half of what had been agreed for the total cost of the commission. But once the mold had been made up for this bronze, additional plaster copies could be reproduced for the patron at a trifling expense. In the dining room at Syon, six niches contain four handmade marble copies of antique statues in Italy and France (fig. 62): *Capitoline Flora*, *Apollino* (Florence), *Diana Chasseresse* (Versailles), and the *Muse Euterpe*. The two remaining niches house a statue of *Ceres* by Bartolomeo Cavaceppi and a copy by Joseph Wilton of Michelangelo's *Bacchus*.[62] Wilton's marble *Bacchus* was copied at a cost of £150 from a cast in the Duke of Richmond's Academy at Whitehall, which reportedly contained the only cast of the figure in England.[63] According to *The Works in Architecture of Robert and James Adam* (London, 1778), eating rooms "are always finished with stucco [rather than damask and tapestry], and adorned with statues and paintings, that they may not retain the smell of the victuals."[64] Practicalities aside, the copies of Ceres, Diana, and Bacchus retain the favored pastimes of the dining room: eating and drinking.

We have already come across the *Apollino* or *Medici Apollo* as one of the plaster casts from Florence that Lyttleton had wanted but had been unable to acquire for his hall at Hagley since there were no existing molds. The *Apollino* for the dining room at Syon was not selected by the patron, Lord Northumberland at home in Britain, but by the contact, James Adam, in Rome. As with Lyttleton's order, Northumberland's commission was confined to statues whose specifications would fit the niches in the dining room. A letter from James Adam to Robert Adam relates the difficulties encountered when the antique *Apollino* was enlarged in its reproduction for Lord Northumberland:

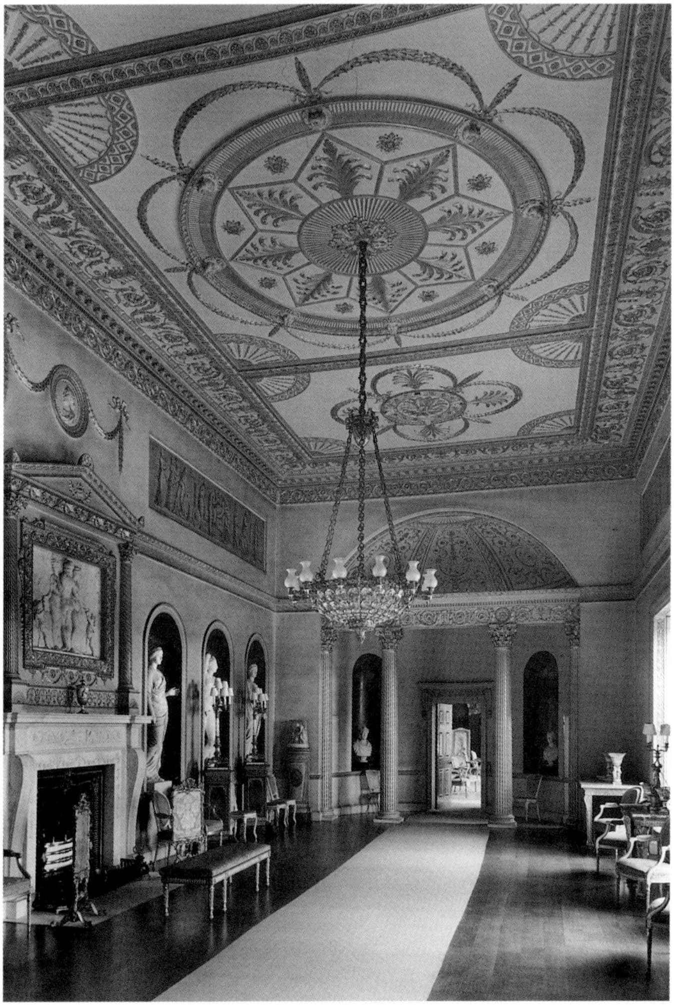

Figure 62 Marble copies confined to niches in the dining room at Syon House. Photograph: A. F. Kersting.

I am realy uneasy from what you write me of L.[d] Northumberland's account of the Florence statue. You know very well that the choice of these statues were left to me, at the same time confined me to a certain size of nich, which of consequence fix'd the size of the statue & also its attitude. The only way I had to judge of this, was from the Vol.[e] of statues in the Museum Florentinum, & both Cav. Zucchi & I fix'd upon this one now doing [Apollino], as the most agreeable attitude of any that cou'd be confined to the size of the nich. I therefor wrote [Francis] Harwood desiring him to examen it, & let me know what he thought of it, his answer was that it was small but of good workmanship & an elegant attitude & wou'd make a very

> agreable statue of the size wanted. from this report, I desir'd he might proceed, & hop'd much from him, who I had piqu'd to execute this well & who I knew to be realy a clever workman. Breton who happen'd to be lately at Florence & saw this figure assur'd me it wou'd be a good one, & I don't imagine he wou'd be apt to give a Brother Sculptor undeserv'd praise. This makes me wish that my L.[d] wou'd have at least allow'd it to come to Eng[d] where if it was condemn'd, I'm perswaded he cou'd easily dispose of it without any loss, which will not be so easy at Florence. This statue, freight &c won't cost my L.[d] upwards of £150 & in London you know the common price of statues are £250 & £300. But what in this affair concerns me most is lest my L.[d] shou'd discover a small difference of size betwixt the other originals & copys, which tho' not so different as that at Florence yet may have some little difference in order to addapt them to their niches, a liberty which I never coud have dreamt wou'd have diminish'd the merit of a copy. as to any other article they are in no ways alter'd from the Antique & no liberty taken. In short I leave it entirely to you to mannage my L.[d] the best way you can.[65]

James Adam selected the *Apollino* for reproduction for Lord Northumberland on the basis of Adam's secondhand encounter with it as an engraved copy (fig. 63): plate 8 in volume 3 of Gori's *Museum Florentinum* (Florence, 1734). In this instance, a deluxe library volume devoted to a collection in Florence was utilized by the middleman in Rome as a catalog for modern reproductions. The engraved copy may well have confirmed that the Apollino's attitude was the most agreeable that could be confined to the size of the niche, being a freestanding sculpture supported by a tree trunk, but it gave no indication of the dimensions of the original.[66] Rather, Adam wrote to the copier, Francis Harwood in Florence, asking him to examine it. As Adam tells it, the choice of the *Apollino* was ultimately determined by the copier with access to the ancient prototype. Lest Harwood's professional judgment should be called into question by the patron, Adam's letter proceeds to cite the favorable opinion of fellow sculptor Luc-François Breton, who saw the *Apollino* face-to-face in the Tribuna and endorsed its reproduction. One of the difficulties this case illuminates is the degree to which a commission for copies was managed, or *mis*managed, by the middleman in Rome.

Unlike James Adam choosing the *Apollino* for reproduction for Northumberland with the endorsement of the sculptor-copier but without seeking the patron's initial consent, the Scottish architect John Baxter was more circumspect. He was instructed in 1765 by his father, also John Baxter, "to find out the best antique masculine figures in rome, as companions to stand in niches" in Sir James Clerk's new dining room at Penicuik outside Edinburgh.[67] Baxter forwarded sketches from an unnamed sculptor of the *Apollino*, the *Borghese Faun*, the *Apollo Belvedere,* and the

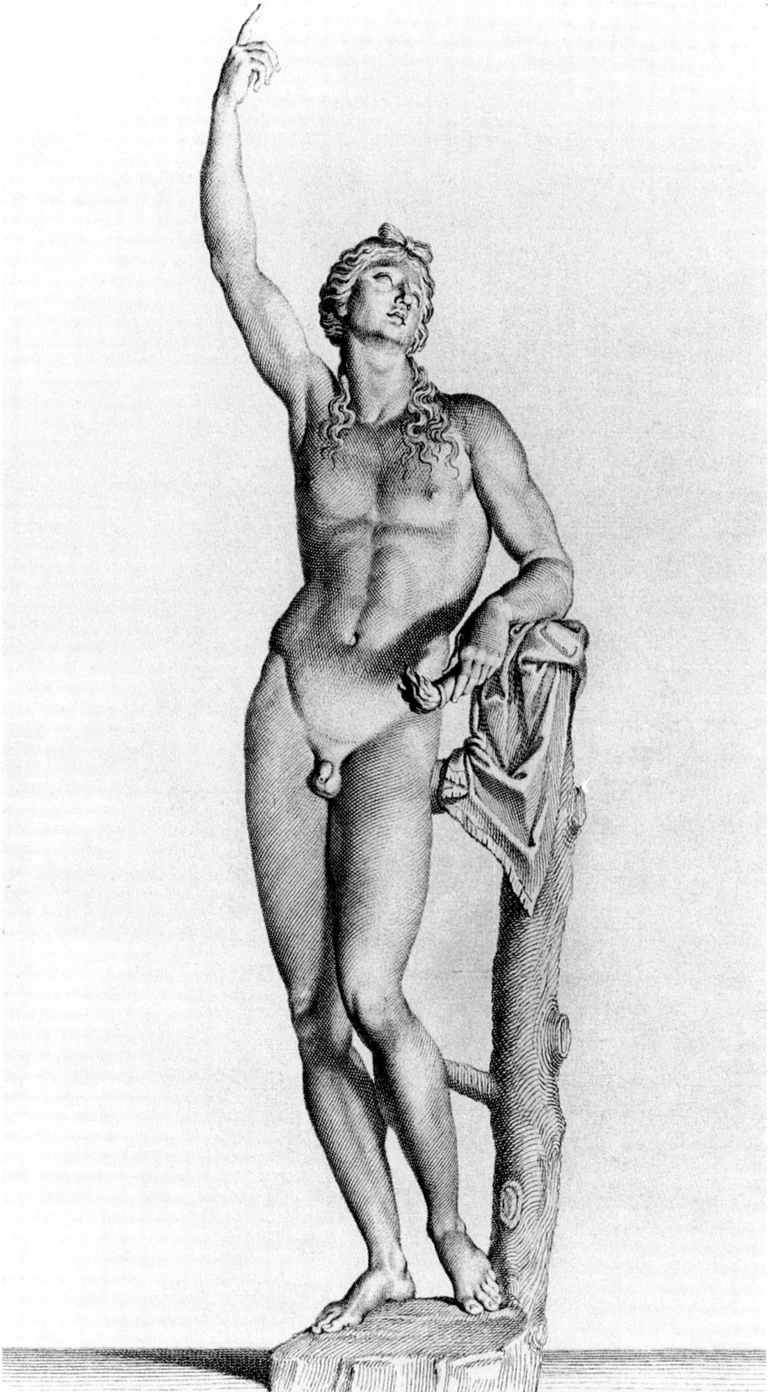

Figure 63 *Apollino*: "the most agreeable attitude of any that cou'd be confined to the size of the nich." *Museum Florentinum* (Florence, 1734), vol. 3, plate 8. The Warburg Institute.

Figure 64 Sketches of the *Apollino*, the *Borghese Faun*, the *Apollo Belvedere,* and the *Capitoline Antinous* supplied to Sir James Clerk from Rome, 1765. By permission of Sir R. M. Clerk Bt.

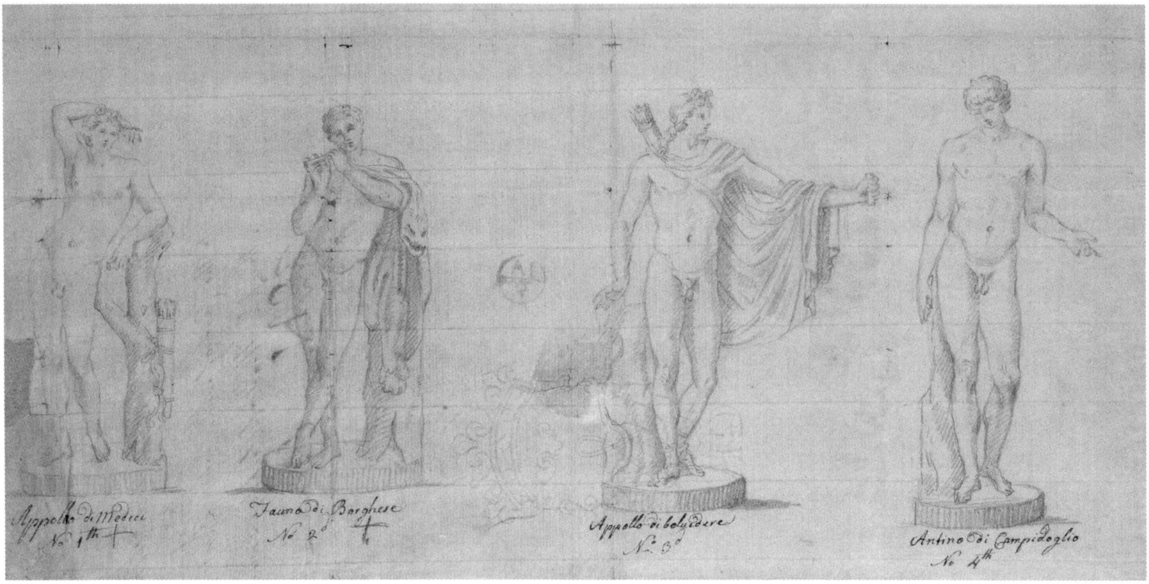

Capitoline Antinous (fig. 64). As a concession to the strict moral codes of cold Caledonia, he also added a note bene that these naked male statues were "to have dresserie on their middle parts." Waiting for Sir James's reply regarding his preference for the two male sculptures, Baxter wrote that he had already "sett to work the sculptor with the [Farnese] flora which I think there can be no doubt of being the best that can be chose." The Flora's impeccable credentials were (seemingly) matched by those of the anonymous sculptor, who Baxter describes as "the best in Rome for coppying statues and he has sent to Carrara for the best marble" in advance "as it takes a sculptor seven or eight months to do a statue." By 30 March 1770, John Clerk wrote from Rome to his uncle that he was "glad to hear that Sr James's statues [of the *Apollino* and the *Borghese Faun*—with the appropriate 'dresserie'] please they are Copys of fine things but much inferior to several in Rome. After seeing the Appollo of the Belvidera most of the other statues seem to have been carved by Sandy Thompson or some such Artist."[68] This is another instance of the contemporary copy in Britain being superseded by viewing the ancient masterpieces in Rome.

What the Adam brothers' patron, Lord Northumberland, apparently objected to was how far his *Apollino*, copied by the sculptor Francis Harwood (fig. 65), had adapted the height of the ancient statue in Florence to five feet (1.52 m). In the patron's eyes, such license was enough to diminish the merit of a copy whose original was famed for its small size (1.41 m). Given that this minute (11 cm) discrepancy was of such concern to Northumberland, what worried James Adam most was whether "my L.[d] shou'd discover a small difference of size betwixt the other originals & copys." Adam maintained that "as to any other article they are in no ways alter'd from the Antique and no liberty taken." The hardest client to please was one who commissioned a copy and had it tailor-made for a predetermined space but wanted to appropriate in perfect form the esteem of the original. Adam's letter further elucidates the cachet of the copy as exotic souvenir.[69] A copy handmade in Florence for the sum of £150 would be more easily sold at a profit in London, where the "common price" was said to be £250 or £300.

In another documented commission for copies that predates those at Syon and Penicuik, the unique bronze cast is said to *surpass* its ancient model and this is unprecedented. The commission dates from the late 1750s, when John Parker was employed at Rome as an agent by the Irish aristocrat James Caulfield, first Earl of Charlemont. Parker wrote regularly to his patron, who had recently completed his grand tour, of the progress of outstanding commissions. On 28 February 1756, for instance, Parker informed him that the British sculptor Simon Vierpyl had sent the plaster casts of "the little Apollo and the Mercury in the Farnese Gallery which I judged the best companion and which your lordship will find the print of in the 'Raccolta di statue di Roma.'"[70] Vierpyl's casts united the *Apollino* and *Mercury* as a pair in a novel arrangement that was physically impossible for their ancient marble prototypes, which were housed in elite collections in Florence and Rome. Parker referred his patron to the print of the Mercury *Mercury* published as plate 57 in Domenico de Rossi's *Raccolta di statue di Roma* (1704; fig. 66): a folio volume that was part of Charlemont's library collection. On this occasion, the engraved copy, disseminated outside Italy by publication, was cited as a guidebook for the patron, anticipating a plaster copy from Rome. In the same letter, Parker went on to describe the problems encountered in obtaining a license to mold new copies in the Farnese gallery. By 4 October 1758, he described the situation vis-à-vis the bronze cast of the Farnese *Mercury*:

> The Mercury cost more than I apprehended at first, as on the agreement, not being before the statue to examine it, since taken out of the garden, and put up in the gallery, I did not know it had been broke in several parts, viz.: the body split from the bottom of the belly to the throat, the leg it stands on, broke under the knee, the arm also, that holds the wand; and the whole so badly mended as to lap over a finger thick in the juncture; so that to remedy this in our cast, I was obliged first to cast it in soft wax, and have it all retouched by signore Pietro Braeir [Bracci], the best sculptor now here, and then remould this cast retouched to get a proper cast in the hard composition of wax they cast the metal from. . . the above all done, this cast is turned out much better than the original.[71]

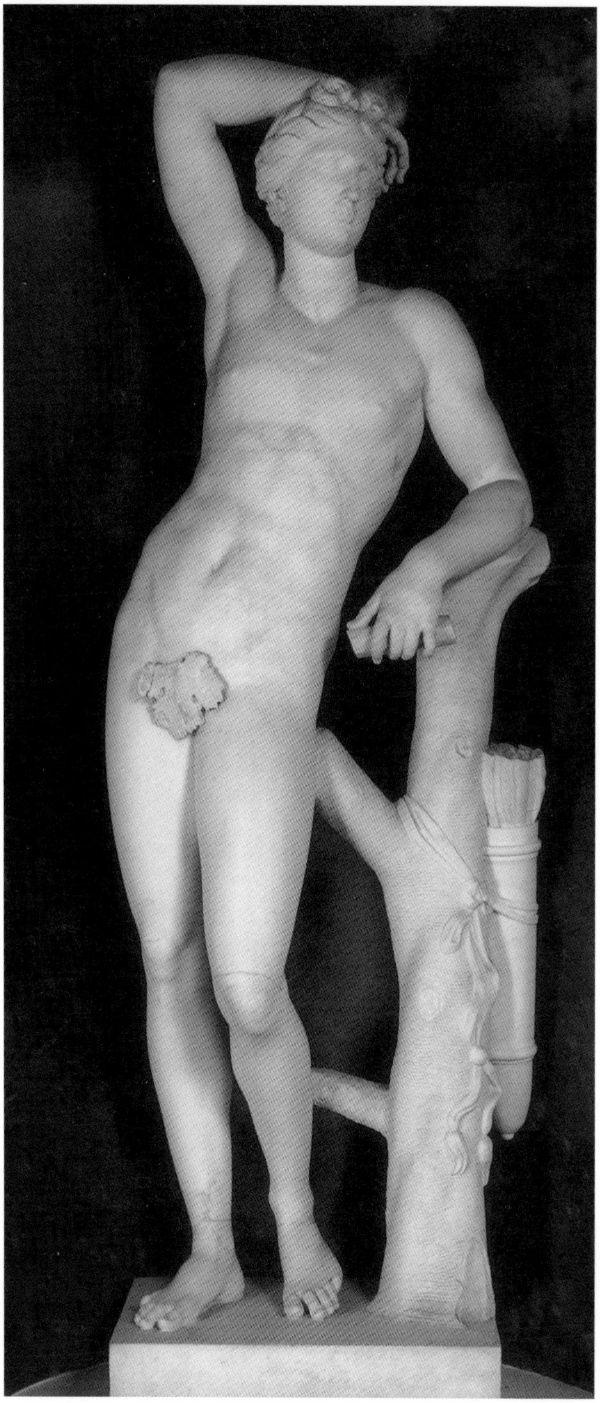

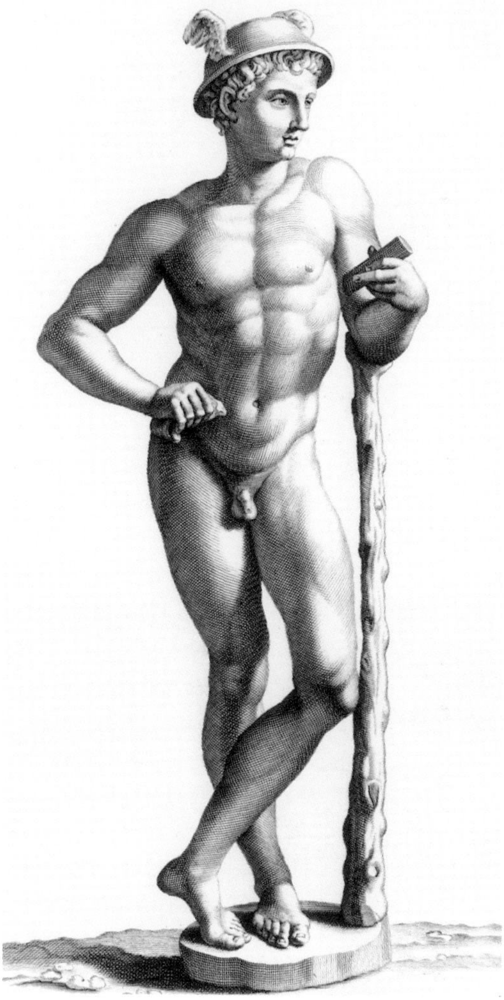

Figure 65 *(left)* Marble copy of the *Apollino* by Francis Harwood. Collection of the Duke of Northumberland. Photograph: Photographic survey, Courtauld Institute of Art.

Figure 66 *(right)* *Mercury*. Domenico de Rossi, *Raccolta di statue di Roma* (Rome, 1704), plate 57. The Warburg Institute.

Charlemont's retouched cast was superior to the original, badly mended *Mercury*. In its new, pristine condition, it was arguably closer to the ancient original prior to its later, clumsy restorations. Again we see not only the esteem of the modern copy but also esteem for the copier Pietro Bracci, who is described as "the best sculptor now here."[72] Charlemont's *Mercury* had the additional advantage over the original of rotating; by means of iron pins which screwed into a base "it may be turned round, to examine it on all sides, without any danger of its falling, or the person that views it changing his place."[73] However, the model for Charlemont's bronze copy that was cast in wax, retouched, remolded in wax, and copied, was itself a sixteenth- or seventeenth-century bronze copy of the marble *Mercury* in the Uffizi in Florence.[74] The Uffizi *Mercury* was one of the readymade casts that Lyttleton had ordered from Florence in 1756. So when Parker writes that Charlemont's *Mercury* is "turned out much better than the original," the original he is referring to is actually a copy.

This commission highlights additional problems encountered when thinking about the relationship between original antique sculptures and their postantique reproductions. A canonical original in its familiar context, the marble *Mercury* in the Uffizi in Florence, for instance, arguably retains some degrees of originality when reproduced in an unfamiliar medium and context—in bronze in the Farnese collection at Rome. Within the context of Charlemont's collection, the Farnese *Mercury* was represented as print, plaster, and bronze; embodying the scale and range of modern reproductions, from mass produced engraving in Rossi's *Raccolta di statue* to readymade plaster cast by Vierpyl, to tailor-made, unique bronze copy by Pietro Bracci.

The further cachet of the copy is articulated for us by Simon Vierpyl, the sculptor who cast the *Apollino* and *Mercury* in plaster for Lord Charlemont and who copied the *Apollino* and *Dancing Faun* in marble for Wentworth Woodhouse. While in Rome, Charlemont's tutor, Edward Murphy, commissioned Vierpyl to copy in clay some twenty-two statues and seventy-eight busts from the Capitoline museum, whose ancient sculpture collection was described in glowing literary terms as "the great book of antiquarians."[75] Some years after the commission was executed, Murphy wrote to Vierpyl enquiring about the value of his imperial series "modelled for me at Rome from the true antique originals by your most masterly hands."[76] Part of Vierpyl's reply, dated 15 August 1774, reads as follows:

> Your happy and, I believe, singular thought (of getting the whole original series copied, and this by one artist only) has never before, not to this day been executed by any sculptor except me. So that your imperial series is the only one of the kind now in the world: which gives it an immense additional value, especially as it is probable

> in the highest degree that an equal series will never again be made; for . . . I am certain that no eminent artist will hereafter stand four years, winter and summer (as I have done) in the chilling Capitoline Museum to model so many busts and statues with his own hand, except he be tempted with such a reward as none but a monarch, or other man of vast superfluous wealth, can conveniently pay. And as for any series made by a great number of different hands . . . I hope I may without vanity say, that it can stand in no comparison with yours. So that as yours now is, so it most probably will remain, the only series of the kind in the world.[77]

Indulging Vierpyl's vanity in flattering both himself and the patron, this letter (predictably) emphasizes the uniqueness of Wright's commission. Unlike the similarly unique collection at, for example, Syon House—which united in bronze, plaster, gilt, and marble copies of originals dispersed throughout Europe and executed by a number of foreign and native sculptors in Rome—Wright's collection reproduced an imperial series en bloc, executed in situ over four years—if we believe Vierpyl—by one sculptor. These statues and busts, individually copied in terracotta, a material Vierpyl considered "much more natural" than marble, came together to furnish a collection of reproductions that truly was "the only one of the kind now in the world." According to Vierpyl, its international status was unlikely to be threatened in the future, given the working conditions imposed on the sculptor and the excess of funds needed by the patron. Rather, Wright's series copied from ancient originals would itself become antiquities and would "last in their original perfection for thousands of years."

When Edward Murphy died in 1777, his collection of imperial statues and busts passed to his former pupil, Lord Charlemont. Charlemont displayed Vierpyl's seventy-eight busts in the Rockingham Library at Charlemont House in Dublin (fig. 67), designed by James Gandon and completed in the early 1780s.[78] The library was named after Joseph Nollekens's portrait bust of the Whig leader Lord Rockingham, which took pride of place in a niche over the chimneypiece. Although esteemed by the dealer James Tyrell as "fine historical ornaments in a Hall and . . . good company for men of Worth & Letters," busts of ancients particularly gravitated towards the *library*.[79] In *Travels through Italy* (London, 1766), John Northall claimed that of all the entertainments the country had to offer, the observation of antique statues was the most agreeable.

> To see the emperors, consuls, generals, orators, philosophers, poets and other great men, whose fame in history engaged our earliest notice, standing as it were in their own person before us, gives a man a cast of almost 2000 years backwards, and mixes the past ages with the present. We can see the beauties too of those early times; to

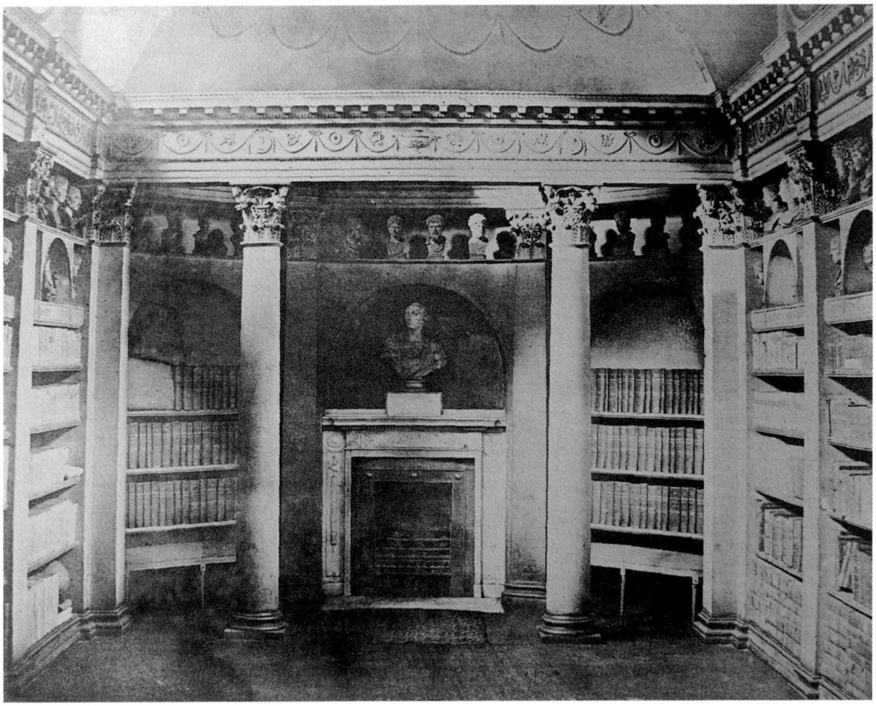

Figure 67 The Rockingham Library at Charlemont House, Dublin, c. 1865. By permission of the Royal Irish Academy © RIA.

> say nothing of the ideal ones, the nymphs and goddesses. Besides the countenance, we see in the statues the habits of those times, which give a complete idea of the whole person, and in that respect make every portrait a history piece.[80]

For classically educated British travellers already intimate with those in Northall's inventory, the ancient sculptures in Italian collections brought them face-to-face with material representations of their schoolboy heroes. As such, portrait busts of eminent ancients were seen as embodying the lessons of Roman history in material form; for Tobias Smollett the Medici collection of busts seemed "a most excellent commentary upon Roman historians, particularly Suetonius and Dion Cassius."[81] The dealer Tyrell wrote from Florence to Ralph Howard encouraging him to commission marble copies of busts by Giovanni Piamontini for the hall of his Irish Palazzo:

> The Tully [Cicero] & Seneca being intended for your Uncle Lord Chief Justice Singleton, I presume you'll have another pair for your own Palazzo, to inspire good morals & Patriotisme to certain Bucks who begin to prefer amor pecuniae to

> the inestimable amor Patriae . . . Antonia is a handsome Busto; and the life of that vertuous Pagan Lady would be an exceeding good model for our Christian ones; she was wife to brave honest Drusus, and mother of the incomparable Germanicus; nor was it her fault if her Father Anthony was as great a Rascal as was ever tuck'd up at Tyburn; Caesar and he deserv'd such a Fate ten thousand times more than Jonathan Wild & Turpin; and to the honour of her memory be it said that by her noble insinuations the Husband & son intended to repair all the mischief that was done by the former well match'd pair; I think therefore that it would be an elegant compliment to the Ladies to see a Busto of this worthy one in your house; and as Cicero was a friend to vertue in all shapes I am sure he'll have no objection to her company, altho' the Daughter of the worst of men & his Enemy; another Busto, a greek one well preserved, is that of the famous Lesbian Sappho, who was a prodigy of parts & deservedly called the 10th Muse; surely this would be agreeable to our women & all the admirers of the belles Lettres; herein youll find drawings of the four [Cicero, Seneca, Antonia, and Sappho], & if you chuse to have them, Sig. Piamontini shall coppy them, to the utmost perfection of Art, for one hundred and twenty sequins Bustoes, Pedestals, & Stands; and all exceedingly well polished.[82]

Tyrell's letter proffers a brief survey of Antonia's biography as a subtext to her bust copied by Piamontini. This Roman woman is described and defined in terms of her relationship with famous Roman men—variously as wife, mother and daughter. It is striking that Tyrell characterizes Antonia's bust and that of the Greek poetess Sappho as compliments, or models, to the *women* in Howard's company. Like one Richard Bull's daughter "become quite knowing in the history of Greece and Rome" from reading the volumes of the *Museum Worsleyanum*, women were not entirely excluded from the lessons of the classical tradition.[83] In fact, there is evidence that many eighteenth-century British women were classically educated. Although there was no formal schooling or counterpart to educational institutions like Eton or Westminster for aristocratic girls, they and their contemporaries from the upper and middling classes were taught Latin either in classes at school or at home by private tutors or a family member. Others were self-taught. It is often difficult to identify these learned ladies (as they were pejoratively known) and to assess the extent of their classical education, since women were not encouraged to think of themselves as learned.[84] Yet some eighteenth-century girls, like their brothers, would have been inculcated in their youth in a classical program of thought. Hence Lady Anne Miller's *Letters from Italy* have been quoted many times in this narrative, and Lady Louisa Conolly's and Lady Sarah Bunbury's roles in the decoration of the "pompeian" gallery at Castletown House are discussed in chapter 4.

In *Notes of a Journey through France and Italy* (London, 1824) William Hazlitt describes history as "vague and shadowy, but sculpture gives life and body to it; the names and letters in timeworn books start up real people in marble."[85] A century earlier, Sir John Clerk went so far as to suggest that ancient material artifacts might supersede textual sources and linguistic aids, being "a better way to form our knowledge upon that we can have from any Grammars or Dictionaries or whatsoever or even from any of the antient authors."[86] Clerk's library at Penicuik outside Edinburgh housed his collection of ancient artifacts along with books in all departments of literature, including various editions of the classics. In a draft letter composed in Latin to a friend, he explained his motivation behind the assemblage of texts and objects, regarding it "as a mean thing to build up a library of huge volumes on antiquities" and yet to overlook material artifacts, which "themselves speak and for the most part explain themselves; but descriptions, however accurate, present to the mind only confused or shadowy ideas."[87] Within Charlemont's late eighteenth-century library at Charlemont House in Dublin, Vierpyl's clay copies of busts in the Capitoline collection would have been accompanied by the books of the ancient authors who had preserved and perpetuated their imperial stories. An aristocratic library like Charlemont's, which was sold in 1865, would also have housed copies of contemporary grand tour publications devoted to the antique; deluxe volumes like F. Gori's *Museum Florentinum* and Domenico de Rossi's *Raccolta di statue di Roma,* which as we have seen were utilized as catalogs and guidebooks by dealers and collectors of copies of the antique.[88]

The display of sculpture in the neoclassical library like that of Charlemont also adhered to an ancient precedent as recorded in classical texts. In the *Naturalis Historiae* (35.ii.9), Pliny the Elder refers to the dedication and erection in libraries of gold, silver, or bronze statues of those divine men whose immortal spirits still speak in the places where their books are. With the revival of ancient learning in the fifteenth century, Renaissance scholars had crowned the bookshelves of their libraries with busts of eminent ancients.[89] In his *Instructions concerning erecting of a library* (London, 1661), Mazarin's librarian, Gabriel Naudé, recommended that

> good Copies drawn from such as are most famous in the profession of Letters; that thereby a man may at once make judgement of the wit of the Authors by their Books, and by their bodies; figure, and physiognomy by these Pictures and Images, which joyn'd to the description which many have made of their lives, may serve, in my opinion, as a puissant spurre to excite a generous and well-born Soul to follow their *track*, and to continue firm and stable in the wayes and beaten paths of some noble enterprise and resolution.[90]

By displaying Vierpyl's imitation imperial busts in the library at Charlemont House, Charlemont situated his collection and himself in a learned dialogue between, on the one hand, texts and artifacts, and on the other, between antiquity, the so-called Renaissance, and modernity. I will discuss the influence of sixteenth-century Italian collectors on their British eighteenth-century counterparts in more detail in the next chapter.

Thirty years after Edward Murphy commissioned his imperial series in Rome from the sculptor Simon Vierpyl, copies of busts intended for the library could be mail-ordered in a variety of media, including marble, bronze, plaster of paris, and scagliola. Take the following letter, dated 19 September 1781, from the dealer James Byres in Rome to Philip Yorke:

> Inclosed is also a note of some of the best Busts of Gods, & Goddesses, of Poets, Philosophers and learned Men for a Library, as also of some Greek kings and Hero's. You know we have all the Imperial Busts of the higher Empire ascertain'd so it's needless to mention them. the Busts of Poets, Philosophers &c which are commonly in this manner [sketch, see fig. 68, *top*] you may have cast in Bronze for twenty sequins each, or cut in white marble for twenty five sequins each. I must own, I think white Marble is of all substances, the best for sculpture as . . . the light penetrates into it and softens the lines as it does in living figures.—the other Busts, such as the Imperial, the Gods, demi Gods, Goddesses and Hero's, generally are cast in Bronze from twenty five to thirty sequins, but they cannot be well executed in Marble under forty five or fifty, the little augmentation of size as also the time it requires to work the drapery [sketch, see fig. 68, *bottom*] on the shoulders and breast, makes this great difference of price in marble, for in Bronze it is cast and soon repaired, so that the principal difference is in the weight of metal.- the price of Busts in Scagliola, is from a sequin and half to three sequins, and in paris plaister from a sequin to two sequins provided there be molds of them, but if the molds must be made on purpose, they'll cost at least double that price. the casing imbaling & freight of these last will be as much as of Marble or Bronze and the risque of their being broke greater. as you are pleased to ask my opinion, I think for the Busts in the stile of the Philosophers or Hermes as we call them, I would rather give twenty five sequins for marble, than twenty for Bronze, especially as they'll probably be placed on Bookcases at a certain distance from the Eye, where the darkness of Bronze would confuse the features. for the Busts of Hero's &c I must own, paying double the price, seems a great deal; I should be much regulated according to the places they were destined for: if in a strong light near the Eye and the Room finish'd in light colours, I would have them of Bronze, if otherwise, of Marble, but you will be the best judge of all this.[91]

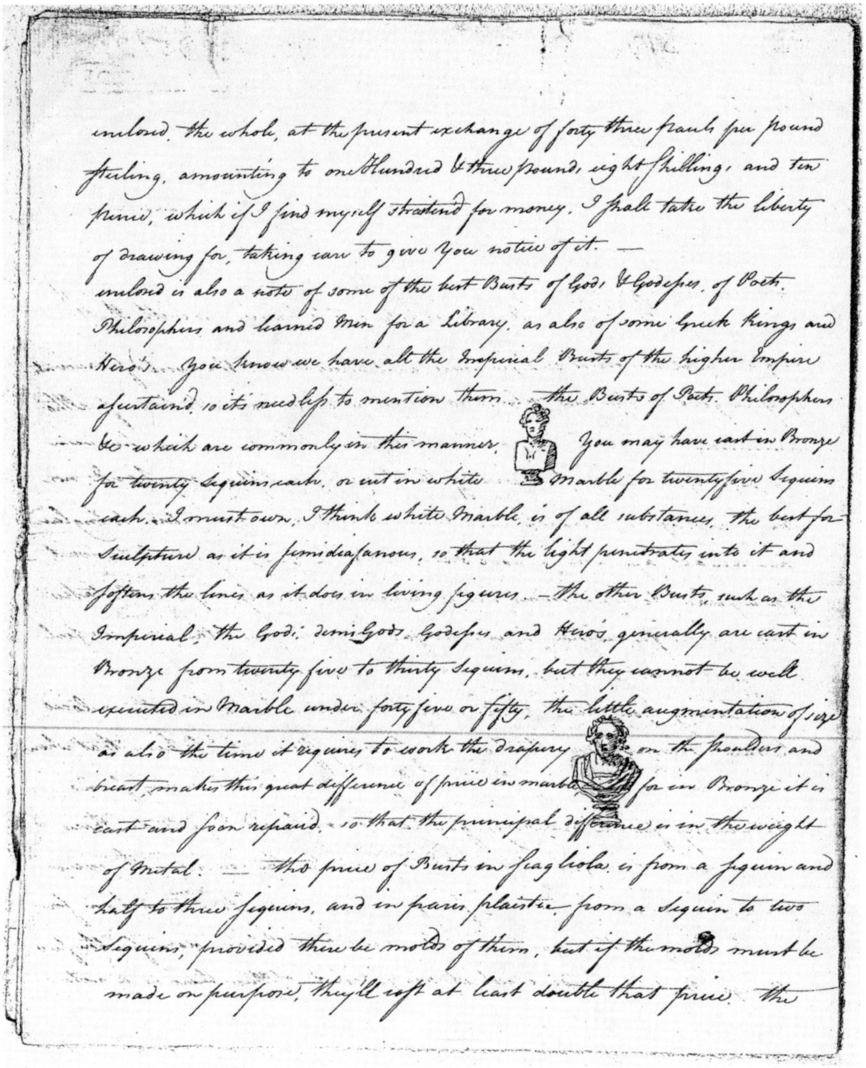

enclosed the whole, at the present exchange of forty three pauls per pound sterling, amounting to one Hundred & three pounds, eight shillings, and ten pence, which if I find myself straitened for money, I shall take the liberty of drawing for, taking care to give You notice of it. —

enclosed is also a note of some of the best Busts of Gods & Godesses, of Poets. Philosophers and learned Men for a Library, as also of some Greek Kings and Hero's. You know we have all the Imperial Busts of the higher Empire ascertained so it's needless to mention them. the Busts of Poets. Philosophers &c which are commonly in this manner, You may have cast in Bronze for twenty Sequins each, or cut in white Marble for twentyfive Sequins each. I must own, I think white Marble is of all substances, the best for Sculpture as it is semidiaphanous, so that the light penetrates into it and softens the lines as it does in living figures. — The other Busts, such as the Imperial, the Gods, demi Gods, Godesses and Hero's, generally are cast in Bronze from twenty five to thirty Sequins, but they cannot be well executed in Marble under forty five or fifty, the little augmentation of size as also the time it requires to work the drapery on the shoulders and breast, makes this great difference of price in marble for in Bronze it is cast and soon repaired, so that the principal difference is in the weight of Metal. — the price of Busts in Scagliola is from a sequin and half to three sequins, and in paris plaister from a Sequin to two Sequins, provided there be molds of them, but if the molds must be made on purpose, they'll cost at least double that price. the

Figure 68 Sketches by James Byres of Busts after the Antigne undraped and draped. Public Record Office of Northern Ireland.

While Vierpyl's busts for Murphy reproduced members of the Roman imperial family, Byres's letter organized the busts for sale and export into two collectable series: "Poets, Philosophers &c" and "the Imperial, the Gods, demi Gods, Goddesses and Hero's." A handmade bust from either series executed in marble was more expensive than a bronze cast, particularly for the latter series given the "the time it requires to work the drapery on the shoulders." A readymade scagliola and plaster of paris bust was at the cheaper end of the market, provided that the molds were already made up. As with commissions for casts of antique statues, the risk of plaster and scagliola busts breaking is mentioned. Byres advised Yorke to make a decision according to the intended location of the busts. Their height on top of bookcases and the colors of the decorative scheme ultimately determined the material of the copies. In this, we see how by the 1780s the reproduction of antique busts in Rome could be manipulated according to the whims of the absent patron and the aesthetic scheme of his library.

In a letter to his mother of 4 April 1767, Lord Kildare wrote, "There are here [Rome] two famous portrait painters. The one you have heard of; his name is Pompeio Battoni. The other is one Maron, a German, who is much cheaper—some reckon much better."[92] Having started the discussion of the cachet of the copy with Batoni's grand tour portrait of Thomas Dundas, it seems appropriate to close with an image of another classically educated British gentleman by Kildare's other famous portrait painter, Anton von Maron, the pupil and brother-in-law of Anton Raphael Mengs.[93] In von Maron's portrait of *William Constable and Winifred as Cato and Marcia* (1773; fig. 69), the English gentleman and his sister are represented as a historical Roman hero and his wife. Given that the painted portrait is always a visual re-presentation, or copy, of its subject, so Constable and his sister are both copied and cast *as* Cato and Marcia.[94] Constable, who was classically educated at the Roman Catholic school of Douai in northern France, would have known Cato as a late-republican hero canonized in the texts of Cicero, Lucan, Plutarch, Sallust, and Seneca. The great-grandson of Cato the Censor, Cato was an exemplary Roman republican living in an age characterized by vice and corruption. He tried to implicate Julius Caesar in the conspiracy of 63 B.C. in which Cataline tried to establish himself as caesar, as a result of which Cato was effectively exiled to Cyprus. Cato became leader of the republican cause after Pompey's death, but rather than accepting *clementia Caesaris*, he committed suicide in 46 B.C.[95] His end was deemed unworthy to readers of *A New Roman History by question and answer* (London, 1740), a textbook designed principally for use in schools.[96] In the bottom right of von Maron's painting are the discarded fasces, a potent symbol of Roman political authority and here a formal sign that Cato's term of office is over.[97] The portrait also recalls the classical literary tradition that created and disseminated Cato's fame into modernity. Inscribed onto a painted scroll in the hand of Constable-as-Cato is a quotation from Horace's *Odes* (2.i.23–24), "Cuncta Terrarum Subacta praeter Atrocem Animum Catonis" (All of the world has been subdued apart from Cato's ferocious spirit). In the preface of the 1741 edition of *The Odes, Epodes and Carmen Seculare*, Horace is credited with being "the only Poet who can form the Gentleman."[98] During the period 1660–1800 there were more new translations of Horace (thirty-seven) than any other Latin or Greek author.[99] Cicero came in a close second in the classical hit parade with thirty-five.

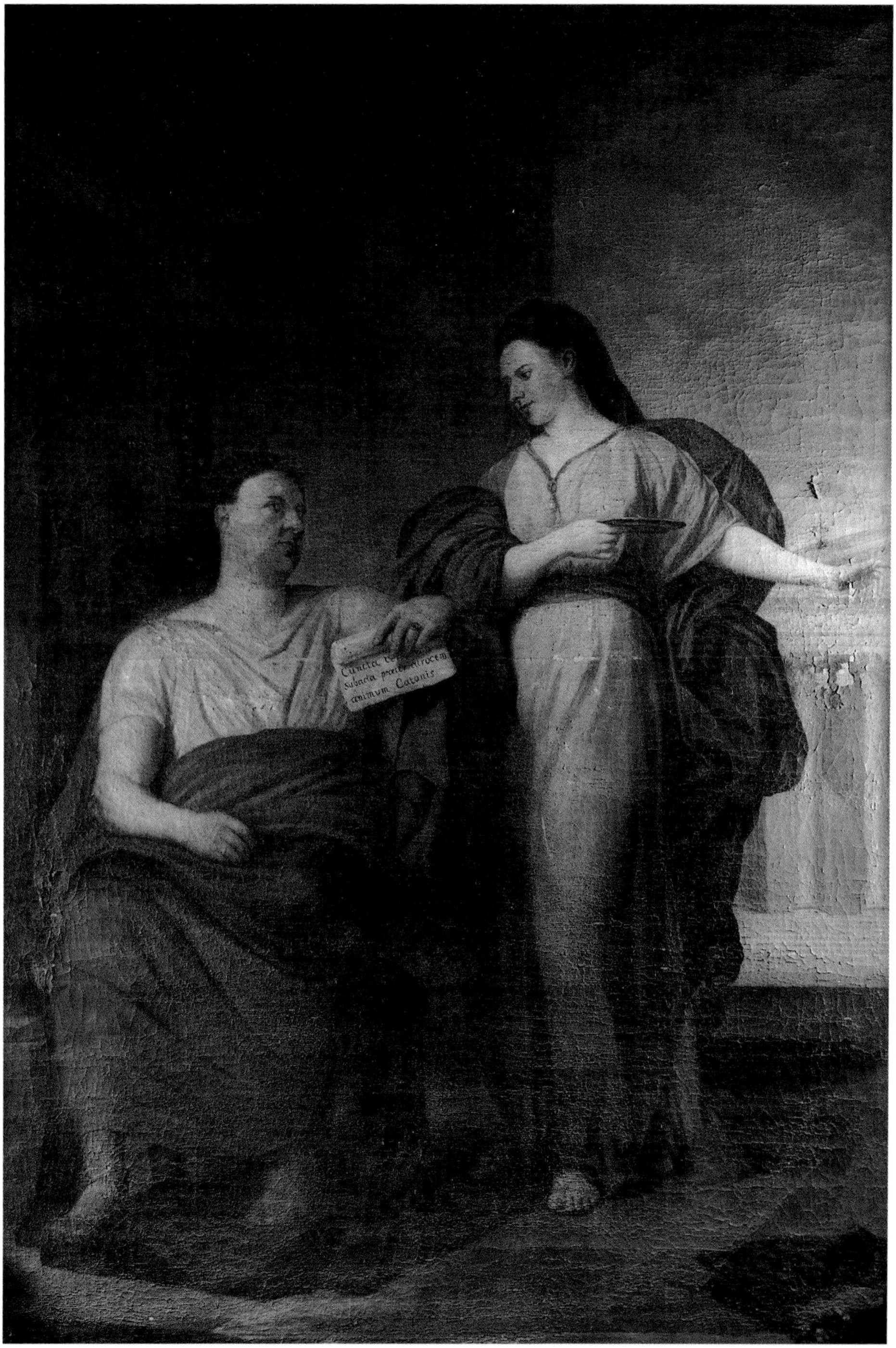
Cuncta te
subacta
animum Catonis

Constable commissioned his portrait from the Austrian court painter during one of his three grand tours to Italy. Its execution was delayed when an unexpected commission from Vienna required von Maron to produce a full-length portrait "of the late Emperour for an apartment that the Empress Queen is fitting up."[100] Precisely why our classically educated Yorkshire gentleman requested this specific historical model for his grand tour portrait remains open to interpretation. The discarded fasces may well be a reference to the exclusion of Roman Catholics from high office in Britain.[101] Constable the excluded Roman Catholic in a form of self-imposed exile in Italy is imaged as Cato the exiled and excluded Roman. Less obliquely, Constable may have cast himself as Cato as a means of appropriating the lasting, classicizing, fame of his model: a fate denied to Constable in public life in late eighteenth-century Britain but not in grand tour portraiture.[102]

Figure 69 *(left)* Anton von Maron, *William Constable and Winifred as Cato and Marcia*, 1773. Burton Constable Foundation. Photograph: Photographic survey, Courtauld Institute of Art.

Figure 70 *(bottom)* The Vatican *Menander*. The Conway Library, Courtauld Institute of Art. Photograph: Dr. Nicholas Penny.

In von Maron's portrait, it is not only the historical Roman hero that is borrowed from the classical tradition, since Constable's representation is itself a painted copy with Constable's portrait of an ancient marble statue *Menander* then in the Negroni collection (fig. 70). This seated sculpture, which is now identified as a portrait of an unknown Greek, whose head was recarved in the late-republican or early imperial period, was unearthed with a sculpture of another Greek poet, Poseidippos, in the late sixteenth century on the Viminial Hill in Rome.[103] The British sculpture collector Henry Blundell described in a letter to Charles Townley how he had seen the pair of marble poets at Rome in 1786 when they were in the possession of the dealer Thomas Jenkins.[104] Jenkins had acquired them from the Negroni collection in a dealer's coup that, as he wrote to Townley, made "as much Noise in Rome, as a Pitt or Fox in London."[105] Blundell's letter describes how the sculptures failed to answer his high expectations of them; expectations predicated on their reproduction ("y^{e} many casts & models"), their reputation in the Negroni

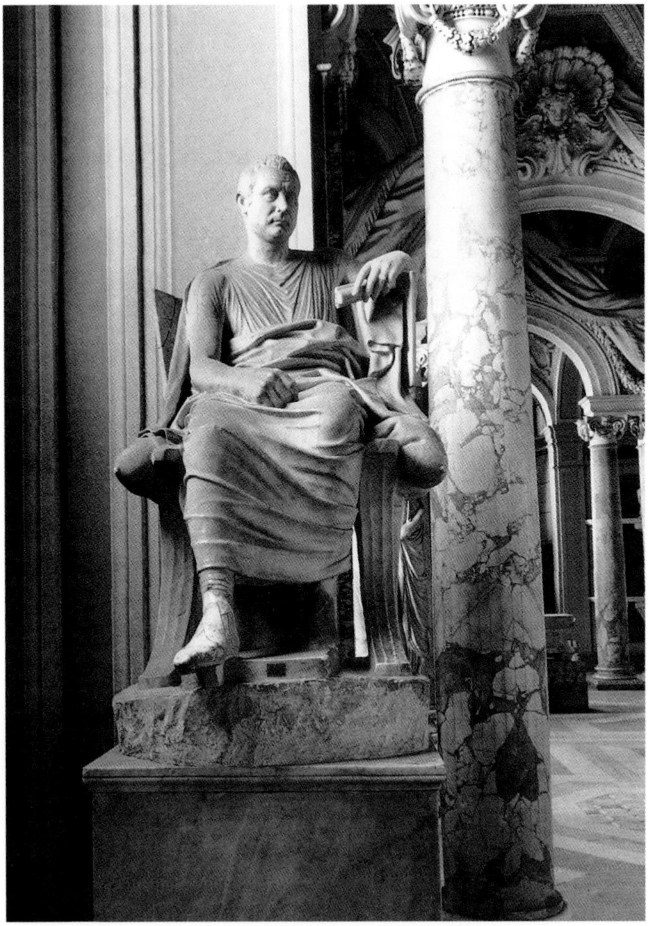

collection, and their price—an extraordinary £2000. His letter concedes them to be "2 respectable pieces of antiquity" having "a noble effect in that broad style of sculpture at y^{e} end of a gallery," but neither their respectability nor their nobility could, in his eyes, be justified by their price tag. Three years after Blundell's 1786 visit to Rome, his agent, Father Thorpe, wrote informing him that the pair of poets had been sold to the pope.[106] Thorpe's letters offers a summary of their merits: "In the ease of their sitting, & in their being a pair of equal size." But he also refers to their postantique defects—the sculptures were "too hastily rubbed by unskilfull Artists" when the figures were restored and exhibited in the Villa Negroni. The Reverend G. W. D. Evans later saw the poets in the Galleria della Statue of the Vatican museum "sit[ting] in their arm chairs, as they might be supposed to have done in their own studies."[107]

The *Menander* and *Poseidippos* were two more of the repertoire of ancient sculptural masterpieces to be serially reproduced in the late eighteenth century. Though

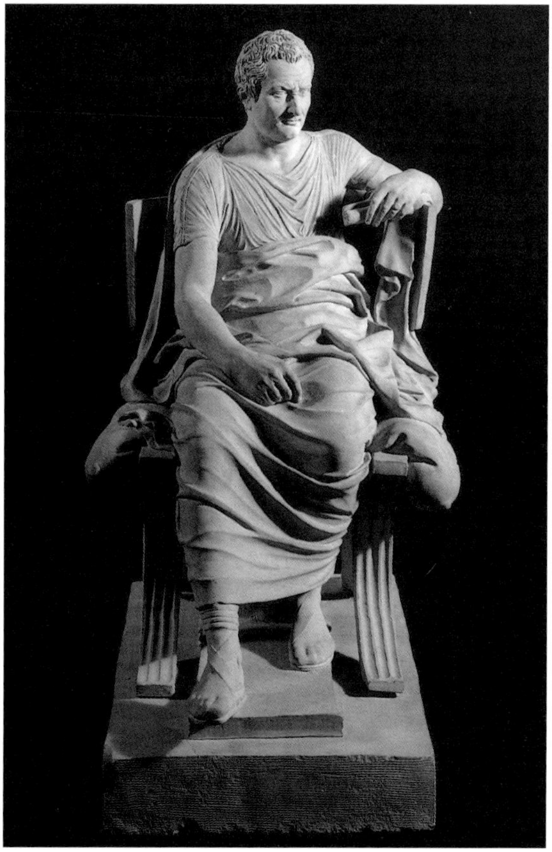

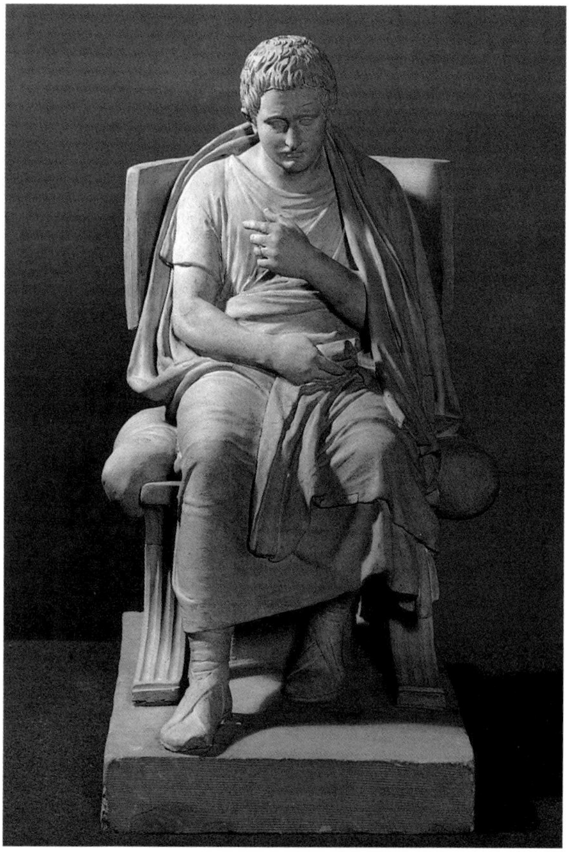

Blundell's letter describes being unable to reconcile the merits of the original sculptures with their £2000 price tag, they were still represented in his collection in the form of reduced, terracotta copies by the Roman sculptor Bartolomeo Cavaceppi (figs. 71a, 71b).[108] A statuette of the *Menander* in plaster of paris also survives at Burton Constable and may have provided a handy model for Constable's painted portrait. His dealer, James Byres, supplied him with lists of similar statuettes done in the antique style sold by Cavaceppi and Constantino Mazzoni. The Baron d'Ulanski visited the Volpato firm in Rome who manufactured examples "in unglazed China paste (biscotto)." These porcelain souvenirs, which he wrote "interest the dilettante, and do not disgrace even an elegant drawing-room," could be ordered in different groupings.[109] A miniature bronze *Menander* by Giacomo or Giovanni Zoffoli (fig. 72) forms part of a *garniture de cheminée* of five bronzes in the Saloon at Saltram House in Devon, where our Menander (29.1 cm tall) is paired with the *Seated Agrippina* (28.8 cm tall) after the original in the Capitoline Museum.[110] In the 1794 French-lan-

Figures 71a (*far left*) *Menander*. Terracotta copy by Bartolomeo Cavaceppi (51 cm high). National Museums Liverpool (The Walker).

Figure 71b (*left*) *Poseidippos*. Terracotta copy by Bartolomeo Cavaceppi (51 cm high). National Museums Liverpool (The Walker).

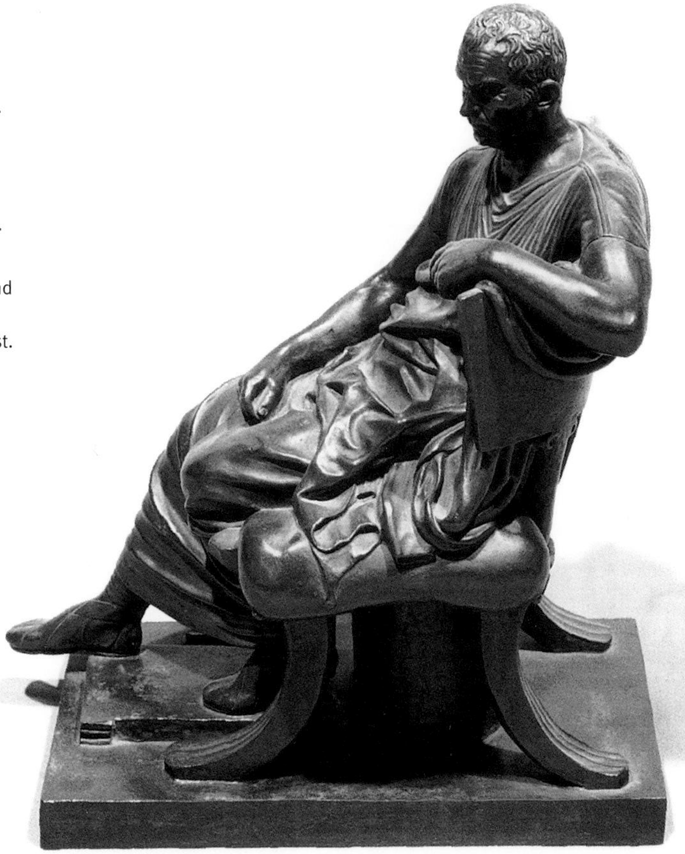

Figure 72 (*right*) *Menander*. Bronze miniature, by Giacomo and Giovanni Zoffoli (29.1 cm high). Saltram House, The National Trust.

guage catalog of bronze statuettes manufactured by Francesco Righetti, "Meneandre du Museum Vatican" is listed for sale at 20 sequins.[111] In much the same way that these miniature copies reproduce the ancient statue of *Menander* while translating its size and material, so Constable's representation by von Maron is a unique copy on canvas of an ancient statue that was serially reproduced.

While Constable's attitude is a recognizable copy of a celebrated ancient sculpture, Winifred's representation as Cato's wife Marcia appears to be influenced by ancient paintings newly discovered at the resuscitated sites of Pompeii and Herculaneum. The fact that access was restricted to both the original paintings in the Portici Museum and to their engraved reproductions in the *Antichità di Ercolano esposte* may explain why we are unable to identify the exact model for Winifred's representation. With her billowing drapery and sacrificial dish she suggests the Herculaneum dancers or twelve dancing Bacchants (figs. 73a, 73b). These small full-length female figures painted on black backgrounds were much admired by von Maron's acquaintance, Winckelmann, as "the work of some great master, for they are as light as thought itself, and as beautiful as if they had been done by the hands of the Graces."[112]

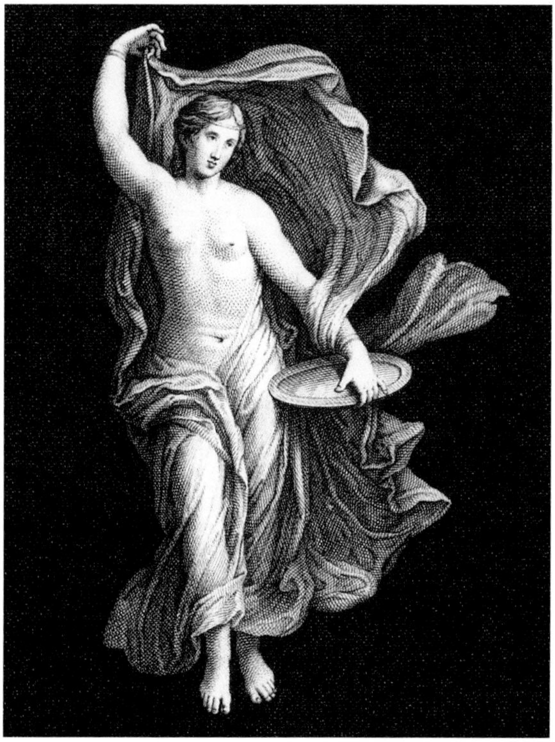

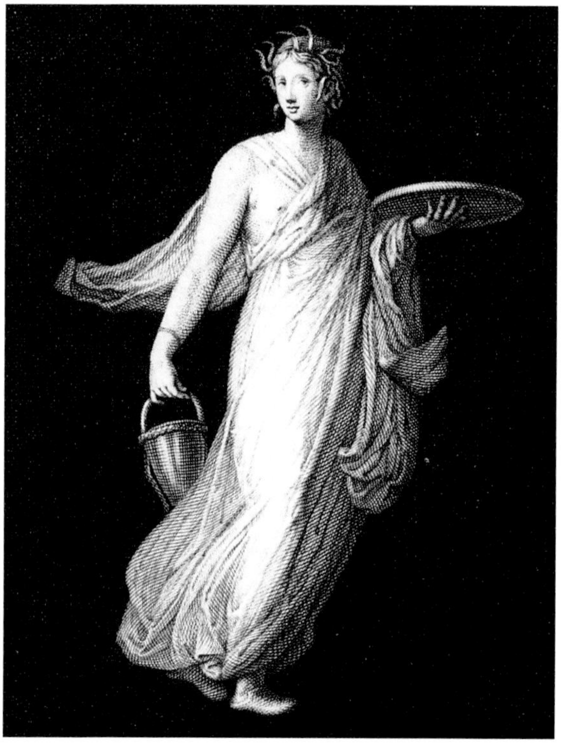

Figures 73a *Antichità di Ercolano esposte* (Naples, 1757), vol. 1, plate 19. The Warburg Institute.

Figure 73b *Antichità di Ercolano esposte* (Naples, 1757), vol. 1, plate 23. The Warburg Institute.

Just as Northall described every ancient statue in the museums of Rome as a history piece, so Anton von Maron's painting of William and Winifred Constable as Cato and Marcia is what we might call a piece of neoclassical art history.[113] It preserves the portraits, what Northall calls the countenance, of the Yorkshire Catholic gentleman and his sister and also the habits of the late eighteenth century. That is, when as a result of the styles of thought inculcated at public, or in Constable's case, at Catholic school, the antique functioned as a cultured *habitus* for members of the educated classes.[114] This educated elite did not simply collect copies of antique sculptures and busts "as seen" in royal and elite collections on the grand tour in Italy. They had them translated into a variety of aesthetic media, tailor-made by being enlarged to fit existing architectural and domestic spaces and juxtaposed in unusual pairs and different groupings. These novel reconfigurations ensured that the cachet of the copy complied with an elite British agenda of social emulation, aristocratic competition, and in the case of William Constable's grand tour portrait, self-representation.

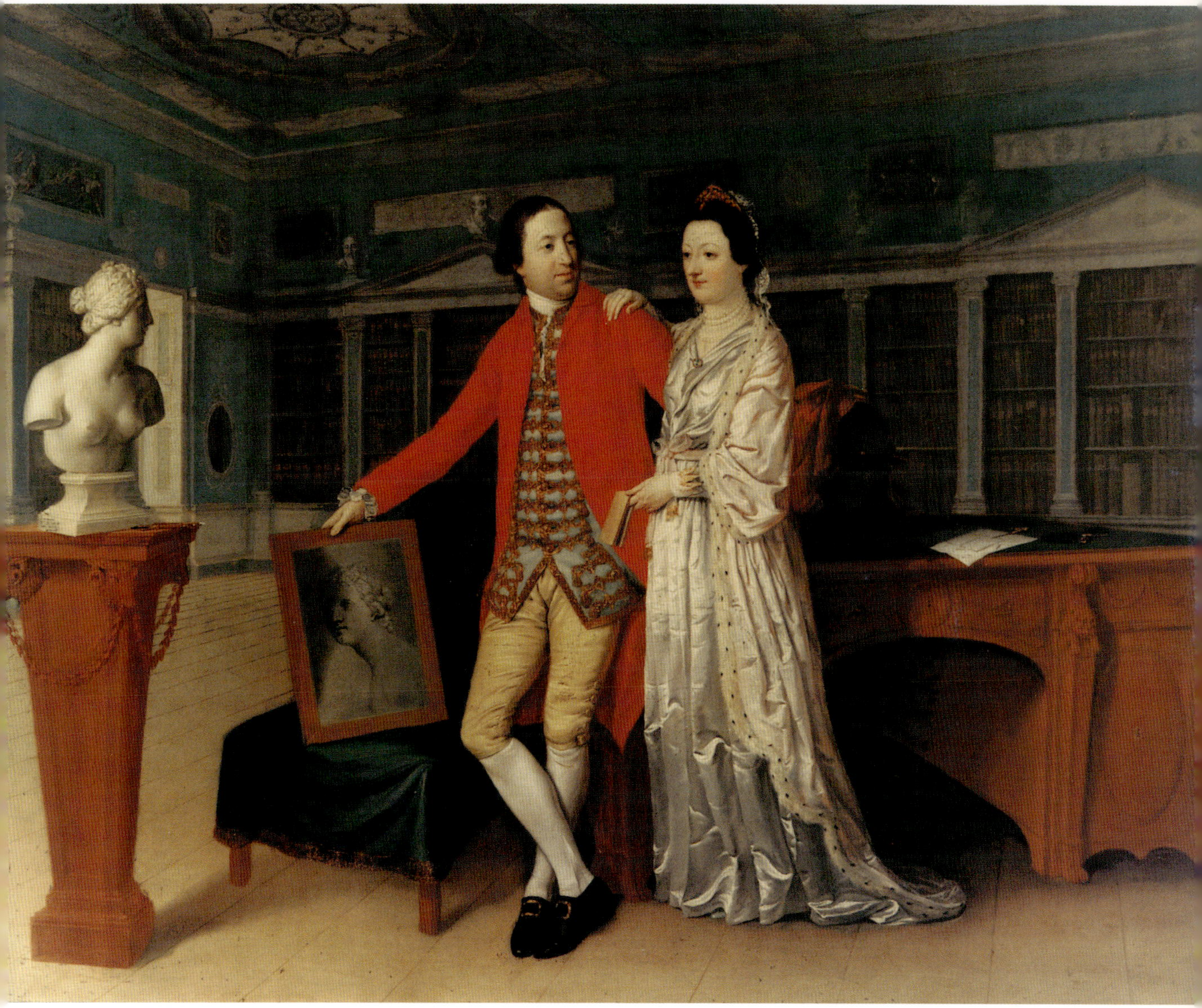

PLATE 1 “Certainly one of the greatest ornaments to a gentleman or to his family is a fine library.” Hugh Douglas Hamilton, *Sir Rowland and Lady Winn in the Library at Nostell Priory*, 1767–68. © Nostell Priory, The St. Oswald Collection (The National Trust).

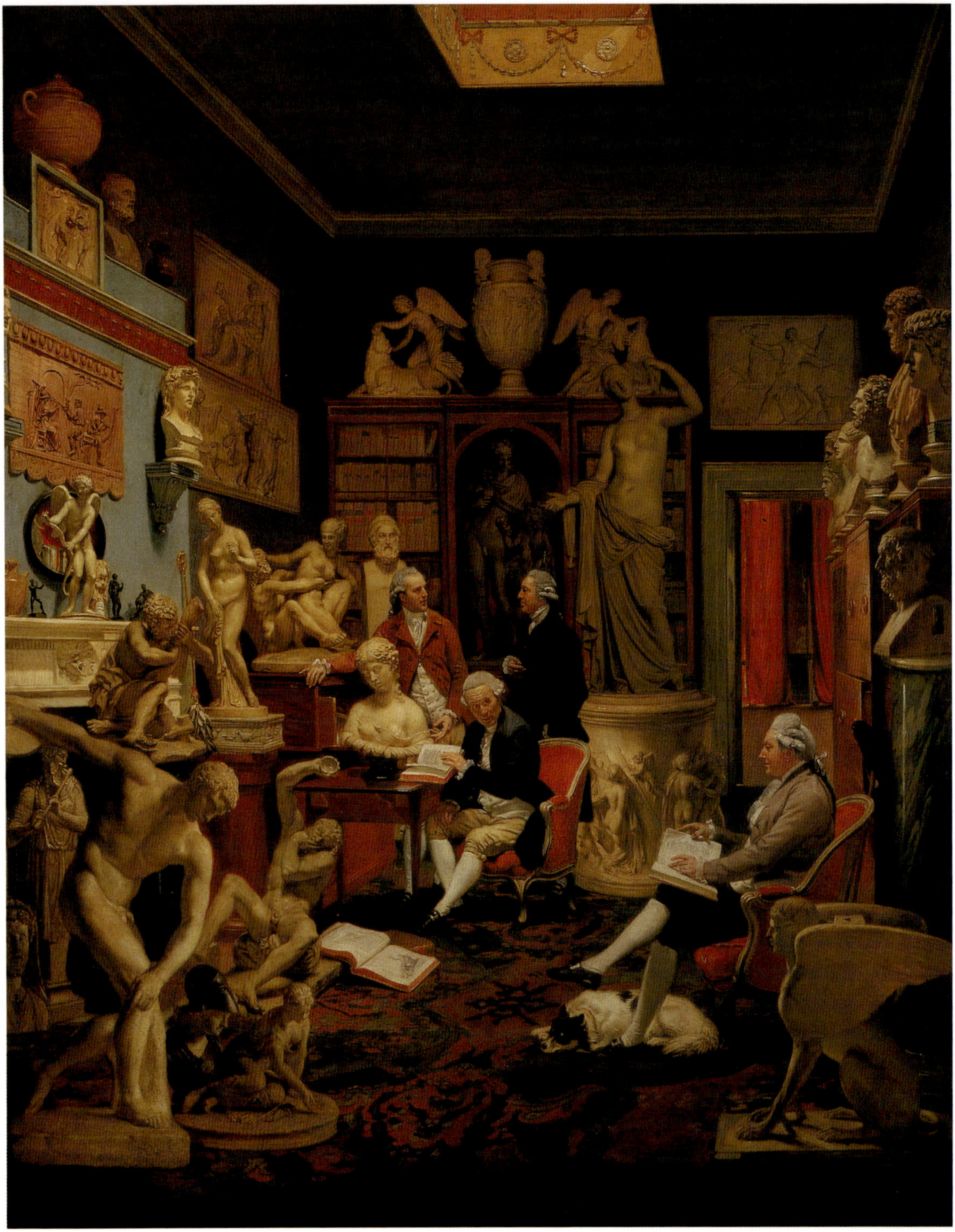

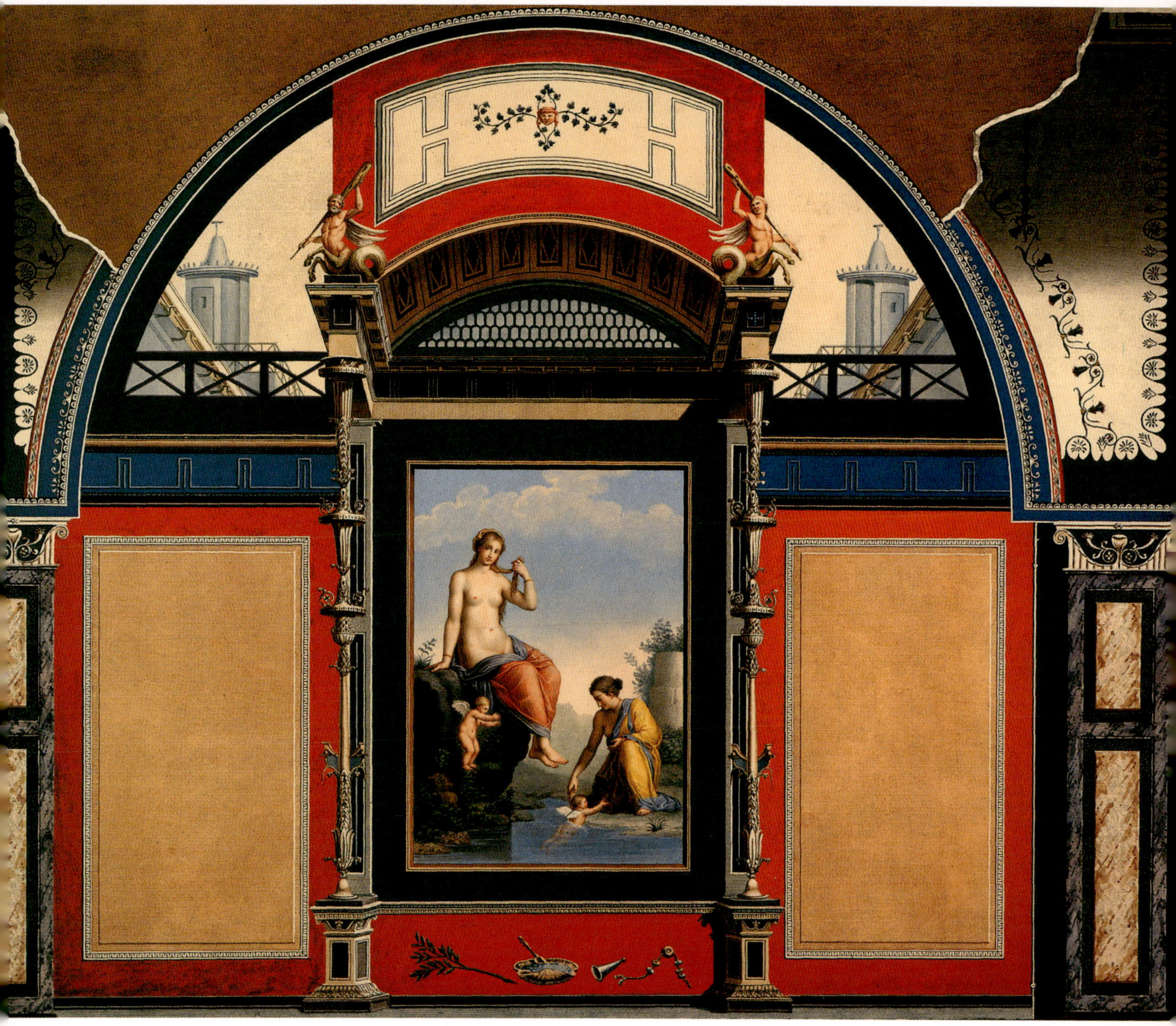

PLATE 3 "An idea of the taste of the ancients in this type of mixed ornamental and figural painting": an ancient wall scheme from the Villa Negroni, published by Camillo Buti. By courtesy of the Trustees of Sir John Soane's Museum.

PLATE 2 Johann Zoffany, *Charles Townley's Library at 7, Park Street, Westminster*, 1781–83/98. Towneley Hall Art Gallery & Museums, Burnley Borough Council.

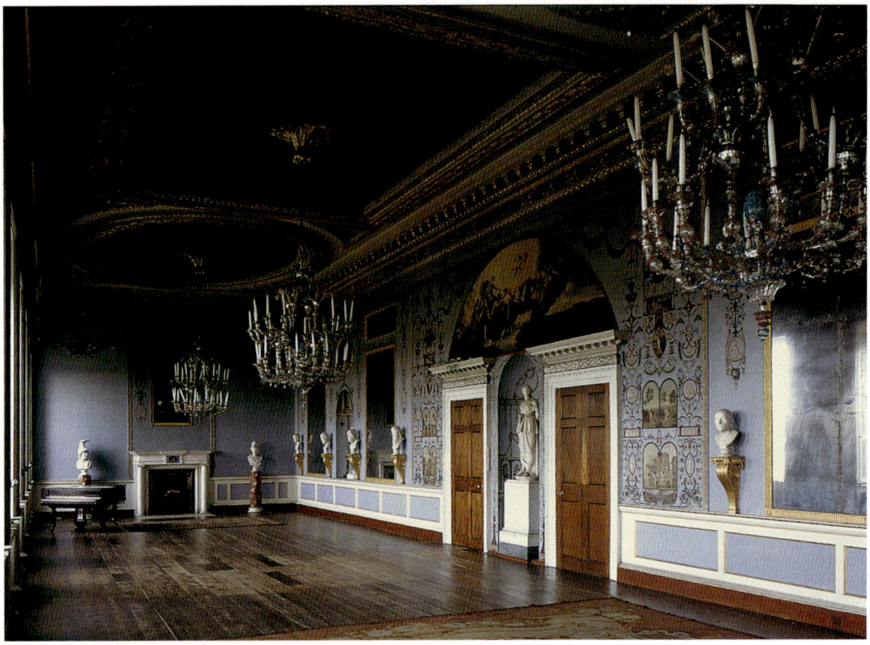

PLATE 4 The long gallery at Castletown House, Co. Kildare. David Davison / Country Life Picture Library.

PLATE 5 Vignette from the little drawing room at Audeley End, as reproduced in *Plans, Views and Drawings of the House and Grounds at Audeley-End in Essex* (1809). © English Heritage.

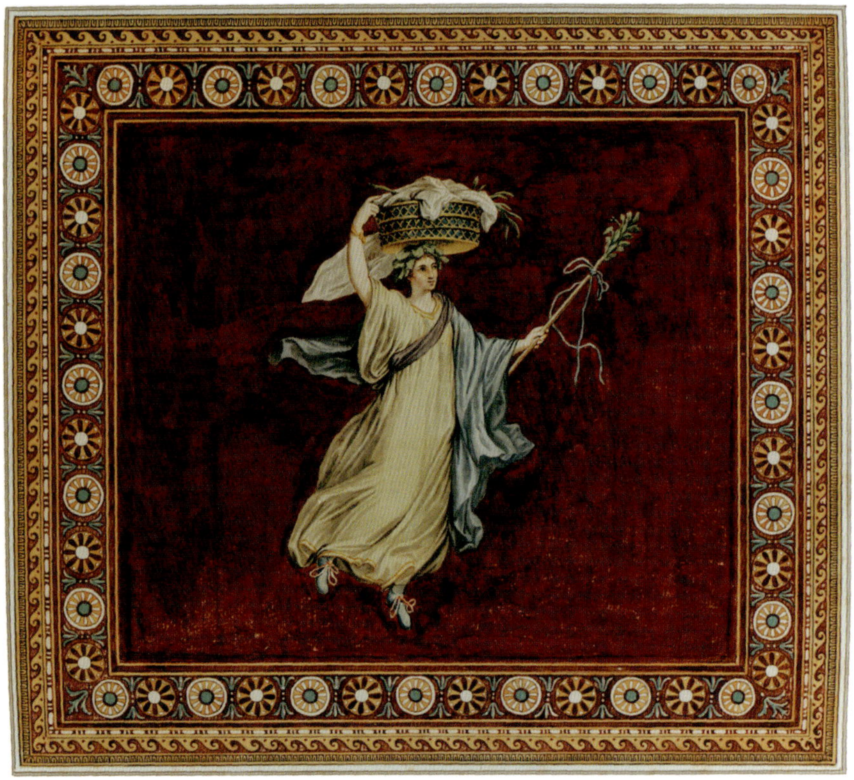

I wonder that no body in England take example from yourself in acquiring one or two real fine things especially as it is in the power of every private gentleman to do so, but I am afraid that we want that kind of sensibility which the Greeks had in perfection.

Gavin Hamilton to
Charles Townley,
letter dated 25 May 1793[1]

6

The Cream of Antiquity

Charles Townley and His August Family of Ancient Marbles

On 20 April 1782 the dealer Thomas Jenkins wrote from Rome to one of his British clients, the collector of ancient sculpture, Charles Townley:

> Sig.[a] Angelica [Kauffman] & Her Husband are here, their sentiments regarding your Collection & its Master are such as I am much interested in, and convinces me, that fine things will in time make their way, and I hope you will constantly have reason to be satisfied with having indulged your passions for the fine productions of the Ancients; indeed the contemplation of such, seems a kind of conversing with the celebrated Genius's of those remote times, and gives an ideal long life, as the Imagination produces a continuation or connection with the ages in which such interesting works were produced; but it does not become me to declaim on a subject, which you are so much master of.[2]

Johann Zoffany's painting *Charles Townley's Library at 7 Park Street, Westminster* (1781–83/98; plate 2) images this ideal conversation between the collector and those in his intimate circle with the "Genius's of those remote times" represented by his collection of ancient marble sculptures. This dialogue is mediated by both the learned library setting and the books prominently displayed in the painting. Townley on the right and Baron d'Hancarville in the center are both represented seated with open books. Indeed, the latter, installed in the very heart of the painting, celebrates the centrality of d'Hancarville's mystical theories about ancient art in interpreting the artifacts in Townley's collection. Having interred himself into the pages of one deluxe folio, Sir William Hamilton's *Collection of Etruscan, Greek and Roman Antiquities*, as we saw in chapter 2, d'Hancarville the antiquarian author was reborn in London at the expense of Townley and Richard Payne Knight.[3] "Few books, if any are void of faults," Townley wrote to Thomas Jenkins:

> there are some in this [d'Hancarville's *Recherches sur l'origine, l'esprit et les progrès des arts de la Grèce* (3 vols., London, 1785–86)], particularly typographical ones, and some passages that had better been omitted, but you will, I think, find in it more discoveries, and informations towards understanding the monuments of the ancients, and the reasons of their compositions, than in all the books thave been wrote on the subject.[4]

"The work is really most interesting, & I am perfectly of your Opinion," Jenkins (predictably) replied to Townley, "he has thrown a new light & opened a new road, for understanding the Mythology of the Ancients."[5] D'Hancarville's *Recherches* proffered a reading of ancient monuments based on a system of comparative mythology. According to this system, the Greek god Dionysus, his Roman counterpart Bacchus, and Brahma of the Hindus were variations of a universal creative force that d'Hancarville identified as "Êtrer Générateur."[6] "You have much enriched d'Hancarville's Recherches by the ornamenting them with your Homer &c," the collector Sir Richard Worsley wrote to Townley.[7] In turn, d'Hancarville's *Recherches* influenced the interpretation of the flying figures ornamenting the painted ceiling of Lord Aylesford's "pompeian" gallery at Packington Hall in Warwickshire (1785–88; fig. 46 above). Said by Richard Payne Knight to be "much commended for its Ingenuity . . . & much abused for its prolixity & inaccuracy," d'Hancarville's book, he continued, "can never have a very great sale in any one country, at least in the present age, for the persons who turn their attention to such sorts of studies are not a thousandth part of those who read novels & pamphlets, which I believe are the only very profitable kinds of writing."[8]

Zoffany's painting of Townley's library, which gives visual form to an exclusive culture of learned conversation, displays two additional companions, Thomas Astle and Charles Greville. Keeper of records at the Tower of London, Astle was the author of a book about philology, *The Origin and Progress of Writing* (London, 1784). His colleague Charles Greville, the nephew of Sir William Hamilton and former lover of Hamilton's prize exhibit, Emma (see chapter 3), wrote to Townley that "your collection . . . must be resorted to both for the History of the art & for the Illustration of the true principles of Taste of the Ancients."[9] Zoffany represents him with one arm around *Clytie* bust (fig. 4 above), while his other hand caresses the diaphanous drapery of Townley's marble "wife."

All too often, Zoffany's *Townley* is discussed in terms of biographies of Townley, d'Hancarville, Astle, and Greville rather than books, so let's return to our bookish dialogue. Opposite Townley on the left-hand side of the canvas and resting on the plinth of a statue of a drunken faun is a folio that has been identified as a copy of volume 6 (1771) of the *Antichità di Ercolano esposte* (fig. 20 above).[10] When Jenkins acquired the sculpture of the drunken faun in 1774, he described it in a letter to Townley as of "the size of nature, he is in the action of just falling on his back, with one hand to his mouth the other arm up, which latter & the feet are wanting, as soon as I get the Model made, shall send you a sketch of it in two views, the head was never broke of, the stile of Sculpture is true Greek and of the Good, or High times, you know what I mean by it, the hand held up must have a cup or bunch of grapes in it, for tho' the old Gentleman has had his fill, he still wishes for more."[11] Jenkins's classification of the style of sculpture points to the impact of another learned library folio: Johann Joachim Winckelmann's *Geschichte der Kunst des Alterthums* (Dresden, 1764). In this so-called bible of late eighteenth-century neoclassicism, Winckelmann conceptualized a history of ancient art according to a system of evolutionary traditions, from archaic, to classic, to decadent phases.[12] In this and other letters to Townley, Jenkins adopts a Winckelmannian system of classification; the drunken faun, for instance, is said to represent the good, or high period, one of the two distinct styles in the classic Greek tradition; the other being the beautiful style. In Zoffany's painting the *Antichità* volume lies open at plate 42 (fig. 20 above), an engraving of a drunken faun in bronze excavated from Herculaneum. When the traveller Charles Burney saw this sculpture in the royal museum at Portici, he ranked it "equally perfect with any of the finest statues in the world, such as those at Florence and the Belvedere."[13] By installing this open volume into his painting, Zoffany images a dialogue between the bronze faun in the royal museum at Naples and his marble counterpart at Park Street, Westminster. "Things that were celebrated amongst the Ancients, were frequently copied," Thomas Jenkins reminded Townley, "instances of which you must have often observed, & I believe they were frequently done in haste, to answer the impatience of such as wanted them, probably as furniture. This will account for incorrectness and other defects."[14] In the dialogue between bronze and marble, original and copy, a further connection is made: between the renowned Neapolitan collection, described by Goethe as "the alpha and omega of all collections of antiquities," and that of Charles Townley.[15]

In Zoffany's painting, conversations with the ancients are as much mediated by open library volumes as by the learned setting of the library itself. With reference to the way that Roman authors like Cicero in his *De divinatione* situated their discussions in their libraries, so the neoclassical library remains the site for conversing with the ancients.[16] On 17 June 1775, the dealer Gavin Hamilton replied to Townley, "You tell me that your books are to be put in cases & a statue or bust before them. I am now content, & wish you joy in so fine a room w.[h] is so perfect that after a great deal of puzling I have not been able to alter it for the better, it is perfect, in short it is antique."[17] This reading, where collections of books and marbles replicate the perfect precedent that is antiquity, has particular resonances when we look again at Zoffany's *Townley* (plate 2). In removing some of the ancient sculptures from the *various* exhibition rooms of Townley's house at 7 Park Street, including the hall, the street parlor, the dining room, the street drawing room, the library, and the park drawing room, Zoffany has re-presented the collection in the *library*.[18] We know from contemporary watercolors by William Chambers that the chef d'oeuvres of Townley's collection were never exhibited in the library. Rather, they were placed in the ground-floor dining room, which overlooked St. James' Park (fig. 74). In Chambers's 1794 watercolor, the view of the dining room is from the windows looking through toward the entrance hall. We see the majority of the sculptures displayed on pedestals and exhibited in a formal, symmetrical lineup against the walls. The walls themselves are punctuated with marble reliefs and with busts elevated on wall brackets. Townley's discobolus takes center stage, flanked on either side by the horizontal figures of the sleeping *Endymion* and the falling-down drunken faun (fig. 20 above). Chambers's watercolour is testimony to the display of Townley's principal sculptures in the dining room and also to their visibility to a wider public; in the background of the image, we see a couple examining specimens from the collection, while a woman seated on the pedestal of the discobolus appears to be taking instruction in drawing from her male companion. Chambers produced an equivalent painting of Townley's entrance hall but not the library. According to the boyhood memories of J. T. Smith, a former pupil of the sculptor Joseph Nollekens, the marbles in the library "were not so numerous as those in the dining parlour, but they consisted of some choice specimens."[19] Thomas Coke, first Earl of Leicester, described in 1715 a fine library as "certainly one of the greatest ornaments to a gentleman or to his family."[20]

Townley's late eighteenth-century library as represented by Zoffany is more than an ornament for the gentleman; the intellectual heart of the ancient sculpture collection has been established in the then-present—where fragments of the whole collection of books and sculptures affect a connection with the ancient past. We learn from Sir Henry Ellis in his guidebook to the Townley Gallery in the British

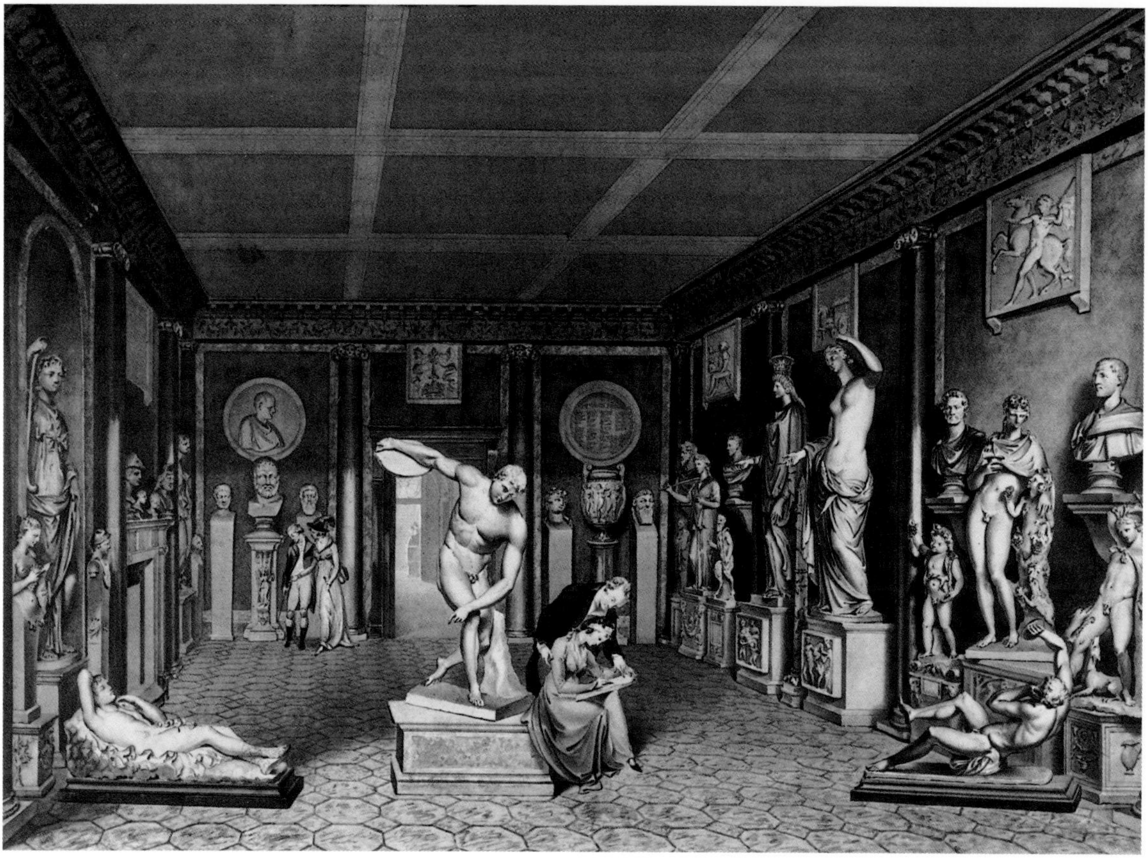

Figure 74 William Chambers, *The Townley Marbles in the Dining Room of 7 Park Street, Westminster*, 1794. By courtesy of the Trustees of the British Museum.

Museum that after the exhibition of the marbles Townley's "time was chiefly occupied in arranging a library, which comprised almost every curious work on the subject of the arts. His books he consulted with equal industry and judgment."[21] Townley obtained a bibliography of curious works on his grand tours of Italy and via mail order with his dealers like Thomas Jenkins. He purchased black market copies of the first six volumes of the *Antichità di Ercolano esposte* in Naples in March 1768 for 240 ducats and at the same time subscribed at a cost of 48 ducats to Sir William Hamilton's *Collection of Etruscan, Greek and Roman Antiquities*.[22] "All the Books you order shall be procured forthwith, & when got carefully packed, & sent as you direct," Jenkins reassured Townley when he was at home in London.[23] After Townley's death in 1805, the books in his library passed to his heir and uncle, John Townley. As we saw in chapter 1, the bibliotheca Townleiana was dispersed in a number of auctions throughout the nineteenth century.

Charles Townley delineated the circumstances of Zoffany's painting in a letter to another of his dealers in Rome, James Byres: "Mr Zoffany is painting in the stile of his Florence Tribune, a room in my house, wherein he introduces what objects he chuses in my collection. It will be a picture of extraordinary effect and truth."[24] Critiques of the painting from its inception have repeatedly drawn attention to what Townley calls the "effect" of the image in its apparent disregard for the truth.[25] In other words, they focus on how Zoffany fabricated the locations, arrangement, and even in some cases the sizes of the ancient marble sculptures in order to accommodate them into his painting of the library. For instance, the larger-than-life *Venus* towering behind Thomas Astle actually stood on the right-hand side of the dining room, opposite the fireplace and next to the caryatid (as represented in fig. 74). In his painting, Zoffany not only brought the *Venus* excavated by Gavin Hamilton at Ostia in 1776 out of the ground-floor dining room and upstairs into the library but he also deployed Townley's marble wellhead as her plinth. This mode of display was often utilized for smaller objects like the sphinx crouching in the right foreground, but never for such a large and heavy piece like the *Venus*. Brian Cook has calculated that Zoffany had to reduce her size by one-fifth to incorporate her into the painted library.[26]

In his letter to James Byres, Townley identified the precedent for his painting as a celebrated image from Zoffany's repertoire, *The Tribuna of the Uffizi* (1772–78/79; fig. 75). As one of the unmissable sights of the grand tour in Italy, the Tribuna and its contents had acquired quasi-religious status in the canons of connoisseurship; according to Thomas Broderick in the 1750s, the gallery in Florence was "the greatest repository of curiosities in the world."[27] Commissioned in 1772 by Queen Charlotte as an elite guidebook to picture hanging, Zoffany's work-in-progress was often referred to in letters and accounts of British tourists visiting the gallery.[28] Consequently it became as much of a sight on the grand tour of Florence as the prize collection it represented in miniature. The traveller Robert Harvey went so far as to suggest that Zoffany's painting was "the most curious thing in this Tribune and perhaps in all Italy."[29] Lord Winchilsea, one of the cast of British travellers represented *in* the painting, described in a letter how Zoffany's detailing of parts of the gallery re-created a "compleat and exact" impression of the whole:

Figure 75 Johann Zoffany, *The Tribuna degli Uffizi*, 1772–8/9. The Royal Collection © 2004, Her Majesty Queen Elizabeth II.

> He not only copies a great many Pictures & Statues & the Room &c. which is a great deal to do, but even the Frames & every the most minute thing Possible the small bronzes, the Table &c. to make it be a compleat & exact representation of the Room, & besides that he is obliged to put several of the Pictures in perspective, & to make a distinction between the life & the heads in the Pictures, & what is most difficult of all to make them appear as if they were painted on different kinds of

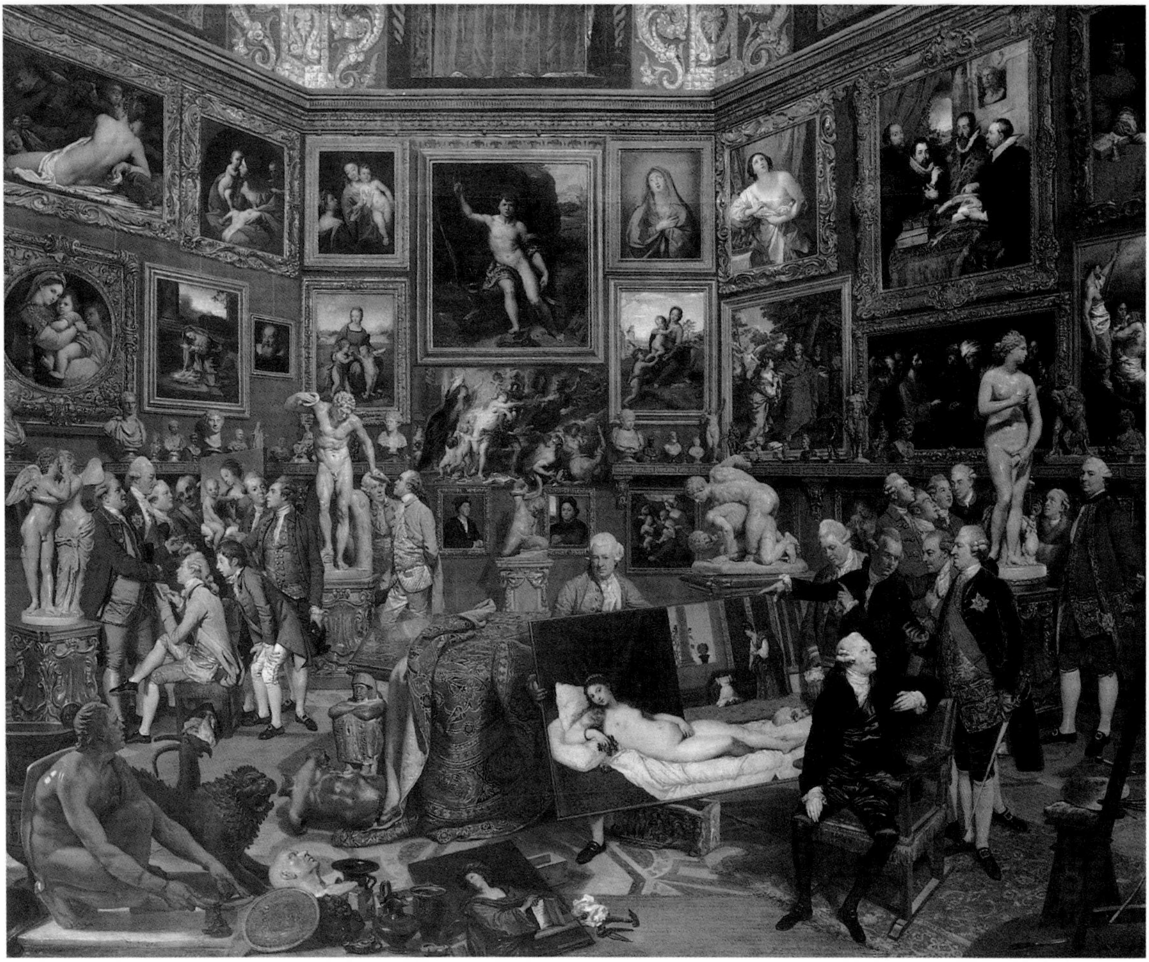

Canvass in the Originals. When it is done it will be a very pretty thing, & will give a very good idea of the Originals.[30]

In fact, Zoffany's *Tribuna*, like his later picture of Townley's library, is not a complete and exact representation of the collection onto canvas at all but rather an imaginative re-creation. Sir Horace Mann, whose portrait is also featured in the ensemble, observed how Zoffany created a phantom collection of paintings by importing pictures from the Pitti Palace in Florence to join those in the Tribuna.[31] Furthermore, the size and shapes of these painted masterpieces were necessarily redrawn to fit the frame of Zoffany's contemporary version. In this, Zoffany imaginatively represented both the totality and the arrangement of the Medici collection.

By evoking the Tribuna in his painting of Townley's library, Zoffany enshrines Townley's collection within a genealogical tradition of collecting that emulates the cosmopolitan model of the grand duke of Tuscany as well as the royal British model of the patron. The Tribuna as single exhibition room provides the precedent for Zoffany's imaginative installation of Townley's sculptures into the painted library. On 10 May 1775, Gavin Hamilton wrote that he had received Townley's plan of a "great room," a proposal (later abandoned) for arranging his collection in a single gallery, "w.^{h} I like much as a library, tho as a gallery of statues it is liable to a few objections, in particular with regard to the intermediate spaces between the niches where I coud wish to see a statue or bust on its pedestal as in the Medici gallery, & the books in the closets."[32]

A notice in the *Public Advertiser* for June 1785 identified the model for the Townley painting as Zoffany's *Tribuna*, but reattributed the model for the *collection* to an English, rather than cosmopolitan, history of *sculpture* collections. "Mr Townley's marbles and statuary—the Wilton House of London—are a most remarkably fine subject of a picture in the manner of Zoffani's gallery of Florence—with some portraits grouped in front—the specimens of ancient art in the background."[33] The eighth Earl of Pembroke's collection at Wilton House was the largest of its type in early eighteenth-century Britain and was consolidated with acquisitions from the collections of Lord Arundel, Cardinal Mazarin, and the Roman Giustiniani family.[34] Displayed throughout the house and gardens, Pembroke's marbles were an evocative metonym of antiquity. For John Dodd in 1735, "To describe this Place [Wilton] would be to write the Greek and Roman History."[35] The sculptures at Wilton translated and transported the experience of classic ground in Italy to Wiltshire in England; as Stukeley observed in his *Itinerarium curiosum* (1776), "Wilton is become tramontane Italy."[36] Likewise, Townley's collection at 7 Park Street, Westminster (now 14 Queen Anne's Gate) brought tramontane Italy in the urban space of the capital city.[37]

While the Earl of Pembroke's collection at Wilton was compiled from earlier cosmopolitan collections of antiquities accumulated in England, France, and Italy, the majority of sculptures in Townley's collection derived from classic ground beyond the Alps. According to a letter of one of Townley's contemporaries, Henry Temple, second Viscount Palmerston, the greatest pleasure he enjoyed during his grand tour derived from the ancient marbles in Italy.

> Besides their merit [he writes] they had the charm of novelty to recommend them. I had seen before I came to Italy Pictures allmost as good as those at Rome but I never saw a statue worth looking at till I cross'd the Alps which gave me the least idea of the powers of the art. I believe that in the real comforts and conveniences of life we

surpass the ancients and we have many admirable inventions of which they were totally ignorant. But certainly in the arts which they practised and in all the magnificence of luxury, we have nothing to do but wonder and submit.[38]

Palmerston refers to the ancients versus moderns debate that, as we saw in chapter 4, was especially applicable to some of the artifacts unearthed at Pompeii and Herculaneum. During a four-week residence at Rome in 1764 and at a cost of £515.0.0, Palmerston acquired over thirty ancient statues, a modern copy by Joseph Nollekens of a *Boy on a Dolphin,* and marble busts, sarcophagi, medallions, vases, and tables (figs. 76a, 76b).[39] A recent catalog of Palmerston's ancient marbles cites Montfaucon's *Antiquité expliquée et représentée en figures* (Paris, 1719–24) as a kind of guidebook to the collection at Broadlands in Hampshire.[40] Montfaucon's encyclopedic work was certainly read by British collectors of sculpture; Henry Blundell of Ince Blundell

Figures 76a, 76b Viscount Palmerston's memorandum for *Prices Marbles & Pictures*, 1764. University of Southampton Library, Archives and Manuscripts, BR101/34. By courtesy of the Trustees of the Broadlands Archives.

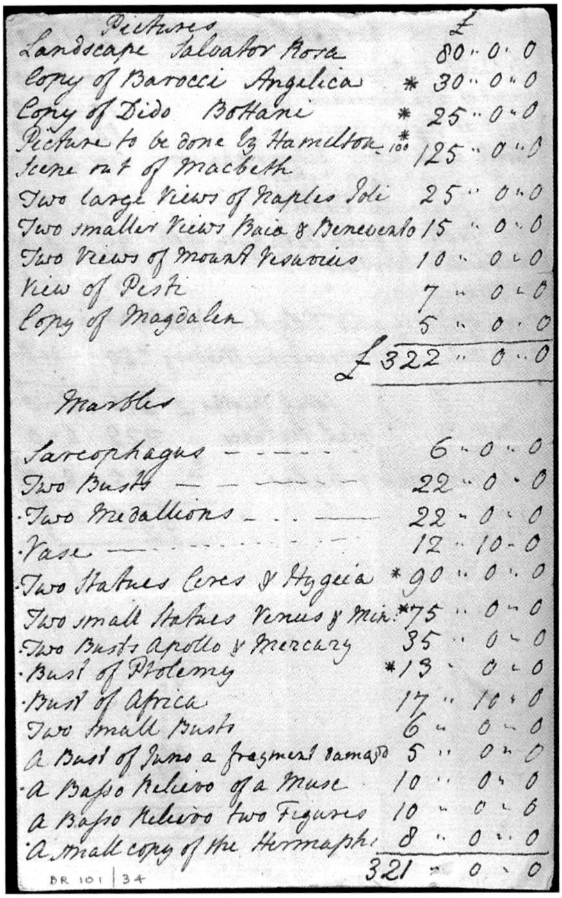
Pictures £
Landscape Salvator Rosa 80 .. 0 . 0
copy of Barocci Angelica * 30 .. 0 .. 0
Copy of Dido Bottani * 25 .. 0 .. 0
Picture to be done by Hamilton *100 125 .. 0 .. 0
Scene out of Macbeth
Two large Views of Naples Soli 25 .. 0 .. 0
Two smaller Views Baia & Benevento 15 .. 0 .. 0
Two Views of Mount Vesuvius 10 .. 0 .. 0
View of Pesti 7 .. 0 .. 0
Copy of Magdalen 5 .. 0 .. 0
£322 .. 0 .. 0

Marbles
Sarcophagus 6 . 0 . 0
Two Busts 22 . 0 . 0
Two Medallions 22 . 0 . 0
Vase 12 . 10 . 0
Two Statues Ceres & Hygeia *90 .. 0 . 0
Two small Statues Venus & Min: *75 .. 0 . 0
Two Busts Apollo & Mercury 35 .. 0 . 0
Bust of Ptolemy *13 . 0 . 0
Bust of Africa 17 .. 10 . 0
Two small Busts 6 . 0 . 0
A Bust of Juno a fragment damaged 5 .. 0 . 0
A Basso Relievo of a Muse 10 .. 0 . 0
A Basso Relievo two Figures 10 . 0 . 0
A small copy of the Hermaphr. 8 .. 0 .. 0
321 . 0 . 0
BR 101 | 34

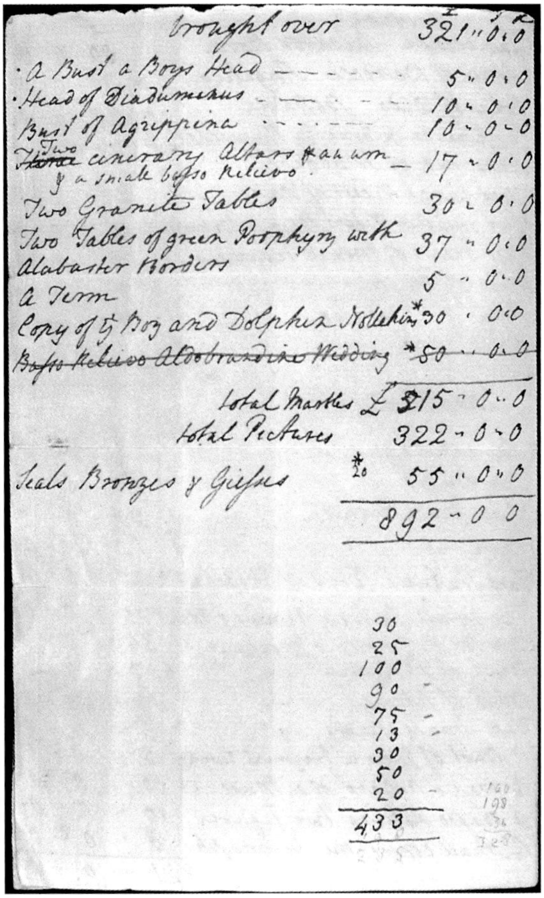
brought over 321 .. 0 . 0
A Bust a Boys Head 5 .. 0 . 0
Head of Diadumenus 10 . 0 . 0
Bust of Agrippina 10 . 0 . 0
~~Three~~ Two cinerary Altars *an urn & a small basso relievo 17 . 0 . 0
Two Granite Tables 30 . 0 . 0
Two Tables of green Porphyry with Alabaster Borders 37 . 0 . 0
A Term 5 . 0 . 0
Copy of ye Boy and Dolphin Nollekins *30 . 0 . 0
~~Basso Relievo Aldobrandini Wedding *50 .. 0 . 0~~
total Marbles £ 515 . 0 .. 0
total Pictures 322 . 0 . 0
Seals Bronzes & Gessus *20 55 .. 0 . 0
892 . 0 . 0

30
25
100
90
75
13
30
50
20
433

Hall in Lancashire informed Charles Townley that during the winter of 1795–96 he had great pleasure looking over Montfaucon's "wonderful work."[41] Six years later, Blundell referred again to Montfaucon and his method of classifying antiquities, when compiling a catalog of his own collection.[42] But however much Montfaucon's *Antiquité expliquée* may have impressed Blundell with its method of classification, or *in*formed Viscount Palmerston's collection as a guidebook, in order to situate Townley's marbles and those of his contemporaries within a neoclassical culture of collecting, we need look beyond specific books in the sculpture collector's library. We must refer instead and once again to our methodological framework deriving from the sociology of education. Based on this approach, any discernible program of collecting sculptures is determined by the programs of thought inculcated by a classical education; a "wonderful work" like Montfaucon's *Antiquité expliquée* is necessarily supplanted by a *library* of classical textbooks that embody the content of that education.

Like John Dodd for whom a description of Wilton in 1735 "would be to write the Greek and Roman History," ancient marbles in Italian collections had long been "Speak[ing] Roman History more palpably than any author."[43] What denotes British classicism in the period that forms our timeframe is precisely this dialogue or conversation with the texts of the ancients. In turn, what denotes British neoclassicism of the same period is an extension or conversion of this conversation into material *possession(s)*. For a Roman Catholic collector like Townley, classically educated at the seminary and school of Douai in northern France, antiquity was part of his intellectual makeup; to quote his contemporary the Reverend Alison, it was "so much the possession of our minds."[44] Townley is said to have been "too ardent a lover of antiquity to remain a spectator of its fairest forms without courting the possession."[45] His passion for the fine productions of the ancients began to be indulged when he first went to Italy in 1767–68 at the age of thirty.[46] According to the sixth Duke of Devonshire, himself a prolific collector of ancient and modern sculpture, it was "at Rome [where] the love of marble possesses most people like a new sense, and a knowledge is acquired of the value of the ancient marbles."[47] In possessing ancient marble sculptures from Rome, the classically educated collector imparted the knowledge derived the studies of his youth into this new-found "sensation for sculpture."[48]

Letters to Townley preserved in his archive are peppered with references and quotations from the classical literary tradition, a library of works in which the classically educated were quite literally saturated. "I hope all my acquaintance in your Museum with whom tho mute (& as Ovid says[49] nec Vox nec Verba Sequuntur) I have so often conversed by the expression of their countenances are well—especially the Beautiful Clytie [fig. 4 above]," wrote "your old fellow traveller," William

Sandys to Townley, "happy in the thoughts of stealing a peep at them soon."[50] *Clytie* was named after a nymph in Ovid's *Metamorphoses* who pined for love of Helios and was turned into a flower.[51] The collector Sir Richard Worsley wrote to Townley reproaching him "in the same manner & almost in the same words that Cicero does Atticus, where he says, you knew I was at Rome, but I did not know whether you where in Epirus, at Amalthea, or at Athens, only changing Rome for Appuldurcombe, Amalthea for Townley [in Lancashire] & London for Athens."[52] Months before Townley died, the poet Samuel Rogers "rejoice[d] to think you are mending, & mending *my way*, for a horse & a cow are in my mind better doctors than Galen & Hippocrates, & long have I wished to be able to say with Vergil, Lac mihi non aestate nouum non frigore defit."[53] Whether reproaching or rejoicing, mute or conversing, the works of Roman authors like Ovid, Cicero, and Virgil provided an expression for every occasion. These are fragments in Latin of the elite, learned dialogue that denotes the pervading influence of classicizing thought styles beyond the classroom and into later life.

How this dialogue with its educational basis was subsequently translated into the material currency of ancient sculpture—into neoclassicism—is usefully represented in a pair of sculptures formerly in the collection of another of Townley's contemporaries, the second Earl of Shelburne, later first Marquess of Lansdowne.[54] Following the death of his wife in 1771, this Whig leader and future prime minister embarked on a five-month tour of Italy during which he contracted the dealer Gavin Hamilton to supply 16 antique statues, 12 busts, 12 basso-relievos, 11 historical pictures, and 4 landscapes for the proposed gallery of his London townhouse in Berkeley Square, Mayfair.[55] Unlike twenty-five-year-old Viscount Palmerston, who as we have seen acquired the bulk of his marbles while in situ in Italy, the mature Shelburne, like Townley and also Henry Blundell, left commissions with the dealer in Rome to be realized long after the collector had completed his grand tour. Thomas Jenkins wrote to Townley of his "sincere pleasure . . . that your collection proves such a fund of entertainment to you . . . it would be fortunate for many, whose money is laid out in momentary amusements, if they followed your example" of perseverance, rather than one-off collecting.[56] Shelburne's dealer, Gavin Hamilton, had ambitious plans for the proposed London gallery of antique statues: "I don't mean a collection such as has been hitherto made by myself and others. I mean a collection that will make Shelburne House famous not only in England but all over Europe."[57] When plans for the Europe-famed gallery were abandoned, Hamilton was prepared to adapt the commission as necessary, writing to his patron on 1 July 1773 "that a library may be ornamented with statues and busts so as to form something elegant and beautiful . . . I think that places for books may be made so as not to interfere with the sculpture."[58] In a space "that will answer both the ends of

Library and Gallery," certain books in the library influenced the subject matter of the adjacent sculptures. For instance, in a letter of 25 March 1776, Hamilton wrote that "something entirely new and uncommon" had been dispatched to Shelburne:

> It is a Diomede carrying off the Palladium. Your Lordship when in Rome mentioned to me particularly subjects of this sort as interesting to you, but besides the subject, give me leave to add that the sculpture is first-rate, and exactly in the style and size of the Cincinnatus to which I mean it as a composition, being a Greek hero to match the Roman. The legs and arms are modern, but restored in perfect harmony with the rest. He holds the Palladium in one hand, while he defends himself with the right holding a dagger. Your Lordship will ask me why I suppose this statue to be a Diomede. I answer because it would be to the last degree absurd to suppose it any thing else, as I believe your Lordship will easily grant when you see it. Every view of it is fine and I could wish it to be placed so as to be seen all round. With regard

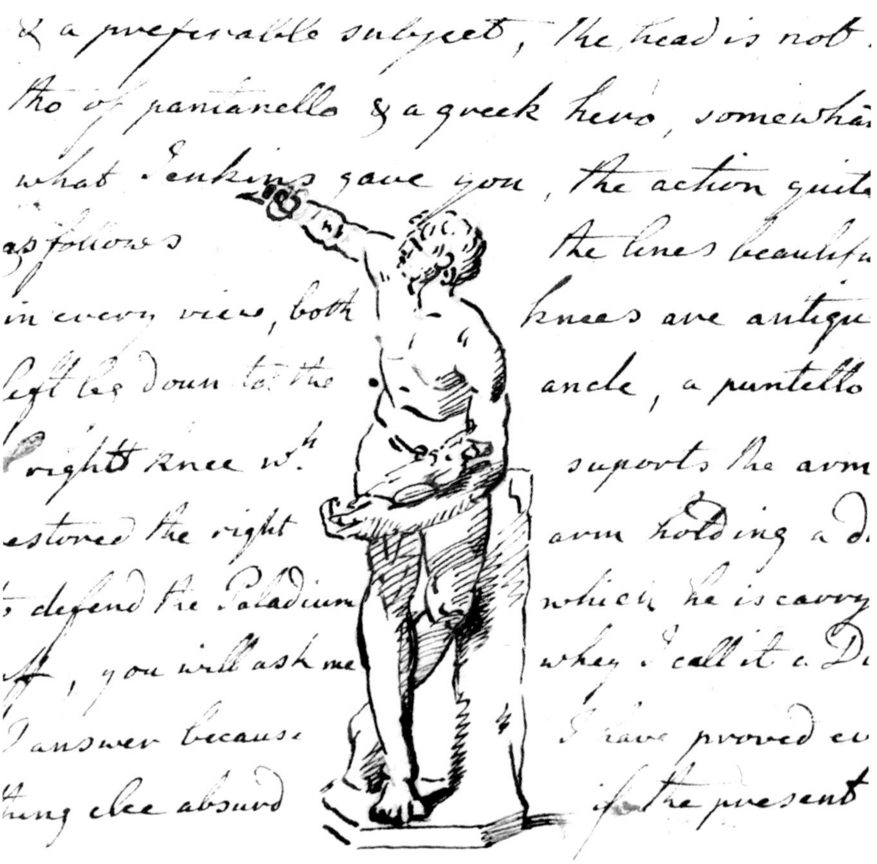

Figure 77 "Something singular and uncommon": *Diomedes Carrying Off the Palladium,* as sketched by Gavin Hamilton in a letter to Charles Townley, 25 March 1776. By courtesy of the Trustees of the British Museum.

> to the price, I have put it at £200, but as I have made so many draughts of late, I shall suspend every view of interest till it arrives and meets with your Lordship's approbation. All I beg is that it may be placed near the Cincinnatus. The contrast will add beauty to each. Your Lordship will excuse the liberty I have taken, as my principal motive is to increase your collection with something entirely new and uncommon.[59]

"Your Lordship when in Rome mentioned to me particularly subjects of this sort as interesting to you," Hamilton reminded Shelburne five years later when the *Diomedes* (fig. 77) had already been dispatched. For those of us whose reference to and reverence for the ancients has not been instilled by an eighteenth-century classical education, the inference of this statement may require some explanation. As Hamilton's letter points out, Diomedes was one of the heroes in Homer's *Iliad*. Together with Odysseus he was responsible for stealing the Palladium from the city of Troy. The security of Troy depended on the safekeeping of this image of the goddess Athena: if stolen, the Greeks could capture and sack the city. In addition to its literary referents, the style and size of the *Diomedes* was cited by the dealer as a companion for a *Cincinnatus* excavated from Hadrian's Villa at Tivoli and already in Shelburne's possession (fig. 78). For Hamilton described the depiction of the Roman hero as "no less than a Cincinnatus taken from the plough, the same as that at Versailles, of better sculpture, though not so well preserved, of the same artist that made the Gladiator at the Villa Borghese. The head is almost the same."[60] Unlike the legendary Diomedes, Cincinnatus was a political figure from Roman history; "taken from the plough" in 458 B.C. to defend the Romans, he was elected dictator but resigned his office after sixteen days and returned to his farm beyond the river Tiber. In this pair of sculptures for the Earl of Shelburne's collection we see the thinking behind the neoclassical sculpture collection, embodying in marble all manner of ancients preserved in the texts of the classical literary tradition. "I know your Lordship [Shelburne] is not so fond of portraits in general," wrote Gavin Hamilton on 4 March 1773, "but a statue of so great an Emperor and

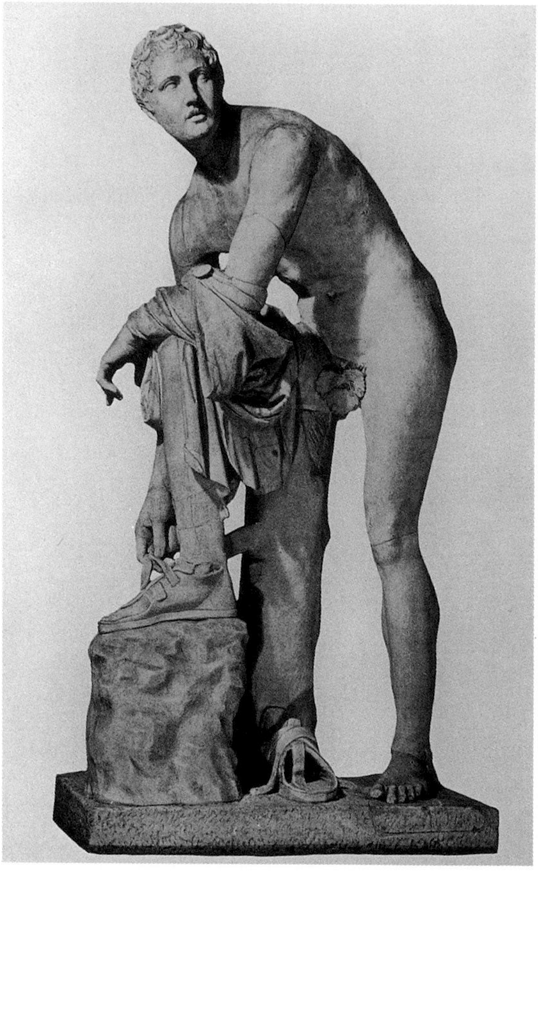

Figure 78 "A Cincinnatus taken from the plough." *The celebrated collection of ancient marbles the property of the most Hon. The Marquis of Lansdowne*, Christie's, 5 March 1930, lot 49. Institute of Classical Studies Library.

so great a Philosopher [as the second-century A.D. Marcus Aurelius] I think deserves a place in any gallery."[61]

Novelty has been a persistent theme in our study of late eighteenth-century neoclassicism. We see it in Hamilton's justification of his embarkation of the *Diomedes*: "My principal motive is to increase your collection with something entirely new and uncommon."[62] The novelty of ancient sculptures in contemporary Rome relied to a great extent on their excavation and restoration. The marbles collected by Townley and his contemporaries were new in the sense of being new to the market and also being resurrected by excavation, much like the buried cities of Pompeii and Herculaneum. The dealers who negotiated the dispersal of sculptures from some of Rome's oldest collections like those of the Palazzo Mattei, the Villas d'Este and Negroni, and the Barberini and Giustiniani families also embarked on excavations in and around the city. "I look upon it as a lottery so have thrown my dice," wrote Hamilton in 1773 of the gamble that was an excavation project.[63] Two years later, he was "resolved to leave no stone unturn'd in the literal sense of the word."[64]

Having been resurrected by excavation, the ruined or fragmentary sculptures were then reconstructed and improved by professional sculptor-restorers in Rome like Bartolomeo Cavaceppi or Carlo Albacini.[65] As we've seen with reference to Shelburne's *Diomedes*, it was the dealer rather than the collector who determined how an archaeological fragment should be cleaned, restored, and attributed. Only once a sculpture had undergone the necessary doctoring would it be viewed by its would-be possessor either firsthand in Rome or in drawings supplied by the dealer. The collector Henry Blundell was atypical when he "recommend[ed] to every one, to buy with their own eyes, or not to buy at all . . . It is a rule with me not to expend yw^e^ sum of 5 or 600 £ in ye purchase of a thing, I have not seen, nor had any correct drawing of to judge, if it w.^d^ please me; I w.^d^ sooner take a trip to Rome to see it, than buy it at such a price & with such doubts."[66] In the case of the *Diomedes,* Shelburne enjoyed neither the privilege of a visit to Rome or the practice of receiving correct drawings. The restoration of this sculpture has been attributed to Bartolomeo Cavaceppi.[67] But since the restorer's identity is nowhere documented—restoration techniques and chisel marks being far from substantive—this and other retrospective attributions say more about the discipline of art history than about the contemporary dialogue with the ancients. Ironically, it is Blundell, who so feared "ye puffs & tricks of all kinds of dealers," who we find boasting to Townley of contemporary sculptors in Rome who had left their mark on his marbles.[68] Writing on 15 April 1800 that the head of his bust of the moon goddess Diana Lucifera (fig. 79) was a modern work by Cavaceppi, Blundell proceeded to make the astonishing—and entirely groundless—claim that "this [bust] and most

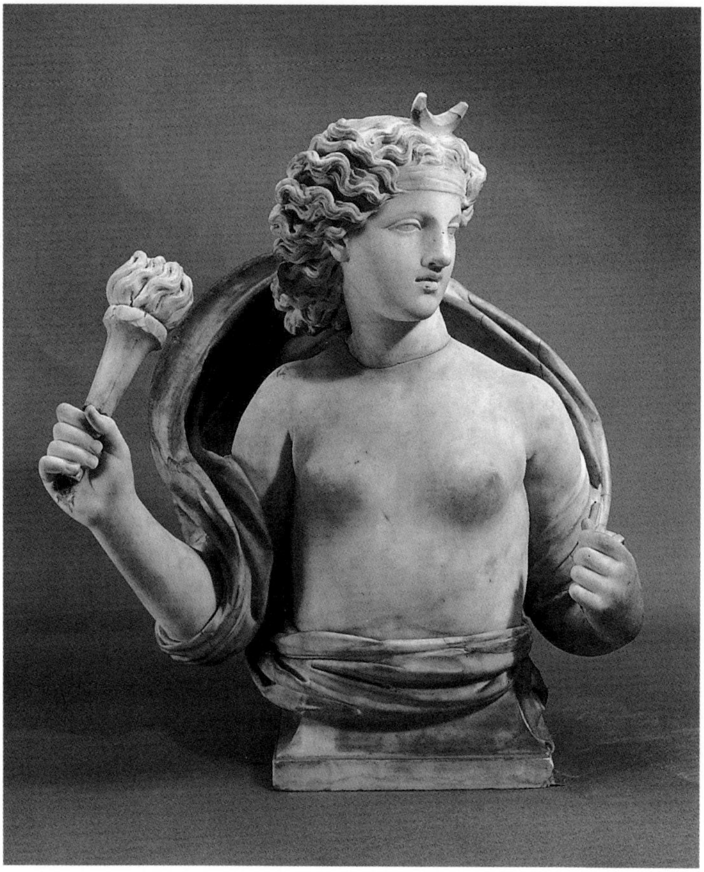

Figure 79 "The head is modern, but the sculpture of the body is very fine": Henry Blundell's bust of the moon goddess, *Diana Lucifera,* with her crescent horns and flaming torch. National Museums Liverpool (The Walker).

other of my restores was done under the direction of [Antonio] Canova, who after retouched many of them himself."[69]

In *Engravings and Etchings*, Blundell describes the often indiscriminate nature of restoration, where naive collectors—"people [who] see with their ears"—were duped by dealers in their desire for named pieces.[70] To meet the demand, sculptural fragments became blank canvases inventively patched together as a cast of ancients and identified by the addition of a defining prop. Blundell writes,

> It is often found difficult to ascertain the primeval characters, or real names, of ancient busts and statues . . . [W]here there remains no distinguishing symbol or attribute on the marble, names are often given them by caprice, or from their restores: For instance, a celebrated statue bought at Rome from Mr. Jenkins, was at that time called a *Venus*, owing to the arm being restored with a mirror in the hand. This figure was afterwards thought not delicate enough for a *Venus*; the mirror was

> removed, and it was pronounced a *Hebe*, that character being more suitable for it. The owner some time after called it an *Isis*, as a character more mysterious. At present it belongs to the British Museum, and is denominated an *Ariadne*.—Likewise a *Torso* (which by different restorers might have been adapted to various characters) by placing it on an austere head, and restoring the arms with a dagger on one hand, became a *Brutus*, which was artfully contrived by Mr. Jenkins to suit certain people. This shews the uncertainty of names given to ancient marbles. When no symbol or attribute can be distinguished on them, it is generally allowed to every virtuoso to give such names to his busts and statues as he thinks most appropriate.[71]

The sculptural fragment was necessarily completed and attributed for its exhibition as furniture in the elite English interior. But as Blundell wrote to Townley,

> I am quite of your opinion, that every *statue* should have some remains of its real character, otherwise without its head & extremities, it becomes a mere trunk or fragment; and may be made into an emperor, or a merry Andrew, or a *Brutus*, as that at Nuby is so dub'd, by having a severe countenanced head put on its shoulders and hands on with a dagger in them; yet as a *Brutus* by some is extold to the skies. A remark of yours comeing from Nuby, I shall never forget.[72]

Marcus Junius Brutus was one of the leading conspirators in the murder of the dictator Julius Caesar in 44 BC. A statue of the defender of the Roman republic formed part of a sculpture collection belonging to William Weddell at Newby Hall in Yorkshire that was purchased en bloc from Thomas Jenkins in Rome in 1765 (fig. 80).[73] Unlike Weddell's patchwork *Brutus*, an anonymous naked male torso reborn as a Brutus with the addition of a head and an incriminating dagger, Townley's sculptures retained as far as possible remains of their real character. Knowing all too well Townley's desire for "things of a superior class," Hamilton described how he

Figure 80 "A severe countenanced head put on its shoulders and hands on with a dagger in them": the so-called *Brutus* from William Weddell's collection at Newby Hall. Forschungsarchiv für antike Plastik, Archaeological Institute, University of Cologne.

> never proposed to you my Diomed with the Paladium . . . the head is not its own tho of pantanello & a greek hero . . . the action quite new as follows the lines beautifull in every view, both knees are antique & the left leg down to the ancle, a puntello on the right knee w.[h] suports the arm. I have restored the right arm holding a dagger to defend the Paladium which he is carrying off. you will ask me why I call it a Diomed I answer because I have proved every thing else absurd if the present insience should raise your curiosity to see a more correct drawing I will send it to you, & woud even venture to send you the original but I am afraid that its being in your possession & refused by you will prevent the sale to any body else. upon the whole I woud advise you to keep your money for acquisitions of greater consequence. what I write you

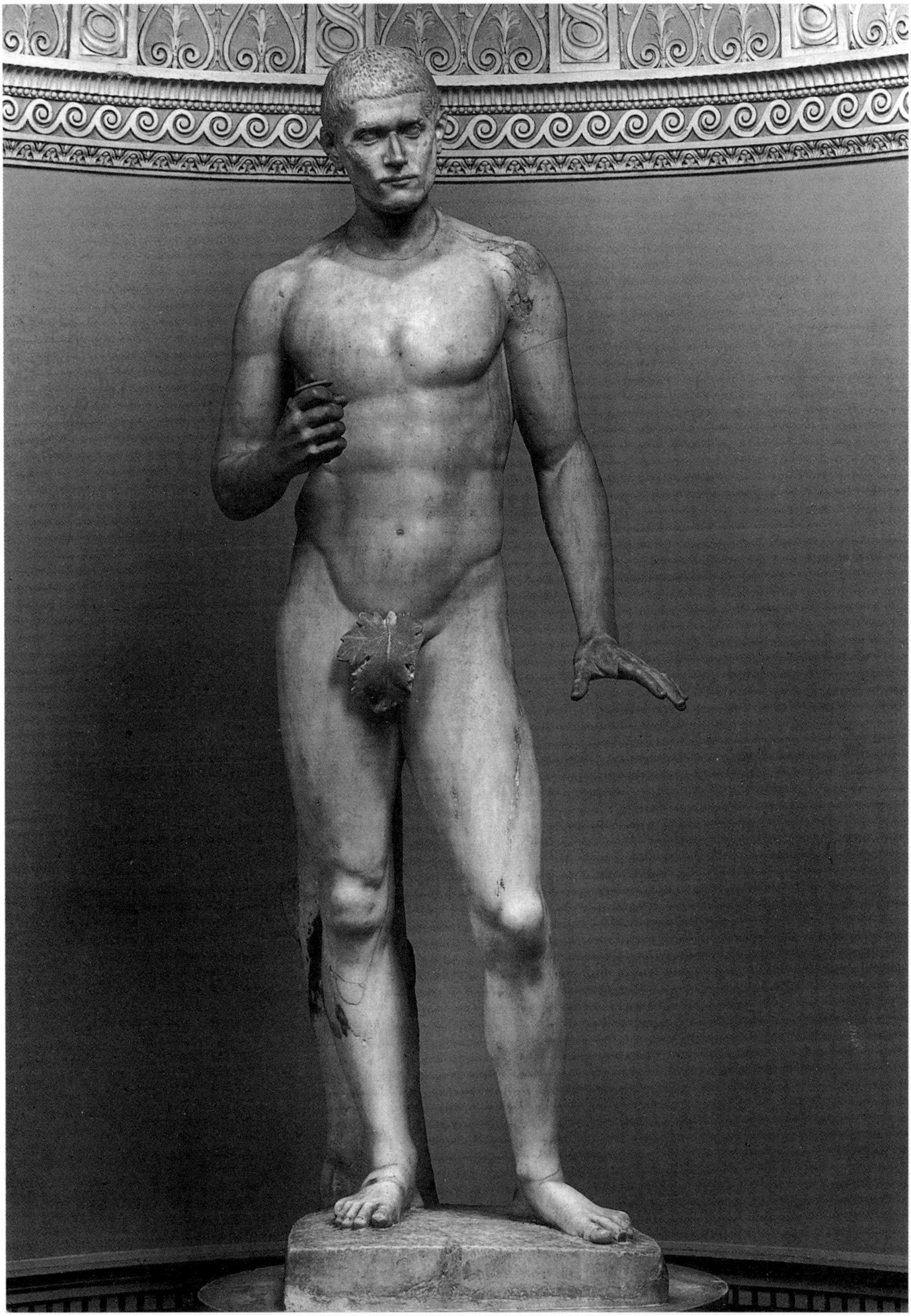

> is meerly out of delicacy, that you may be preferred in this as well as in every thing else. I found this admirable torso in my first works at ostia, comonly called by my men the gobbo. the back is fine in an extraordinary degree, but corroded by salnitro. it is left by the artist w.h the marks of the scarpello. in the stile of the Laocoon [fig. 54 above] & sleeping faun of the Barberini the price of it I imagin will be £200.[74]

The varying descriptions of the *Diomedes* that Hamilton supplied first in this letter to Townley and four months later when the statue was en route to Lord Shelburne give an indication of how the agendas of individual collectors affected their different relationships with their dealers. The version for Townley reveals information about the *Diomedes* never divulged to Shelburne—the port of Ostia as its provenance and the extent of its extensive restorations, including the head. Hamilton's fear that Townley's rejection would effectively blackball the sculpture may be read *either* as the degree to which Townley single-handedly manipulated the English market, or as yet more "puffs & tricks" from the dealer. A later letter from Jenkins clarifies Townley's acquisition policy:

> The Minerva in my Cava tho' really good sculpture, is not of that *Portato* that you wish, tho the preservation makes it an interesting figure for any Gentleman that wants an elegant object for a Library or for furniture, but I know what you want, it must be of the first water or it will not do, and you may be assured if such offers, you will have the refusal of it.[75]

On one level, Zoffany's painting (plate 2) is proof of the proprietorial pride of collecting elegant objects for a library or for furniture in late eighteenth-century Britain. As Henry Blundell wrote to Townley on 5 March 1787: "I agree with you entirely, in ye purchasing *respectable objects*; Every man, I apprehend, wishes to purchase, what is good, let it be in marble, Painting, a Horse or a Dog. The difficulty is to find out & distinguish what is truly good & respectable, without being misled by ye Puffs of ye sellers or ye imaginary value often set upon things, from a great price being askd."[76] Zoffany's painting realizes this ambition, being a painting of the collector's possessions—his marbles, dog ("Kam"), and library—to add to his whole collection. But since any new acquisition had to be, as Gavin Hamilton put it, quoting the Earl of Bristol, the cream and not the skimmed milk of antiquity, so Zoffany's *Townley* is an ideal representation of the restoration of antiquity in modernity via the model of the Renaissance collection: the Medici gallery.[77]

In the acquisition of sculptures with their real character as far as possible preserved intact, Townley's marbles forged a dialogue with the ancients *and* with ancient models of collecting. The great protector of the fine arts and in particular the art of sculpture was the second-century A.D. Roman emperor Hadrian.[78] His extensive travels had furnished his imperial villa at Tivoli with imitations of buildings from throughout the empire and it was said to be "ornamented with the finest works of sculpture he could procure from all parts," especially from Greece.[79] By the late eighteenth century, Hadrian's imperial collection formerly at Tivoli had been unearthed by excavations, dispersed, and reinstalled into elite collections throughout parts of his former empire. Artifacts in Italy reputedly from Hadrian's collection of ancient Greek statuary included the Furetti *Centaurs*, the Vatican *Antinous,* and the *Flora*.[80] Any artifact with an imperial provenance, be it authentic or fabricated, inevitably carried an elite cachet. Hamilton invoked images of imperial domesticity to whet Townley's appetite for finds from Santa Maria della Villa near the temple of Fortune at Preneste:

> This Villa was built by Augustus & where he pass'd part of the summer, & where his guest Horace probably read all Homer. Tiberius recovered his health in this place, & continued to be a favourite spot, of all the Emperours down to the latter age. My friend Hadrian among others has been there, & as usewall has ornamented it with sculpture, but as yet have found nothing of great value.[81]

Zoffany's *Townley* (plate 2), staged in the collector's library, represents a visual reworking of this theme of sculptural decoration and study.

The ancient Roman emperors Augustus, Tiberius, and Hadrian were materially embodied in Townley's collection in the form of portrait busts: his most celebrated example of this genre was the bust *Homer* (fig. 81). Richard Payne Knight wrote to Townley in 1784 that he was very impatient to see what d'Hancarville would say about the busts of Homer:

> There can be no doubt I suppose of their being intended by the Artists to represent that Poet, but the doubt is whether they are real or ideal portraits. Pliny [the Elder] says the latter, but his Authority in Matters of this kind is not unquestionable. I wish in this instance that it could be

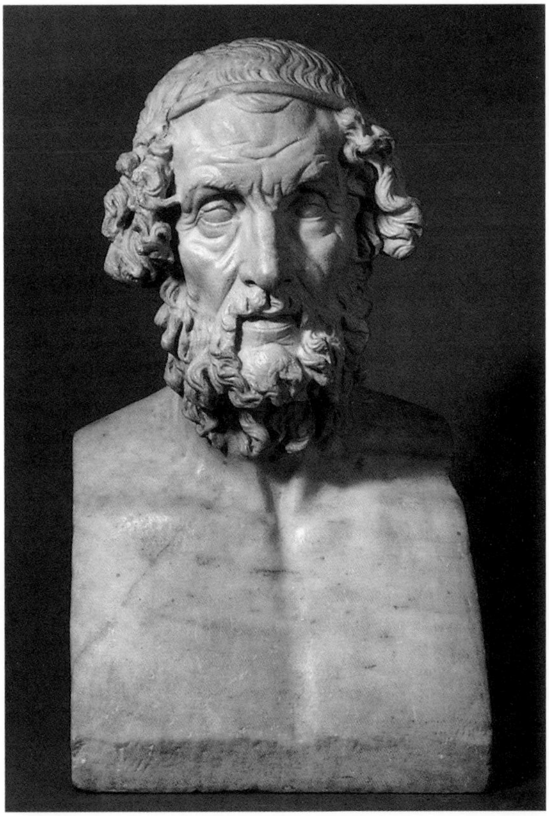

Figure 81 "The finest bust of the greatest of men": Townley's *Homer*. © Copyright The Trustees of the British Museum.

> proved wrong, for I should have great pleasure in looking at those Heads if I could suppose them real resemblances of the Man who was certainly the greatest Prodigy Human Nature has ever produced. all who can understand & feel his Poetry must be of this opinion, nil oriturum alias, nil ortum tale fatentes.[82]

Payne Knight's quotation from Horace (*Epistles* II. I. 17) articulates his admiration for the ancient Greek poet. Marble busts in general had the ability to bring collectors face-to-face with the ancients (fig. 82), including those authors whose works they esteemed so highly.

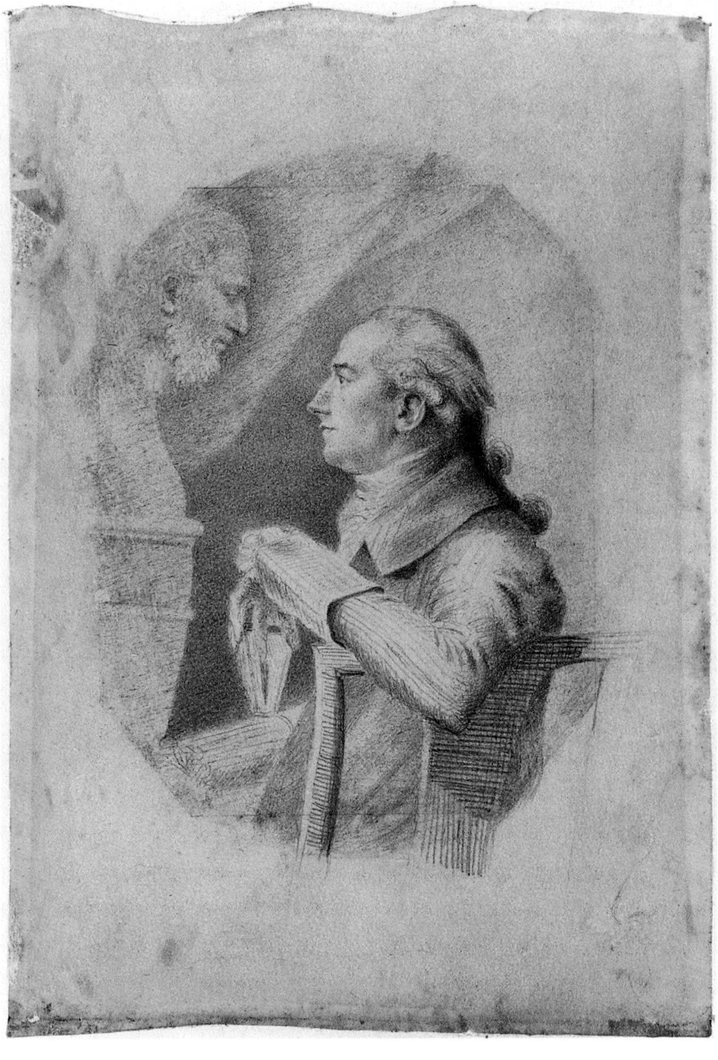

Figure 82 A miniature portrait by John Brown of Townley with an unidentified bust in the background, c. 1786. National Galleries of Scotland.

Payne Knight's letter further introduces art historical debates about ancient portraiture—whether the busts of Homer are taken from life or posthumous—issues that he revisits via Pliny's text. As we saw in chapter 5, it was part of the same passage in book thirty-five of Pliny's *Naturalis Historiae* that influenced the display of busts of ancients within the neoclassical library. J. T. Smith tells us that among the busts installed in Townley's library at Park Street were those of Antoninus Pius, Titan, Caracalla's wife Plautilla, Lucius Verus, and that of Homer, "which has been so repeatedly and admirably engraven."[83] In Zoffany's painting of the library (plate 2), the bust of Homer is isolated from the lineup of busts on the far right and is displayed on its own pedestal immediately behind Townley. In fact, the profile of the bust of Homer mirrors exactly that of the collector. Richard Payne Knight received an "excellent" engraving of Townley's bust of Homer in November 1786. He wrote in response,

> It gives one a perfect Idea of the original, tis the first engraved Head of the old Bard that looks like a great Poet instead of a blind ballad singer. I cannot help wishing that Pliny had been less communicative, & left at least the Pleasure of imagining that we had some resemblance of that wonderful being who produced the Iliad & Odyssie.[84]

Townley's *Homer* was also engraved for the collector's visiting card (fig. 83) with his other favorite busts *Clytie* (fig. 4 above) and *Pericles*; the triumvirate represented among the debris of ancient architecture. According to one of Townley's manuscript catalogs of his collection, the marble bust of Pericles, with his name inscribed in Greek on the base of the terminus, corresponds exactly with the descriptions of his character in the ancient texts of Thucydides and Plutarch. The characteristic mode of his representation—with a helmet—is attributed by Plutarch (*Life of Pericles* III.2) as caused by the need to hide the defect of the extraordinary length of Pericles' head.[85] In these discussions of Townley's busts of Homer and Pericles we see the correlations and contradictions between reading ancient texts and collecting ancient artifacts. While Townley reads the bust of Pericles as a three-dimensional illustration of the ancient literary evidence, Payne Knight wants the material evidence of Townley's bust to supersede Pliny's discussion of real and ideal portraits of Homer.

By the late 1820s, J. T. Smith describes Townley's visiting card with its engraved busts as "greatly coveted by the collectors of such *bijoux*."[86] In the second half of the eighteenth century, "the most valuable acquisition a man of refined taste can make, is a peice of fine Greek Sculptour," according to Hamilton—who was hardly a disinterested party.[87] With valuable acquisitions in mind, Zoffany reworked his painting in July 1798, installing in the left foreground a representation of one of Townley's

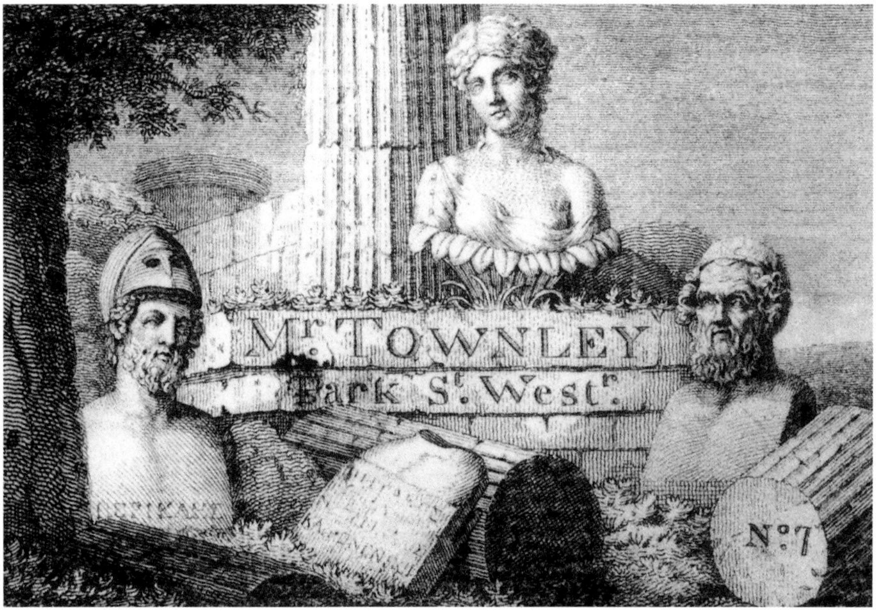

Figure 83 "Greatly coveted by the collectors of such *bijoux*": Charles Townley's visiting card. Towneley Hall Art Gallery & Museums, Burnley Borough Council.

Figure 84 "A momentary & wonderful exertion of the human faculties": Townley's *Discobolus*. © Copyright The Trustees of the British Museum.

last and most prized purchases: a *Discobolus* (fig. 84), excavated from Hadrian's Villa at Tivoli.[88] Citing the "universal opinion in Rome," Thomas Jenkins attributed Townley's discobolus to the same anonymous Greek sculptor who created the *Borghese Gladiator* (fig. 55 above).[89] Both marbles were celebrated for their animated poses. It "requires the utmost Powers," enthused Jenkins of the discobolus, "to imagine & execute such a momentary & wonderful exertion of the human faculties."[90] The early nineteenth-century Scottish surgeon John Bell described the limbs of the *Gladiator* as "thrown out with an animation which exhibits all their elasticity and youthful strength."[91] Townley's discobolus was the latest in a series of marble torsos, including Shelburne's *Diomedes*, that had previously been misidentified and erroneously restored on account of their fragmentary condition.[92] Following the discovery in 1781 of a discobolus with its head intact, these versions were identified in an Italian edition of Winckelmann's *Geschichte der Kunst des Alterthums* as marble copies of a bronze statue by the fifth-century B.C Greek sculptor, Myron. Evidence of the original bronze sculpture of Winckelmann's classic period of Greek art was lost, but references to it were preserved in the much later texts of the first-century A.D. Roman rhetorician Quintilian (*Institutio Oratoria* II.13. 8–10) and in Lucian (*Philopseudes* 18). Townley's discobolus, whose restored head faced away from the discus rather than back towards it, was puffed as being a improved adaptation rather than a slavish copy of Myron's original bronze.[93]

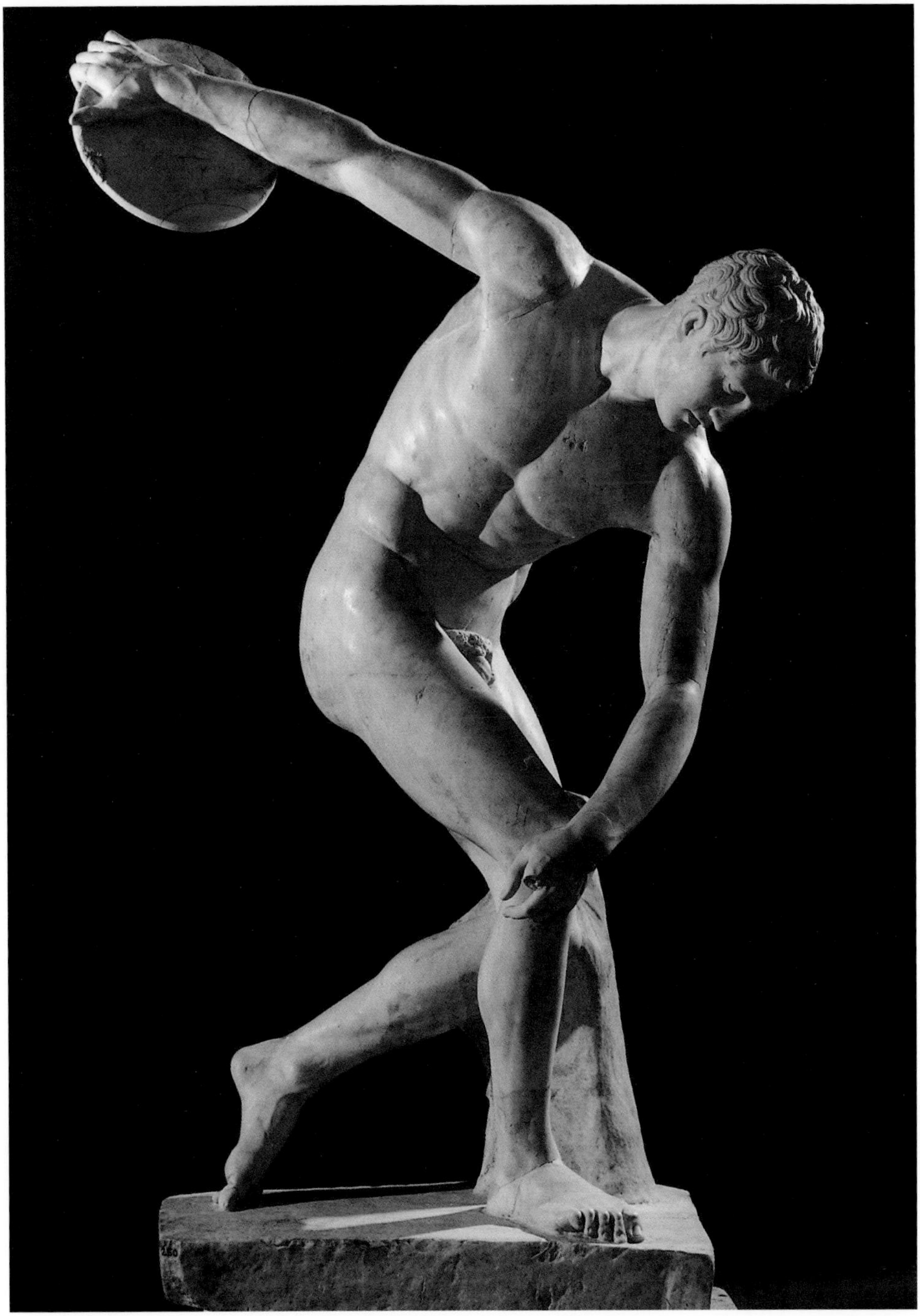

In collecting and contemplating the sculptural productions of the ancient Greeks and Romans, Charles Townley and his fellow collectors Henry Blundell, Viscount Palmerston, Lord Shelburne, and William Weddell participated in what Thomas Jenkins called "a kind of conversing with the celebrated Genius's of those remote times."[94] In the course of this narrative, we have been introduced to the Roman emperors Hadrian and Marcus Aurelius, to ancient heroes from the realms of Greek legend (Diomedes), and Brutus and Cincinnatus from the annals of Roman history, not forgetting the great poet Homer. In the repetition of sculptures like the discobolus and the drunken faun, we see "the passion the ancients had" for certain subjects; "a guide that never fails [insisted Jenkins] and those that do not discover this excellence in their Works, are deprived of much pleasure."[95] But while some of Townley's contemporaries gained pleasure in the possession of sculptures of illustrious ancients with whose names and actions they had been long familiar, Townley's collection conversed with the ancients in a multitude of conversations and on many different levels. In addition to situating the dialogue in the library, in the company of antiquarian authors like d'Hancarville, and surrounded by books like the *Antichità di Ercolano eposte*, Zoffany's famous painting and the published notices about it position Townley's collection of classical sculptures within other postantique traditions of collecting. Equally at home in Britain, at Wilton House, or abroad in Italy, be it the Tribuna of the Uffizi or the finds from Pompeii and Herculaneum, Zoffany's *Townley* may also be situated within a cosmopolitan pictorial tradition of representing collectors and their collections. In Daniel Mytens's portrait of Townley's ancestor, *Lord Arundel in His Gallery* (circa 1615), for instance, the seated Arundel presides over a barrel vaulted gallery at Arundel House, south of the Strand in London. The gallery is shown lined on either side with life-size classical statues and terminating in an arch that looks through to the Thames and beyond.

In another of the two hundred surviving letters written to Townley, Thomas Jenkins referred again to his "passion for the Ancients, & your not being indifferent to the Moderns, nor they to you."[96] With all this talk of antiquity, we should not lose sight of the collection and, in particular, Townley's proprietorial role as collector in conversing with the *moderns*. The sixth Duke of Bedford reckoned a taste for the fine arts an "interesting pursuit . . . not incompatible with those of hunting, shooting, or politics."[97] Henry Blundell cited the poacher as a metaphor for his pursuits when protesting (too much) at being labeled a *collector*:

> I am not pleased at yr [Townley] saying I am *now become fairly a collector*; What I have done was only, as it were, ye sport of a day, as I w.d not be thought to be Idle while abroad; And you might as well tell me, I am *now become fairly a Poacher*, because I go

> out on ye 1st day of shooting & kill all ye Game I can, tho' I scarce ever kill a bird after words.[98]

Writing to the Earl of Shelburne in 1778, Gavin Hamilton characterized "putting you once more in mind of the fine arts and of Rome" as an interruption in the "noble occupation" of Whig politician.[99] When a subsequent Parliamentary session was adjourned, Hamilton hoped "you will find a leisure moment to think of the fine arts and of Rome."[100] As Roman Catholics, Blundell and Townley never juggled the suitably classical demands of *otium* and *negotium*, leisure and business. Unlike Sir Richard Worsley, who in later life neglected collecting in the pursuit of politics, Townley and Blundell were permanently excluded from public office.[101] Based at Ince Blundell Hall in Lancashire, Blundell busied himself with the demands of the estate and family. Rather than installing his own collection at the family seat of nearby Towneley Hall also in Lancashire, its metropolitan location meant the fine arts could become Townley's full-time occupation. From "my Love of sculpture painting &c I am like a child in a brilliant Toy shop," wrote Worsley of London in the 1780s.[102] "Tis no small satisfaction to me frequently to hear your [Townley's] collection mentioned as it ought," flattered Jenkins, "and that the Publick looks up to you as a model of taste."[103]

From the roll call of names represented in the correspondence in Townley's archive, we know that it was not only the public who were said to look up to him. Contemporary sculpture collectors, James Smith Barry, Sir Richard Worsley, and Henry Blundell variously referred, deferred, and especially in Blundell's case, exhausted Townley's "friendship, taste & Judgements."[104] Like Viscount Palmerston and William Weddell, Barry was in his twenties when he first travelled to Italy in 1771. Joined by family friend Townley the following year, they seem to have enjoyed a relationship of protégé and mentor in marble matters.[105] Jenkins surmised that if Barry came to Rome without Townley, "his collection will not make such acquisitions as it might otherwise do."[106] In contrast, letters to Townley from Sir Richard Worsley refer to the "Reciprocal Love that we have for good things"; to "that delightful softness of the Greek chissel which you & I feel, & that I am sorry to observe in this Country is seldom felt and less understood."[107] Wishing in 1790 to consult with him on, among other matters, the publication of the *Museum Worsleyanum*, a year later Worsley wrote of his gratitude to Townley for persuading him to buy Sir William Hamilton's collection of antique gems.[108] While Worsley casts himself as "so great a dabbler in Virtù," a self-proclaimed "young . . . Dabler" was Henry Blundell.[109] Fragments from Blundell's letters have been quoted throughout this chapter. In their earliest surviving correspondence of the 1780s and 1790s, Blundell repeatedly agrees with Townley's advice pertaining to his collection, but after the turn of the century, the two men are unable to agree on any aspect of its publication.[110] From the evidence of these and other letters, Townley's archive shows him to be influencing the content, arrangement, and publication of the ancient artifacts in the collections of several of his contemporaries.[111] Cultivating the tastes of those "not so deep nor of so universal a taste as yourself," as Gavin Hamilton wrote obsequiously to Townley of Charles Greville, who is represented in Zoffany's painting (plate 2).[112]

Townley's refined sensation for sculpture and the London location of his collection meant he made additional connections with a number of social and political heavyweights as well as with professionals in the related fields of painting, sculpture, and architecture. Members of the aristocratic English establishment were directed to Park Street by Townley's dealers in Rome, in particular by Thomas Jenkins. Travellers of the first rank and fortune given Townley's "address to see Policletus & Co," included Lord and Lady Spencer, the Earl of Darnley of Cobham Hall in Kent, and the Duke of Dorset of Knole, also in Kent.[113] Hans Ludwig von Walmoden from Hanover was one of Townley's many distinguished foreign visitors. In using 7 Park Street as what was effectively his London showroom, Jenkins instructed Townley in negotiations with potential purchasers. In 1789, for instance, he had two statues for sale: one of the Roman emperor Trajan from the Villa Mattei and the other of the Athenian orator Demosthenes from the Villa Negroni. Jenkins requested that Townley mention the statues and show the drawings of them to Henry Holland, the architect who was employed by the fifth Duke of Bedford at Woburn Abbey. Jenkins describes being "encouraged to take this Liberty, knowing you have a Pleasure in Promoting fine things coming to England. The Uncommon Merit of the Demosthenes will justify its Price, the Trajan is so reasonable, that a Copy of it would cost more money; The Portrait of so Great an Emperor would be a noble Ornament for the Habitation of the Prince of Wales or a King."[114] For the Earl of Shelburne (by now Lord Lansdowne), Townley negotiated the purchase from Thomas Jenkins in 1792 of a £500 sculpture *Herakles* (fig. 85) excavated with Townley's discobolus (fig. 84 above) from Hadrian's Villa at Tivoli. This life-size statue of Herakles holds a lion skin in one hand and a club in the other, his head, feet, and hands preserved intact. Townley reckoned the *Herakles* a rare survival "of the fine ancient style of Greek sculpture," proclaiming it to be a copy of a celebrated original by a "good Greek artist anterior to the time of the Caesars."[115]

Figure 85 Engraving of the Lansdowne *Herakles,* "executed by some Good Greek artist anterior to the time of the Caesars." The Warburg Institute.

It has been demonstrated how Townley's many conversations with the ancients *and* the moderns went far beyond that of an interesting pursuit, like hunting or shooting—politics being ruled out on account of this faith. Yet his collection of ancient sculptures was firmly implicated into another competitive eighteenth-century sport: possession. Having introduced Townley to fellow collectors, assured of the mutual "pleasure [in] visiting each other Penates & that your passion for them

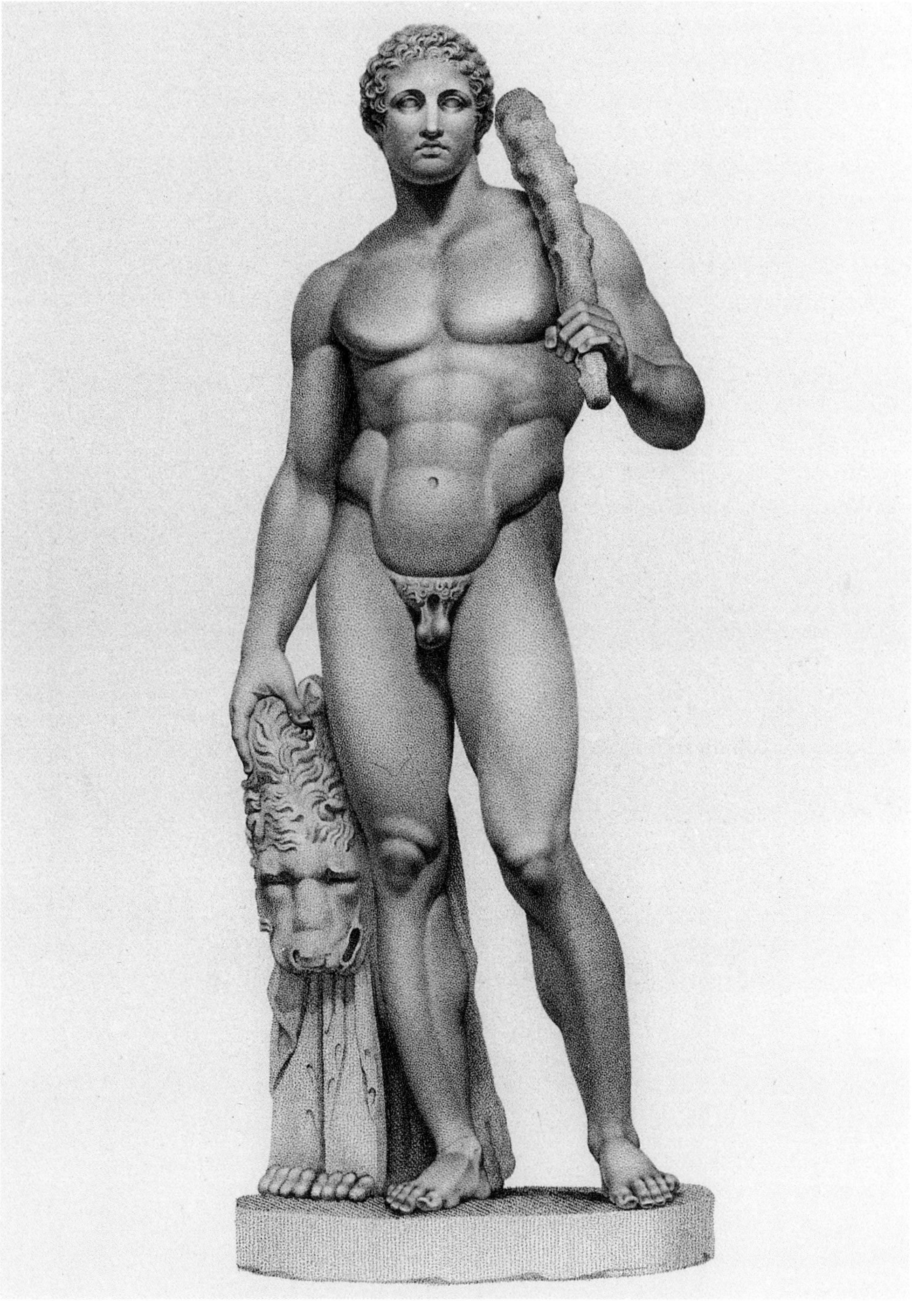

will not diminish," Thomas Jenkins later entreated he "fairly judge of your wife as you did of your Mistress, which I am sensible is no easy task, but as far as possible suppose you ware in possession of the collection [of the Duke of Dorest] at Knole or [William Weddell at] Newby, and not that at Whitehall, would you not cast a lustful eye after them."[116] For the bachelor-collector Townley chastised by his dealer for being "a little inclined to fornication in *virtu* and apt to see other people's wifes with the eye of a mistress" this was sound advice.[117] After all, it was his bust of the nymph *Clytie* (fig. 4 above) that he used jocosely to refer to as his wife.[118] Among the correspondence in the Townley archive, Townley's sculptures are variously characterized as his metaphorical family, as a court of sculpture sessions, and a church of pagan idols.[119] Following anti-Catholic Gordon riots in Westminster in June 1780, Gavin Hamilton wrote of threat of the indigenous barbarians: "Hop[ing] however the storm will blow over & that you will once more smile on the unruly ill governed Brittons, I hope likewise that provision will be made for to prevent for the future such horrid outrages, & that you will continue to enjoy your select collection of elegant Greek ideas, in the midst of fanatism & anarchy, we may say with Lucretius, *Tantum potuit Religio suadere malorum*."[120]

By studying the correspondence in the Townley archive in the British Museum, we eavesdrop on some of Townley's many conversations with the moderns, which more often that not have some connection with the material culture of the ancients. The contents of one letter in particular enable us to conceptualize Townley's archive as a form of luxury sculptural monument executed in the classicizing tradition and in doing so, will bring the discussion to its conclusion. Written by one Samuel Solly of Great Ormond Street, London, and dated only 4 September, the letter outlines a plan to Townley following a visit to the nearby premises of the sculptor Joseph Nollekens. In it, Solly advocates the erection of a mausoleum as part of the (costly) construction of one's reputation: "The thousands if you have them heaped up in a Corner where can you bury them better than in a Mausoleum, will you be inferior to Castle Howard, Nollekens is now come from Lord Fitzwilliams [Wentworth Woodhouse in Yorkshire] to place his statue in the Mausoleum erected to the Marquis [of Rockingham] the rich [Charles Anderson] Pelham of [Brocklesby Park] Lincolnshire is to have a superb one that is to cost £30,000."[121]

Townley never did follow to the letter Solly's scheme for erecting a mausoleum in honour of himself and his ancestors. When it came to marble memorials, he already possessed prize specimens of ancient sculpture, which enabled him to converse with illustrious ancient Greeks and Romans. Their purchase for the nation for twenty thousand pounds and deposit in the British Museum ensured that Townley's relatives "would have the perpetual enjoyment of the collection without any of the care, trouble, or expence of it," as Payne Knight wrote to Townley's brother, after his death in 1805.[122] Almost two hundred years later, in 1992, the museum purchased what is now known as the Townley archive. This paper mausoleum provides written testimony of the warmth of Townley's passion and sometime fornication for the ancients: a passion that was translated into material possessions but that was initially formulated by Townley's classical education. In many ways, this Who's Who of British neoclassicism is less a dynastic mausoleum like that at Brocklesby Park in Lincolnshire, with its monuments to Pelham's distant and more recent relatives, than it is a collective cenotaph, like that in the park of Wentworth Woodhouse. Here, Nollekens's posthumous portrait sculpture of the former Whig prime minister, the Marquis of Rockingham, is accompanied by busts of his friends and political allies in what has been described as a temple of political friendship.[123] The Rockingham mausoleum is also recognized by art historians as the model for the fifth Duke of Bedford's Temple of Liberty in the conservatory at Woburn Abbey in Bedfordshire.[124] Bedford's architect, Henry Holland, contacted Townley at the request of the sixth duke, who inherited his brother's unfinished project in 1802. Wanting "the effect of an antient Temple adopted for a modern purpose," the duke was said by Holland to have "a much higher opinion of your [Townley's] judgment than of that of any other person."[125] When couched in these terms, Townley's paper mausoleum preserves and perpetuates evidence of an entire neoclassical culture of collecting; an educated, nonpolitical Parliament in which Townley is characterized, literally and by the mass of existing documentation, as its first minister.

CONCLUSION

Fabricating the Antique has challenged the still prevalent notion of British neoclassicism as a purely decorative encounter with the ancient Greeks and Romans. It contends that such a notion *mis*conceives of neoclassicism as pedantic, random, and faddish, as if it were little more than a two-dimensional backdrop largely devoid of broader cultural significance. The dangers of conceptualizing the phenomenon through a nineteenth-century filter have also been highlighted. Rather than the nineteenth century's retrospective and monolithic classification, neoclassicism during the period from 1760 to 1800 has been understood as a fluid and pervasive style of thought. While not disagreeing with the position that the architecture of Robert Adam and the pottery of Josiah Wedgwood remain its best-known manifestations in England, I have situated them and lesser-known examples in the wider historical, cultural, and intellectual context of eighteenth-century Britain.[1]

In seeking to flesh out the bare surface of a stylistic classification, I have located neoclassicism in the discipline of material culture. Identifying its educational origin provides an interpretative framework in which the mental and linguistic exercises of the eighteenth-century classroom sheds meaning on the material culture of the country house drawing room. This narrative has equipped us with the methodological approaches and strategies with which to cast classicism— defined here as the use and abuse of ancient learning—as a style of thought inculcated by a classical education. As a form of what may be termed intellectual programming, classicism has been seen to map out itineraries—figurative and literal—for later encounters with the antique. With this in mind, the cultural institution for educated Britons that was the grand tour in Italy has been re-presented as a form of classical pilgrimage; the collections of ancient artifacts acquired on classic ground as the extension or conversion of classicism into neoclassicism: of programs of thought "so much the possession of our minds, from the studies and amusements of our youth" into material possessions.[2]

In focusing on the culture of education, imitation, competition, and conversation, which saw the material culture of the ancients packaged for possession by an elite British audience, we have had continual recourse to the *library*. In its physical and architectural space, its contents and decoration, the eighteenth-century library encapsulated the neoclassical enterprise—in much the same way as the laboratory had for the experimental life a century before. Cited by authors and imaged by artists, including Edward Gibbon, Giovanni Battista Piranesi, and Hugh Douglas Hamilton, the library was the prime site for the reception, preservation, and display of antiquity. In other words, the library embodied antiquity in its textual *and* material incarnations, housing editions of ancient texts in Latin and Greek and in translation alongside contemporary publications of antiquity. In much the same way that a classical education was materially embodied in school textbooks, so ancient architecture, sculpture, and painting encountered on the grand tour in Italy was packaged in deluxe library volumes. These volumes preserved and perpetuated fragile classical monuments in book form. Collected as ornaments for the aristocratic library, at the same time, their engraved plates were utilized as pattern books by British manufacturers and architects, including Josiah Wedgwood and Robert Adam, mass producing and reproducing a whole range of imitation antique artifacts and paintings for the elite interior, including the library.

In commissions for copies of ancient sculptural masterpieces like the *Medici Venus* and *Apollino*, these folios were consulted as catalogs by middlemen in Italy who in turn cited them as guidebooks for the absent patrons whose instructions they followed—not always to the letter. Exploring how the unique copies of statues and busts in marble and bronze were tailor-made to comply with the agendas of their British patrons reminds us of the complexities and subtleties at work in instances of neoclassicism in the late eighteenth century. Neoclassicism, then as now, was never a case of slavishly replicating the material culture of the ancients but rather a carefully molded simulacrum, as much prized for its novel as its canonical associations. Johann Zoffany's famous painting of Charles Townley's library (plate 2) visually reinforces the centrality of the library space, with its collections of folios and artifacts, to the neoclassical endeavor. It gives visual form to the conversations with the ancients that educated sculpture collectors like Townley participated in. Townley's expertise in marble matters allowed him a public role in British society from which he was otherwise excluded on account of his Roman Catholic faith. His first-rate sculpture collection is testimony to the collecting of representations of Greek and Roman emperors, heroes and poets, as both a learned pursuit and a highly competitive social pastime.

For Townley, his bust of the nymph Clytie (fig. 4) was a prized possession, a mute wife presiding over his family of ancient marble sculptures. We saw in the introduction how Clytie has latterly become a palimpsest for the irreconcilable views of specialist scholars, who seem intent on classifying her as definitively ancient or modern. It has been demonstrated throughout this book how she and other artifacts of neoclassicism resist this dogmatic line of interrogation: her silence being the perfect riposte to notions of a monolithic neoclassicism. By literally incorporating the dialectic of the new versus the ancient that lies at the heart of neoclassicism, her status as an emblematic object derives precisely from the way she resists such categorization. She also reminds us how debates over authenticity can obscure the ludic potential of the apparent split between the original and the copy, the genuine and the fake, when in fact it was often employed as a deliberate strategy in neoclassicism. This is plain in our final example: the folding doors at the west end of the long gallery at Syon House in Middlesex (fig. 86). Syon is a property already familiar

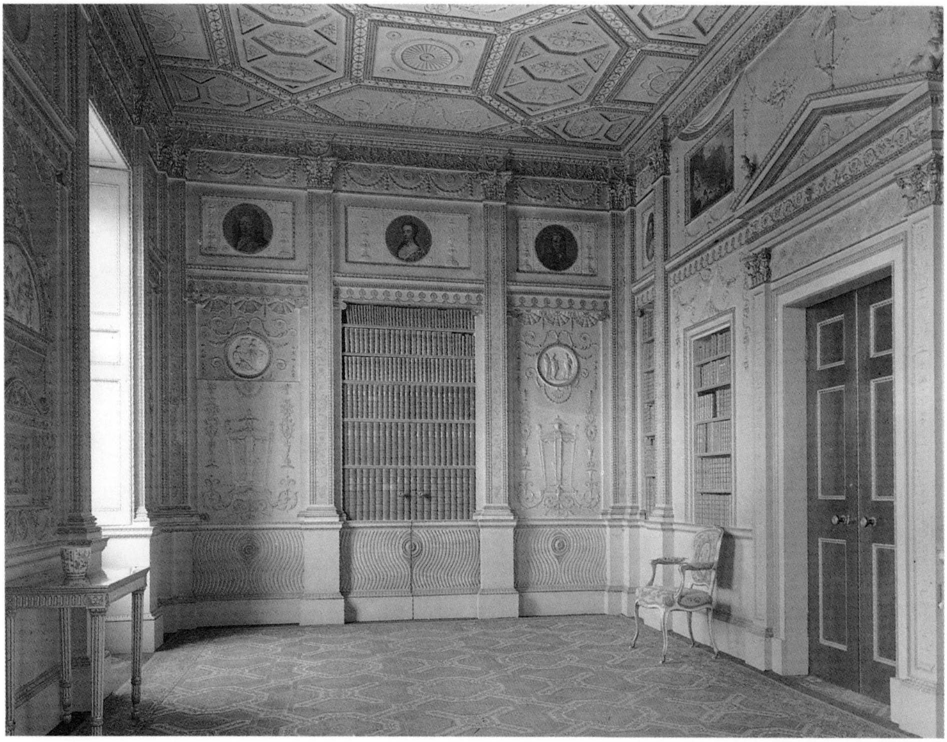

Figure 86 "A curious catalogue of the *auctores deperditi*": View of the mimic volumes inscribed with the titles of the lost texts of Greek and Roman authors in the west end of the long gallery at Syon House. Country Life Picture Library.

to us from Robert Adam's interiors for Lord Northumberland, including the dining room, which was furnished with marble copies of sculptures, including the *Apollino* commissioned by his brother, James Adam, in Italy (see chap. 5). Robert Adam was also responsible for refurnishing the interior of Syon's long gallery as a library. Ostensibly, the doors at the far west end consist of further bookshelves containing books. But on closer examination, it can be seen that the volumes consist only of book spines. They are in fact mimic volumes, each inscribed with the titles of lost works by ancient Greek and Roman authors. These folding doors, which open onto the garden, have been described as a 'curious catalogue of the *auctores deperditi*.'[3] Masquerading as the prized lost texts of the classical literary tradition, they remind us of the program of late eighteenth-century neoclassicism, with its emphasis on the library and learning. They also playfully remind us that everything is not always what it seems. In this instance Adam exploits the *losses* rather than the survivals of the classical literary tradition, reinscribing the works of the *auctores deperditi* as part of the material culture of eighteenth-century neoclassicism. Here again the library is the prime site for the reception, preservation, and display of antiquity. But the library–cum–long gallery at Syon is both repository *and* laboratory—transforming textual losses into material possessions.

ABBREVIATIONS

BM, TY	British Museum, Townley Archive
Keele	Wedgwood Archive, Keele University Library
NAS	National Archives of Scotland

NOTES

INTRODUCTION

1. Hugh Honour, *Neo-classicism* (London: Penguin, 1991), 14.

2. A. H. Layard, "Pompeii," *Quarterly Review* 115 (1864): 346.

3. Adolf Michaelis, *Ancient Marbles in Great Britain* (Cambridge: Cambridge University Press, 1882), 164. This passage is quoted and discussed by Wolfgang Ernst, "Adolf Michaelis: Die konfrontation Deutscher archäologie mit Britischen antikensammlungen," *Zeitschrift des Deutschen Vereins für Kunstwissenschaft* 46 (1992): 85–87.

4. *Penny Magazine* 363 (1837): 458, described Soane's house as "a model house" and an "architectural kaleidoscope." On Soane's room of architectural models, see John Elsner, "A Collector's Model of Desire: The House and Museum of Sir John Soane," in *The Cultures of Collecting*, ed. John Elsner and Roger Cardinal, 155–76 (London: Reaktion, 1994). Soane's cork model of Pompeii has been attributed to Domenico Padiglione, employee of the Neapolitan court, see Valentin Kockel, "Rom über die Alpen tragen: Korkmodelle antiker im. 18. und 19. jahrhundert," *Rom über die Alpen tragen: Fürsten sammeln antike Architektur; Die Aschaffenburger Korkmodelle, mit einem Bestandskatalog*, ed. Werner Helmberger and Valentin Kockel (Landshut and Ergolding: Arcos, 1993), 21–22. Margaret Richardson, "Model Architecture," *Country Life* 183 (1989): 224, refers to Soane's acquisition of the model from the estate of John Saunders.

5. Pierre Bourdieu, *Distinction: A Social Critique of the Judgment of Taste* (London: Routledge and Kegan Paul, 1989), 2: "a work of art has meaning and interest only for someone who possesses the cultural competence, that is, the code, into which it is encoded."

6. Thomas Jenkins to Charles Townley, 14 August 1772, British Museum, Townley archive (hereafter BM, TY) 7/313. Jenkins was evidently "in treaty" for *Clytie* on behalf of another of his English clients, the collector Lyde Browne. Browne was to lose out on this occasion.

7. Mark Jones, ed., *Fake? The Art of Deception,* exhibition catalog (London: British Museum Press, 1990), no. 3.

8. Susan Walker, "Clytie—A False Woman," in *Why Fakes Matter: Essays on Problems of Authenticity*, ed. Mark Jones, 32–40 (London: British Museum Press, 1992).

9. Nicholas Penny argues this position in the *Burlington Magazine* 126 (1984): 55 and 132 (1990): 506.

10. Sir Henry Ellis, *The Townley Gallery* (London: Library of Entertaining Knowledge, 1836), 1: 9.

11. Samuel Rogers to Charles Townley, undated, BM, TY 7/1579.

12. William Sandys to Charles Townley, 16 October 1780, BM, TY 7/1204. The Ovid passage is *Metamorphosis* 11. 326.

13. Susan J. Hill, *Catalogue of the Townley Archive at the British Museum,* British Museum Occasional Paper, 138 (London: British Museum Publications, 2002), vii.

14. Alex Potts, *Flesh and the Ideal: Winckelmann and the Origins of Art History* (New Haven and London: Yale University Press, 1994), 9–10.

15. Potts, *Flesh and the Ideal*, 13.

16. Sam Smiles, *The Image of Antiquity: Ancient Britons and the Romantic Imagination* (New Haven and London: Yale University Press, 1994), ix–x.

17. Philip J. Ayres, *Classical Culture and the Idea of Rome in Eighteenth-Century England* (Cambridge: Cambridge University Press, 1997), xiii.

18. Dana Arnold, *The Georgian Country House: Architecture, Landscape and Society* (Stroud: Sutton, 1998), 107.

19. David Irwin, *English Neoclassical Art: Studies in Inspiration and Taste* (London: Faber, 1966), 19. Irwin's recent *Neoclassicism* (London: Phaidon, 1997), 4–9, begins with a discussion of the label as a *style* in the visual arts.

20. Matthew Craske, *Art in Europe, 1700–1830: A History of the Visual Arts in an Era of Unprecedented Urban Economic Growth* (Oxford: Oxford University Press, 1997), 7.

21. My quotations are harvested from Potts, *Flesh and the Ideal*, 21; Thomas Crow, *Emulation: Making Artists for Revolutionary France* (New Haven and London: Yale University Press, 1995), 102; Abigail Solomon-Godeau, "Male Trouble: A Crisis in Representation," *Art History* 16 (1993): 292; N. B. Nisbet, *German Aesthetic and Literary Criticism: Winckelmann, Lessing, Hamann, Herder, Schiller, Goethe* (Cambridge: Cambridge University Press, 1985), 5; David Watkin, *Thomas Hope, 1769–1831, and the Neo-Classical Idea* (London: Murray, 1968), 141.

22. Aidan Day, *Romanticism* (London: Routledge, 1996), 74: "there was in the eighteenth century more than one Neoclassicism."

23. Christopher Stray, *Classics Transformed: Schools, Universities and Society in England, 1830–1960* (Oxford: Clarendon Press, 1998), 15.

24. Potts, *Flesh and the Ideal*, 222–23, and idem, "Winckelmann's Construction of History," *Art History* 5 (1982): 399. Useful bibliography on French neoclassicism includes Carol Ockman, "Profiling Homoeroticism: Ingres' *Achilles Receiving the Ambassadors of Agamemnon*," *Art Bulletin* 75 (1993): 259–74; Solomon-Godeau, "Male Trouble," 286–312; Thomas Crow, "Revolutionary Activism and the Cult of Male Beauty in the Studio of David," in *Fictions of the French Revolution*, ed. Bernadette Fort, 55–83 (Evanston, Ill.: Northwestern University Press, 1991); and Edouard Pommier, "Winckelmann et la vision de l'Antiquité classique dans la France des Lumières et de la Rèvolution," *Revue de l'Art* 83 (1989): 9–20.

25. Ronald T. Ridley, *The Eagle and the Spade: Archaeology in Rome during the Napoleonic Era* (Cambridge: Cambridge University Press, 1992), 1.

26. Valerie Huet, "Napoleon I: A New Augustus?" in *Roman Presences: Receptions of Rome in European Culture, 1789–1945*, ed. Catharine Edwards, 53–69 (Cambridge: Cambridge University Press, 1999).

27. Christopher M. S. Johns, *Antonio Canova and the Politics of Patronage in Revolutionary and Napoleonic Europe* (Berkeley: University of California Press, 1998), 93–98 and 104–9.

28. See, for example, Anthony Grafton, "Polyhistory into *Philolog*: Notes on the Transformation of German Classical Scholarship, 1780–1850," *History of Universities* 3 (1983): 159–92; Suzanne L. Marchand, *Down from Olympus: Archaeology and Philhellenism in Germany, 1750–1970* (Princeton, N.J.: Princeton University Press, 1996), 4; and Nisbet, *German Aesthetic and Literary Criticism*, 6.

29. Alex Potts, "Political Attitudes and the Rise of Historicism in Art History," *Art History* 1 (1978): 191; Stephen Bann, "The Sense of the Past: Image, Text, and Object in the Formation of Historical Consciousness in Nineteenth-Century Britain," in *The New Historicism*, ed. Harold Aaram Veeser (London: Routledge, 1989), 105; and Wolfgang Ernst, "Frames at Work: Museological Imagination and Historical Discourse in Neoclassical Britain," *Art Bulletin* 75 (1993): 483.

30. Lawrence E. Klein, *Shaftesbury and the Culture of Politeness: Moral Discourse and Cultural Politics in Early Eighteenth-Century England* (Cambridge: Cambridge University Press, 1994), 41.

31. Nicholas Thomas, *Entangled Objects: Exchange, Material Culture and Colonialism in the Pacific* (Cambridge, Mass., and London: Harvard University Press, 1991), 143. Thomas's book should be read in conjunction with B. M. Benedict, "The "Curious Attitude" in Eighteenth-Century Britain: Observing and Owning," *Eighteenth-Century Life* 14 (1990): 59–98; Urs Bitterli, *Cultures in Conflict: Encounters between European and Non-European cultures, 1492–1800* (Cambridge: Polity, 1989); David Mackay, *In the Wake of Cook: Exploration, Science and Empire, 1780–1801* (London: Croom Helm, 1985); Bernard Smith, *European Vision and the South Pacific* (New Haven and London: Yale University Press, 1985); P. J. Marshall and Glyndwr Williams, *The Great Map of Mankind: British Perceptions of the World in the Age of Enlightenment* (London: Dent, 1982); and Robin Fisher and Hugh Johnston eds., *Captain James Cook and His Times* (London: Croom Helm, 1979).

32. Harriet Guest, "The Great Distinction: Figures of the Exotic in the Work of William Hodges," *Oxford Art Journal* 12 (1989): 41–42. See also Patricia Fara, "Benjamin West's Portrait of Joseph Banks," *Endeavour* 24 (2000): 1–3; and Beth Fowkes Tobin, *Picturing Imperial Power: Colonial Subjects in Eighteenth-Century British Painting* (Durham: Duke University Press, 1999), 87.

33. Marshall and Williams, *The Great Map of Mankind*, 299.

34. As Howard D. Weinbrot points out, the labels "Augustan" and "Augustanism" are loaded "with a panoply of inferences, hypotheses, and critical and scholarly methods (or lack of them) that dictate conclusions and evaluation of recalcitrant evidence." See his *Augustus Caesar in "Augustan" England: The Decline of a Classical Norm* (Princeton, N.J.: Princeton University Press, 1978), 240; Joseph M. Levine, *The Battle of the Books: History and Literature in the Augustan Age* (Ithaca, N.Y.: Cornell University Press, 1991); Laird Okie, *Augustan Historical Writing: Histories of England in the English Enlightenment* (London: University Press of America, 1991); Martin C. Battestin, *The Providence of Wit: Aspects of Form in Augustan Literature and the Arts* (Oxford: Clarendon Press, 1974); Richard Feingold, *Moralized Song: The Character of Augustan Lyricism* (New Brunswick: Rutgers University Press, 1989); Howard Erskine-Hill, *The Augustan Idea in English Literature* (London: Edward Arnold, 1983); Ian Watt, "Two Historical Aspects of the Augustan Tradition," in *Studies in the Eighteenth Century*, ed. R. F. Brissenden, 67–88 (Toronto: University of Toronto Press, 1968); and Paul Fussell, *The Rhetorical World of Augustan Humanism: Ethics and Imagery from Swift to Burke* (Oxford: Clarendon Press, 1965).

35. Richard Hewlings, "Chiswick House and Gardens: Appearance and Meaning," in *Lord Burlington: Architecture, Art and Life*, ed. Toby Barnard and Jane Clark, 1–149 (London: Hambleton, 1995); John Harris, "The Transformation of Lord Burlington: From the Palladio and Jones of His Time to the Modern Vitruvius," in *The Georgian Villa*, ed. Dana Arnold, 41–47 (Stroud: Alan Sutton,

1996); John Harris, *The Palladian Revival: Lord Burlington, His Villa and Garden at Chiswick* (Montreal, Quebec: Centre Canadien d'Architecture and London: Royal Academy of Arts, 1994); Giles Worsley, "Taking the Ancients Literally: Archaeological Neoclassicism in Mid-Eighteenth-Century Britain," in *New Light on English Palladianism*, ed. Charles Hind, 64–80 (London: Georgian Group, 1990); and Rudolf Wittkower *Palladio and English Palladianism* (London: Thames and Hudson, 1974).

36. For styles of thought, see Karl Mannheim, *Ideology and Utopia: An Introduction to the Sociology of Knowledge* (London: Routledge, 1991), 45, and idem, Mannheim, *Conservatism: A Contribution to the Sociology of Knowledge* (London: Routledge, 1986), 111 and 191.

37. Christopher Stray, "Scholars and Gentlemen: Towards a Sociology of English Classical Scholarship," in *Aspects of Nineteenth-Century British Classical Scholarship*, ed. H. D. Jocelyn (Liverpool: Liverpool Classic Monthly, 1996), 26.

38. John Cannon, *Aristocratic Century: The Peerage of Eighteenth Century England* (Cambridge: Cambridge University Press, 1984), 35.

39. Pierre Bourdieu, "Systems of Education and Systems of Thought," in *Knowledge and Control: New Directions for the Sociology of Education*, ed. Michael F. D. Young (London: Collier Macmillan, 1971), 191–92.

40. Jonathan Gathorne-Hardy, *The Public School Phenomenon, 597–1977* (Harmondsworth: Penguin, 1977), esp. 24 and 38.

41. R. M. Ogilvie, *Latin and Greek: A History of the Influence of the Classics on English Life from 1600–1800* (London: Routledge and Kegan Paul, 1964), 40.

42. Stray, *Classics Transformed*, 48.

43. My summary here is based largely on H. C. Maxwell Lyte, *A History of Eton College* (3rd ed., London: Macmillan & Co., 1899), esp. 319–21; and M. V. Wallbank, "Eighteenth Century Public Schools and the Education of the Governing Elite," *History of Education* 8 (1979): 1–19.

44. Gathorne-Hardy, *The Public School Phenomenon*, 39.

45. Bourdieu, "Systems of Education and Systems of Thought," 204.

46. Quoted by Wallbank, "Eighteenth Century Public Schools and the Education of the Governing Elite," 5.

47. Lyte, *History of Eton College*, 321.

48. Bourdieu, "Systems of Education and Systems of Thought," 194.

49. H. T. Parker, *The Cult of Antiquity and the French Revolutionaries: A Study in the Development of the Revolutionary Spirit* (Chicago: University of Chicago Press, 1937), 8–36.

50. Bourdieu, "Systems of Education and Systems of Thought," 196.

51. Andrew Wilton and Ilaria Bignamini, ed., *The Grand Tour: The Lure of Italy in the Eighteenth Century* (London: Tate Gallery, 1996), 33; and Jeremy Black, *The British Abroad: The Grand Tour in the Eighteenth Century* (Stroud: Alan Sutton, 1992).

52. Ayres, *Classical Culture and the Idea of Rome*, sees travel to Italy as fleshing out one's classical reading.

53. J. D. Prown, "Mind in Matter: An Introduction to Material Culture Theory and Method," in *Material Life in America, 1660–1860*, ed. Robert Blair St. George, 17–37 (Boston: Northeastern University Press, 1988).

54. Judy Attfield, "Beyond the Pale: Reviewing the Relationship between Material Culture and Design History," *Journal of Design History* 12 (1999): 373. See also her *Wild Things: The Material Culture*

of Everyday Life (Oxford: Berg, 2000).

55. Moira Vincentelli, *Women and Ceramics: Gendered Vessels* (Manchester: Manchester University Press, 2000), 2.

56. Steven Shapin and Simon Schaffer, *Leviathan and the Air-Pump: Hobbes, Boyle and the Experimental Life* (Princeton, N.J.: Princeton University Press, 1985), 39 and 334.

57. Of these books, the following have been most useful: Chloe Chard, *Pleasure and Guilt on the Grand Tour: Travel Writing and Imaginative Geography, 1600–1830* (Manchester: Manchester University Press, 1999); M. L. Pratt, *Imperial Eyes: Travel Writing and Transculturation* (London: Routledge, 1992); B. M. Stafford, *Voyage into Substance: Art, Science, Nature and the Illustrated Travel Account, 1760–1840* (Cambridge Mass., and London: MIT Press, 1984); P. G. Adams, *Travel Literature and the Evolution of the Novel* (Lexington: University Press of Kentucky, 1983); P. G. Adams, *Travellers and Travel Liars, 1660–1800* (New York: Dover, 1980); and Charles L. Batten, *Pleasurable Instruction: Form and Convention in Eighteenth-Century Travel Literature* (Berkeley and London: University of California Press, 1978).

CHAPTER 1

1. Quoted in W. O. Hassall, "Portrait of a Bibliophile II. Thomas Coke, Earl of Leicester, 1697–1759," *Book Collector* 8 (1959): 251.

2. John Berger, *Ways of Seeing* (London: BBC and Harmondsworth: Penguin, 1972), 107. For a rigorous discussion of the Gainsborough painting, see Ann Bermingham, *Landscape and Ideology: The English Rustic Tradition, 1740–1860* (London: Thames and Hudson, 1986), 28–30. Bermingham warns against using this atypical image to exemplify the genre of the outdoor conversation piece. I, however, am using it as a representation of land as "property."

3. *Nostell Priory* (London: The National Trust 1997), 12. Lindsay Boynton and Nicholas Goodison, "Thomas Chippendale at Nostell Priory," *Furniture History* 4 (1968): 10–61, transcribe the correspondence and bills between Sir Rowland and the Chippendale firm. See also Christopher Gilbert, "New Light on the Furnishings at Nostell Priory," *Furniture History* 26 (1990): 53–64; and Lindsay Boynton and Nicholas Goodison, "The Furniture of Thomas Chippendale at Nostell Priory," *Burlington Magazine* 111 (1969): 281–85 and 351–60.

4. Marcia Pointon, *Hanging the Head: Portraiture and Social Formation in Eighteenth-Century England* (New Haven: Yale University Press, 1993), 162.

5. Hamilton's bill is transcribed in full in Alastair Laing, "Sir Rowland and Lady Winn: A Conversation Piece in the Library at Nostell Priory," *Apollo* 151 (2000): 15.

6. Leeds district archives, NP/C3/1/5/1/19/1.

7. *Memoirs, Journals and Correspondence of Thomas Moore*, ed. Lord John Russell (London, 1853–56), 2: 365. Quoted by J. R. Hale, "Art and Audience: The *Medici Venus*, c. 1750–c. 1850," *Italian Studies* 31 (1976): 37, note 1; and John Northall, *Travels through Italy, containing new & curious observations on that country* (London, 1766), 1: 58.

8. The Hamilton painting and its later copy are discussed in more detail in Viccy Coltman, "Status, Stasis and Statue: The Nostell Priory Conversation Piece(s)," *Visual Culture in Britain* 3 (2002): 37–52.

9. Zoffany's *Townley* and the marbles it represents are discussed at length in chapter 6 below.

10. *Sophie in London, 1786, being the diary of Sophie von la Roche*, trans. Clare Williams (London: Jonathan Cape 1933), 219.

11. Jenkins to Charles Townley, 23 January 1782, BM, TY7/411.

12. Gerard Vaughan, "The Townley Zoffany: Reflections on *Charles Townley and His Friends*," *Apollo* 144 (1996): 32.

13. John Britton, *The Union of Architecture, Sculpture and Painting, exemplified by a series of illustrations with descriptive account of the house and galleries of John Soane* (London: The Author, 1827), vii. On Soane's library, see Eileen Harris, "Sir John Soane's Library: 'O Books! Ye Monuments of Mind,'" *Apollo* 131 (1990): 242–47.

14. Rev. Archibald Alison, *Essays on the nature and principles of taste* (London: J. J. G. & G. Robinson and Edinburgh: Bell & Bradfute, 1790), 27. On Alison's *Essays*, see Kay Dian Kriz, *The Idea of the English Landscape Painter: Genius as Alibi in the Early Nineteenth Century* (New Haven: Yale University Press, 1997), esp. 83–84.

15. Bann compares the antiquarian endeavor with the collecting of classical sculptures in "The Sense of the Past," 105.

16. James Raven, "Modes of Reading and Writing in the Eighteenth-Century Private Library," in *Lesen und Schreiben im 17. und 18. Jahrhundert*, ed. Paul Goetsch (Tübingen: G. Narr, 1994), 49. The following have been useful in thinking generally about libraries and their contents: Nicolas Barker, *Treasures from the Libraries of National Trust Country Houses* (New York: The Royal Oak Foundation & the Grolier Club, 1999); P. H. Reid, "The Development of a National Heritage Policy for Libraries and Book Collections of Country Houses" (Ph.D. diss., Robert Gordon University, 1999), esp. "Historical Development of Country House Libraries," 64–96; Anthony Grafton, *Commerce with the Classics: Ancient Books and Renaissance Readers* (Ann Arbor: University of Michigan Press, 1997); Dora Thornton, *The Scholar in His Study: Ownership and Experience in Renaissance Italy* (New Haven: Yale University Press, 1997); Robin Myres and Michael Harris, eds., *Antiquaries, Book Collectors and the Circles of Learning* (Winchester: St. Paul's Bibliographies, 1996); James Raven, Helen Small, and Naomi Tadmor, eds., *The Practice and Representation of Reading in England* (Cambridge: Cambridge University Press, 1996); Roger Chartier, *The Order of Books: Readers, Authors and Libraries in Europe between the Fourteenth and Eighteenth Centuries* (Cambridge: Polity Press, 1994); Robin Myres and Michael Harris, eds., *Property of a Gentleman: The Formation, Organisation and Dispersal of the Private Library, 1620–1920* (Winchester: St. Paul's Bibliographies, 1991); Robin Myres and Michael Harris, eds., *Bibliophily* (Cambridge: Chadwyck-Healey, 1986); Isabel Rivers, ed., *Books and Their Readers in Eighteenth-Century England* (Leicester: Leicester University Press, 1982); André Masson, *The Pictorial Catalogue: Mural Decoration in Libraries*, trans. David Gerard (Oxford: Clarendon, 1981); Mark Girouard, *Life in the English Country House: A Social and Architectural History* (New Haven: Yale University Press, 1978); Roger Chartier and Denis Roche, "New Approaches to the History of the Book," in *Constructing the Past: Essays in Historical Methodology*, ed. Jacques Le Goff and Pierre Nora, 198–214 (Cambridge: Cambridge University Press, 1985); and Raymond Irwin, *The Origins of the English Library* (London: George Allen & Unwin, 1958).

17. See A. N. L. Munby, "The Library," in *The Destruction of the Country House*, ed. Roy Strong, Marcus Binney, and John Harris, 107–10 (London: Thames and Hudson, 1974).

18. Quoted from a MS in the possession of John Yorke.

19. David Pearson, *Provenance Research in Book History: A Handbook* (London: British Library, 1998), 173. My account of the formation and dispersal of the library at Osterley Park House is based on William Clarke, *Repertorium Bibliographicum; or, Some Account of the Most Celebrated British Libraries* (London: William Clarke 1819), 1: 312–13.

20. Edward Harwood, *A View of the Various Editions of the Greek and Roman Classics* (London: G. Robinson, 1775), xi–xii.

21. Seymour di Ricci, *English Collectors of Books and Manuscripts, 1530–1930, and Their Marks of Ownership* (Cambridge: Cambridge University Press, 1930), 88. See also J. E. Bailey, "The Towneley Library," *Palatine Notebook* 3 (1886): 187–92. Bailey describes the sale as "one of the most deplorable dispersions of an old family library."

22. Clarke, *Repertorium Bibliographicum*, 2: 551.

23. Chetham's Library, Bailey Collection, Mun. A.2.93; and Chetham's Library, Mun. A.3.137, Crossley and Bailey collections.

24. Edward Gibbon, *The History of the Decline and Fall of the Roman Empire,* ed. David Womersley, 3 vols. (London: Allen Lane, 1994), 3: 908–9.

25. Gibbon, *History of the Decline and Fall*, 3: 909. For discussions of this passage, see Karen O' Brien, "Gibbon's Prospects: Rhetoric, Fame and the Closing Chapters of *The Decline and Fall*," in *Edward Gibbon: Bicentenary Essays*, ed. David Womersley (Oxford: Voltaire Foundation, 1997), 239; and Joseph M. Levine, "Edward Gibbon and the Quarrel between the Ancients and Moderns," *Humanism and History: Origins of Modern English Historiography* (Ithaca: Cornell University Press, 1987), esp. 188.

26. Anthony Grafton, *Commerce with the Classics: Ancient Books and Renaissance Readers* (Ann Arbor: University of Michigan Press, 1997), 226, notes that humanistically educated readers see reception and creativity, reading and writing as intimately connected.

27. See Peter Ghosh, "The Conception of Gibbon's *History*," in *Edward Gibbon and Empire,* ed. Rosamund McKitterick and Roland Quinault (Cambridge: Cambridge University Press, 1997), 289.

28. Christopher Kelly, "A Grand Tour: Reading Gibbon's *Decline and Fall*," *Greece & Rome* 44 (1997), 53.

29. Horace Walpole to William Mason, in *Horace Walpole's Correspondence*, 28: 243. It should be noted that Walpole was less enthusiastic in a letter to Lady Ossory dated 4 March 1796 (34: 215–16) about the later volumes, where Gibbon's "want of method, his leaping back and forwards to different periods, by embracing such a mass of matter, confounds and bewilders his readers."

30. Potts, *Flesh and the Ideal*, 13.

31. Gibbon, *History of the Decline and Fall*, 1: 428. Francis Haskell, "Gibbon and the History of Art," in *Edward Gibbon and "The Decline and Fall of the Roman Empire,"* ed. G. W. Bowersock, John Clive, and Stephen R. Graubard, 193–205 (Cambridge, Mass.: Harvard University Press, 1977), considers Gibbon's artistic taste in relation to the aesthetic conventions of the grand tour, rather than the absence of art history in the *Decline and Fall*, but see further chapter 6, "The Dialogue between Antiquarians and Historians," in Francis Haskell, *History and Its Images: Art and the Interpretation of the Past* (New Haven: Yale University Press, 1993), 159–200.

32. Gibbon, *History of the Decline and Fall*, 3: 909.

33. Potts, *Flesh and the Ideal*, 189–90.

34. Edward Gibbon, *A Vindication of Some Passages in the Fifteenth and Sixteenth Chapters of "The History of the Decline and Fall of the Roman Empire"* (London: W. Strahan, 1779), 89. Most useful works consulted on Gibbon in his cultural and intellectual context include David Womersley, *Gibbon and the "Watchmen of the Holy City": The Historian and His Reputation, 1776–1815* (Oxford: Oxford University Press, 2002); Patricia Craddock, "Contemplative Heroes and Gibbon's Historical Imagination," in *The Historical Imagination in Early Modern Britain: History, Rhetoric, Fiction*, ed. Donald R. Kelley and David Harris Sacks, 343–59 (Cambridge: Woodrow Wilson Centre Press and Cambridge University Press, 1997); Kelly, "A Grand Tour," 39–58; Rosamund McKitterick and Roland Quinault,

eds., *Edward Gibbon and Empire* (Cambridge: Cambridge University Press, 1997); Philip Hicks, *Neo-classical History and English Culture from Clarendon to Hume* (Basingstoke: Macmillan, 1996); Patricia B. Craddock, *Edward Gibbon: Luminous Historian, 1772–1794* (Baltimore: John Hopkins University Press, 1989); Roy Porter, *Edward Gibbon: Making History* (London: Weidenfeld and Nicholson, 1988); W. B. Carnochan, *Gibbon's Solitude: The Inward World of the Historian* (Stanford: Stanford University Press, 1987); J. G. A. Pocock, *Virtue, Commerce and History: Essays on Political Thought and History, Chiefly in the Eighteenth Century* (Cambridge: Cambridge University Press, 1985); R. T. Ridley, "The Genesis of an Historian: Gibbon's English Journal," *Mundus antiquus* 2 (1978): 64–78; G. W. Bowersock, John Clive, Stephen R. Graubard, eds., *Edward Gibbon and "The Decline and Fall of the Roman Empire"* (Cambridge, Mass.: Harvard University Press, 1977); and J. W. Johnson, *The Formation of English Neo-Classical Thought* (Princeton: Princeton University Press, 1967).

35. J. E. Norton, ed., *The Letters of Edward Gibbon* (London: Cassell & Co., 1956), 2: no. 592, 360.

36. Edward Gibbon, *An Essay on the Study of Literature* (London, 1764), 48.

37. Gibbon, *History of the Decline and Fall*, 1: 253.

38. Gibbon, *Vindication of Some Passages*, 96–97.

39. Howard B. Gotlieb, *William Beckford of Fonthill, Writer, Traveller, Collector, Caliph, 1760–1844 . . . A Brief Narrative and Catalogue of an Exhibition* (New Haven: Yale University Press, 1960), no. 237.

40. Brian Fothergill, *Beckford of Fonthill* (London: Faber 1979), 255; Robert J. Gemmett, ed., *Sale Catalogues of Libraries of Eminent Persons,* vol. 3 of *Poets and Men of Letters* (London: Sotheby Parke Bernet Publications Ltd., 1972), 2. Gemmett cites Beckford, who "bought it [Gibbon's library] to have something to read when I passed through Lausanne" and in doing so, "I read myself nearly blind."

41. Norton, *Letters of Edward Gibbon*, 1: no. 210, 353

42. Norton, *Letters of Edward Gibbon,* 2: no. 592, 360.

43. Norton, *Letters of Edward Gibbon,* 2: no. 592, 360, 3: no. 722, 145.

44. Quoted by Craddock, *Edward Gibbon*, 218–19. But see John Murray, ed., *The Autobiographies of Edward Gibbon* (London: J. Murray, 1896), memoir B, 165: "The review of my library must be reserved for the period of its maturity; but in this place I may allow myself to observe that I am not conscious of having ever bought a book from a motive of ostentation; that every volume before it was deposited on the shelf, was either read or sufficiently examined."

45. John Owen, *Travels into different parts of Europe in the years 1791 and 1792* (London, 1796), 1: 218. Duchess of Devonshire to Lord Sheffield, 18 July 1792, East Sussex Record Office, AMS 5440/198.

46. Gibbon, *History of the Decline and Fall*, 3: 23; Kelly, "A Grand Tour," 52.

47. Murray, *Autobiographies of Edward Gibbon*, memoir E, 338–39.

48. Murray, *Autobiographies of Edward Gibbon*, memoir E, 337–38.

49. Norton, *Letters of Edward Gibbon*, 2: 265–66.

50. *Pamphleteer* 4 (1813): 283.

51. Edward Gibbon, *An Essay on the Study of Literature* (London, 1764), 25–26.

52. Johann Wolfgang von Goethe, *Italian Journey*, ed. W. H. Auden and Elizabeth Mayer (London: Collins, 1962), 150.

53. Murray, *Autobiographies of Edward Gibbon*, memoir F, 51–52.

54. Christopher Stray, *Classics Transformed: Schools, Universities and Society in England, 1830–1960* (Oxford: Clarendon Press, 1998), 54.

55. Cited by Jeremy Black, *Maps and History: Constructing Images of the Past* (New Haven: Yale University Press, 1997), 18.

56. Christopher Stray, "Scholars and Gentlemen: Towards a Sociology of English Classical Scholarship," in *Aspects of Nineteenth-Century British Classical Scholarship,* ed., H. D. Jocelyn (Liverpool: Liverpool Classic Monthly, 1996), 26. On styles of thought, see Karl Mannheim, *Ideology and Utopia: An Introduction to the Sociology of Knowledge* (London: Routledge, 1991), 45; and Karl Mannheim, *Conservatism: A Contribution to the Sociology of Knowledge* (London: Routledge, 1986), 111 and 191.

57. Bourdieu, "Systems of Education and Systems of Thought," 192.

58. Bourdieu, "Systems of Education and Systems of Thought," 194 and 198.

59. Bourdieu, "Systems of Education and Systems of Thought," 196.

60. Bourdieu, "Systems of Education and Systems of Thought," 189 and 201.

61. James Russel, *Letters from a young painter abroad to his friends in England,* 2d ed. (London, 1750), 2: 368. This point is made by Chloe Chard, *Pleasure and Guilt on the Grand Tour: Travel Writing and Imaginative Geography, 1600–1830* (Manchester: Manchester University Press, 1999), 83: "The intensity conferred on Italy by its classical past, travel writings suggest, is derived not only from the intensified character of that past and its writings, but also from the pleasure that the traveller derives from reminders of texts with which he is already familiar."

62. Russel, *Letters from a young painter abroad,* 2: 180.

63. The Earl of Mornington to Lord Greville, Naples, 4 January 1791, in *The Manuscripts of J. B. Fortescue Esq . . . preserved at Dropmore,* Historical Manuscripts Commission, Fourteenth Report, appendix, part V (London: HMSO, 1894), 2: 5.

64. Warwickshire County Record Office, 125C/2/1–2. North adds that "near ye banks of the river *Silarus* Ld Dartmouth had ye^{e} Classical pleasure [like Io in Aeschylus's *Prometheus Bound*] of being stung by a Gad-Fly."

65. Murray, *Autobiographies of Edward Gibbon,* memoir C, 265. On Gibbon and maps, see Carnochan, *Gibbon's Solitude,* 31.

66. Gibbon, *History of the Decline and Fall,* 3: 84; Kelly, "A Grand Tour," 48–49.

67. Gibbon, *History of the Decline and Fall,* 3: 1084.

68. Geoffrey Keynes, *The Library of Edward Gibbon: A Catalogue,* 2nd ed. (Godalming: St. Paul's Bibliographies, 1980), 18 and 288. Gibbon's "travelling library" was furnished as follows: 1, Horace; 2, Virgil; 3, Terence; 4, Juvenal and Persius; 5–6, Caesar; 7, Nepos: 8, Sallust; 9–13, Ovid; 14–15, Curtius; 16, Catullus, Tibullus and Propertius; 17, Lucretius; 18, Phaedrus; 19–20, Lucan; and 21–24, Tacitus. For earlier and later examples, see H. M. Nixon and W. A. Jackson, "English Seventeenth-Century Travelling Libraries," *Transactions of the Cambridge Bibliographical Society* 7 (1979): 294–304; and John Pemble, *The Mediterranean Passion: Victorians and Edwardians in the South* (Oxford: Clarendon, 1987), 68–69.

69. Rev. John Chetwode Eustace, *A Classical Tour through Italy* (London: J. Mawman, 1815), 1: 4–5. See also Thomas Watkins, *Travels through Swisserland, Italy, Sicily, the Greek Islands, to Constantinople* (London: T. Cadell, 1792), 2: 91: "As I looked about us, many descriptive passages in Virgil, Horace, Sylvius Italicus, and Claudian, came fresh into my memory, or if imperfectly recollected, we could refer to these authors, and also to many other, as the carriage is quite a rolling library."

70. Lucas Pepys, letter of 2 March 1768, in *A Later Pepys: The Correspondence of Sir William Weller Pepys, Bart.,* ed. Alice C. C. Gaussen (London and New York: John Lane, 1904), 1: 345–46.

71. *Correspondence of William Pitt, Earl of Chatham* (London: J. Murray, 1838), 1: 62–63. Reference to Virgil is *Aeneid* I, v, 738–739.

72. Samuel Sharp, *Letters from Italy, describing the customs and manners of that country in the years 1765 and 1766* (London: R. Cave, 1766), 51.

73. Murray, *Autobiographies of Edward Gibbon*, memoir C, 267. See P. B. Craddock, "Edward Gibbon and the 'Ruins of the Capitol,'" in *Roman Images*, ed. Annabel Patterson (Baltimore: John Hopkins University Press, 1984), 63–82. Gibbon's guide around Rome was the Scottish antiquarian James Byres, who, as Ford observes, must have learned as much from Gibbon as Gibbon learned from him. See Brinsley Ford, "James Byres, Principal Antiquarian for the English Visitors to Rome," *Apollo* 99 (1974): 451.

74. Gibbon, *History of the Decline and Fall*, 1: 1073.

75. Gibbon, *History of the Decline and Fall*, 3: 909.

76. Alison, *Essays*, 28–29.

77. Earl of Mornington to Lord Greville, 3 July 1791, *The Manuscripts of J. B. Fortescue Esq . . . preserved at Dropmore,* Historical Manuscripts Commission, Fourteenth Report, appendix, part V (London: HMSO, 1894), 2: 119.

78. James Boswell, *Boswell on the Grand Tour: Italy, Corsica and France, 1765–6*, ed. Frank Brady and Frederick A. Pottle (London: William Heinemann, 1955), 62.

79. Eustace, *Classical Tour through Italy*, 1: 56–58. Reference to Gibbon is *Decline and Fall*, volume VI, chapter lxxi, 1062, note 3.

80. Boswell, *Boswell on the Grand Tour*, 68.

81. By the early nineteenth century, Gibbon was both pilgrim and site of pilgrimage. Using Gibbon's *Memoirs* as a guidebook, travelers visited his Lausanne residence for souvenirs of "The Historian." See Craddock, *Edward Gibbon*, 240.

82. Leeds district archives, WYL5013/2902/48.

83. Gibbon, *History of the Decline and Fall*, 3: 1062, note 3. Anthony Grafton's *The Footnote: A Curious History* (London: Faber & Faber 1997), 1, begins with the historical footnote as represented in Gibbon's *Decline and Fall.*

84. [Joseph Wilcocks], *Roman Conversations; or, A short description of the Antiquities of Rome and the characters of Many Eminent Romans intermixed with references of classical authors and various moral reflections in a supposed conversation between some English Gentlemen at Rome* (London, 1792), 1: xv.

85. As Catharine Edwards notes in her *Writing Rome: Textual Approaches to the City* (Cambridge: Cambridge University Press, 1996), 113, Rome was a place where the outsider might become more Roman than the Romans.

86. Boswell, *Boswell on the Grand Tour*, 65.

87. Conyers Middleton, *A Letter from Rome shewing an exact conformity between Popery and Paganism: or, the Religion of the present Romans to be derived entirely from that of their heathen ancestors,* 4th ed. (London, 1741), 128–29.

88. Eustace, *Classical Tour through Italy*, 2: 326–27.

89. Quoted by Jeffrey Morrison, *Winckelmann and the Notion of Aesthetic Education* (Oxford: Clarendon Press, 1996), 10.

90. Gibbon, *History of the Decline and Fall*, 1: cvi.

91. Russel, *Letters from a young painter abroad*, 2: 369.

92. Alison, *Essays*, 393.

93. Bourdieu, "Systems of Education and Systems of Thought," 196.

94. Gibbon, *History of the Decline and Fall*, 3: 1070.

CHAPTER 2

1. Draft of an undated letter (probably 1763–64) quoted in Brian Connell, *Portrait of a Whig Peer: Compiled from the Papers of the Second Viscount Palmerston* (London: Andre Deutsch, 1957), 40.

2. Wilton and Bignamini, *Grand Tour*, no. 164.

3. Luigi Balsamo, "Dealing across Frontiers: Italian Bookselling in the Eighteenth Century," in *A Genius for Letters: Booksellers and Bookselling from the Sixteenth to the Twentieth Century*, ed. Robin Myres and Michael Harris (Winchester: St. Paul's Bibliographies, 1995), 15–31, does not consider the trade in grand tour books, but for a list of "Some English, Welsh, Scottish and Irish book-collectors in Italy, 1467–1850," see Dennis E. Rhodes in *Bookbindings and Other Bibliophily: Essays in Honour of Anthony Hobson*, ed. Dennis E. Rhodes (Vienna: Edizioni Valdonega, 1994), 247–76.

4. Warwickshire County Record Office, CR 136/ B3014.

5. Charles Parker to Sir Roger Newdigate, 1783, Warwickshire Country Record Office, CR 136/ B2091.

6. Charles Parker to Sir Roger Newdigate, 22 November 1783, Warwickshire County Record Office, CR 136/ B2101. On the Piranesian candelabra that Newdigate presented to Oxford University in 1777, see Michael McCarthy, "Sir Roger Newdigate and Piranesi," *Burlington Magazine* 114 (1972): 466–72.

7. Charles Parker to Sir Roger Newdigate, 18 February 1784. Warwickshire County Record Office, CR 136/ B2015. The volume referred to is discussed in depth in Bernard D. Frischer and Iain Gordon Brown, eds., *Allan Ramsay and the Search for Horace's Villa* (Aldershot: Ashgate, 2001).

8. Roger Paulin, "Goethe's and Stolberg's Italian Journeys and the Romantic Ideology of Art," in *Travel Fact and Travel Fiction: Studies on Fiction, Literary Tradition, Scholarly Discovery and Observation in Travel Writing*, ed. Zweder von Martels (Leiden and New York: E. J. Brill, 1994), 207.

9. Charles Parker to Sir Roger Newdigate, 30 January 1784, Warwickshire County Record Office, CR 136/B2014A.

10. James Byres to William Constable, 11 June 1785, East Riding of Yorkshire Archives Service DDCC/145/6.

11. Ivan Hall and Elisabeth Hall, *Burton Constable Hall: A Century of Patronage* (Hull: Hull City Museums and Beverley: Hutton Press, 1991), 72.

12. M. J. Boyd, "'The Catholic Maecenas of His Age': Cuthbert Constable (c. 1680–1747) of Burton Constable," in *Burton Constable Hall: The Eighteenth and Nineteenth Centuries*, ed. A. G. Credland, East Yorkshire Local History Series, 51 (1998), 30–31.

13. The sales were held at Sotheby's on 24 and 27 June 1889.

14. Mark Bence-Jones, *The Catholic Families* (London: Constable, 1992), 42.

15. P. R. Harris, ed., *Douai College Documents, 1639–1794* ([London]: Catholic Record Society, 1972), 139–41.

16. Cecil Torr, *Catalogue of the Classical Antiquities from the Collection of the Late Sir Gardner Wilkinson* (Harrow: J. C. Wilbee, 1887), 9.

17. Torr, *Catalogue of the Classical Antiquities*, 5.

18. Bourdieu, "Systems of Education and Systems of Thought," 194.

19. Ibid. Christopher Stray, "Scholars and Gentlemen: Towards a Sociology of English Classical Scholarship," in *Aspects of Nineteenth-Century British Classical Scholarship,* ed. H. D. Jocelyn (Liverpool: Liverpool Classic Monthly, 1996), 17, describes the country house library as forming "part of the landscaping and statuary" of the English gentleman. A further example of this is Arthur Devis's portrait of Newdigate, *Sir Roger Newdigate in his Library at Arbury Hall* (c. 1756–58); see further, Michael J. McCarthy, "The Gothic Revival Library," *Ex Libris* 2 (1989): 4–11; Gervase Jackson-Stops, ed., *The Treasure Houses of Britain: Five Hundred Years of Private Patronage and Art Collecting* (Washington: National Gallery of Art; and New Haven: Yale University Press, 1985), no. 329; *Polite Society by Arthur Devis: Portraits of the English Country Gentleman and His Family* (Preston: Harris Museum and Art Gallery, 1983), no. 38.

20. Robert Wood, *The Ruins of Balbec: Otherwise Heliopolis in Coelosyria* (London, 1757), introduction.

21. Maria Grazia Lolla, "Monuments and Texts: Antiquarianism and the Beauty of Antiquity," *Art History* 25 (2002): 432.

22. For summaries of Montfaucon's *L'Antiquité expliquée et representée en figures* (Paris: Florentin Delaulne, 1719), see J. M. Pailler, "L'archéologue par delà les frontières: *L'Antiquité expliquée*," in *Dom Bernard de Montfaucon: Actes du colloque de Carcassonne, octobre 1996*, ed. Daniel-Odon Hurel and Raymond Rogé (Saint-Wandrille Rançon: Éd. De Fontenelle; and Paris: Didier Sorbonne, 1998), 1: 225–41; Alain Schnapp, *The Discovery of the Past: The Origins of Archaeology* (London: British Museum Press, 1996), 235–36; and Francis Haskell, *History and Its Images: Art and the Interpretation of the Past* (New Haven: Yale University Press, 1993), esp. 131–32.

23. Montfaucon, *L'Antiquité*, 1: vi.

24. Iain Gordon Brown, *Monumental Reputation: Robert Adam and the Emperor's Palace* (Edinburgh: National Library of Scotland, 1992); and Eileen Harris, *British Architectural Books and Writers, 1556–1785* (Cambridge: Cambridge University Press, 1990) have been invaluable for the purposes of my own research.

25. Harris, *British Architectural Books and Writers*, 73. Robert Adam to Margaret Adam, NAS, GD18/4766.

26. James Adam to Robert Adam, 13 August 1760, NAS, GD18/4868; James Adam to Robert Adam, 11 September 1756, NAS, GD18/4817.

27. Harris, *British Architectural Books and Writers*, 78.

28. Robert Adam, *Ruins of the Palace of the Emperor Diocletian at Spalatro in Dalmatia* (London: The Author, 1764), 1.

29. Adam, *Ruins of the Palace*, 2; 25 June 1758, James to Robert Adam, NAS, GD18/4849.

30. Brown, *Monumental Reputation*, 11 and 28; quotation from NAS, GD18/4874.

31. Brown, *Monumental Reputation*, 47. Robert Adam to James Adam, 11 December 1758, NAS, GD18/4854.

32. Quoted by Dora Wiebenson, *Sources of Greek Revival Architecture* (London: A. Zwemmer, 1969), 113.

33. James Adam to Robert Adam, 13 August 1760, NAS, GD18/4868.

34. Brown, *Monumental Reputation*, 46.

35. Harris, *British Architectural Books and Writers*, 75.

36. Adam, *Ruins of the Palace*, 4.

37. Robert Adam to James Adam, 1 November 1757, NAS, GD18/4843.

38. James Holloway, *Patrons and Painters: Art in Scotland, 1650–1760* (Edinburgh: Scottish National Portrait Gallery, 1989), no. 99. In *Burlington Magazine* 120 (1978): 762, John Kerslake discusses the problems of attribution and identification of the volume.

39. Edward Young, *Conjectures on Original Composition* (London: A. Millar and J. Dodsley, 1759), 43.

40. Robert Adam to James Adam, 19 October 1755, NAS, GD18/4789.

41. John Wilton-Ely, *Piranesi as Architect and Designer* (New Haven: Yale University Press, 1993), 25.

42. John Wilton-Ely, *Giovanni Battista Piranesi: The Complete Etchings* (San Francisco: Alan Wofsy, 1994), 1: 327.

43. Potts, *Flesh and the Ideal*, 191.

44. In committing this act of *damnatio memoriae* Piranesi was deliberately following an ancient precedent: the third-century A.D. emperor Caracalla expunged his brother Geta's memory by removing his inscriptions from the arch of their father, Septimius Severus. Wilton-Ely, *Giovanni Battista Piranesi*, 2: 803.

45. Wilton-Ely, *Giovanni Battista Piranesi*, 2: 802.

46. According to Maurice James Craig, *The Volunteer Earl, being the Life and Times of James Caulfeild, First Earl of Charlemont* (London: Cresset Press, 1948), 85–97, the entire business between Piranesi and Charlemont remains something of a "mystery." For more recent attempts to unravel this mystery, see Jonathan Scott, *Piranesi* (London: Academy Editions, 1975), esp. 108–16; and Cynthia O'Connor, *The Pleasing Hours: The Grand Tour of James Caulfeild, First Earl of Charlemont, 1728–1799: Traveller, Connoisseur and Patron of the Arts* (Cork: Collins Press, 1999).

47. Wilton-Ely, *Piranesi as Architect and Designer*, 29–31.

48. *Piranesi* (Northampton, Mass.: Smith College Museum of Art, 1961), no. 176.

49. Lady Anne Miller, *Letters from Italy, describing the manners, customs, antiquities, paintings &c. of that country, in the years MDCCLXX and MDCCLXXI, to a friend residing in France* (London: Edward & Charles Dilly, 1776), 3: 38. On Rome as a "museum," see Jerome J. McGann, "Rome and Its Romantic Significance," in *Roman Images*, ed. Annabel Patterson (Baltimore: John Hopkins University Press, 1984), 84.

50. Tobias Smollett, *Travels through France and Italy*, ed. Frank Felsenstein (Oxford: Oxford University Press, 1981), 240.

51. Horace Walpole, *Anecdotes of Painting in England . . . collected by the late Mr. George Vertue* (Strawberry Hill: Thomas Farmer, 1771), 4: vi. Charles Heathcote Tatham in his *Etchings of Ancient Ornamental Architecture* (London: T. Gardiner, 1799), 3–4, similarly wrote of Piranesi, "He has sometimes sacrificed accuracy, to what he conceived the richer productions of a more fertile and exuberant mind."

52. Joseph Forsyth, *Remarks on Antiquities, Arts and Letters during an excursion in Italy in the years 1802 and 1803*, 3rd ed. (Geneva: Ledouble, 1824), 167.

53. Quoted by David Irwin, "Flaxman: Italian Journals and Correspondence," *Burlington Magazine* 100 (1958): 216.

54. Goethe, *Italian Journey*, 492.

55. Charles Brown, letter of 27 October 1823, in Maurice Buxton Forman, ed., *Some Letters and Miscellanea of Charles Brown* (London: Oxford University Press, 1937), 41–42. For an account, "Forgetting Rome and the Voice of Piranesi's 'Speaking Ruins,'" see Tanya Cooper in *The Art of Forgetting*, ed. Adrian Forty and Susanne Küchler (Oxford: Berg, 2001), 107–25.

56. James Stuart and Nicholas Revett, *The Antiquities of Athens* (London, 1762), v note (a).

57. James Stuart to Thomas Anson of Shugborough, 6 October 1764. Staffordshire Record Office, D615/P(S)/1/6/15.

58. Stuart and Revett, *Antiquities of Athens*, 4: xxiii.

59. Horace Walpole, letter of 14 June 1740, *Horace Walpole's Correspondence*, 13: 224.

60. Russel, *Letters from a young painter abroad*, 1: 218.

61. *Annual Register* 3 (1760): 162; *Le Antichità di Ercolano esposte* (Naples: Reale Accademia Ercolanese di Archeologia, 1757), 1: 278.

62. Richard Brilliant, "Herculaneum: Archaeological, Art Historical and Cultural Oroperties," in *Ercolano, 1738–1988: 250 anni di ricerca archeologica*, ed. Luisa Franchi dell' Orto (Rome: "L'Erma" di Bretschneider, 1993), 121, describes the volumes as a museum without walls.

63. *Horace Walpole's Correspondence*, 22: 457; Harold Acton, *The Bourbons of Naples, 1734–1825* (London: Methuen & Co., 1956), 89.

64. Goethe, *Italian Journey*, 150; Owen, *Travels into different parts of Europe*, 2: 113. On the volumes as a monument, see Denise Kaspar, "Felix Urbium Restitutio—'Le Antichità di Ercolano' zwischen Museum und Öffentlichkeit; Die ersten nachrichten der grabungen am Golf von Naples und die "Pompejimode" im 18. jahrhundert," in *Antikensammlungen im 18. Jahrhundert*, ed. Herbert Beck et al. (Berlin: Mann, 1981), 22.

65. *Gentleman's Magazine* 43 (1773): 9.

66. Wendy Wassyng Roworth, ed., *Angelica Kauffman: A Continental Artist in Georgian England* (London: Reaktion, 1992), 21.

67. Sir Horace Mann to Horace Walpole, 15 May 1762, *Horace Walpole's Correspondence*, 22: 35.

68. Sir Henry Ellis, *The Townley Gallery* (London: Library of Entertaining Knowledge, 1836), 1: 232. Gerard Vaughan, "The Townley Zoffany: Reflections on *Charles Townley and his friends*," *Apollo* 144 (1996): 34.

69. BM, TY10/2, p. 7.

70. Thomas Jenkins to Charles Townley, 14 February 1770, BM, TY7/301.

71. For a detailed discussion of this painting, see chapter 6.

72. Ian Jenkins and Kim Sloan, eds., *Vases and Volcanoes: Sir William Hamilton and His Collection* (London: British Museum Press, 1996), no. 51.

73. Pierre François [Hughes] D'Hancarville, ed., *Collection of Etruscan, Greek and Roman Antiquities from the Cabinet of the Hon. W. Hamilton, His Britannick Majesty's Envoy Extraordinary and Plenipotentiary at the Court of Naples*, 4 vols. (Naples, 1766–76), 1: vi.

74. D'Hancarville, *Collection*, 1: ii.

75. D'Hancarville, *Collection*, 1: xviii.

76. On publication as a means of preservation, see Maria Grazia Lolla, "'Monuments' and 'Texts': Antiquarianism and Literature in Eighteenth and Early Nineteenth-Century Britain" (Ph.D. diss., Cambridge University, 1997), esp. 58, 87 and 98, and her "Monuments and Texts: Antiquarianism and the Beauty of Antiquity," *Art History* 25 (2002): 431–49.

77. Quoted by Constantine, "Winckelmann and Sir William Hamilton," 74.

78. D'Hancarville, *Collection*, 1: "Avertissement."

79. D'Hancarville, *Collection*, 1: xxii.

80. D'Hancarville, *Collection*, 1: viii.

81. Constantine, "Winckelmann and Sir William Hamilton," 68.

82. D'Hancarville, *Collection*, 1: x.

83. François Lissarrague and Marcia Reed, "The Collector's Books," *Journal of the History of Collections* 9 (1997): 276.

84. D'Hancarville, *Collection*, 1: 150.

85. Lissarrague and Reed, "The Collector's Books," 275–94; and Nancy H. Ramage, "The Initial Letters in Sir William Hamilton's "Collection of Antiquities,'" *Burlington Magazine* 129 (1987): 446–56.

86. D'Hancarville, *Collection*, 1: 70.

87. Nisbet, *German Aesthetic and Literary Criticism*, 247.

88. Here Gibbon refers in a footnote to having "often perused with pleasure a chapter of Quintilian (*Institutio Oratoria* 10.1), in which that judicious critic enumerates and appreciates the series of Greek and Latin classics."

89. Gibbon, *History of the Decline and Fall*, 3: 286.

90. Jenkins and Sloan, *Vases and Volcanoes*, 46.

91. Jenkins and Sloan, *Vases and Volcanoes*, no. 31 and figure 48.

92. D'Hancarville, *Collection*, 3: 3.

93. D'Hancarville, *Collection*, 1: xviii.

94. Sir Richard Worsley to Sir William Hamilton, 18 January 1794, BM Add. MSS. 51, 315; Hamilton to Worsley, 26 December 1802. Lincoln Record Office, Worsley papers, 55. 21. Worsley's purchase of Sir William Hamilton's gem collection is discussed in Jenkins and Sloan, *Vases & Volcanoes*, 101–4.

95. Lincoln Record Office, Worsley papers, 23. In the introduction to the *Museum Worsleyanum*, Worsley writes of being "Impelled [to travel] by a love of the Fine Arts." In reality, his extended travels abroad provided an opportunity to escape the very public scandal that was his divorce from Lady Worsley. The details of the scandal are referred to in Nicholas Penny, ed., *Reynolds* (London: Weidenfeld and Nicolson, 1986), no. 118; and *Masterpieces from Yorkshire Houses: Yorkshire Families at Home and Abroad, 1700–1850* (York: City Art Gallery, 1994), no. 17.

96. Sir Richard Worsley to Charles Townley, undated, BM, TY7/2045. The phrase "Brother Virtuoso" comes from a letter of Worsley's to Hamilton, 25 December 1800, Lincoln Record Office, Worsley papers, 55. 16. Worsley also joined the "Diplomatic Line" as British envoy at Venice from 1793 to 1797.

97. Sir Richard Worsley to Sir Joseph Banks, 15 January 1788, Isle of Wight County Record Office, JER/WA/39/6.

98. BM, TY7/2075. The work was divided into six classes. In volume one, class 1 was devoted to reliefs, 2 to busts, 3 to Egyptian and Greek sculpture, and 4 to gems. In volume 2, class 5 illustrated the Parthenon sculptures, and finally, class 6 consisted of the views by Reveley. *A Catalogue Raisonné of Paintings, Sculptures, Drawings &c &c at Appuldurcombe House* was published in London in 1804.

99. When Worsley died in 1805, the collection was inherited by his niece who married the Earl of Yarborough; it was published by A. H. Smith as *A Catalogue of the Antiquities in the Collection of the Earl of Yarborough at Brocklesby Park* (London, 1897). The letter quoted is dated 15 November 1823. Lincoln Record Office, Yarborough papers, 9/6.

100. Lincoln Record Office, Worsley papers, 31.

101. Richard Bull to Worsley, 15 November 1823. Lincoln Record Office, Yarborough papers, 9/6.

CHAPTER 3

1. D'Hancarville, *Collection*, 1: viii.

2. Jonathan Richardson, *Works* (London: T. Davies, 1773), 7. Quoted in Richard Wendorf, *The Elements of Life: Biography and Portrait-Painting in Stuart and Georgian Britain* (Oxford: Clarendon, 1991), 9–10.

3. *The Memoirs of Elisabeth Vigée-le Brun*, trans. Sian Evans (Bloomington: Indiana University Press, 1989), 102.

4. D. M. Stuart, ed., *Dearest Bess: The Life and Times of Lady Elizabeth Foster, afterwards Duchess of Devonshire* (London: Methuen, 1955), 59.

5. Henry Blundell to Charles Townley, 5 March 1787, BM, TY7/ 1317; Jenkins and Sloan, *Vases and Volcanoes*, 75 and 252.

6. Marcia Pointon, *Strategies for Showing: Women, Possession and Representation in English Visual aulture* (Oxford: Oxford University Press, 1997), 205–8.

7. Charles Greville to Sir William Hamilton, 11 March 1786. Alfred Morrison, *Catalogue of the collection of autography letters and historical documents formed between 1865 and 1882 by A. Morrison* (London: Printed for private circulation, 1893), volume 1, no.147.

8. Goethe, letter dated 27 May 1787. Goethe, *Italian Journey*, 315–16. The antique paintings from Pompeii as one of the sources for Emma's attitudes are discussed in Lori-Ann Touchette, "Sir William Hamilton's 'Pantomime Mistress': Emma Hamilton and Her Attitudes," in *The Impact of Italy: The Grand Tour and Beyond*, ed. Clare Hornsby (London: British School at Rome, 2000), 123–46.

9. *The Remains of the Late Mrs. Richard Trench* (London: Parker, Son & Bourn, 1862), 108.

10. Letter dated 16 March 1787, Goethe, *Italian Journey*, 208.

11. Quoted in Connell, *Portrait of a Whig Peer*, 276.

12. Henry Blundell to Charles Townley, 4 May 1790, BM, TY7/1320.

13. The expression "attitudinal celebrity" is from Pryse Lockhart Gordon, *Personal Memoirs or reminiscences of men and manners at home and abroad* (London, 1830), 2: 385; Samuel Sharp, *Letters from Italy, describing the customs and manners of that country in the years 1765 and 1766* (London: R. Cave, 1766), 75–76.

14. Emma to Charles Greville, 4 August 1787. Morrison, *Catalogue of the collection*, volume 1, no. 168.

15. *Memoirs of Elisabeth Vigée-le Brun*, 103.

16. James Irvine, letter dated 8 April 1791. British Library, Cumberland Papers, Add. MSS. 36. 496 f 307. On Hewetson, see Brian de Breffny, "Christopher Hewetson," *Irish Arts Review* 3 (1986): 52–75.

17. Jenkins and Sloan, *Vases and Volcanoes*, 252.

18. Goethe, *Italian Journey*, 372.

19. Alexander Day to Sir William Hamilton, 31 January 1792. British Library, Add. MSS. 41199 f 87.

20. Richardson, *Works*, 7.

21. Most recently by Flora Fraser, *Beloved Emma: The Life of Emma Lady Hamilton* (London: Weidenfeld and Nicolson, 1987).

22. *Memoirs of the Comtesse de Boigne, 1781–1814*, ed. M. C. Nicoullaud (London: William Heinemann, 1907), 1: 83; J. Mordaunt Crook, *The Greek Revival: Neo-classical Attitudes in British Architecture, 1760–1870* (London: J. Murray, 1972), 28.

23. See Nancy Ramage, "Publication Dates of Sir William Hamilton's Four Volumes," *Ars*

Ceramica 8 (1991): 35. Francis Haskell, "The Baron d'Hancarville: An Adventurer and Art Historian in Eighteenth Century Europe," in *Oxford, China and Italy: Writings in Honour of Sir Harold Acton*, ed. Edward Chaney and Neil Ritchie (London: Thames and Hudson, 1984), 182, observes, "It is not surprising that Josiah Wedgwood should have been among those who acquired them [Hamilton plates]—though the true extent of the influence exerted by these on English taste has been more frequently asserted than investigated." For recent investigations of the cosmopolitan influences, see Cristiani Morigi Govi, "Le 'style étrusque,'" in *Les étrusques et l'Europe* (Paris: Réunion des musées nationaux, 1992), esp. 300; and Pascal Griener, *Le Antichità etrusche, greche e romane, 1766–1776, di Pierre Hugues d'Hancarville: La pubblicazione della ceramiche antiche della prima collezione Hamilton* (Rome: Edizione dell'Elefante, 1992), esp. 104–9, "Arti decorative."

24. Joshua Reynolds, *Discourses*, ed. Pat Rogers (London: Penguin, 1992), 167.

25. D'Hancarville, *Collection*, 1: xvi.

26. D'Hancarville, *Collection*, 1: vi.

27. D'Hancarville, *Collection*, 1: xviii.

28. Reynolds, *Discourses*, 167.

29. For a survey of imitation from antiquity to the Renaissance, see Patricia Lee Rubin, *Giorgio Vasari: Art and History* (New Haven: Yale University Press, 1995), esp. 246–48. Also useful is James Ackerman, "Imitation," in *Antiquity and Its Interpreters*, ed. Alina Payne, Ann L. Kuttner, and Rebekah Smick (Cambridge: Cambridge University Press, 2000), 9–16.

30. Gibbon, *History of the Decline and Fall*, 3: 908–9.

31. Horace Walpole, *Anecdotes of Painting in England*, ed. R. N. Wornum (London: Chatto, 1876), 1: xvii. See also Rudolph Wittkower, "Imitation, Eclecticism and Genius," in *Aspects of the Eighteenth Century*, ed. E. R. Wasserman (Baltimore: John Hopkins University Press; and London: Oxford University Press, 1965), 143–62.

32. Wittkower, "Imitation, Eclecticism and Genius," 143.

33. D'Hancarville, *Collection*, 1: xiv.

34. D'Hancarville, *Collection*, 1: vi.

35. J. H. W. Tischbein, *Collection of Engravings from Ancient Vases discovered in the kingdom of the Two Sicilies between 1789–90* (Naples, 1793), 1: preface.

36. In his *Outlines from the figures and compositions upon the Greek, Roman, and Etruscan Vases of the late Sir William Hamilton* (London, 1804), ii–iii, Thomas Kirk described the frames as follows: "The various beautiful borders which surround these designs, were not so placed in the original vases, but serve there, merely to ornament the handles, and other parts, nor were the border and figures, which are always upon the same Plate in this work, always upon the same vase. Nothing can exceed the different borders, in simplicity, in variety, in elegance, in richness, or in beauty, and all modern ornaments sink in the comparison."

37. D'Hancarville, *Collection*, 1: vi and 1: xviii.

38. The gap between the rhetoric of the text and the improved reality of the engravings has been too long overlooked. For R. M. Cook, *Greek Painted Pottery* (London: Methuen, 1960), 292, the drawings are "recognisably close rather than pedantically accurate." Clare L. Lyons, "The Museo Mastrilli and the Culture of Collecting in Naples, 1700–1755," *Journal of the History of Collections* 4 (1992): 9, is right to see the images as "schematised or strongly idealised," but she, like Cook, neglects the "law [of the volumes] . . . to be as exact as possible" (D'Hancarville, *Collection*, 1: viii).

39. Tischbein, *Collection of Engravings from Ancient Vases*, 1: 38. This volume established that

Hamilton's vases were Greek rather than Etruscan in origin. As we shall see, however, the misnomer "Etruscan" continued to be used long after 1793.

40. Michael Vickers and David Gill, *Artful Crafts: Ancient Silverware and Pottery* (Oxford: Clarendon Press, 1994), 11.

41. D'Hancarville, *Collection*, 2: 46. Reynolds explains that (*Discourses*, 164) "it is from his [Raphael] having taken so many models, that he became himself a model for all succeeding painters; always imitating, and always original."

42. On the Meidias hydria, see Jenkins and Sloan, *Vases and Volcanoes,* no. 55, p. 180.

43. D'Hancarville, *Collection*, 2: 144. This point was illustrated by the inclusion of a line drawing of Raphael's painting of *Atilla and the Pope* in volume 2.

44. David Irwin, ed., *Winckelmann: Writings on Art* (London: Phaidon 1972), 112. See further, Constantine, "Winckelmann and Sir William Hamilton," 55–83.

45. Jenkins and Sloan, *Vases and Volcanoes*, no. 55.

46. D'Hancarville, *Collection*, 2: 168.

47. Tischbein, *Collection of Engravings from Ancient Vases*, 1: 10.

48. D'Hancarville, *Collection,* 1: xvi.

49. D'Hancarville, *Collection*, 1: 168–70.

50. Irwin, *Winckelmann*, 113.

51. Lord Kildare to his mother, 24 February 1767, in Brian Fitzgerald, ed., *Correspondence of Emily, Duchess of Leinster* (Dublin: Stationery Office, 1957), 3: 459.

52. Lord Kildare, letter dated 13 July 1768, Fitzgerald, *Correspondence*, 3: 529.

53. Lord Fitzwilliam, letter dated 9 February 1768. Quoted with permission of the owners of the Fitzwilliam (Milton) Archive held at Northamptonshire Record Office.

54. P. J. Wendler to Matthew Boulton, 4 July 1767, Birmingham City archives (UK), MS 3782/12/23/98.

55. D'Hancarville, *Collection*, 1: xvi.

56. Quoted by Robert Rowe, *Adam Silver, 1765–1795* (London: Faber & Faber, 1965), 61; and Nicholas Goodison, *Ormolu: The Work of Matthew Boulton, 1728–1775* (London: Phaidon, 1974), 47.

57. See Rowe, *Adam Silver*, plate 42. Hugh Tait, "The 'Etruscan Service' of King Ferdinand IV and Josiah Wedgwood," *Ars Ceramica* 3 (1986): 31, wrongly assumes that "the process of copying involved Wedgwood and his artists in modifying and adapting the original to such an extent that the style became, indeed, 'elegant' and even, gentle, more an Adam style than a truly classical style."

58. Translated from Friedrich von Alten, ed., *Aus Tischbein's Leben und Briefwechsel* (Leipzig, 1872), 56–57.

59. *Mere Hall Knutsford, Cheshire: Christie's, 23 May 1994*, sale catalog (n.p.: Christie's, 1994), 213.

60. *Mere Hall Knutsford, Cheshire*, 132–51. See Jenkins and Sloan, *Vases and Volcanoes*, 61 and figure 28.

61. Charles Heathcote Tatham to Henry Holland, 4 April 1796, Tatham correspondence, Soane Museum library.

62. J. A. Kiechler, "The Murals at Newtimber Place," *Sussex Archaeological Society* 113 (1976): 175–81.

63. *Heaton Hall: A Short Account of Its History and Architecture* (Manchester: Manchester City Art Gallery, 1984), 20–22.

64. Quoted by John Wilton-Ely, "Pompeian and Etruscan Tastes in the Neo-classical Country House Interior," in *The Fashioning and Functioning of the English Country House*, ed. Gervase Jackson-Stops (Washington, D.C.: National Gallery of Art, 1989), 60. On Raphael's loggia, Nicole Dacos's two monographs, *La Découvert de la Domus Aurea et la formation des grotesques à la Renaissance* (London: Warburg Institute, 1969) and *Le Logge di Raffaello maestro e bottega di fronte all'antico* (Rome: Istituto poligrafico dello Stato, Libreria, 1977), remain fundamental. In English is Bernice F. Davidson, *Raphael's Bible: A Study of the Vatican Logge* (University Park: Pennsylvania State University Press, 1985). On the post-Renaissance reception of Raphael, Martin Rosenburg, *Raphael and France: The Artist as Paradigm and Symbol* (University Park: Pennsylvania State University Press, 1995), esp. chapter 7, "Foreign Neoclassicists' Views of Raphael," 119–43; and Hilary Fraser, *The Victorians and Renaissance Italy* (Oxford: Blackwell, 1992), esp. chapter 2, "The Spirit of Raphael," 43–90, have been most useful although neither deal in detail with eighteenth-century Britain.

65. Hetty Joyce, "Grasping at Shadows: Ancient Paintings in Renaissance and Baroque Rome," *Art Bulletin* 74 (1992): 219. See also her "From Darkness to Light: Annibale Carracci, Bellori, and Ancient Painting," in *Art History in the Age of Bellori: Scholarship and Cultural Politics in Seventeenth-Century Rome*, ed. Janis Bell and Thomas Willette (Cambridge: Cambridge University Press, 2002), 170–88.

66. Charlotte A. Eaton, *Rome in the nineteenth century . . . in a series of letters written during a residence in Rome in the years 1817 and 1818* (Edinburgh, 1820), 2: 92.

67. Quoted by Ferdinando Bologna, "The Rediscovery of Herculaneum and Pompeii in the Artistic Culture of Europe in the Eighteenth Century," in *Rediscovering Pompeii*, ed. Luisa Franchi dell' Orto and Antonio Varone (Rome: "L'Erma" di Bretschneider, 1992), 79. The image referred to, of the woman selling cherubs as chickens, located in *Antichità di Ercolano esposte*, 3: plate 7.

68. Leslie Campbell Hatfield, "A Set of Silver Condiment Vases from Kedleston Hall," *Bulletin of the Boston Museum of Fine Arts* 79 (1981): 10.

69. Hatfield, "A Set of Silver Condiment Vases," 16.

70. See, for example, Michael Vickers and David Gill, "Value and Simplicity: A Historical Case Study," in *Artful Crafts: Ancient Silverware and Pottery* (Oxford: Clarendon Press, 1994), 1–32; Nancy Ramage, "Wedgwood and Sir William Hamilton: Their Personal and Artistic Relationship," *Proceedings of the Thirty-fifth Annual Wedgwood International Seminar* (1990): 71–90; Nancy Ramage, "Owed to a Grecian Urn: The Debt of Flaxman and Wedgwood to Hamilton," *Ars Ceramica* 6 (1989): 8–12; Hatfield, "A Set of Silver Condiment Vases," 16; and D. Graeme Keith, "Wedgwood and the Classical Revival," *Sixth Wedgwood International Seminar* (April 1961): 86.

71. Ramage, "Wedgwood and Sir William Hamilton," 71–90. In an often-quoted letter to Wedgwood of 23 May 1786, Hamilton wrote, "It is with infinite satisfaction that I reflect upon having been in some measure instrumental in the introducing a purer taste of forms & Ornaments by having placed my Collection of Antiquities in the British Museum, but a Wedgewood and a Bentley were necessary to diffuse that taste so universally and it is to their liberal way of thinking & and acting that so good a taste prevails at present in Great Britain." Keele 30-22495.

72. Charles Greville to Sir William Hamilton, 3 December 1775, in Morrison, *Catalogue of the collection*, volume 1, no. 59.

73. Josiah Wedgwood, letter dated 19 May 1770, Keele, E25-18301. On the relationship between Wedgwood and his aristocratic patrons, including Sir William Hamilton, see Neil McKendrick, "Josiah Wedgwood and the Commercialisation of the Potteries," in *The Birth of a Consumer Society: The Commercialization of Eighteenth-Century England*, ed. Neil McKendrick, John Brewer, and J. H. Plumb (London: Europa, 1982), 111, 115, and 128.

74. Roy Porter, "The Enlightenment in England," in *The Enlightenment in National Context*, ed. Roy Porter and Mikulàš Teich (Cambridge: Cambridge University Press, 1981), 9.

75. Gibbon, *Vindication of Some Passages, 82.*

76. Gibbon, *Vindication of Some Passages*, 89.

77. Murray, *Autobiographies*, memoir B, 162.

78. Norton, *Letters of Edward Gibbon*, 2: no. 360; Murray, *Autobiographies of Edward Gibbon*, memoir B, 164.

79. Wedgwood to Thomas Bentley, 6 August 1770, Keele 18315-25.

80. Keele E1/31201. H. A. Johnson, "Books Belonging to Wedgwood & Bentley the 10th of Augt 1770," *Ars Ceramica* 7 (1990): 13–23.

81. Wedgwood to Thomas Bentley, 2 August 1770, Keele 18314-25.

82. *Monthly Review* 42 (1770): 514.

83. Contrary to Eliza Meteyard's assertion, *The Wedgwood Handbook: A Manual for Collectors* (London: George Bell & Sons, 1875), 273, note 1, the vases were not sold on the death of the marquis but remain at Bowood House in their original location. The collection was brought to my attention by John Betts.

84. Third Marquis of Lansdowne to Wedgwood II, 14 May 1813, Keele 24904-126.

85. D'Hancarville, *Collection*, 1: vi.

86. Third Marquis of Lansdowne to Wedgwood, August 1813, Keele 21187-29.

87. Lord Dartmouth to Wedgewood II, 10 January 1820, Keele 25049-33.

88. The location of the plates referred to are vol. 1, plate nos. 22, 30, 33, 52, 59, 72, 75, 91, 97; vol. 2, plate nos. 59 and 75; and vol. 3, plate nos. 69, 72, 101.

89. Lord Dartmouth to Wedgewood II, 31 January 1820, Keele 25050-33. The memorandum reference is 25052-33.

90. Sir William Hamilton, preface to Tischbein, *Collection of Engravings from Ancient Vases*, vol. 1.

91. Wedgwood II to Lord Dartmouth, 19 April 1820, Keele 25052-33.

92. Wedgwood I to Erasmus Darwin, July 1789, Keele E26-19002.

93. Lord Dartmouth to Wedgwood II, 26 April 1820, Keele 25053-33.

94. Rev. Richard Warner, *Excursions from Bath* (Bath and London, 1801), 214.

95. Horace Walpole to Rev. William Mason, 16 July 1778, *Horace Walpole's Correspondence*, 28: 413–14.

96. *The Works in Architecture of Robert and James Adam* (London, 1779), volume 2, preface.

97. Eileen Harris and John Martin Robinson, "New Light on Wyatt at Fawley," *Architectural Review* 27 (1984): 263–67.

98. Emily J. Climenson, ed., *Passages from the diaries of Mrs. Lybbe Powys* (London: Longmans & Co., 1899), 148.

99. Quoted by Harris and Robinson, "New Light on Wyatt at Fawley," 265.

100. Maurice Tomlin, *Catalogue of Adam Period Furniture* (London: Victoria and Albert Museum, 1972), 84, notes that the table was either designed for the room or installed after the room was completed.

101. Margaret L. Mare and W. H. Quarrell, *Lichtenberg's Visits to England as Described in His Letters and Diaries* (Oxford: Clarendon Press, 1938), 98, letter dated 16 October 1775.

102. Norman Scarfe, ed., *Innocent Espionage: The La Rochefoucauld Brothers' Tour of England in 1785* (Woodbridge: Boydell, 1995), 113–14.

103. This point is made by James Millingen, *Ancient Unedited Monuments: Painted Greek Vases* (London, 1822–26), 54, note 3.

104. Henry Clay to Sir William Hamilton, August 1775, Birmingham, 1 August 1775. Bibliothèque Centrale du Muséum National d'Histoire Naturelle, Paris, Krafft Bequest. See Morrison, *Catalogue of the collection*, volume 1, nos. 56 and 59.

105. Thomas Hardwick, journal entry, 1778, Royal Institute of British Architects, London, H1/4.

106. D'Hancarville, *Collection*, 1: vi.

107. Sam Smiles, *The Image of Antiquity: Ancient Britons and the Romantic Imagination* (New Haven: Yale University Press, 1994), 220.

CHAPTER 4

1. John Moore, *A View of Society and Manners in Italy*, 3rd. ed. (London: W. Strahan & T. Cadell, 1790), 2: 177. I. C. McIlwaine, *Herculaneum: A Guide to the Printed Sources*, 2 vols. (Naples: Bibliopolis, 1988), provides a comprehensive bibliography on the primary sources. For a summary of "Viggatore e illustratori inglesi," see Lucio Fino, *Ercolano e Pompei: Vedute neoclassiche e romantiche* (Naples: Electa Napoli 1988), 21–28. Chantal Grell's *Herculaneum et Pompéi dans les récits des voyages français du XVIIIe siècle* (Naples: Centre Jean Berard and Rome: Diffusion ERMA di Bretschneider, 1982) provides a French perspective on the finds.

2. Joseph Forsyth, *Remarks on Antiquities, Arts and Letters during an excursion in Italy in the years 1802 and 1803*, 2nd ed. (London, 1816), 286.

3. *Horace Walpole's Correspondence*, 13: 224.

4. Catharine Taylor, *Letters from Italy* (London, 1841), 71.

5. [Lewis Engelbach,] *Naples and the Campagna Felice in a series of letters addressed to a friend in England in 1802* (London: R. Ackerman, 1815), 59.

6. Christopher Charles Parslow, *Rediscovering Antiquity: Karl Weber and the Excavations of Herculaneum, Pompeii and Stabiae* (Cambridge: Cambridge University Press, 1995), 41.

7. [Engelbach,] *Naples and the Campagna Felice*, 112.

8. Thomas Martyn, *A Tour through Italy containing full directions for travelling in that . . . country* (London, 1791), 305.

9. Eric M. Moorman, "Destruction and Restoration of Campanian Mural Paintings in the Eighteenth and Nineteenth Centuries," in *The Conservation of Wall Paintings: Proceedings of a Symposium Organized by the Courtauld Institute of Art and the Getty Conservation Institute*, ed. Sharon Cather (Getty Conservation Institute, 1991), 94.

10. Lady Anne Miller, *Letters from Italy, describing the manners, customs, antiquities, paintings &c. of that country, in the years MDCCLXX and MDCCLXXI, to a friend residing in France* (London: Edward & Charles Dilly, 1776), 2: 273–74.

11. Ibid., 2: 298. Later that day, Lady Miller and her party were left with a guide "who softened a little towards us" (2: 300) and briefly allowed them to make observations, but feared "being sent to the gallies" for doing so (2: 304).

12. Letter dated 7 February 1756. Mr. Dobson's letter is transcribed in Mary Elisabeth Lucy, *Biography of the Lucy Family of Charlecote Park, in the county of Warwick* (London: E. Faithfull & Co.,

1862), 93.

13. Charles Burney, *Music, Men and Manners in France and Italy, 1770*, ed. H. Edmund Poole (London: Folio Society, 1969), 187. Mario Praz, *On Neoclassicism* (London: Thames and Hudson, 1969), 72, cites the reactions of other tourists to this patent.

14. Miller, *Letters from Italy*, 2: 252.

15. Denise Kaspar, "Felix Urbium Restitutio: 'Le Antichità di Ercolano' zwischen Museum und Öffentlichkeit; Die ersten nachrichten der grabungen am Golf von Naples und die "Pompejimode" im 18. jahrhundert," in *Antikensammlungen im 18. Jahrhundert*, ed. Herbert Beck et al. (Berlin: Mann, 1981), 21–31.

16. Thomas Martyn and John Lettice, preface to *The Antiquities of Herculaneum*, (London, 1773), v, explain how the Neapolitan royal adversary attempted to stifle their English translation of the work originally published "in a language not universally read" (Italian).

17. Charles-Nicolas Cochin and Jérôme-Charles Bellicard, *Observations upon the antiquities of the town of Herculaneum* (London: D. Wilson & T. Durham, 1753), 58–59.

18. Martyn, *Tour through Italy*, 305, describes the painting of Theseus and the minotaur as a historical piece.

19. Cochin and Bellicard, *Observations*, 61–62.

20. Ibid., 72.

21. James Russel to his son, 14 June 1753, British Library, Add. MSS. 41, 169: "The greatest number of these [Bellicard's] Plates are of the size of a Duodecimo; four are somewhat larger; but there are ten not three inches square. . . besides their smallness, they seem to be very ill ingraved. The Author owns, that he was not permitted to make any use of a pensil, when he viewed the subterranean curiosities; so that his drawings were all done from his own memory, and consequently can not be very exact."

22. Mr. Freeman at Naples to Lady Mary Capel, 1750, quoted in *Philosophical Transactions of the Royal Society* 47 (1751–52): 159.

23. Camillo Paderni to Allan Ramsay, 20 February 1740, cited in *Philosophical Transactions of the Royal Society* 41 (1739–41): 486–87.

24. Mr. Freeman, letter dated 18 April 1751, quoted in *Philosophical Transactions of the Royal Society* 47 (1751–52): 156–58.

25. Elisabeth Chevallier, "Les peintures découvertes à Herculanum, Pompéi et Stabies vues par les voyageurs du XVIIIe siècle: Influence des critéres d'appreciation en vigueur à cette époque," in *L'influence de la Gréce et de Rome sur l'occident moderne*, ed. Raymond Chevallier (Paris: Les Belles Lettres, 1977), 177.

26. Cochin and Bellicard, *Observations*, 105.

27. Rev. John Chetwode Eustace, *A Classical Tour through Italy* (London: J. Mawman, 1813), 1: 584.

28. Cochin and Bellicard, *Observations*, 110.

29. Burney, *Music, Men and Manners*, 189.

30. Ibid.

31. Henry Swinburne, *Travels in the two Sicilies in the years 1777,1778, 1779 and 1780*, 2nd ed. (London: T. Cadell, 1790), 3: 142–43.

32. P. J. Marshall, "Taming the Exotic: The British and India in the Seventeenth and Eighteenth Centuries," in *Exoticism in the Enlightenment*, ed. G. S. Rousseau and Roy Porter (Manchester: Man-

chester University Press, 1990), 61.

33. Horace Walpole, *Anecdotes of Painting in England. . . collected by the late Mr. George Vertue* (Strawberry Hill: Thomas Farmer, 1771), 4: 113. On receptions of India, see Marshall, "Taming the Exotic," 46–65; and Partha Mitter, *Much Maligned Monsters: History of European Reactions to Indian Art* (Oxford: Clarendon Press, 1977).

34. Miller, *Letters from Italy*, 2: 280–81.

35. William Chambers, preface to *Designs of Chinese Buildings, Furniture, Dresses, Machines, and Utensils* (London: Published for the Author, 1757), no pagination. On his *Designs*, see R. C. Bald, "Sir William Chambers and the Chinese Garden," in *Discovering China: European Interpretations in the Enlightenment*, ed. Julia Ching and Willard G. Oxtoby (Rochester: University of Rochester Press, 1992), 144. On the reception of the exotic, I have looked at James Walvin, *Fruits of Empire: Exotic Produce and British Taste, 1660–1800* (Basingstoke: Macmillan, 1997); Frances Mannsåker, "Elegancy and Wildness: Reflections of the East in the Eighteenth-Century Imagination," in *Exoticism in the Enlightenment*, ed. G. S. Rousseau and Roy Porter (Manchester: Manchester University Press, 1990), 175–95; Madeleine Jarry, *Chinoiserie: Chinese Influence on European Decorative Art, Seventeenth and Eighteen Centuries* (New York: Vendome, 1981); Oliver Impey, *Chinoiserie: The Impact of Oriental Styles on Western Art and Decoration* (London: Oxford University Press, 1977), esp. chapters 11 and 12; Richard C. Rudolph, *China and the West: Culture and Commerce*, (Los Angeles: University of California Press, 1977); and John Villiers, "Oriental Influences on English Taste," *History Today* 25 (1975): 164–76.

36. Chambers, preface to *Designs of Chinese Buildings*, no pagination.

37. See John Harris, "Sir William Chambers and Kew Gardens," in *Sir William Chambers, Architect to George III*, ed. John Harris and Michael Snodin (New Haven: Yale University Press, 1996), 55–67.

38. *The Antiquities of Herculaneum,* trans. Thomas Martyn and John Lettice (London, 1773), 170–71.

39. Cochin and Bellicard, *Observations,* 84.

40. Ibid., 87.

41. *Monthly Review* 52 (1775): 633.

42. The members of the Accademia Ercolanese were described in the *Annual Register* 3 (1760): 162, as "long eminent in the republic of letters." See further in chapter 2.

43. Eustace, *A Classical Tour through Italy*, 2: 156; James Fenimore Cooper, *Excursions in Italy* (London: Richard Bentley, 1838), 2: 54.

44. Roy Porter, "The Exotic as Erotic: Captain Cook at Tahiti," in *Exoticism in the Enlightenment*, ed. G. S. Rousseau and Roy Porter (Manchester: Manchester University Press, 1990), 118.

45. Russel, *Letters from a young painter abroad*, 1: 164.

46. Camillo Paderni to Thomas Hollis, 18 October 1754. *Philosophical Transactions of the Royal Society* 48 (1754): 823.

47. Burney, *Music, Men and Manners*, 189.

48. Henry Matthews, *The Diary of an Invalid, being the journal of a tour in pursuit of health in Portugal, Italy, Switzerland and France in the years 1817 and 1818,* 2nd ed. (London, 1820), 178.

49. Francis Haskell, "Art Patronage and Collecting in Bourbon Naples during the Eighteenth Century," in *The Golden Age of Naples: Art and Civilization under the Bourbons, 1734–1805* (Detroit: Institute of Arts, 1980), 1: 16; Carlo Pietrangeli, "Archaeological Excavations in Italy, 1750–1850," in *The Age of Neo-Classicism* (London: Arts Council of Great Britain, 1972), xlvi–lii.

50. Sir William Gell, *Pompeiana: The topography, edifices and ornaments of Pompeii, the result of excavations since 1819* (London: Jennings and Chaplin, 1832), 1: xvi.

51. Richard Brilliant, "Herculaneum: Archaeological, Art Historical and Cultural Properties," in *Ercolano, 1738–1988: 250 anni di ricerca archeologica*, ed. Luisa Franchi dell' Orto (Rome: "L'Erma" di Bretschneider, 1993), 118.

52. Richard Fellowes, letter dated 1771, quoted by Nancy H. Ramage, "Goods, Graves and Scholars: Eighteenth-Century Archaeologists in Britain and Italy," *American Journal of Archaeology* 96 (1992): 655–56.

53. Thomas Watkins, *Travels through Swisserland, Italy, Sicily, the Greek Islands, to Constantinople*, 2nd ed. (London: T. Cadell, 1794), 1: 425.

54. Peter Beckford, *Familiar Letters from Italy to a friend in England* (Salisbury: J. Easton, 1805), 2: 354.

55. Kenelm Digby, letter dated 17 March 1790, Birmingham City archives (UK), Digby papers, B 113a.

56. W. Beckford, *Letters and observations written in a short tour through France and Italy* (Salisbury: Privately printed, 1786), 81; and John Owen, *Travels into different parts of Europe in the years 1791 and 1792* (London, 1796), 2: 114.

57. Goethe, *Italian Journey*, 198.

58. Edward Bulwer-Lytton, *The Last Days of Pompeii* (Paris: Baudry's European Library, 1834), 1: 20–21. On *The Last Days*, see Laurence Goldstein, "The Impact of Pompeii on the Literary Imagination," *Centennial Review* 23 (1979): 233–36. Solomon's apothegm is cited in the accounts of early nineteenth-century travelers like Matthews, *Diary of an Invalid*, 184; and Rev. G. W. D. Evans, *The Classic and Connoisseur in Italy and Sicily* (London, 1835), 2: 143.

59. Mary Wollstonecraft Shelley, *Rambles in Germany and Italy* (London, 1844), 2: 279.

60. George Augustus Sala, *Rome and Venice, with other wanderings in Italy, 1866–67* (London, 1869), 426.

61. John Moore, *A View of society and manners in Italy*, 3rd ed. (London: W. Strahan & T. Cadell, 1790), 2: 180–81.

62. On the "Pompeian" room at Packington, see David Watkin, "Bonomi at Packington," *Georgian Group Journal* (1989): 102–5; John Wilton-Ely, "Pompeian and Etruscan Tastes in the Neoclassical Country House Interior," in *The Fashioning and Functioning of the English Country House*, ed. Gervase Jackson-Stops (Washington, D.C: National Gallery of Art, 1989), 65–70; and Desmond Fitz-Gerald, "A Gallery after the Antique," *Connoisseur* 181 (1972): 2–13.

63. W. L. Pressly, "Facts and Recollections of the XVIIIth Century in a Memoir of John Francis Rigaud Esq., RA," *Walpole Society* 50 (1984): 74.

64. On the content and reception of d'Hancarville's *Recherches*, see chapter 6 below, and Peter Funnell, "The Symbolical Language of Antiquity," in *The Arrogant Connoisseur: Richard Payne Knight, 1751–1824*, ed. Michael Clarke and Nicholas Penny (Manchester: Manchester University Press, 1982), 52–56; and Francis Haskell, "The Baron d'Hancarville: An Adventurer and Art Historian in Eighteenth Century Europe," in *Oxford, China and Italy: Writings in Honour of Sir Harold Acton*, ed. Edward Chaney and Neil Ritchie (London: Thames and Hudson, 1984), 187–89.

65. Richard Payne Knight, letter dated 1784, BM, TY7/2081.

66. Richard Payne Knight, letter dated 8 March 1785, BM, TY7/2083.

67. The published source for the scheme was identified by Desmond Fitz-Gerald, "A Gallery

after the Antique," *Connoisseur* 181 (1972): 8.

68. Father Thorpe, letter dated 25 April 1775, Sir Brinsley Ford archive, Paul Mellon Centre.

69. *Philosophical Transactions of the Royal Society* 47 (1751–52): 157.

70. James Byres to William Constable, 20 September 1777, East Riding of Yorkshire Archives Service DDCC/145/6.

71. Ann Sumner and Greg Smith, eds., *Thomas Jones, 1742–1803: An Artist Rediscovered* (New Haven: Yale University Press, 2003), no. 62; and Andrew Wilton and Ilaria Bignamini, eds., *The Grand Tour: The Lure of Italy in the Eighteenth Century* (London: Tate Gallery, 1996), no. 173.

72. Hetty Joyce, "The Ancient Frescoes from the Villa Negroni and Their Influence in the Eighteenth and Nineteenth Centuries," *Art Bulletin* 65 (1993): 423.

73. Buti, *Manifesto,* cited in Joyce, "The Ancient Frescoes from the Villa Negroni," 426.

74. 23 July 1777, BM, TY7/371.

75. Thomas Jenkins to Charles Townley, 30 September 1777, BM, TY7/375.

76. Charles Parker to Sir Roger Newdigate, 13 February 1783, Warwickshire County Record Office, CR136/ B2077.

77. *Sophie in London, 1786, being the diary of Sophie von la Roche,* trans. Clare Williams (London: Jonathan Cape, 1933), 226.

78. Emily J. Climenson, ed., *Passages from the diaries of Mrs. Lybbe Powys* (London: Longmans & Co., 1899), 231.

79. Damie Stillman, "Robert Adam and Piranesi," in *Essays in the History of Architecture Presented to Rudolf Wittkower*, ed. Douglas Fraser, Howard Hibbard, and Milton J. Levine (London: Phaidon 1967), 203.

80. Father Thorpe, letter dated 19 March 1773, Sir Brinsley Ford archive, Paul Mellon Centre.

81. D. Jacques, *A Visit to Goodwood near Chichester, the seat of his Grace the Duke of Richmond* (London, 1822), 26.

82. Lady Louisa Conolly to the Duchess of Leinster, 21 January 1773, in Brian Fitzgerald, ed., *Correspondence of Emily, Duchess of Leinster* (Dublin: Stationery Office, 1957), 3: 67.

83. Fitzgerald, *Correspondence of Emily*, 3: 141.

84. A. M. Keller, "The long Gallery of Castletown House," *Bulletin of the Irish Georgian Society* 22 (1979): 11–44. As related in chapter 3, when Lord Kildare subscribed to the Hamilton volumes in 1767, he asked his mother to mention them to her sister Lady Louisa Conolly "as she is fond of pretty ornaments, etc."

85. D. Stephen Pepper, *Guido Reni: A Complete Catalogue of His Works* (Oxford: Phaidon, 1984), no. 40.

86. John Owen, *Travels into different parts of Europe in the years 1791 and 1792* (London, 1796), 2: 43.

87. Tobias Smollett, *Travels through France and Italy*, ed. Frank Felsenstein (Oxford: Oxford University Press, 1981), 278. See Sybille Ebert-Schifferer, Andrea Emiliani, and Erich Schleier, *Guido Reni e l'Europe: Fama e fortuna* (Frankfurt: Schirn Kunsthalle and Bologna: Nuova Alfa editonale, 1988), C17.

88. Russel, *Letters from a young painter abroad*, 1: 227.

89. Mario Praz, On *Neoclassicism* (London: Thames and Hudson, 1969), 80.

90. William Chambers, *Treatise on the Decorative Part of Civil Architecture* (London: Joseph Smeeton, 1791), 135.

91. William Blackett to his father, 8 January 1785, Northumberland Record Office, ZBL 239.

CHAPTER 5

1. John Evelyn, *Diary*, ed. E. S. de Beer (Oxford: Clarendon Press, 1955), 2: 235.

2. Anthony M. Clark, *Pompeo Batoni: A Complete Catalogue of His Works* (Oxford: Phaidon, 1985), no. 278; Robert Adam to Margaret Adam, 5 March 1755, NAS, GD18/4766.

3. Martyn, *Tour through Italy*, 210. Burney, *Music, Men and Manners*, 131, described them as "the very first statues in the universe!" On the *Laocoön's* entrance into the pantheon of masterpieces in the Renaissance, see Richard Brilliant, *My Laocoön: Alternative Claims in the Interpretation of Artworks* (Berkeley: University of California Press, 2000); and Sonia Maffei, "La fama di Laocoonte nei testi del Cinquecento," in *Laocoonte: Fama e stile*, ed. Salvatore Settis (Rome: Donzelli, 1999).

4. Thomas Broderick, *The Travels of Thomas Broderick Esq., in a late tour through several parts of Europe* (London: M. Cooper, 1754), 2: 82.

5. Edward Wright, *Some Observations made in travelling through France, Italy &c. in the years 1720, 1721, and 1722* (London: Thomas Ward and E. Wicksteed, 1730), 1: 267. A second edition of Wright's *Observations* was published in 1764.

6. Smollett, *Travels*, 273. Elsewhere in his *Travels*, 230, Smollett describes Keysler as "so laboriously circumstantial in his descriptions, that I never could peruse them, without suffering the headache, and recollecting the old observation, That the German genius lies more in the back than in the brain."

7. Johann Georg Keysler, *Travels through Germany, Bohemia, Hungary, Switzerland, Italy and Lorrain*, 3rd ed. (London: G. Keith, 1760), 2: 296–97. The reference to Pliny is *Naturalis Historiae* 36, 37.

8. As Alex D. Potts points out in "Greek Sculpture and Roman Copies I: Anton Raphael Mengs and the Eighteenth Century," *Journal of the Warburg and Courtauld Institutes* 43 (1980): 152, the idea that ancients had frequently copied famous masterpieces was familiar in the eighteenth century.

9. Goethe, *Italian Journey*, 129.

10. Here, I am eliding the German and English grand tour experiences in that both cultures reconstructed the ancient past through representations. Although similar in this respect, we should not lose sight of the many *differences* between them.

11. Arthur Young, *Travels in Italy and France during the years 1787, 1788 and 1789* (Everyman's Library, 1915), 274.

12. John Boyle [Earl of Cork and Orrey], *Letters from Italy in the years 1754 and 1755*, ed. John Duncombe (London: B. White, 1773), 79.

13. Ibid., 76.

14. J. B. S. Morritt to his mother, 18 November 1795, in John B. S. Morritt, *A Grand Tour Letters and Journeys, 1794–6*, ed. Peter J. Hogarth (London: Century, 1985), 260.

15. Forsyth, *Remarks on Antiquities*, 274–75. In a letter to William Constable (11 June 1785), James Byres wrote "young Piranesi . . . is publishing a collection of forty of the best antient statues, they are well done." East Riding of Yorkshire archives office, DDCC 145/6.

16. Jacques Derrida, "The Parergon," *October* 9 (1979): 15, states that plastic arts do "not necessarily prescribe an order of reading. I can place myself in front of it, begin with the top or bottom, at times moved around." Quoted in Susan Stewart, *On Longing: Narratives of the Miniature, the Gigantic, the Souvenir, the Collection* (Baltimore: John Hopkins University Press, 1984), 143.

17. Wright, *Some Observations*), 1: 267–68.

18. Burney, *Music, Men and Manners*, 208.

19. James Martin, journal entry, 6 July 1764, volume 4, Sir Brinsley Ford archive, Paul Mellon Centre.

20. For a discussion of the "essential copy," see Norman Bryson, *Vision and Painting: The Logic of the Gaze* (London: Macmillan, 1983), 13–36.

21. Gerard Vaughan, "The Restoration of Classical Sculpture in the Eighteenth Century and the Problem of Authenticity," in *Why Fakes Matter: Essays on Problems of Authenticity*, ed. Mark Jones (London: British Museum Press, 1992), 42.

22. Moore, *A View of Society and Manners in Italy*, 2: 74.

23. Clark, *Pompeo Batoni*, 41.

24. Clark, *Pompeo Batoni*, no. 299.

25. Clark, *Pompeo Batoni*, 50.

26. One of the Vatican's earliest acquisitions of antique sculpture, *Cleopatra* was exhibited in the early sixteenth century in the Belvedere courtyard, where she was installed as a fountain as seen in Batoni's portrait of Dundas. On the later arrangement of statuary in the Belvedere courtyard, see Alex Potts, "Die Skulpturenaufstellung in der Glyptothek," in *Glypthothek München, 1830–1980*, ed. Klaus Vierneisel and Gottlieb Leinz (Munich: Glypthothek, 1980), 258–83; Jeffrey Collins, "The Gods' Abode: Pius VI and the Invention of the Vatican Museum," in *The Impact of Italy: The Grand Tour and Beyond*, ed. Clare Hornsby (London: British School at Rome, 2000), 173–94; Alex Potts, "The Classical Ideal on Display," *Viewing Antiquity: The Grand Tour, Antiquarianism and Collecting, Ricerche di storia dell'Arte* 72 (2000), 29–36.

27. The following have been useful in thinking about antique casts and the issues of reproduction: Anthony Hughes and Erich Ranfft, eds., *Sculpture and Its Reproductions* (London: Reaktion, 1997); Mary Beard, "Casts and Cast-Offs: The Origins of the Museum of Classical Archaeology," *Proceedings of the Cambridge Philological Society* 39 (1993): 1–29; Nicholas Penny, "Imposing Décor," *Country Life* 184 (1990): 250–53; Peter Connor, "Cast-Collecting in the Nineteenth Century: Scholarship, Aesthetics and Connoisseurship," in *Rediscovering Hellenism: The Hellenic Inheritance and the English Imagination*, ed. Graeme Wilber Clarke (Cambridge: Cambridge University Press: 1989), 187–235; *Retaining the Original: Multiple Originals, Copies and Reproductions*, Studies in the History of Art, 20 (Washington, D.C.: National Gallery of Art, 1989); Paul Duro, "'Un Livre Ouvert à l'instruction': Study Museums in Paris in the Nineteenth Century," *Oxford Art Journal* 10 (1987): 44–58; Susan Lambert, *The Image Multiplied: Five Centuries of Printed Reproductions of Paintings and Drawings* (London: Trefoil, 1987); Pierre Bourdieu, *Distinction: A Social Critique of the Judgement of Taste* (London: Routledge and Kegan Paul, 1989); Jean Baudrillard, *Simulations* (New York: Semiotext(e) Inc., 1983), 83–92; Walter Benjamin, "The Work of Art in the Age of Mechanical Reproduction," in *Illuminations*, ed. Hannah Arendt (London: Cape, 1970), 219–53; John Kenworthy-Browne, "Matthew Brettingham's Rome Account Book, 1747–1754," *Walpole Society* 49 (1983): 37–132; Francis Haskell and Nicholas Penny, *Taste and the Antique: The Lure of Classical Sculpture, 1500–1900* (New Haven: Yale University Press, 1981), esp. 79–91; M. Pabst Battin, "Exact Replication in the Visual Arts," *Journal of Aesthetics and Art Criticism* 38 (1979): 153–58; Roland Barthes, *Image, Music, Text* (London: Fontana, 1977).

28. Broderick, *Travels*, 2: 82.

29. Clark, *Pompeo Batoni*, 296.

30. For a critical rereading of a Batoni portrait, see Christopher M. S. Johns, "Portraiture and the Making of Cultural Identity: Pompeo Batoni's *The Honourable Colonel William Gordon* (1765–66) in Italy and North Britain," *Art History* 27 (2004): 382–411. Johns's description of Batoni portraits as "vanity vehicles" is readily applicable to that of Dundas.

31. Goethe, *Italian Journey*, 136 and 490.

32. Wright, *Some Observations*, 2: 412. See further, T. P. Connor, "Edward Wright and Lord Parker in Italy, 1720–22," *Apollo* 148 (1998): 23–30.

33. Broderick, *Travels*, 2: 158.

34. Charles Avery, "The Duke of Marlborough as a Collector and Patron of Sculpture," in *The Evolution of English Collecting: The Reception of Italian Art in the Tudor and Stuart Periods*, ed. Edward Chaney (New Haven: Yale University Press, 2003), 427–64; Dimitrios Zikos, "Antikenkopien in Bronze des Massimiliano Soldani Benzi," in *Von allen Seiten schön: Rückblicke auf Ausstellung und Kolloquium*, ed. Volker Krahn (Cologne: Letter Stiflung, 1996), 125–38; Andrew Ciechanowiecki and Gay Seagrim, "Soldani's Blenheim Commission and Other Bronze Sculptures after the Antique," in *Festschrift Klaus Lankheit*, ed. Wolfgang Hartmann (Cologne: DuMont Schauberg, 1973), 180–84.

35. Boyle [Earl of Cork and Orrey], *Letters*, 77.

36. Wright, *Observations*, 412.

37. James Martin, journal entry, 19 July 1764, volume 4, Sir Brinsley Ford archive, Paul Mellon Centre.

38. Quoted in Haskell and Penny, *Taste and the Antique*, 60.

39. Wright, *Some Observations*, 2: 412.

40. Stewart, *On Longing*, 91.

41. Lord Rockingham to Lord Malton, 5 July 1749, Sheffield Archives, Wentworth Woodhouse Muniments/M2/515. The Wentworth Woodhouse Muniments have been accepted in lieu of Inheritance Tax by HM Government and allocated to Sheffield City Council.

42. Lord Malton, letter of August 19 1749, Sheffield Archives, WWM/M2/518.

43. On Strafford's copies of the statures *Antinous, Apollo, Ceres,* and *Priestess*, see Hugh Honour, "English Patrons and Italian Sculptors in the First Half of the Eighteenth Century," *Connoisseur* 141 (1958): 223.

44. Sheffield Archives, WWM/M2/519.

45. 18 September 1749. Sheffield Archives, WWM/M2/521.

46. Michael Charlesworth, "Elevation and Succession: The Representation of Jacobite and Hanoverian Politics in the Landscape Gardens of Wentworth Castle and Wentworth Woodhouse," *New Arcadian Journal* 31–32 (1991): 7–65.

47. Nicholas Penny, "Lord Rockingham's Sculpture Collection and *The Judgement of Paris* by Nollekens," *J. Paul Getty Museum Journal* 19 (1991): 7. All these sculptures feature in Haskell and Penny, *Taste and the Antique*. Their late eighteenth-century provenance is given in brackets.

48. Goethe, *Italian Journey*, 152.

49. J. A. Galiffe, *Italy and its Inhabitants, an account of a tour in that country in 1816 and 1817* (London, 1820), 1: 249.

50. "Lord Rockingham's Sculpture Collection," 7.

51. Giambologna's *Samson and a Philistine* is in the Victoria and Albert Museum (A.7.1954), so too is Foggini's *Samson and the Philistines,* formerly at Wentworth Woodhouse (A1-1991). Gervase

Jackson-Stops, ed., *The Treasure Houses of Britain: Five Hundred Years of Private Patronage and Art Collecting* (Washington, D.C.: National Gallery of Art; and New Haven: Yale University Press, 1985), no. 214.

52. The quotation is Sir Thomas Wentworth in 1624. Cited in Malcolm Baker, "'A Peece of wondrous art': Giambologna's Samson and a Philistine and Its Later Copies," *Antologia di Belle Arti* 23–24 (1984): 67.

53. Angela Hass, "Michelangelo's Samson and the Philistine: Conception, Meaning and Subsequent Influence," *Apollo* 137 (1993): 383–86.

54. Penny, "Lord Rockingham's Sculpture Collection," 6.

55. Broderick, *Travels,* 2: 168.

56. Bruce Boucher, *The Sculpture of Jacopo Sansovino* (New Haven: Yale University Press, 1991), 2: 317, no. 6. *Bacchus* is now in the Museo Nazionale del Bargello in Florence.

57. *Horace Walpole's Correspondence*, 20: 539.

58. *Horace Walpole's Correspondence*, 20: 547.

59. Joseph Nollekens to Thomas Anson, 26 July 1765, Staffordshire Record Office, D615/P(S)/1/6/1.

60. Broderick, *Travels,* 2: 96. Martyn, *Tour through Italy*, 210.

61. James Adam, letter of 5 June 1762. NAS, GD18/4935. For a summary of Valadier's English commissions, see Roberto Valeriani, "Marmo e bronzo per l'Inghilterra," in *L'oro di Valadier: Un genio nella Roma del Settecento* (Rome: F. lli Palombi, 1997), 148–49.

62. According to Seymour Howard, the *Ceres* at Syon is an invented composition by Cavaceppi. See his "Bartolomeo Cavaceppi and the Origins of Neoclassical Sculpture," in *Antiquity Restored: Essays on the Afterlife of the Antique* (Vienna: IRSA, 1990), 101–2.

63. Edward Edwards, *Anecdotes of Painters* (London: Leigh and Sotheby, 1808), xvii, note. See Joan Coutu, "'A Very Grand and Seigneurial Design': The Duke of Richmond's Academy at Whitehall," *British Art Journal* 1 (2000): 47–54.

64. *The Works in Architecture of Robert and James Adam* (London, 1778), ed. Robert Oresko (London: Academy Editions, 1975), 48.

65. James Adam to Robert Adam, 25 December 1762. NAS, GD18/4951. John Fleming and Hugh Honour refer to Northumberland's *Apollino* in "Francis Harwood: An English Sculptor in XVIII Century Florence," in *Festschrift Ulrich Middeldorf*, ed. Antje Kosegarten and Peter Togler (Berlin: De Gruyter, 1968), 1: 510–16.

66. Matthews, *Diary of an Invalid*, 43, describes the Apollino as "a model of symmetry."

67. 3 January 1765. NAS, GD18/5015.

68. NAS, GD18/5494/3.

69. Stewart, *On Longing*, 146–50.

70. John Parker to first Earl of Charlemont, 28 February 1756, *The Manuscripts and Correspondence of James, First Earl of Charlemont*, ed. Sir J. T. Gilbert (London : H.M.S.O., 1891–94), 1: 225, no. 44.

71. *Manuscripts and Correspondence*, 1: 250, no. 54.

72. The copier is identified as Bracci by Parker in a letter of 5 April 1758, *Manuscripts and Correspondence*, 1: 245, no. 52. For a summary of his career, see Edgar Peters Bowron and Joseph J. Rishel, eds., *Art in Rome in the Eighteenth Century* (London: Merrell Holberton, 2000), 122–23.

73. *Manuscripts and Correspondence*, 1: 250, no. 54. On rotating pedestals, see Penny, "Lord Rock-

ingham's Sculpture Collection," 27.

74. Haskell and Penny, *Taste and the Antique*, 266–67.

75. Edward Murphy to Vierpyl, 10 February 1756. Jean Jacques Barthélemy, *Voyage en Italie . . . imprimé sur ses lettres originales écrites au Comte de Caylus* (Paris, 1801), 95.

76. Edward Murphy to Vierpyl, 25 July 1774, *Manuscripts and Correspondence*, 1: 322, no. 130i.

77. Vierpyl, 15 August 1774, *Manuscripts and Correspondence*, 1: 323, no. 130ii.

78. The Rockingham library is referred to by Sean O'Reilly, "Charlemont House—A Critical History," in *Images and Insights* (Dublin: Hugh Lane Gallery 1993), 43–54; and Edward McParland, *James Gandon: Vitruvius Hibernicus* (London: Zwemmer, 1985), 119–20. Vierpyl's busts were presented to the Royal Irish Academy in 1868; see Helen Byrne, "Simon Vierpyl: Busts, c. 1751–55," in *Charlemont, 1728–1799*, ed. Siobhán O'Rafferty and Bernadette Cunningham (Dublin: Royal Irish Academy, 1999), 19–26. The twenty-two statues are untraced.

79. Dr. James Tyrell to Ralph Howard, 7 September 1752, National Library of Ireland, PC 227. For a survey of portrait sculpture, ancient and modern, in the institutional and the private library, see Malcolm Baker in *The Making of the Wren Library: Trinity College, Cambridge*, ed. David McKitterick (Cambridge: Cambridge University Press, 1995), 110–37. Clive Wainwright, "The Library as Living Room," in *Property of a Gentleman: The Formation, Organisation and Dispersal of the Private Library, 1620–1920*, ed. Robin Myres and Michael Harris (Winchester: St. Paul's Bibliographies, 1991), 15.

80. John Northall, *Travels through Italy, containing new & curious observations on that country* (London, 1766), 362

81. Smollett, *Travels*, 233.

82. Dr. James Tyrell to Ralph Howard, National Library of Ireland, PC 227.

83. See chapter 2.

84. Jane Stevenson, *Poetissae: Women and the Language of Authority* (forthcoming); Jane Stevenson, "Women Latin Poets in Britain in the Seventeenth and Eighteenth Centuries," *Seventeenth Century* 16 (2001): 1–36; Sylvia Harcstark Myers, *The Bluestocking Circle: Women, Friendship, and the Life of the Mind in Eighteenth-Century England* (Oxford: Clarendon, 1990).

85. William Hazlitt, *Notes of a Journey through France and Italy* (London, 1824), 258.

86. "The Country Seat a poem by Sir John Clerk (1726)," NAS, GD18/4404/2 note 25.

87. J. M. Gray, ed., "Memoirs of the Life of Sir John Clerk," *Scottish History Society* 13 (1892): 237–38.

88. Charlemont's library was due to be sold at Sotheby's on 11 August 1865. Owing to a fire at the auctioneer's warehouse on 27 June, there was a sale of books and manuscripts on 11 August and a second sale of salvaged and damaged lots on 27 September. See Seymour di Ricci, *English Collectors of Books and Manuscripts, 1530–1930, and Their Marks of Ownership* (Cambridge: Cambridge University Press, 1930), 155.

89. The Renaissance display of busts after the texts of ancient authors is referred to in Seymour Howard, "Ancient Busts and the Cavaceppi and Albacini Casts," *Journal of the History of Collections* 3 (1991): 199; and Dora Thornton, *The Scholar in His Study: Ownership and Experience in Renaissance Italy* (New Haven: Yale University Press, 1997), 101.

90. Gabriel Naudé, *Instructions concerning erecting of a library . . . and now interpreted by J. Evelyn* (London, 1661), 85.

91. James Byres to Philip Yorke, 19 September 1781, Public Record Office of Northern Ireland, D2433/69/19.

92. Fitzgerald, *Correspondence of Emily*, 3: 464.

93. Bowron and Rishel, *Art in Rome in the Eighteenth Century*, 398.

94. Richard Wendorf, *The Elements of Life: Biography and Portrait-Painting in Stuart and Georgian Britain* (Oxford: Clarendon, 1991), 9–10.

95. Anton J. L. van Hooff, *From Autothanasia to Suicide: Self-Killing in Classical Antiquity* (London: Routledge, 1990), 52–3; and Robert J. Goar, *The Legend of Cato Uticensis from the First Century B.C. to the Fifth Century A.D.* (Brussels: Latomus, 1987).

96. *A New Roman history by question and answer . . . extracted from ancient authors and the most celebrated among the modern* (London: T. Astley, 1740), 282.

97. A. J. Marshall, "Symbols and Showmanship in Roman Public Life: The Fasces," *Phoenix* 38 (1984): 120–41.

98. *The Odes, Epodes and Carmen Seculare of Horace* (London: Joseph Davidson, 1741), 1: iii.

99. Cited by Philip J. Ayres in *Classical Culture and the Idea of Rome in Eighteenth-Century England* (Cambridge: Cambridge University Press, 1997), 31–32.

100. James Byres to William Constable, 1771(?), East Riding of Yorkshire Archives Service DDCC/145/6.

101. Ivan Hall, "A Yorkshireman with Roman Tastes," *Country Life* 161 (1977): 221.

102. David Connell, "The Grand Tour of William and Winifred Constable, 1769–71," in *Burton Constable Hall: The Eighteenth and Nineteenth Centuries*, ed. A. G. Credland, East Yorkshire Local History, 51 (1998): 55, note 29, suggests that "the precise scene depicted should not necessarily be taken too seriously as a analogy for William . . . by adopting the pose of a comic poet, he has his tongue firmly in-cheek."

103. Klaus Fittschen, "Zur rekonstruktion Griechischer dichterstatuen," *Mitteilungen des Deutschen Archäologischen Instituts, Athenische Abteilung* 107 (1992): 229–71.

104. Henry Blundell to Charles Townley, 25 November 1787, BM, TY7/1318.

105. Thomas Jenkins to Charles Townley, 12 November 1785, BM, TY7/428.

106. Father Thorpe to Henry Blundell, 5 August 1789, private collection.

107. Evans, *Classic and Connoisseur*, 1: 57.

108. *An Account of the statues, busts, bass-relieves, cinerary urns and other ancient marbles and paintings at Ince. Collected by H[enry] B[lundell]* (Liverpool, 1803), lxix and lxx.

109. Baron d'Ulanski, *Travels in Upper Italy, Tuscany and the Ecclesiastical State in a series of letters written to a friend in the years 1807 and 1808* (London, 1816), 2: 106–7. See further, Maria Elisa Tittoni, "La fabbrica di biscuit di Giovanni Volpato," in *Giovanni Volpato, 1735–1803* (Bassano del Grappa: Ghedina & Tassotti, 1988), 34–36; and Elisa Tittoni Monti, "Volpato e Roma," in *Piranesi e la culture antiquaria* (Rome: Multigrafica, 1985), 405–19.

110. Hugh Honour, "Bronze Statuettes by Giacomo and Giovanni Zoffoli," *Connoisseur* 148 (1961): 201.

111. Haskell and Penny, *Taste and the Antique*, appendix, 343.

112. Johann Joachim Winckelmann, *Critical Account of the situation and destruction by the first eruptions of Mount Vesuvius, of Herculaneum, Pompeii and Stabia* (London, 1771), 38.

113. Northall, *Travels through Italy*, 362.

114. Bourdieu, "Systems of Education and Systems of Thought," 194.

CHAPTER 6

1. BM, TY7/668. In writing this chapter, Brian F. Cook, *The Townley Marbles* (London: British Museum Publications, 1985), has been a useful introduction. Published before the British Museum acquired the Townley archive, Cook's book draws on Townley's notebooks and the series of manuscript catalogs to the collection. Jonathan Scott, *The Pleasures of Antiquity: British Collectors of Greece and Rome* (New Haven: Yale University Press, 2003), provides a survey of British collectors of Greece and Rome in the second half of the eighteenth century, including Charles Townley, in his chapters 5 and 6.

2. Thomas Jenkins to Charles Townley, letter dated 20 April 1782, BM, TY7/413.

3. TY7/2080/2 and TY7/2080/3: "I [Payne Knight] will gladly take a part of the Burden [d'Hancarville] which you [Townley] have supported so long."

4. Charles Townley to Thomas Jenkins, letter dated 21 October 1785, BM, TY7/427/2.

5. Thomas Jenkins to Charles Townley, letter dated 25 November 1786, BM, TY7/446.

6. See Francis Haskell, "The Baron d'Hancarville: An Adventurer and Art Historian in Eighteenth Century Europe," in *Oxford, China and Italy: Writings in Honour of Sir Harold Acton*, ed. Edward Chaney and Neil Ritchie, 177–91 (London: Thames and Hudson, 1984); and Peter Funnell, "The Symbolical Language of Antiquity," in *The Arrogant Connoisseur: Richard Payne Knight, 1751–1824*, ed. Michael Clarke and Nicholas Penny, 65–81 (Manchester: Manchester University Press, 1982).

7. Sir Richard Worsley to Charles Townley, letter dated 28 December 1789, BM, TY7/2042.

8. Richard Payne Knight, letter dated 1 March 1785, BM, TY7/2082; BM, TY7/2086.

9. Charles Greville to Charles Townley, letter dated 12 August 1778, BM, TY7/1044.

10. The *Antichità* volume was identified by Gerard Vaughan, "The Townley Zoffany: Reflections on *Charles Townley and His friends*," *Apollo* 144 (1996): 34.

11. Thomas Jenkins to Charles Townley, 27 August 1774, BM, TY7/336.

12. Potts, *Flesh and the Ideal*, 13.

13. Burney, *Music, Men and Manners*, 189.

14. Thomas Jenkins to Charles Townley, 24 February 1787, BM, TY7/451.

15. Goethe, *Italian Journey*, 326.

16. Grafton, *Commerce with the Classics*, 43.

17. Gavin Hamilton to Charles Townley, 17 June 1775, BM, TY7/591.

18. *A Catalogue of the antient marbles contained in each room of Mr Townley's house in Park Street Westminster with an account of the places where they were found, or formerly stood*. Towneley Hall Art Gallery & Museums.

19. J. T. Smith, *Nollekens and His Times* (London: Century, 1986), 168.

20. Quoted in W. O. Hassall, "Portrait of a Bibliophile II. Thomas Coke, Earl of Leicester, 1697–1759," *Book Collector* 8 (1959): 251.

21. Sir Henry Ellis, *The Townley Gallery* (London: Library of Entertaining Knowledge, 1836), 1: 10.

22. BM, TY10/2, p. 7, "An account of Books bought at Naples."

23. 28 December 1791, BM, TY7/509.

24. Quoted in Wilton and Bignamimi, *Grand Tour*, exhibition catalog no. 215, p. 260.

25. Smith, *Nollekens and His Times,* 164, "Zoffany . . . painted a picture called 'Mr. Townley's Gallery of Statues'; it was a portrait of the Library, though not strictly correct as to its contents, since

all the best of the marbles displayed in various parts of the house were brought into the picture by the artist, who made it up into a picturesque composition according to his own taste." Brian F. Cook, "The Townley Marbles in Westminster and Bloomsbury," in *Collectors and Collections,* ed. Richard Camber, British Museum Yearbook, 2 (London : Published for the Trustees of the British Museum by British Museum Publications, 1977), esp. 38–52.

26. Cook, "The Townley Marbles," 38 and 41.

27. Broderick, *Travels*, 2: 158.

28. Oliver Millar, *Zoffany and His Tribuna* (London: Routledge and K. Paul, 1967), 6, explains that neither Queen Charlotte nor King George III had visited the Tribuna, but rather had commissioned the painting from Zoffany as they were then arranging their own collection of pictures!

29. Robert Harvey, letter dated 9 August 1773. Quoted in Andrew W. Moore, *Norfolk and the Grand Tour: Eighteenth-Century Travellers Abroad and Their Souvenirs* (Norwich: Norfolk Museums Service, 1985), exhibition catalog no. 109, p. 154.

30. Lord Winchilsea, letter dated 2 January 1773. Quoted in Millar, *Zoffany*, 13. Winchilsea is the far left of the group of tourists clustered around the *Medici Venus*.

31. Horace Mann to Horace Walpole, 10 December 1779, *Horace Walpole Correspondence*, 24: 540. Mann is in the right foreground, at the edge of the group around Titian's *Venus of Urbino*. He stands to attention with the Order of Bath on his chest.

32. Gavin Hamilton, letter dated 10 May 1775, BM, TY7/588.

33. Quoted by Mary Webster, "Zoffany's Painting of Charles Towneley's Library in Park Street," *Burlington Magazine* 106 (1964): 316.

34. On the Wilton collection, see James Kennedy, *A Description of the Antiquities and Curiosities in Wilton-House* (Salisbury, 1769); Philip J. Ayres, *Classical Culture and the Idea of Rome in Eighteenth-Century England* (Cambridge: Cambridge University Press, 1997), 133–34; and now Jens-Arne Dickman, "'Lord Pembrokes design to form a School of Sculpture"—Erweb, Aufstellung und Funktion von Antiken in Wilton House während des 17. und 18. Jhs," in *Antikensammlungen des europäischen Adels im 18. Jahrhundert als Ausdruck einer europäischen Identität*, ed. Dietrich Boschung and Henner von Hesberg, 115–29 (Mainz am Rhein: Philip von Zabern, 2000).

35. John Dodd, letter dated 1735, BM Add. MSS., 5957. Quoted by Esther Moir, *The Discovery of Britain, 1540–1840* (London: Routledge and K. Paul 1964), 75.

36. William Stukeley, *Itinerarium curiosum: Or an account of the antiquities, and remarkable curiosities in nature, or art, observed in travel through Great Britain*, 'Centuria I', 'Iter VI' (London: Baker and Leigh, 1776), 135.

37. Dan Cruickshank, "Queen Anne's Gate," *Georgian Group Journal* (1992): 56–67.

38. Henry Temple, second Viscount Palmerston, letter dated 22 June 1764. Quoted in Brian Connell, *Portrait of a Whig Peer: Compiled from the Papers of the Second Viscount Palmerston* (London: Andre Deutsch, 1957), 54.

39. Dagmar Grassinger, *Antike Marmorskulpturen auf Schloss Broadlands*, Corpus signorum imperii Romani Great Britain, vol. 3, fasc. 4 (Mainz am Rhein: Philip von Zabern, 1994), 24–27, esp. 25. For the Nollekens sculpture, see Edgar Peters Bowron and Joseph J. Rishel, eds., *Art in Rome in the Eighteenth Century* (London: Merrell Holberton, 2000), no. 141, with bibliography.

40. Grassinger, *Antike Marmorskulpturen*, 47.

41. Henry Blundell to Charles Townley, 3 April 1796, BM, TY7/1326. Blundell's collection was acquired by the Merseyside County Museum in Liverpool in 1959. It is currently being published in

a series of volumes, see Jane Fejfer and Edmund Southworth, *The Ince Blundell Collection of Classical Sculpture*, vol. 1, *The Portraits* (London: HMSO, 1991). Volume 2 will be devoted to the ash chests, volume 3 to statuary, volume 4 to reliefs and sarcophagi, and volume 5 to the history of the collection and its modern pieces.

42. 4 March 1802, BM, TY7/1349.

43. John Raymond, *An Itinerary contayning a voyage made through Italy in the yeare 1646 and 1647* (London, 1648), 78.

44. Alison, *Essays*, 393.

45. T. D. Whitaker, *An History of the original parish of Whalley* (London: Nichols, Son and Bentley, 1818), 484.

46. Thomas Jenkins to Townley, 20 April 1782, BM, TY7/413. Townley's ancestor through his maternal grandmother was the renowned sculpture collector, Thomas, Earl of Arundel, so collecting was in the blood (so to speak). Townley renewed his passion for the ancients on classic ground in Italy in two later tours, in 1771–74 and 1777.

47. W. G. S. Cavendish (sixth Duke of Devonshire), *Handbook of Chatsworth and Hardwick* (London: Privately Printed, 1845), 80.

48. Alison, *Essays*, 393. The phrase "sensation for sculpture" comes from one of Thomas Jenkins's letters to Townley of 9 October 1772, BM, TY7/316.

49. *Metamorphosis* 10.326.

50. William Sandys to Charles Townley, 16 October 1780, BM, TY7/1204.

51. *Metamorphosis* 4.264–270.

52. Sir Richard Worsley to Charles Townley, 2 September 1791, BM, TY7/2052. Appuldurcombe was Worsley's Isle of Wight home.

53. 18 October 1804, BM, TY7/1578. The Virgil quotation can be found at *Ecolgues* II.22.

54. The Lansdowne marbles were sold at Christie's on 5 March 1930 under the title of its sale catalog, *The celebrated collection of ancient marbles the property of the most Hon. The Marquis of Lansdowne*.

55. See Antonia Tatham, *A Brief History and description* of *Lansdowne House* (London: Legal & General, 1988).

56. Thomas Jenkins to Charles Townley, 25 November 1786, BM, TY7/446.

57. Gavin Hamilton (second Earl of Shelburne), 18 January 1772, quoted in A. H. Smith, *A Catalogue of the Ancient Marbles at Lansdowne House* (London: Privately printed, 1889), 54. Damie Stillman, "The Gallery for Lansdowne House: International Neoclassical Architecture and Decoration in Microcosm," *Art Bulletin* 52 (1970): 75–80.

58. Smith, *Catalogue of the Ancient Marbles at Lansdowne House*, 67.

59. Gavin Hamilton to the second Earl of Shelburne, 25 March 1776. Quoted in Smith, *Catalogue of the Ancient Marbles at Lansdowne House*, 78. The sculpture remained unsold at the Christie's sale (5 March 1930) and is now at Bowood House, Wiltshire.

60. Gavin Hamilton to the second Earl of Shelburne, 18 January 1772. Quoted in Smith, *Catalogue of the Ancient Marbles at Lansdowne House*, 55. The *Cincinnatus* is now in the collection of the Ny Carlsberg Glyptothek (inv. no. 2798) as a sandal-tying Hermes.

61. Gavin Hamilton to the second Earl of Shelburne, 4 March 1773. Quoted in Smith, *Catalogue of the Ancient Marbles at Lansdowne House*, 65.

62. Gavin Hamilton to the second Earl of Shelburne, 25 March 1776. Quoted in Smith, *Catalogue of the Ancient Marbles at Lansdowne House*, 78.

63. Gavin Hamilton, letter written in 1773, BM, TY7/554.

64. Gavin Hamilton, letter written on 28 October 1775, BM, TY7/598.

65. On the practice and polemic of restoration, see Bartolomeo Cavaceppi, "Dell' arte di ben restaurare le antiche statue" in his *Raccolta d'antiche statue, busti, bassirelievi ed altre sculture restaurate da Bartolomeo Cavaceppi*, 3 vols. (Rome, 1768–72); Janet Burnett Grossman, Jerry Podany, and Marion True, eds., *History of the Restoration of ancient stone sculptures* (Los Angeles: J. Paul Getty Museum, 2003); Thomas Weiss, ed., *Von der Schönheit weissen Marmors zum 200. Todestag Bartolomeo Cavaceppis* (Mainz am Rhein: Philip von Zabern, 1999); Maria Giulia Barberini et al., eds., *Bartolomeo Cavaceppi, scultore romano, 1717–1779* (Rome: Fratelli Palombi, 1994); Gerard Vaughan, "The restoration of classical sculpture in the eighteenth century and the problem of authenticity," in *Why Fakes Matter: Essays on problems of authenticity*, ed. Mark Jones (London: British Museum Press, 1992), 41–50; Gerard Vaughan, "Albacini and his English patrons," *Journal of the history of collections* 3 (1991): 183–97; Carlos A. Picón, *Bartolomeo Cavaceppi: Eighteenth-century restorations of ancient marble sculpture from English private collections* (London: The Gallery, 1983); Seymour Howard, *Bartolomeo Cavaceppi: Eighteenth-century restorer*, (New York: Garland Pub., 1982).

66. Henry Blundell, letter dated 25 November 1787, BM, TY7/1318. On Blundell's collection, see Edmund Southworth, "The Ince Blundell Collection: Collecting Behaviour in the Eighteenth Century," *Journal of the History of Collections* 3 (1991): 219–34; Seymour Howard, "Henry Blundell's Sleeping Venus," in *Antiquity Restored: Essays on the Afterlife of the Antique* (Vienna: IRSA, 1990), 117–29; and Gerard Vaughan, "Henry Blundell's Sculpture Collection at Ince Hall," in *Patronage and Practice: Sculpture on Merseyside*, ed. Penelope Curtis, 13–21 (Liverpool: Tate Gallery, 1989).

67. Bowron and Rishel, *Art in Rome in the Eighteenth Century*, no. 121, with bibliography.

68. Henry Blundell to Charles Townley, 25 November 1787, BM, TY7/1318.

69. Henry Blundell, letter dated 15 April 1800, BM, TY15/11/1. For the bust of *Diana Lucifera*, see *An account of the statues, busts, bass-relieves, cinerary urns and other ancient marbles and paintings at Ince. Collected by H. B.* (Liverpool, 1803), clx. Blundell purchased a modern sculpture of *Psyche* from Canova "the first in his profession." See Blundell's *Account*, xvii.

70. Henry Blundell to Charles Townley, 19 October 1774, BM, TY7/339.

71. Henry Blundell, *Engravings and Etchings. . . in the collection of Henry Blundell Esq. at Ince* (Liverpool, 1809), 1: preface. Ellis, *Townley Gallery*, 1: 173, note 36, claims that the statue Blundell refers to first is the Townley *Venus*.

72. Henry Blundell to Charles Townley, 6 December 1799, BM, TY15/11/1.

73. 19 October 1774, BM, TY7/339(1). See Dietrich Boschung, "Die Antikensammlung in Newby Hall: Ein Beispiel englisher Antikenrezeption im 18. Jh.," *International Journal for the Classical Tradition* 8 (2002): 359–74. Weddell's collection was exhibited in a sculpture gallery designed by Robert Adam. In a letter of 15 July 1779 (BM, TY7/387), Jenkins wrote to Townley of the "Pity Weddell shou'd have been induced to over charge his Gallery with Ornaments, but the Adam's I am told have done it every where." See further Robin Middleton, "The Sculpture Gallery at Newby Hall," *AA Files: Annals of the Architectural Association School of Architecture* 13 (1986): 48–60.

74. Gavin Hamilton to Charles Townley, letters dated 6 April 1775, BM, TY7/585; 28 November 1775, BM, TY7/599. Hamilton failed to inform Shelburne that the head of the Diomedes was not its own.

75. Gavin Hamilton to Charles Townley, 23 July 1777, BM, TY7/371.

76. BM, TY7/ 1317.

77. From a letter dated 22 April 1780 (BM, TY7/641): "The Bishop of Derry now Earl of Bristol has seen your collection he says you have got all the cream & he onely the skim'd milk & now begins to wish he had paid better & purchased less."

78. Gavin Hamilton to Charles Townley. Letter transcribed by A. H. Smith, "Gavin Hamilton's Letters to Charles Townley," *Journal of Hellenic Studies* 21 (1901): 315.

79. Thomas Jenkins to John Dick, 15 November 1766, Stafford Record Office, D615/P(A)/2.

80. On the "spoils" from Hadrian's villa, see Haskell and Penny, *Taste and the Antique*, 64–65; William L. Macdonald and John A. Pinto, *Hadrian's Villa and Its Legacy* (New Haven: Yale University Press, 1995), esp. chapter 9, "Art Dispersed."

81. Gavin Hamilton to Charles Townley, 25 May 1793, BM, TY7/668.

82. Richard Payne Knight to Charles Townley, 30 November 1784, BM, TY7/2081. The reference to Pliny is *Naturalis Historiae* XXXV.ii.9.

83. Smith, *Nollekens and His Times*, 168.

84. Richard Payne Knight to Charles Townley, letter from November 1786, BM, TY7/2092.

85. Townley manuscript catalog, BM, TY12/5.

86. Smith, *Nollekens and His Times*, 168, note 1.

87. Letter dated 3 July 1794, transcribed by Smith, "Gavin Hamilton's Letters to Charles Townley," 317.

88. See Townley's diary entry for 9 July 1798: "Mr Zoffani continued to paint the Discobolus and began it again for the third time." BM, TY1/10.

89. BM, TY7/534.

90. Jenkins, letter dated 12 July 1794, BM, TY7/535.

91. John Bell, *Observations on Italy* (Edinburgh: William Blackwood; and London: T. Cadell, 1825), 261–62.

92. Seymour Howard, 'Some Eighteenth-Century Restorations of Myron's *Discobolus*," in *Antiquity Restored: Essays on the Afterlife of the Antique* (Vienna: IRSA, 1990), 70–77.

93. 27 September 1794, BM, TY7/536.

94. Thomas Jenkins, letter, BM, TY7/413.

95. Jenkins to Townley, 12 July 1794, BM, TY7/535; 19 October 1774, BM, TY7/339.

96. Thomas Jenkins to Charles Townley, 17 July 1776, BM, TY7/358.

97. Sixth Duke of Bedford, letter of 28 January 1823. Quoted by Elizabeth Angelicoussis, *The Woburn Abbey Collection of Classical Antiquities*, Corpus signorum imperii Romani Great Britain, vol. 3, fasc. 3 (Mainz am Rhein: Philip von Zabern, 1992), 29. The fifth Duke of Bedford began the collection at Woburn Abbey in the 1780s. The sixth duke continued to collect ancient sculptures and commissioned works from contemporary sculptors.

98. Henry Blundell, letter of 2 January 1787, BM, TY7/1316. Jane Fejfer discusses collections of classical sculpture as a leisure pursuit in the countryside equivalent to sporting activities in her "Restoration and Display of Classical Sculpture in English Country Houses," in *History of the Restoration of Ancient Stone Sculptures*, ed. Janet Burnett Grossman, Jerry Podany, and Marion True (Los Angeles: J. Paul Getty Museum, 2003), 94 and 101.

99. Gavin Hamilton to the Earl of Shelburne, 26 May 1778. Smith, *Catalogue of the Ancient*

Marbles at Lansdowne House, 84.

100. Gavin Hamilton, letter of 10 [January 1780?]. Smith, *Catalogue of the Ancient Marbles at Lansdowne House*, 86.

101. BM, TY7/2057.

102. Sir Richard Worsley, letter of 21 December 1789, BM, TY7/2041.

103. Jenkins to Charles Townley, 23 January 1782, BM, TY7/411.

104. Sir Richard Worsley to Charles Townley, 4 August 1790. BM, TY7/2049.

105. Gerard Vaughan, "James Smith Barry as a Collector of Antiquities," *Apollo* 126 (1987): 4–11.

106. Jenkins, letter of 25 September 1772, BM, TY7/315.

107. Sir Richard Worsley to Charles Townley, 21 November 1789, BM, TY7/2040; 20 June 1790, BM, TY7/2048.

108. Sir Richard Worsley to Charles Townley, BM, TY7/2049; Sir Richard Worsley to Charles Townley, 2 September 1791, BM, TY7/2052.

109. Undated, BM, TY7/2045. 5 March 1787, BM, TY7/1317.

110. 4 May 1790, BM, TY7/1320. 7 March 1802, BM, TY7/1350.

111. For example, on 6 June 1775 (BM, TY7/346), Thomas Jenkins wrote that James Smith Barry wanted Townley's assistance in arranging his collection in Cheshire—as did Blundell at Ince (TY7/1321).

112. Gavin Hamilton to Charles Townley, 7 October 1775, BM, TY7/596.

113. 14 February 1770, BM, TY7/301; Lord and Lady Spencer, TY7/428; Earl of Darnley, TY7/499; Duke of Dorset TY7/308.

114. Thomas Jenkins, letter of 4 March 1789, BM, TY7/485.

115. Quoted by Seymour Howard, *The Lansdowne Herakles* (Malibu: J. Paul Getty Museum, 1978), 15. The Lansdowne *Herakles* is now in the J. Paul Getty Museum (70.AA.109).

116. Thomas Jenkins to Charles Townley, 9 November 1768, BM, TY7/298, and 27 August 1774, BM, TY7/336. Townley lived at Whitehall, London before he moved to Park Street in 1777.

117. Thomas Jenkins to Charles Townley, 6 June 1775, BM, TY7/346. Jenkins refers to Lyde Brown's bust *Lucius Verus,* which was sold with other pieces from his collection at Wimbledon to Catherine the Great in 1784.

118. Ellis, *Townley Gallery*, 1: 9.

119. See, for instance, TY7/2079, 2081 and 2082.

120. 10 September 1780, BM, TY7/644. The Lucretius quotation is from *De Rerum Natura* 1.101. On the Gordon riots, I have looked at Colin Haydon, *Anti-Catholicism in Eighteenth-Century England, c. 1714–80: A Political and Social Study* (Manchester: Manchester University Press, 1993), 204–44; and Ian Gilmour, *Riot, Risings and Revolution: Governance and Violence in Eighteenth-Century England* (London: Hutchinson 1992), 342–70.

121. Samuel Solly to Charles Townley, BM, TY7/1592. The mausolea that Solly's letters refer to are all discussed in Nicholas Penny, *Church Monuments in Romantic England* (New Haven: Yale University Press 1977), esp. 50–54 and 61–62. In addition, see Charles Saumarez Smith, *The Building of Castle Howard* (London: Faber, 1990), 168–92; R. B. Wragg, "The Rockingham Mausoleum (1784–1793)," *Yorkshire Archaeological Journal* 52 (1980): 157–66; and John Lord, "The Building of the Mausoleum at Brocklesby, Lincolnshire," *Church Monuments* 7 (1992): 85–96.

122. Payne Knight to Townley's brother, 17 May 1805, BM, TY18/3. See *Report from the Committee*

to whom the petition of the Trustees of the British Museum, respecting the late Mr. Townley's collection of ancient sculptured marbles, was referred (June 1805).

123. On this monument, see Penny, *Church Monuments in Romantic England*, 62.

124. John Kenworthy-Browne, "The Temple of Liberty at Woburn Abbey," *Apollo* 130 (1989): 27–32.

125. Henry Holland to Charles Townley, 18 April 1802, BM, TY7/963. See Townley's plan of the temple in the conservatory, TY14/3/4 and TY7/850, where he is said to have given Holland "some very useful hints." Ruth Guilding, *Marble Mania: Sculpture Galleries in England, 1640–1840* (London: Sir John Soane's Museum, 2001), no. 99.

CONCLUSION

1. David Irwin, *English Neoclassical Art: Studies in Inspiration and Taste* (London: Faber, 1966), 19.

2. Alison, *Essays*, 393.

3. George James Aungier, *The History and Antiquities of Syon Monastery* (London: J. B. Nichols & Son, 1840), 120.

SELECT BIBLIOGRAPHY

This select bibliography is organised into three distinct sections: manuscript sources, printed primary sources, and printed secondary sources. A complete list of manuscript sources is provided. I have included references to primary printed sources that are frequently cited. The list of secondary sources is by no means exhaustive; references to additional books and articles will be found in the endnotes. This third section of the bibliography is intended to indicate the substantive texts that have shaped my narrative and its methodological framework. Hence, key readings from discrete disciplines are provided, including the history of art, the history of the book, cultural tourism, and the sociology of education. It is my hope that the bibliography will signpost the direction of my own research and assist those wishing to pursue the topic further.

PRIMARY SOURCES

Manuscripts

Bibliothèque Centrale du Muséum National d'Histoire Naturelle, Paris, Krafft Bequest, Hamilton papers.

Birmingham City archives: Matthew Boulton papers and Digby MSS.

British Library, Additional Manuscripts: Cumberland, Hamilton, Northumberland and Russel.

British Museum: Charles Townley MSS.

East Riding of Yorkshire Archives Service, Beverley: Chichester-Constable MSS.

East Sussex Record Office: Sheffield MSS.

Isle of Wight County Record Office: Worsley MSS.

Keele University Library: Wedgwood archive.

Leeds district archives: Nostell Priory MSS.

Lincoln Record Office: Worsley MSS and Yarborough MSS.

National Archives of Scotland, Edinburgh: Clerk of Penicuik MSS.

National Library of Ireland: Wicklow MSS.

Northamptonshire Record Office: Fitzwilliam MSS.

Northumberland Record Office: Blackett MSS.

Paul Mellon Centre: Sir Brinsley Ford archive.

Public Record Office of Northern Ireland: Caledon Castle MSS.

Royal Institute of British Architects: Hardwick MSS.

Sheffield Archives: Wentworth Woodhouse MSS.

Sir John Soane's museum library: C. H. Tatham correspondence.

Staffordshire Record Office: Anson MSS.

Warwickshire County Record Office: Newdigate MSS.

Printed primary sources

Adam, Robert. *Ruins of Dioclesian's Palace at Spalatro in Dalmatia*. London: The Author, 1764.

Alison, Rev. Archibald. *Essays on the nature and principles of taste*. London: J. J. G. & G. Robinson; and Edinburgh: Bell & Bradfute, 1790.

Le Antichità di Ercolano esposte. 8 vols. Naples: Reale Accademia Ercolanese di Archeologia, 1757–92.

Beckford, Peter. *Familiar Letters from Italy to a friend in England*. 2 vols. Salisbury: J. Easton, 1805.

Beckford, W. *Letters and observations written in a short tour through France and Italy*. Salisbury: Privately printed, 1786.

Boswell, James. *Boswell on the Grand Tour: Italy, Corsica and France, 1765–6*. Edited by Frank Brady and Frederick A. Pottle. London: William Heinemann, 1955.

Boyle, John [Earl of Cork and Orrey]. *Letters from Italy in the years 1754 and 1755*. Edited by John Duncombe. London: B. White, 1773.

Britton, John. *The Union of Architecture, Sculpture and Painting, exemplified by a series of illustrations with descriptive account of the house and galleries of John Soane*. London: The Author, 1827.

Broderick, Thomas. *The Travels of Thomas Broderick Esq., in a late tour through several parts of Europe*. 2 vols. London: M. Cooper, 1754.

Burney, Charles. *Music, Men and Manners in France and Italy, 1770*. Edited by H. Edmund Poole. London: Folio Society, 1969.

Chambers, William. *Designs of Chinese Buildings, Furniture, Dresses, Machines and Utensils*. London: The Author, 1757.

Cochin, Charles-Nicolas, and Jérôme-Charles Bellicard. *Observations upon the antiquities of the town of Herculaneum*. London: D. Wilson & T. Durham, 1753.

[Engelbach, Lewis]. *Naples and the Campagna Felice in a series of letters addressed to a friend in England in 1802*. London: R. Ackermann, 1815.

Ellis, Sir Henry. *The Townley Gallery*. 2 vols. London: Library of Entertaining Knowledge, 1836.

Eustace, Rev. John Chetwode. *A Classical Tour through Italy*. 3 vols. London: J. Mawman, 1813.

Fitzgerald, Brian, ed. *Correspondence of Emily, Duchess of Leinster*. 3 vols. Dublin: Stationery Office, 1957.

Forsyth, Joseph. *Remarks on Antiquities, Arts, and Letters, during an excursion in Italy, in the years 1802 and 1803*. 2nd ed. London, 1816.

Gibbon, Edward. *The History of the Decline and Fall of the Roman Empire*. Edited by David Womersley. 3 vols. London: Allen Lane, 1994.

———. *A Vindication of some passages in the fifteenth and sixteenth chapters of the History of the Decline and Fall of the Roman Empire*. London: W. Strahan, 1779.

Goethe, Johann Wolfgang. *Italian Journey*. Translated by W. H. Auden and Elizabeth Mayer. London: Collins, 1962.

D'Hancarville, Pierre François [Hughes]. *Collection of Etruscan, Greek and Roman Antiquities from the Cabinet of the Hon. W. Hamilton, His Britannick Majesty's Envoy Extraordinary and Plenipotentiary at the Court of Naples*. 4 vols. Naples, 1766–76.

Keysler, Johann Georg. *Travels through Germany, Bohemia, Hungary, Switzerland, Italy and Lorrain*. 3rd ed. 4 vols. London: G. Keith, 1760.

Lewis, Wilmarth Sheldon et al., eds. *Horace Walpole's Correspondence*. 48 vols. London: Oxford University Press, 1937–83.

Martyn, Thomas. *A Tour through Italy, containing full directions for travelling in that . . . country*. London, 1791.

Matthews, Henry. *The Diary of an Invalid, being the journal of a tour in pursuit of health in Portugal, Italy, Switzerland and France in the years 1817 and 1818*. 2nd ed. London, 1820.

[Miller, Lady Anne]. *Letters from Italy, describing the manners, customs, antiquities, paintings &c. of that country, in the years MDCCLXX and MDCCLXXI, to a friend residing in France*. 3 vols. London: Edward & Charles Dilly, 1776.

Montfaucon, Bernard de. *L'Antiquité expliquée et representée en figures*. 10 vols. Paris: Florentin Delaulne, 1719–24.

Moore, John. *A View of Society and Manners in Italy*. 2 vols. London: W. Strahan & T. Cadell, 1781.

Morrison, Alfred. *Catalogue of the collection of autograph letters and historical documents formed between 1865 and 1882 by A. Morrison*. 2 vols. London: Printed for private circulation, 1893–94.

Morritt, John B. S. *A Grand Tour Letters and Journeys, 1794–6*. Edited by Peter J. Hogarth. London: Century, 1985.

Murray, John, ed. *The Autobiographies of Edward Gibbon*. London: J. Murray, 1896.

Museum Worsleyanum, or a collection of antique basso relievos, bustos, statues and gems, with views of places in the Levant taken on the spot in the years 1785–7. 2 vols. London, 1796–1804.

Northall, John. *Travels through Italy, containing new and curious observations on that country*. London, 1766.

Norton, Jane Elizabeth, ed. *The Letters of Edward Gibbon*. 3 vols. London: Cassell & Co., 1956.

Owen, John. *Travels into different parts of Europe in the years 1791 and 1792*. 2 vols. London, 1796.

Piranesi, Giovanni Battista. *Lettere di giustificazione scritte a Milord Charlemont*. Rome, 1757.

———. *Antichità Romane*. 4 vols. Rome, 1756.

Reynolds, Joshua. *Discourses*. Edited by Pat Rogers. London: Penguin, 1992.

Russel, James. *Letters from a young painter abroad to his friends in England*. 2nd ed. 2 vols. London, 1750.

Sharp, Samuel. *Letters from Italy, describing the customs and manners of that country in the years 1765 and 1766*. London: R. Cave, 1766.

Smith, Arthur Hamilton. "Gavin Hamilton's letters to Charles Townley." *Journal of Hellenic Studies* 21 (1901): 306–21.

———. *A catalogue of the ancient marbles at Lansdowne House*. London: Privately printed, 1889.

Smith, John Thomas. *Nollekens and His Times*. 2 vols. London: Flaxman & Blake, 1828.

Smollett, Tobias. *Travels through France and Italy*. Edited by Frank Felsenstein. Oxford: Oxford University Press, 1981.

Stuart, James, and Nicholas Revett. *The Antiquities of Athens*. 4 vols. London, 1762–1816.

Watkins, Thomas. *Travels through Swisserland, Italy, Sicily, the Greek Islands, to Constantinople*. 2 vols.

London: T. Cadell, 1792.

Wright, Edward. *Some Observations made in travelling through France, Italy &c. in the years 1720, 1721, and 1722*. 2 vols. London: T. Ward & E. Wickstead, 1730.

SECONDARY SOURCES

Arnold, Dana. *The Georgian Country House: Architecture, Landscape and Society*. Stroud: Sutton, 1998.

Ayres, Philip J. *Classical Culture and the Idea of Rome in Eighteenth-Century England*. Cambridge: Cambridge University Press, 1997.

Batten, Charles L. *Pleasurable Instruction: Form and Convention in Eighteenth-Century Travel Literature*. Berkeley: California University Press, 1978.

Bologna, Ferdinando. "The Rediscovery of Herculaneum and Pompeii in the Artistic Culture of Europe in the Eighteenth Century." In *Rediscovering Pompeii*, edited by Luisa Franchi dell' Orto and Antonio Varone, 79–91. Rome: "L'Erma" di Bretschneider, 1992.

Bourdieu, Pierre. *Distinction: A Social Critique of the Judgement of Taste*. London: Routledge & Kegan Paul, 1989.

———. "Systems of Education and Systems of Thought." In *Knowledge and Control: New Directions for the Sociology of Education*, edited by Michael F. D. Young, 189–207. London: Collier Macmillan, 1971.

Bowron, Edgar Peters, and Joseph J. Rishel,, eds. *Art in Rome in the Eighteenth Century*. London: Merrell Holberton, 2000.

Brilliant, Richard. "Herculaneum: Archaeological, Art Historical and Cultural Properties." In *Ercolano, 1738–1988: 250 anni di ricerca archeologica*, edited by Luisa Franchi dell' Orto, 117–26. Rome: "L'Erma" di Bretschneider, 1993.

Brown, Iain Gordon. *Monumental Reputation: Robert Adam and the Emperor's Palace*. Edinburgh: National Library of Scotland, 1992.

Bryson, Norman. *Vision and Painting: The Logic of the Gaze*. London: Macmillan, 1983.

Campbell Hatfield, Leslie. "A Set of Silver Condiment Vases from Kedleston Hall." *Bulletin of the Boston Museum of Fine Arts* 79 (1981): 4–19.

Cannon, John. *Aristocratic Century: The Peerage of Eighteenth-Century England*. Cambridge: Cambridge University Press, 1984.

Chard, Chloe. *Pleasure and Guilt on the Grand Tour: Travel Writing and Imaginative Geography, 1600–1830*. Manchester: Manchester University Press, 1999.

Chartier, Roger, and Denis Roche. "New Approaches to the History of the Book." In *Constructing the Past: Essays in Historical Methodology*, edited by Jacques Le Goff and Pierre Nora, 198–214. Cambridge: Cambridge University Press, 1985.

Chevallier, Elisabeth. "Les Peintures découvertes à Herculanum, Pompéi et Stabies vues par les voyageurs du XVIIIe siécle: Influence des critéres d' appreciation en vigueur à cette époque." In *L'influence de la Gréce et de Rome sur l'occident moderne*, edited by Raymond Chevallier, 173–200. Paris: Les Belles Lettres, 1977.

Clark, Anthony M. *Pompeo Batoni: A Complete Catalogue of his works*. Oxford: Phaidon, 1985.

Clark, J. C. D. *English Society, 1688–1832: Ideology, Social Structure and Political Practice during the Ancien Regime*. Cambridge: Cambridge University Press, 1985.

Clark, Michael, and Nicholas Penny, eds. *The Arrogant Connoisseur: Richard Payne Knight, 1751–1824*. Manchester: Manchester University Press, 1982.

Connell, Brian. *Portrait of a Whig Peer: Compiled from the Papers of the Second Viscount Palmerston*. London: Andre Deutsch, 1957.

Constantine, David. "Winckelmann and Sir William Hamilton." *Oxford German Studies* 22 (1993): 55–83.

Cook, Brian F. *The Townley Marbles*. London: British Museum Publications, 1985.

Craddock, Patricia B. *Edward Gibbon: Luminous Historian, 1772–1794*. Baltimore: John Hopkins University Press, 1989.

Craske, Matthew. *Art in Europe, 1700–1830: A History of the Visual Arts in an Era of Unprecedented Urban Economic Growth*. Oxford: Oxford University Press, 1997.

Ernst, Wolfgang. "Frames at Work: Museological Imagination and Historical Discourse in Neoclassical Britain." *Art Bulletin* 75 (1993): 481–98.

———. "Adolf Michaelis: Die konfrontation Deutscher archäologie mit Britischen antikensammlungen." *Zeitschrift des Deutschen Vereins für Kunstwissenschaft* 46 (1992): 75–87.

Grafton, Anthony. *Commerce with the Classics: Ancient Books and Renaissance Readers*. Ann Arbor: University of Michigan Press, 1997.

Grassinger, Dagmar. *Antike Marmorskulpturen auf Schloss Broadlands*. Corpus signorum imperii Romani Great Britain, vol. III, fasc. IV. Mainz am Rhein: Philip von Zabern, 1994.

Griener, Pascal. *Le Antichità Etrusche Greche e Romane, 1766–1776 di Pierre Hugues d'Hancarville. La pubblicazione della ceramiche antiche della prima collezione Hamilton*. Rome: Edizione dell'Elefante, 1992.

Harris, Eileen. *British Architectural Books and Writers, 1556–1785*. Cambridge: Cambridge University Press, 1990.

Harris, Eileen, and John Martin Robinson. "New Light on Wyatt at Fawley." *Architectural Review* 27 (1984): 263–67.

Haskell, Francis. *History and Its Images: Art and the Interpretation of the Past*. New Haven: Yale University Press, 1993.

———. "The Baron d'Hancarville: An Adventurer and Art Historian in Eighteenth Century Europe." In *Oxford, China and Italy: Writings in Honour of Sir Harold Acton*, edited by Edward Chaney and Neil Ritchie, 177–91. London: Thames and Hudson, 1984.

———. "Gibbon and the History of Art." In *Edward Gibbon and the Decline and Fall of the Roman Empire*, edited by G. W. Bowersock, John Clive, and Stephen R. Graubard, 193–205. Cambridge, Mass.: Harvard University Press, 1977.

Haskell, Francis, and Nicholas Penny. *Taste and the Antique: The Lure of Classical Sculpture, 1500–1900*. New Haven: Yale University Press, 1981.

Honour, Hugh. *Neo-classicism*. London: Penguin, 1991.

Hornsby, Clare, ed. *The Impact of Italy: The Grand Tour and Beyond*. London: British School at Rome, 2000.

Howard, Seymour. *Antiquity Restored: Essays on the Afterlife of the Antique*. Vienna: IRSA, 1990.

Ingamells, John, ed. *A Dictionary of British and Irish Travellers in Italy, 1701–1800*. New Haven: Yale University Press, 1997.

Irwin, David. *English Neoclassical Art: Studies in Inspiration and Taste*. London: Faber, 1966.

Jenkins, Ian, and Kim Sloan, eds. *Vases and Volcanoes: Sir William Hamilton and His Collection*. London: British Museum Press, 1996.

Jones, Mark, ed. *Why Fakes Matter: Essays on Problems of Authenticity*. London: British Museum Press, 1992.

Joyce, Hetty. "The Ancient Frescoes from the Villa Negroni and Their Influence in the Eighteenth and Nineteenth Centuries." *Art Bulletin* 65 (1993): 423–40.

Kaspar, Denise. "Felix Urbium Restitutio – 'Le Antichità di Ercolano' zwischen Museum und Öffentlichkeit. Die ersten nachrichten der grabungen am Golf von Naples und die "Pompeji-mode" im 18. jahrhundert." In *Antikensammlungen im 18. Jahrhundert*, edited by Herbert Beck et al., 21–31. Berlin: Mann, 1981.

Keller, Ann Margaret. "The Long Gallery of Castletown House." *Bulletin of the Irish Georgian Society* 22 (1979): 1–54.

Kelley, Donald R., and David Harris Sacks, eds. *The Historical Imagination in Early Modern Britain: History, Rhetoric and Fiction, 1500–1800*. Cambridge: Woodrow Wilson Center Press; and Cambridge University Press, 1997.

Kelly, Christopher. "A Grand Tour: Reading Gibbon's *Decline and Fall*." *Greece and Rome* 44 (1997): 39–58.

Kiechler, John Anthony. "The Murals at Newtimber Place." *Sussex Archaeological Society* 113 (1976): 175–81.

Lambert, Susan. *The Image Multiplied: Five Centuries of Printed Reproductions of Paintings and Drawings*. London: Trefoil, 1987.

Langford, Paul. *A Polite and Commercial People: England, 1727–1783*. Oxford: Oxford University Press, 1989.

Lissarrague, François, and Marcia Reed. "The Collector's Books." *Journal of the History of Collections* 9 (1997): 275–94.

Macdonald, William L., and John A Pinto. *Hadrian's Villa and Its Legacy*. New Haven: Yale University Press, 1995.

Mannheim, Karl. *Ideology and Utopia: An Introduction to the Sociology of Knowledge*. London: Routledge, 1991.

———. *Conservatism: A Contribution to the Sociology of Knowledge*. London: Routledge, 1986.

Marshall, Peter James, and Glyndwr Williams. *The Great Map of Mankind: British Perceptions of the World in the Age of Enlightenment*. London: Dent, 1982.

McIlwaine, I. C. *Herculaneum: A Guide to the Printed Sources*. 2 vols. Naples: Bibliopolis, 1988.

McKendrick, Neil. "Josiah Wedgwood and the Commercialisation of the Potteries." In *The Birth of a Consumer Society: The Commercialization of Eighteenth-Century England*, edited by Neil McKendrick, John Brewer, and J. H. Plumb, 100–45. London: Europa, 1982.

McKitterick, Rosamund, and Roland Quinault, eds. *Edward Gibbon and Empire*. Cambridge: Cambridge University Press, 1997.

Michaelis, Adolf. *Ancient Marbles in Great Britain*. Cambridge: Cambridge University Press, 1882.

Millar, Oliver. *Zoffany and His Tribuna*, London: Routledge & K. Paul, 1967.

Myres, Robin, and Michael Harris, eds. *Property of a Gentleman: The Formation, Organisation and Dispersal of the Private Library, 1620–1920*. Winchester: St. Paul's Bibliographies, 1991.

Nisbet, N. B. *German Aesthetic and Literary Criticism: Winckelmann, Lessing, Hamann, Herder, Schiller, Goethe*. Cambridge: Cambridge University Press, 1985.

Ogilvie, R. M. *Latin and Greek: A History of the Influence of the Classics on English Life from 1600*. London: Routledge & K. Paul, 1964.

Parker, H. T. *The Cult of Antiquity and the French Revolutionaries: A Study in the Development of the Revolutionary Spirit*. Chicago: University of Chicago Press, 1937.

Parslow, C. C. *Rediscovering Antiquity: Karl Weber and the Excavations of Herculaneum, Pompeii and Sta-*

biae. Cambridge: Cambridge University Press, 1995.

Patterson, Annabel, ed. *Roman Images*. Baltimore: John Hopkins University Press, 1984.

Penny, Nicholas. "Lord Rockingham's Sculpture Collection and 'The Judgement of Paris' by Nollekens." *J. Paul Getty Museum Journal* 19 (1991): 5–34.

Pointon, Marcia. *Strategies for Showing: Women, Possession and Representation in English Latin and Greek: A History of the Influence of the Classics Visual Culture, 1665–1800*. Oxford: Oxford University Press, 1997.

Porter, Roy "The Enlightenment in England." In *The Enlightenment in National Context*, edited by Roy Porter and Mikulàš Teich, 1–18. Cambridge: Cambridge University Press, 1981.

Potts, Alex. *Flesh and the Ideal: Winckelmann and the Origins of Art History*. New Haven: Yale University Press, 1994.

Pratt, M. L. *Imperial Eyes: Travel Writing and Transculturation*. London: Routledge, 1992.

Praz, Mario. *On Neoclassicism*. London: Thames and Hudson, 1969.

Ramage, Nancy. "Wedgwood and Sir William Hamilton: Their Personal and Artistic Relationship." *Proceedings of the Thirty-fifth Annual Wedgwood International Seminar* (1990): 71–90.

Raven, James, Helen Small and Naomi Tadmor, eds. *The Practice and Representation of Reading in England*. Cambridge: Cambridge University Press, 1996.

Rivers, Isabel, ed. *Books and Their Readers in Eighteenth-Century England*. Leicester: Leicester University Press, 1982.

Rosenblum, Robert. *Transformations in Late Eighteenth Century Art*. Princeton: Princeton University Press, 1967.

Rousseau, G. S., and Roy Porter, eds. *Exoticism in the Enlightenment*. Manchester: Manchester University Press, 1990.

Schnapp, Alain. *The Discovery of the Past: The Origins of Archaeology*. London: British Museum Press, 1996.

Scott, Jonathan. *The Pleasures of Antiquity: British Collectors of Greece and Rome*. New Haven: Yale University Press, 2003.

Shapin, Steven, and Simon Schaffer,. *Leviathan and the Air-Pump: Hobbes, Boyle and the Experimental Life*. Princeton: Princeton University Press, 1985.

Smiles, Sam. *The Image of Antiquity: Ancient Britons and the Romantic Imagination*. New Haven: Yale University Press, 1994.

Stewart, Susan. *On Longing: Narratives of the Miniature, the Gigantic, the Souvenir, the Collection*. Baltimore: John Hopkins University Press, 1984.

Stray, Christopher. *Classics Transformed: Schools, Universities and Society in England, 1830–1960*. Oxford: Clarendon Press, 1998.

———. "Scholars and Gentlemen: Towards a Sociology of English Classical Scholarship." In *Aspects of Nineteenth-Century British Classical Scholarship*, edited by H. D. Jocelyn, 13–27. Liverpool: Liverpool Classic Monthly, 1996.

Thomas, Nicholas. *Entangled Objects: Exchange, Material Culture and Colonialism in the Pacific*. Cambridge, Mass.: Harvard University Press, 1991.

Vaughan, Gerard. "The Townley Zoffany: Reflections on *Charles Townley and His Friends*." *Apollo* 144 (1996): 32–35.

Vickers, Michael, and David Gill. *Artful Crafts: Ancient Silverware and Pottery*. Oxford: Clarendon Press, 1994.

Wallbank, M. V. "Eighteenth Century Public Schools and the Education of the Governing Elite." *History of Education* 8 (1979): 1–19.

Watkin, David. *Thomas Hope, 1769–1831 and the Neo-Classical Idea*. London: Murray, 1968.

Wendorf, Richard. *The Elements of Life: Biography and Portrait-Painting in Stuart and Georgian England*. Oxford: Clarendon Press, 1991.

Wilton, Andrews, and Ilaria Bignamini, eds. *The Grand Tour: The Lure of Italy in the Eighteenth Century*. London: Tate Gallery, 1996.

Wilton-Ely, John. *Giovanni Battista Piranesi: The Complete Etchings*. 2 vols. San Francisco: Alan Wofsy, 1994.

———. *Piranesi as Architect and Designer*. New Haven: Yale University Press, 1993.

———. "Pompeian and Etruscan Tastes in the Neo-classical Country House Interior." In *The Fashioning and Functioning of the English Country House*, edited by Gervase Jackson-Stops, 51–73. Studies in the History of Art, 25. Washington, D.C: National Gallery of Art, 1989.

Wittkower, Rudolph. "Imitation, Eclecticism and Genius." In *Aspects of the Eighteenth Century*, edited by Earl Reeves Wasserman, 143–62. Baltimore: John Hopkins Press; and London: Oxford University Press, 1965.

Womersley, David, ed. *Edward Gibbon: Bicentenary Essays*. Oxford: Voltaire Foundation, 1997.

INDEX